Portraits of the Artist

Portraits of the Artist

Psychoanalysis of Creativity and Its Vicissitudes

JOHN E. GEDO, MD

Introduction by Peter Gay

THE GUILFORD PRESS
New York   London

© 1983 The Guilford Press
A Division of Guilford Publications, Inc.
200 Park Avenue South, New York, N.Y. 10003

Printed in the United States of America

LIBRARY OF CONGRESS CATALOGING IN PUBLICATION DATA

Gedo, John E.
  Portraits of the artist.

  Bibliography: p.
  Includes index.
    1. Creation (Literary, artistic, etc.).   2. Creative
ability.   3. Psychoanalysis.   4. Personality.   I. Title.
BF408.G36 1983   153.3'5   83-1693
ISBN 0-89862-629-3

To the memory of my parents,
A. M. G. *and* M. S. G.,
whose voices have filled these pages

ACKNOWLEDGMENTS

Previous versions of Chapters 6, 12, and 13 appeared in *The Annual of Psychoanalysis* and are reprinted by permission of the Chicago Institute for Psychoanalysis. Previous versions of Chapters 10 and 14 appeared in *American Imago* and are reprinted by permission of the Association for Applied Psychoanalysis, Inc., and Wayne State University Press.

Photographic credits for figures in this book are due to:

Albright–Knox Gallery (21)
Archivi Alinari, Florence (28, 31, 32, 34)
The Art Institute of Chicago (5, 10, 16, 19, 36, 37, 38)
The Chrysler Museum (18)
Detroit Institute of Arts (25)
Documentation photographique de la Réunion des Musées Nationaux (33, 35)
Fogg Art Museum, Harvard University (14)
The Hermitage Museum, Leningrad (11, 27)
Mr. Alexander Lewyt (17)
The Metropolitan Museum of Art (15, 26)
Museum of Fine Arts, Boston (22)
The Museum of Modern Art, New York (6, 20)
The National Gallery, London (1)
Nelson Gallery–Atkins Museum (30)
Norton Gallery and School of Art (8)
Norton Simon Museum of Art (13)
Photoatelier Jörg P. Anders (29)
Renger Foto (24)
Stedelijk Museum, Amsterdam (2, 9, 12)
Wadsworth Atheneum (23)

LIST OF ILLUSTRATIONS

LIST OF ILLUSTRATIONS

LIST OF ILLUSTRATIONS

PREFACE

This book is an effort to use the conceptual tools of contemporary depth psychology to illuminate one aspect of culture: the vicissitudes of the creative process. The current psychoanalytic scene, it should be noted, is one of lively controversy, generally devoid of consensus on most issues. Self-evidently, then, the version of depth psychology presented in this volume is very much my own. In this project, however, it has not been my intention to overburden the reader with issues of psychoanalytic theory, and I have therefore not attempted to justify explicitly my psychoanalytic convictions. Readers interested in the conceptual framework that underlies the viewpoint espoused here may wish to consult my previous studies: *Models of the Mind* (with Arnold Goldberg, 1973), *Beyond Interpretation* (1979), and *Advances in Clinical Psychoanalysis* (1981).

Despite the limited focus I have tried to maintain in this book, I trust that even the nonspecialist reader will easily apprehend that the psychoanalytic universe in which I move is radically different from the universe which circumscribes Freud's great essays in the cultural realm. My subtitle, "Creativity and its Vicissitudes," paraphrases one of the most seminal works in the Freudian canon; in shifting emphasis from the instincts to creativity, I wish to highlight the novel possibilities of a depth psychology based on a hierarchy of personal goals and values in which human biology forms but one of the relevant components.

My optimistic perspective in this matter proceeds in part from extensive therapeutic encounters with a broad range of creative individuals. I hope that the encouraging results of these analytic efforts, though reported here only *en passant*, will lend credence to my contention that psychoanalytic progress in the virtual half century since Freud's death justifies renewed interest in the application of psychoanalysis to a variety of interdisciplinary topics. In this volume, I have restricted myself to an examination of creativity, but I am fully aware of the need to amplify this approach by exploring the psychology of the encounter between the artist and his audience. However, as the French say, in matters of this difficulty, *"c'est le premier pas qui coûte!"*

This is perhaps the best place to record the fact that I could not have taken this first costly step without the assistance—more, the collaboration—of two supporters. I dedicated *Beyond Interpretation* to my wife, Mary Mathews Gedo; at this time, therefore, I shall only say that the present work is, to an even greater extent, the fruit of her unflagging confidence and interest. The inspiration provided by her own pioneering work in correlating a great artist's psychological universe with the form and narrative content of his oeuvre has been one crucial prerequisite for this study, emboldening me to transcend the boundaries of clinical discourse.

The other person whose help has been indispensable in my endeavor is Paul Stepansky. We encountered each other when he served as the staff senior editor whose assistance enabled me to produce the best work of which I was capable in the writing of *Advances in Clinical Psychoanalysis*. Shortly after he completed his contribution to that project, Dr. Stepansky became an independent editor in psychoanalysis. I believe that the present volume should be the first to bear the imprint, "A Paul Stepansky Book." Not only did he encourage me to undertake a venture in an area Freud himself declined to enter—more importantly, he reviewed the inchoate mass of material I initially sent him and actively collaborated in shaping it into what follows. Although he has never injected his own ideas into our joint endeavor, he has been an ideal taskmaster in making me clarify my own, and he has made innumerable felicitous suggestions for improving their presentation.

It was Paul Stepansky who brought the book to the attention of The Guilford Press and its editor in chief, Seymour Weingarten, thus making possible that unclouded working relationship with them that every author needs. Finally, it was Paul Stepansky, a distinguished intellectual historian of psychoanalysis in his own right, who conceived of the plan to solicit a substantive Introduction from Professor Peter Gay, a preeminent American humanist who is also trained in psychoanalysis.

I am singularly pleased by the fact that Professor Gay has paid my work the greatest of compliments, that of voicing not only praise and agreement but also doubts and differences of opinion. I am temperamentally most comfortable when I can feel like an embattled outsider, and Professor Gay's references to my radical position on the current psychoanalytic scene, however tactfully phrased, permit me to portray myself to readers in my preferred guise, that of the innovator.

INTRODUCTION

Peter Gay

The comment quoted most often on psychoanalytic aesthetics is a disclaimer by the master himself. In his paper on Dostoevski, Sigmund Freud noted, with becoming modesty, that before the work of art, "analysis must, alas, lay down its arms." However, it is true that Freud, from his early, immensely fertile observations on *Oedipus Rex* and *Hamlet* to his papers on Leonardo da Vinci's childhood and on Michelangelo's *Moses*, played his psychoanalytic searchlight on artists and men of letters. It is true, too, that his deft resort to lines from Goethe, Shakespeare, and a library of other poets, coupled with his justly celebrated style, made him something of an explorer, or at least a voyager, in the elusive realms of creativity. But these passages and these papers do not constitute a psychoanalytic view of the arts. They do not even imply one. Rather, they serve other of Freud's enterprises such as his efforts to shed light on the vagaries of psychosexual development (the Leonardo paper) or to dramatize such startling discoveries as the Oedipus complex (his remarks on *Hamlet*). A true positivist, a conquistador who both expanded and respected the limits of his science, Freud did not like to theorize in the dark. Before creativity, he laid down his arms.

Freud's followers have not followed him in this. Although all too inclined to search his collected writings for quotable texts and to proffer their little nuggets as though they constituted proof of their assertions, psychoanalysts writing on art and literature have boldly rushed in where Freud had feared to tread. They have, as John Gedo notes with critical commentary—sometimes, I think, as with Maynard Solomon's fascinating *Beethoven*, rather too critical—attempted ambitious psychobiographies; they have tracked their subjects to their most private lairs to discover, if possible, the secrets behind their artistic or literary achievement. The results have rarely been definitive and often less than happy: Psychobiography at its best has provided ample room for controversy even among psychoanalysts, and the mysteries of creativity seem little less remote than before. Witness the divergent conclusions that the Sterbas and Maynard Solomon have reached in their interpretation of Ludwig van Beethoven's pathological involvement with his nephew.

The results of psychobiography should surprise no one: The biographical materials available for a definitive, or even tentative, interpretation of creativity, are scarce, sometimes inconsistent, often quite illegible; they invite conflicting answers. At the same time, these bold biographers have at least shown that a psychoanalytic aesthetic is something better than a utopian fantasy. Dr. Gedo's illuminating essays thus stand in a tradition that, brief and thin though it may be, can already boast some respectable works.

In addition, they illustrate, both implicitly and, with their sensitive observations on method, explicitly, some of the difficulties haunting such an aesthetic. The particular standpoint from which an investigator starts narrows his choice of themes and only too often determines the conclusions reached. The traditional psychoanalyst (to cite the instance with which Dr. Gedo begins) would take the startling incident of Vincent van Gogh's cutting off his ear as an acting out of "oedipal ambivalence." Now, however, with the current emphasis among psychoanalysts on the "adaptive significance of a given piece of behavior," van Gogh's "putative Oedipus complex" would "be regarded, on theoretical grounds, as a factor of minimal relevance for understanding the genesis of the breakdown." The psychoanalysis of art, Dr. Gedo suggests, inevitably reflects the movement in psychoanalysis itself.

This is not entirely reassuring to the cultural or the art historian sympathetic to the psychoanalytic enterprise and seeking light from its findings. Having happily chosen among competing psychologies to inform his work, he is now presented with an urgent invitation to choose more narrowly among competing versions of psychoanalysis. It is obvious that a researcher's work should be informed by a fundamental orientation and that the results should bear its imprint. And this is indeed as it should be: We expect specialized technical inquiries to start from the most advanced position a discipline has reached. Yet has psychoanalysis in recent decades experienced such a linear progression? Has it advanced from "old-fashioned" metapsychology to the more modern amendments that Dr. Gedo and his colleagues have offered to the Freudian canon? Looking at the controversies that have animated psychoanalytic meetings and journals in recent decades, I think we would be well advised to visualize the discipline as Freud visualized the mind: as the multilayered Rome, in which archaic deposits coexist with contemporary buildings and in which recent additions do not destroy all the earlier materials. Of course, there has been progress; Freud's authority is not absolute. He was, rumor to the contrary, not God. But the bulk of his work continues to stand secure. We can now, therefore, it seems to me, say *more* things about the springs of creativity, not merely *other* things, than those who, like K. R. Eissler, continue faithful to Freud in nearly every detail.

Actually, Dr. Gedo does not do himself justice in his introductory remarks. He offers delightful vistas of complexity. He accepts complementary ways of interpreting available material: Leonardo da Vinci's famous "Mona Lisa smile" may well be, as Freud had speculated, the precipitate of a childhood memory of his mother; but it may also be, Gedo adds, that "this stylistic feature of Leonardo's art had its roots in memories from his adolescence in Verrocchio's studio." This demonstrates, I think, a civilized and by no means evasive handling of the evidence: There are, after all—and the psychoanalyst has better reason to know this than anyone—only too many situations in which more than one cause contributes to the making of an event.

Beyond this, Dr. Gedo rightly warns against the danger of reductionism, of basing interpretations entirely on a single aspect of the aesthetic work. If in the past psychoanalytic investigators have concentrated on "narrative content," on the unconscious messages that the subject matter of a painting or a poem was discovered to reveal, they have now widened their purview to include "problems of form." They no longer "see the artist primarily as a spinner of fantasies" but, "instead, as the specially endowed manipulator of varied perceptual elements." Accordingly, Dr. Gedo rejects all simple explanations when a more nuanced and richer one exists. Freud's fundamental concept of overdetermination, which hangs over these pages, once again proves its utility and its astonishing role in Freud's science—astonishing because it is a reversal of the cherished principle of Occam's razor that has governed other scientists for centuries: For the psychoanalyst—and for the psychoanalytic student of artistic creativity—the more complex an explanation, the more likely it is to be correct.

There is yet another way in which Dr. Gedo's papers offer an escape from the bleak conjecture that a researcher's theoretical standpoint must dictate his conclusions. And that way is, to me, the most exciting. He has combined inquiries into the lives of painters and writers with clinical studies. Much of Sigmund Freud's most persuasive work, and much of the best work psychoanalysts have done since his death, was and continues to be informed by clinical experience. Such a clinical background lends psychoanalytic investigations depth, a resonance and a vitality, that researchers who have no such opportunities can only envy. This double access to creativity permits Dr. Gedo (and should encourage others) to shuttle between case histories and biographical analyses, enriching them both. The house of aesthetics has many mansions, and Dr. Gedo proves a stimulating, well-informed guide to all its wings.

Ambitious as Dr. Gedo's systematic reflections on artists are, he has explicitly confined himself to one particular, crucially important dimension of psychoanalytic aesthetics. He has, as his title proudly proclaims, drawn portraits of the artist. But one of the most attractive qualities of his essays is that they invite thoughts beyond their self-imposed limits. A complete psychoanalytic aesthetic would address itself to three dimensions: the artist, his work, and his public. Although Dr. Gedo acknowledges the importance of the work to be done in all these areas and hints that he may address "the psychology of readership" in the future, *Portraits of the Artist* is strictly about "the psychology of creativity." Yet he knows, of course, that it is only from the interplay of all these dimensions, which differ in their relative prominence from artist to artist and require a nice sense of balance, that anything approaching a full interpretation will emerge. The three dimensions of which I speak do not occupy precisely the same level: The study of aesthetic reception is a worthy counterpart to the study of artistic creativity and is in no way derivative from it. For the intentions of the artist, both conscious and unconscious, do not guarantee desired effects; his wishes and conflicts are not necessarily matched by the needs of his audiences. They are likely to overlap; they may even be identical, especially if they address universal human experiences: It was not so much the tragedy of *Oedipus Rex* or of *Hamlet* as their power over their audiences across centuries that first aroused Sigmund Freud's professional interest in them. But the making and the consuming of art and literature often have divergent histories. The accretions of meanings to aesthetic creations with the passage of time would often have astonished the artist had he lived to witness them. The psychology of reception, of the most direct relevance to cultural and political history, thus requires independent investigation.

The work of art itself is more problematic. For, as material, it enters into both the other studies: Dr. Gedo and all other investigators into creativity must take the artistic work—Gauguin's sculptures or Caravaggio's paintings—as testimony, however distorted, to the mind of its creator, to its workings, its conflicts, its collapses. In the same way, the psychoanalytically oriented student of reception, like Norman Holland, inescapably turns to the work as his starting point. Yet there have been psychoanalytic aestheticians—Dr. Gedo mentions Meredith Skura—who have treated texts as though they had cast themselves adrift in order to acquire an analyzable life of their own. The most sophisticated attempt of this sort that I have come across, designed to assign the study of the work the same status as the study of its creator and that of its audience, is Elizabeth Dalton's elegant and economical *Unconscious Structure in "The*

Idiot." As she explains her method, "I have avoided biographical material. Psychoanalytic critics frequently seem to compromise the autonomy of the work of literature as well as its meaning by interpreting it in terms of the author's life, rather than according to the unconscious patterns it can be shown to contain in itself." I have no doubt (even if many literary critics disdain this as a fallacy) that the characters in *The Idiot*, though creatures of Dostoevski's imagination, are in their own way "real." Nor do I doubt that the structure of the novel lends itself to independent analysis. But the three types of psychoanalytic investigations into the arts are not mutually exclusive; nor are they complete by themselves. The polemical methodological debates between psychoanalytic interpreters intent on including, and those intent on excluding, the author's unconscious, or his audiences' responses, seem to me somewhat wasteful. There is no right or wrong kind of psychoanalytic criticism; the question is always simply how well it is done. A work of art or literature is simultaneously autonomous and dependent; it can profit from investigations that both eschew and emphasize biography. And I foresee that these special ways of understanding art and literature, immensely valuable as each can be in itself, must eventually take their places in an overarching synthesis.

In some ways, thinkers have been envisioning such a theory since Aristotle. But now, with the resources of psychoanalysis at our command, the vision may become reality. Unconscious motives and conscious choices, personal wishes, craft demands, social, cultural, and economic imperatives and opportunities may be embraced by a single theory. It will fit comfortably (I believe) into Freud's structural theory and investigate the share of the id, the ego, and the superego in the making and the consuming of art. Robert Waelder sketched a map of such a theory in his *Psychoanalytic Avenues to Art* in 1965, and it is a path that, I predict, a synthetic psychoanalytic theory of aesthetics is likely to pursue.

Dr. Gedo is, I know, less than enthusiastic about Waelder's proposal because such a heavy reliance on Freud's structural model seems to commit the psychoanalytic investigator to the proposition that art must arise out of conflict alone. This, of course, (though less technically put) was the argument that Edmund Wilson advanced in his famous series of essays, *The Wound and the Bow*. But Waelder himself, as Dr. Gedo also notes, sternly rejects reductionism or easy schematic solutions. "Scientific models," Waelder writes at the outset, "hardly ever work equally well in all areas of reality." Freud's structural model, then, is only a provisional, though immensely useful set of capacious—and porous—baskets designed to encompass a bewildering diversity of mental capacities and activities. It is an aid in visualizing psychological functioning. The application of the structural triad may work less well with art, Waelder suggests, than with the neurotic pathology for which it was originally devised. After all, art, though it "seems to extend from an area full of conflict," also enters the domain of "calm which seems to be fairly free of conflict." And Waelder instances, as the two extreme representatives, the tragic Rembrandt and the exuberant Rubens.

Yet, these cautions once offered, Waelder proceeds to pursue his argument by briefly canvassing each element in Freud's structural scheme, indeed beginning his exposition with the very early phase when id and ego are not yet separated. And he is, in my judgment, right to do so. For to postulate the existence of id, ego, and superego does not merely dramatize conflict. To begin with, some conflicts are intrasystemic. More important, there is at times peace—or at least a truce—among the systems of the mind. To seek an understanding of art by exploring the mind's structure is to venture an approach to the varied sources of creation and enjoyment and to the tensions that issue in art either to discharge or to exploit them aesthetically. Waelder was not oblivious that to grant a single system of the mind, particularly the id, the monopoly on aesthetic creation and effectiveness is to devalue art and to misapprehend its very nature.

Art gives pleasure by fulfilling wishes that cannot be met in other ways, and it does so elegantly and without threatening either its maker or its consumer. This overly terse formulation sums up Waelder's argument and suggests the interplay (not necessarily the conflict) among the fundamental institutions of the mind. I offer the nude, whether male or female, as a concrete instance. It is an example to which Waelder also resorts: "The 'formal beauty' of, say, a female nude," he writes, "makes it possible to consummate, without guilt or shame, the sexual pleasure of the view," and he offers a seductive drawing of a standing nude by Corot as an illustration. Having recently studied artistic nudes produced in Corot's century, I want to complicate Waelder's example to support his own case for a structural approach to psychoanalytic aesthetics.

Everyone recalls the reputation of the 19th century, especially of its bourgeoisie, as prudish, hypocritical, and straitlaced. It was, we are told, strenuously opposed to bringing the blush into the young person's cheek. This reputation is largely (if not entirely) undeserved.[1] But it is true that it presented its most anxious spokesmen with something of a problem. Numbers of parents kept their daughters from visiting museums with tantalizing exhibitions. Many critics objected to aggressive nakedness (as in Manet's frank canvas, *Olympia*, or in Clésinger's highly erotic sculpture, *Woman Bitten by a Snake*) as very offensive indeed. Directors of art schools and indignant writers of letters to the editor worried over the indecency of naked models. Artists themselves earnestly discussed the

---

1. I refer to my forthcoming study, *The Bourgeois Experience, Victoria to Freud*, vol. 1, *Education of the Senses*, in which I explore these themes in great detail.

morality of depicting the undraped figure. And yet nudes appeared prominently everywhere: in the salons, on fountains, in monuments.

But, with a handful of scandalous exceptions, these nudes were all "dressed" in mythological, allegorical, historical, or exotic garb. They were Eves, Cleopatras, Odalisques, nymphs, representations of virtue or of purity. Hiram Powers's famous standing life-size nude, *The Greek Slave*, proudly shown at the Great Exhibition in London in 1851 and elsewhere, displayed a lovely young female dressed only in manacles and a sad stare; yet viewers, female and male, approached it with a solemnity verging on reverence. What was at work here was clearly what I call the doctrine of distance—distance as defense. The artistic object was erotic but not dangerous. It was remote even in the associations it produced. It played to sexual voyeurism but did not incite to action. It did not call up perilous incestuous longings but covered erotic desire with the cloak of morality or the faraway in time and place. Thus 19th-century nudes could gratify the id, the ego, and the superego all at once.

A theory devised along these lines should eventually succeed in giving an account of aesthetic consumption as well as of aesthetic creativity; it should convey and explain the unified impression given by that unique conjunction of subject matter, formal properties, and memory–arousal that is the single work of art. And such a theory should also explain the highly differentiated levels of creation and consumption by analyzing the role of the mind in the making and appreciation of art. A pornographic story, for example, contains little artistic work, little ego; it may satisfy the most primitive needs of the id by representing erotic, sadistic, or aggressive acts with little distortions—unconscious fantasies in print. In sharp contrast, a heavy-handed moralizing poem, evasive about realities and intent mainly on "improving" its audience, may principally serve the superego at its most punitive. Similarly, this sort of scheme should clarify the coexistence of contradictory tastes in a single reader or listener. Pleasure, after all, is strangely democratic. A sophisticated student of Beethoven's last quartets may be unable to repress tears at certain tunes in Lehar's *Merry Widow*; the specialist in Proust may find repeated, shame-faced resort to boyish adventure tales, such as the books of Karl May, irresistible. If Beethoven or Proust draw upon all their audiences' resources, Lehar and May live off early memories, recall unfinished, unsuccessfully repressed business. It is, after all, not the artist alone who needs to repeat childhood experiences. Other incidental discoveries will no doubt emerge as this general theory of aesthetic pleasure is worked out in detail.

Although I seem to have traveled far from Dr. Gedo's text, his writings have, as I have said, simply tempted me to explore beyond the boundaries he has staked out for himself. Moreover, his own interests are larger than the psychoanalysis of artistic creativity that is his theme in this book. His

epilogue—eloquent, pessimistic, deeply moving, and not entirely persuasive—attests to that. Much like Sigmund Freud, though of course in
his own way and with his own resources, Dr. Gedo looks beyond couch
to culture. He rightly sees that art is a special kind of work, a transcendence of needs in accord with carefully developed standards of crafts-
manship and self-criticism, reformed in the shaping imagination. It is no
wonder that essayists and biographers have deified artists and talked
high-flying nonsense about the heavenly gift of creativity. Psychoanalysts
can bring such vague and ethereal talk down to earth without reducing
the splendor of mankind's most rewarding sublimations. Wolfgang
Hildesheimer's wonderful recent book on Mozart is a case in point:
Mozart was not a divinity, not an angelic visitor on this earth, but a
musician, with all the mental mechanisms and most of the troubles of
ordinary mortals, yet with a talent that is, and that the psychoanalytic
critic has no hesitation in describing, the remarkable gift of genius. Art,
the psychoanalytic critic knows, is translation, the translation of passions
into artifacts that endure. The rest is commerce.

CONTENTS

CONTENTS

Portraits of the Artist

Psychoanalytic Studies of Creativity: A Retrospect

APPLICATIONS of psychoanalytic psychology to the study of culture have been based on the assumption that a valid psychology can serve as a common explanatory framework—a grammar—for the study of man, including the study of his creative activities. In this sense, psychoanalysis may become as integral to the humanities as calculus is to the natural sciences. In contrast to expansive statements of intention of this kind (cf. Gedo, 1978), the actual results of applied psychoanalytic studies have been rather disappointing. Why should this be the case? There are a number of difficulties attendant to the application of psycho-analysis to humanistic studies, and I wish to begin my survey of recent accomplishments in the interdisciplinary arena—where the study of creativity belongs—by considering some of the more important of them.

To begin with, the introspective–empathic method of psychoanalysis is directly applicable only to the field of biographical studies; this field of applied analysis is therefore urgently in need of guidelines that address its special methodological problems (see Kohut, 1960; Mack, 1971; Gedo, 1972c; Lichtenberg, 1978). The conclusions of analytic biographers must be subject to continuous challenge or confirmation by subsequent scholarship that is informed by newly discovered data about the life of the subject under investigation; they must also be strengthened by progres-sive expansions of psychoanalytic insights in general.

The manner in which progress within psychoanalysis should be re-flected in the work of analytic biographers requires additional comment. Such changes in analytic theory are obviously responsible for frequently shifting fashions with respect to the type of interpretations that are applied to the lives of biographical subjects. It follows that the literal application of the latest clinical theories to historical data is both too easy and too arbitrary. Ubiquitous constellations such as the castration complex will accommodate certain biographical facts with a degree of plausibility every time—not to mention some of the more fanciful so-called dynamics that have been used as interpretive Procrustean beds. But psychoanalytic data always lend themselves to a multitude of plausible interpretations, only a few of which turn out to be valid. In applied analysis, our choices must be dictated not by fashion but by the range of material illuminated by the hypothesis, the compatibility of the hypothesis with the overall fabric of our understanding of the subject's psychology, and the relevance of the issues addressed by the hypothesis to the explanation of unresolved questions about the life history under scrutiny. These strictures notwithstanding, the accumulated insights of psychoanalysis do provide the deepest understanding of the laws of human nature presently available. As such, they serve as an evolving framework that encapsulates the currently imaginable set of alternative hypotheses on which biographers in search of psychological understanding may draw.

An actual illustration may clarify this methodological principle. Until relatively recently, an event such as Vincent van Gogh's self-mutilation was often viewed as an expiatory act for his alleged hostility toward Paul Gauguin, interpreted in terms of oedipal ambivalence (cf. Nagera, 1967). Advances in psychoanalytic thinking have by no means invalidated such interpretations. Beginning with the work of Arlow (1961), however, the emphasis in applied analysis has shifted from identifying the derivatives of childhood conflicts to the examination of the current adaptive significance of a given piece of behavior. From this standpoint, the real issue involved in van Gogh's celebrated outburst is the loss of behavioral integration, a development without precedent in his previous history. It follows that van Gogh's putative Oedipus complex (a human universal, the legacy of which was bound to be implicated in any personality disintegration) would now be regarded, on theoretical grounds, as a factor of minimal relevance for understanding the genesis of his breakdown. Progress in psychoanalytic theory, in other words, directs us to reformulate an explanation of such a series of events in terms of those early childhood factors that determine the nature and potential reversibility of self-cohesion (cf. Gedo & Goldberg, 1973). I can make this point by means of a still simpler analogy: We may privately believe that Wolfgang Amadeus Mozart was an angel, but scientific considerations foreclose the option of attempting to explain his creativity on the basis of a miracle! We must use psychoanalytic theory in a similar manner to impose limits on the potential range of our speculative hypotheses.

In Chapter 1, I shall review the recent evolution of psychoanalytic biography, concentrating on its changing focus from the psychopathology of its subjects to the depth-psychological illumination of the significant public activities of creative figures. In this context, I will attempt to clarify how the most difficult methodological problem of applied analysis has been the issue of relevance. To be sure, the biographies of great men have been regarded as matters of general interest—and patterns for general emulation—ever since the appearance of Plutarch's *Lives*. But psychobiographies are seldom undertaken without more specific aims: It is usually assumed that, in some significant way, the subject's internal life will illuminate certain aspects of his public career. In this sense, biographical studies are the most frequent building blocks from which more complex applications of psychoanalysis to other fields are constructed. To continue with the illustration I have already invoked, we do not study van Gogh's Arles catastrophe as a picaresque episode suitable for the gossip columns; instead, we explore it because a substantial portion of van Gogh's oeuvre—including some of the most significant works of the past century—constitutes a record of and commentary on his relationship with Gauguin and its ultimate failure (see Figures 1 and 2: F.498 and F.499).

Many past efforts in psychobiography have turned out to be trivial or otherwise unsatisfactory because of the author's unthinking assumption that the problem of relevance can be met in applied analysis in the same manner that it is in a case report—that is, that a demonstration of the nature of an individual's possible intrapsychic conflicts has some value per se. This tendency, justly condemned on many occasions by Erik Erikson as the "originological fallacy," has given birth to a spate of shallow pathobiographies.

In areas of the humanities ranging outside of biography—historical studies of culture and politics, studies of creativity and of destructiveness—the depth-psychological approach merely attempts to add the dimension of the protagonist's personal motivations to the multiple factors relevant to understanding his work. In this sense, the crucial unit for study continues to be the personality of the individual agent, and the significance of any one of his actions can best be grasped in the context of his entire life viewed as an empathic gestalt. Thus, from a methodological point of view, it is much riskier to attempt to discern the connection between a single work of art or a single public act and the subjective motives of the person involved than it is to assess the significance of such products within the overall oeuvre of their creator. It is the totality of his productions that can be correlated most legitimately and meaningfully with his personality. Mary Gedo (1980a), for example, has demonstrated the overriding significance of Picasso's changing psychological integration for the evolution of the major styles that typified, successively, his blue, rose, and cubist periods; in comparison with the impressive tightness of these correlations, attempts to discern the psychological meaning of particular paintings on the basis of narrative content seem highly speculative, if not arbitrary. We

Figure 1. Vincent van Gogh, *The Pipe and the Chair*, 1888–1889. Oil on canvas. Reproduced by courtesy of the Trustees, The National Gallery, London.

must pay heed to Vincent van Gogh's telling assertion: "I do not consider [that] my studies are made for their sake, but am always thinking of my work as a whole" (1959b, p. 106).

Hypotheses about the personality organization of creative individuals may be checked by drawing on parallel cases encountered in clinical practice. I shall devote Section II of this work to clinical studies from my own psychoanalytic practice that are illuminating in this respect. Because opportunities for such clinical encounters may not occur very frequently, however, propositions about creativity developed in the course of bio-graphical or clinical work may also be compared to propositions derived from the application of psychoanalytic principles to pragmatic problems in the public arena. Psychoanalytic scholars involved in such research have the opportunity to observe individuals currently engaged in activities analogous to those we investigate in our psychohistorical subjects.[1]

The relevance of studies focused on the meanings of creative activities in the context of a protagonist's overall adaptation cannot be doubted; but such studies still confront the danger of reductionism. It is always difficult to distribute proper weight among the multitude of factors that bear on any public action, and this difficulty is heightened with psychological studies that routinely forego any detailed consideration of matters outside the realm of personal motivations. In principle, of course, it is perfectly legitimate to focus on this realm, just as it is legitimate to limit one's purview to the realm of stylistic or political traditions, philosophical underpinnings, or socioeconomic influences. In practice, however, advo-cates of each vantage point tend to engage in a kind of intellectual imperialism by claiming primacy for their approach and derogating all others. Unfortunately, Freud and many of his analytic successors oc-casionally succumbed to this temptation, in turn provoking rejection by outraged competitors in the marketplace of ideas.

Psychoanalytic contributions to aesthetics could hardly approximate the powerful impact of analytic biographies as long as the heirs of Freud continued to be seduced into focusing exclusively on narrative content in the arts—a temptation difficult to resist because of the importance of unconscious determinants in accounting for such content. Within the past

---

1. Although the methods available in these pragmatic endeavors seldom permit the type of observations made within the therapeutic setting of psychoanalysis, they often do permit the validation of hypotheses through repeated contact with the subject over an extended period of time. All sorts of ancillary methods such as psychological testing may be used to obtain otherwise inaccessible data about the subject's unconscious motivations. Thus, to take one example, it may ultimately be possible to weave together our experiences as consultants within judicial settings with conclusions about the childhood wishes that crystallize into the ambition to become a great judge which we obtain from the analytic treatment of members of the legal profession. It is the confluence of both types of insight that may facilitate a psychohistorical study of a great jurist, a system of jurisprudence, or even of a legal principle.

Figure 2. Vincent van Gogh, *Armchair, Candle and Books*, 1888. Oil on canvas. Collection National Museum Vincent van Gogh, Amsterdam.

generation, however, a series of psychoanalytically informed works has given increasing attention to problems of form. Because I will evaluate these contributions in Chapter 2, here I will merely point out that with this shift toward the importance of formal characteristics in psychoanalytic discussions of art, our views on creativity have also changed. It is no longer possible to see the artist primarily as a spinner of fantasies; he must now be understood, instead, as the specially endowed manipulator of varied perceptual elements. Although the motivations involved in activities of this kind may differ considerably from the motivations traditionally implicated in the creation of wish-fulfilling fantasies, recent psychoanalytic authors have shown that depth psychology nonetheless has much to say about them.

My review of the literature in Section I focuses sharply on that segment of the field of applied analytic studies that has a direct bearing on issues of creativity. The vast majority of works applying psychoanalytic tools to the study of the humanities fall outside of this boundary, because their principal aim is to examine the meaning of the artistic product. Sophisticated methods are currently being developed that will enable scholars to apply psychoanalytic tools directly to a literary text, without, for example, taking into account the biography of its author (see Skura, 1981). These efforts are unquestionably significant, but they pertain to the psychology of readership, not to the psychology of creativity; they must therefore await scrutiny in another context.

Chapter One

Biographical Studies

I

SIGMUND FREUD inaugurated the study of the cultural realm by means of his newly developed psychoanalytic method shortly after the turn of the century. *The Interpretation of Dreams* (1900) already contained brief but original readings of *Oedipus* and *Hamlet*, and Freud's book on jokes (1905) was probably his most significant excursion into aesthetics. In 1907, he published "Delusions and Dreams in Jensen's 'Gradiva,'" intending to demonstrate that his theories about dreams and symptoms had the power to illuminate the meaning of a literary work. The climax of this decade of activity was Freud's essay on Leonardo da Vinci (1910b), the prototype for all subsequent psychoanalytic studies of creativity and its vicissitudes. In order to clarify the evolution of the psychoanalytic approach to creativity, I shall return momentarily to this essay in some detail.

With a few brilliant exceptions, such as the paper of 1928 on Dostoevski, Freud's later efforts in applied analysis focused on the broader area of history and social organization.[1] But his pioneering work in the humanities was enthusiastically taken up by his early followers. Following a 1907 presentation by the eminent musicologist Max Graf, entitled "Methodology of the Psychology of Poets," the Vienna Psychoanalytic Society cogently discussed the application of analysis to the humanities (Nunberg & Federn, 1962, pp. 259–269). Graf emphasized that psychoanalytic psychology does not narrowly focus on pathological conditions; instead, it aspires to understand the human soul in its entirety. Hence analytic studies of the artist and his work were obliged to transcend the

---

1. For a recent survey of Freud's contributions to aesthetics, see Spector (1973).

field that Graf appropriately designated "pathography." In this manner, Graf refused to equate a so-called case history with a comprehensive psychoanalytic portrayal. Astutely, he pointed out that the use of analytic constructs in the cultural sphere could lead to superficiality; by contrast, studies explicitly focused on surface material could attain profundity without resorting to depth psychology. He assumed that creative personalities might prove to be more complex than other people, thereby posing a maximum challenge for those who aspired to understand them.

Graf believed that study of the artist's biography, particularly autobiographical materials, would provide the depth psychologist with the best access to relevant cultural sources. Because of the expectable operation of psychological defenses ("resistances," as they were then called), Graf noted that the central issues in the artist's mental life would probably remain veiled, beyond any inferences that might be drawn from the examination of his works. Repetitive motifs were most likely to be significant as clues to the psychology of their creator; comparative study of the permutations of such motifs might well yield latent meanings more easily than intensive focus on any single thematic variation. But Graf emphasized that the aim of applying psychoanalysis to this realm was the development of a "theory of artistic creation" (Nunberg & Federn, 1962, p. 264). In terms of this objective, the artist's personal psychopathology might effectively preclude understanding, "for illness is inhibition of the productive force" (p. 264). Pathography might clarify such obstructions of creativity, but it had no bearing on the primary issues involved in artistic creation per se.

Despite general agreement with Graf's theses, including Freud's own strong endorsement (p. 265), the half century that followed this Vienna Society lecture can be characterized as the era of pathography in applied analysis. Bergmann (1973) has provided a detailed survey of this period in the history of psychoanalysis. It was an era of excessive optimism, leading to methodologically lax interdisciplinary applications. Bergmann cites Marie Bonaparte's 1933 study of Edgar Allan Poe as a cautionary example, because this work was based on the assumption that an artist's creations have the same significance as the dreams of an analytic patient. Bonaparte relied entirely on Poe's writings in making inferences about the personal conflicts of the author. To the extent that the biographer's aim is to understand the actualities of his subject's life, this method must clearly be adjudged inadequate. We cannot safely assume, in other words, that art is autobiographical; Kris (1952, p. 288) has observed that the great artist in particular is distinguished by the capacity to identify with a wide array of his characters.

Only within the past 25 years has a gradual shift taken place in the direction recommended by Graf in 1907. Probably the most influential agent of this change was the art historian/psychoanalyst Ernst Kris, whose papers were ultimately collected in the volume *Psychoanalytic Explorations in Art* (1952). In the wake of Kris's contributions, discussions of the methodology of psychoanalytic biography (e.g., Gedo, 1972c) have focused on a new set of issues, including the biographer's unconscious motivations in choosing his subject, the contribution of the work to the field in which the subject of the biography was active, the relation of the private meaning of the work of art to its public meaning, and the status of the biographical work as an autobiographical document of its author.

In order to grasp more concretely the course of this radical evolution, we must turn to some of the principal contributions to the field during the period of transition. First, I will focus on select works that chart the increasing ability of psychoanalytic studies to address unanswered questions within the humanities. If I were to draw my illustrative material from the wider field of applied psychoanalytic scholarship, I would certainly include Erik Erikson's celebrated psychohistorical studies of Luther (1958) and Gandhi (1963) among these works. In order to keep the number of relevant variables within reasonable bounds, however, I have elected to confine my analysis to works dealing with artists in the narrow sense of the term.

II

THE EARLIEST WORK I have selected for consideration is a full-scale study of the life of a musician, Editha and Richard Sterba's *Beethoven and His Nephew* (1954). This work deserves consideration because it probably represents the mode of pathobiography at its best. It is in fact an extremely useful example of what depth psychology can contribute to the understanding of a life history, correcting distortions introduced into previous biographies of Beethoven, both consciously and unconsciously, by scholars intent on producing an idealized version of the genius.

The Sterbas were able to arrive at a convincing characterization of the composer because, in Beethoven's case, we possess a remarkable personal record in addition to the usual source materials available to biographers. After the onset of his deafness, people could only communicate with Beethoven in writing, and many of the notebooks in which these conversations were jotted down have been preserved. Even the limited portions of these conversation books available to the Sterbas provided a unique instrument for penetrating into the actualities of Beethoven's everyday life.

The Sterbas chose to focus their biography on the most important human relationship of Beethoven's late years—that involving his brother's son, Karl Beethoven—and they succeeded in creating an empathic picture of the great composer as a maximally vulnerable person with imperative symbiotic needs and a propensity for rageful, quasi-paranoid decompensation. Perhaps because Richard Sterba is himself a distinguished musician, the study scrupulously avoids any discussion of Beethoven's creative work. But this judicious restraint is carried to extremes in the Sterbas' failure to make explicit the way in which Beethoven's struggle to gain custody of his nephew was a reflection of the story line of his most programmatic work, *Fidelio*, composed some 15 years before the custody was finally won. No reader familiar with the opera can miss the implication that the wicked Don Pizarro embodies the composer's own pathological qualities, whereas Florestan and Leonora represent his beloved (i.e., in later years, his nephew) and the latter's wife–mother, respectively. Alternatively, viewed through the screen of Beethoven's projective defenses, the evil jailer represents those who are trying to take a beloved male figure from Beethoven, whereas Fidelio, a woman in man's clothing, portrays the composer's own feminine identification.

It is fascinating to note that Maynard Solomon's more recent (1977) biography of Beethoven, combining musicological expertise with psychoanalytic ambitions, virtually denies the Sterbas' accomplishment. Although Solomon concedes that Beethoven's nephew eventually had to escape the composer's "suffocating embrace" and accepts the fact that the composer's convictions about the boy's mother were often delusional, he disputes the Sterbas' contention that Beethoven underwent a regression in ethical standards in the course of the struggle to gain control of his nephew. In sole support of this unconvincing argument, Solomon cites certain self-serving statements of the composer as evidence of his guilt over what he was doing. It is scarcely surprising, in view of this assumption about Beethoven's guilt, that Solomon's interpretation of *Fidelio* should claim that the patricidal wishes underlying Pizarro's behavior are an echo of Beethoven's boyhood relationship to his own father. Solomon does see that Leonora represents the composer's feminine identification, but he fails to explore the thinly disguised homoerotic themes implicit in the depiction of her. Instead, he chooses to view the need to rescue the so-called father as a reaction formation against oedipal hostility. In Solomon's work, the biographer's need to idealize his subject has taken a new psychoanalytic turn: that of attributing a more or less optimal oedipal constellation to a personality plainly organized according to much more primitive modes.

A perceptible shift toward the more recent mode of psychobiography is already apparent in K. R. Eissler's *Leonardo da Vinci* (1961). Eissler was stimulated to write this book in response to Meyer Schapiro's critique of Freud's prototypical psychoanalytic study of Leonardo (Schapiro, 1956). Schapiro, an art historian, accepted the legitimacy of psychoanalytic investigation of historical figures but concluded that Freud had done his work on Leonardo in a faulty manner by disregarding the import of historical factors (such as stylistic precedents) and making erroneous interpretations of some of Leonardo's works. Eissler's intention in formulating his reply was frankly polemical: He undertook a vigorous defense of Freud's biographical method, claiming that Schapiro disregarded the fact that this method had no pretension of providing complete explanations. Freud, Eissler admonished, had sought to elucidate the *unconscious* motives involved in Leonardo's creations; like the products of all creative behavior, however, Leonardo's art expressed a multiplicity of determinants, including, of course, the influence of traditions. Interestingly, Eissler felt that in certain instances Schapiro himself had ventured unwarranted psychological inferences about Leonardo: When humanists embark on these treacherous waters, they may be bolder than most analysts would dare to be! More characteristically, historians tend to conceptualize human behavior on the basis of external influences alone, an error Eissler aptly described as the application of a stimulus–response psychology. Eissler attempted to diminish the seemingly fruitless controversies between students of the personal sources of the artist's subject matter and students of the historical precedents that lead to these choices by pointing out that some works reveal the personal factor in their creation more readily than others. Among the latter, he singled out commissioned pieces which are obviously more prone to the influence of external determinants.

In the process of defending psychobiography against potential detractors, Eissler subjected Freud's *Leonardo* to a methodological scrutiny that was inadequately rigorous. For instance, he understood Schapiro's objections to Freud's interpretive reliance on Leonardo's recollection of a childhood incident as part of the historian's effort to explain everything on the basis of precedents. But, the general import of this criticism notwithstanding, there *are* legitimate objections to Freud's procedure, for the alleged recollection on which he relied is contained in one of Leonardo's cryptic notes that gives no indication of the author's attitude toward the subject matter of the written recollection. As we know from the nature of free associative material in the psychoanalytic situation, the meaning of a given bit of verbalization depends on whether it is intended as a factual statement, as irony or humor, as an effort to mislead others, or as an imaginative creation. Eissler was far too lenient in accepting at face value Freud's interpretation of a memory purportedly referring to the early oral phase of development—a procedure he would surely condemn if it occurred in the context of contemporary clinical work. He further endorsed Freud's propensity to offer reconstructions of the past that leaped from evidence about adult functioning directly to early childhood. But this too is problematic: The influence of the past may legitimately be inferred from functioning in the present, but one cannot be arbitrary in choosing the particular phase of the past to which the current derivative is correlated. Worst, Eissler absolved Freud of responsibility for uncritically transmitting the errors of the secondary sources on which he relied.

In his own effort to further the psychoanalytic understanding of Leonardo, Eissler made greater use of deductive inference from the accepted clinical generalizations of the day than I would deem safe, given the rate at which such clinical convictions change. The psychology of homosexuals, as seen in 1961, scarcely looks like a reliable guide to understanding any bit of human behavior today. Eissler's work is also partially dated by virtue of its complete and literal adherence to a theory of motivation based on the concept of drive energies; this notion was standard at the time this book was written but has been largely discredited in the intervening two decades. One practical consequence of this *parti pris* is Eissler's ease in making logical inferences based on a simple and internally consistent psychology of postulated instinctual energies. This system of interpretation has not stood up to empirical testing within the psychoanalytic situation; *a fortiori*, it is no longer legitimate to make the theoretical assumption, as Eissler did, that creativity stems from the simple suppression of sexual discharge.

Eissler's intellectual style is generally audacious; he seems comfortable with chains of inference that are, in reality, quite speculative. This quality of mind leads to unhappy results when Eissler derives conclusions about Leonardo's psychology from the subject matter of single works of art— sometimes even from the subject matter of minor sketches. In my view, the presence of a theme within an artist's oeuvre does not in and of itself give any indication of the relative importance of the psychological issues implicated in the subject matter of the theme for the artist in question. As Kris has observed:

> Clinical analysis of creative artists suggests that the life experience of the artist is sometimes only in a limited sense the source of his vision; that his power to imagine conflicts may by far transcend the range of his own experience; or . . . that at least some artists possess the particular gift to generalize from whatever their own experience has been. . . . The artist has created a world and not indulged in a daydream. (1952, p. 288)

Correlations between Leonardo's subject matter and his personal conflicts are much more convincing when they refer to recurrent themes, such as the fantasied horrors he seems to have mastered through humor in his riddles, the *Profetie*. Eissler buttressed his interpretation of the importance of potential traumatization for Leonardo by pointing out that his paintings avoid traumatic scenes altogether: Even his portrayal of combat, *The Battle of Anghiari*, depicts the moment immediately preceding actual violence. We might add that Leonardo thereby seems to have originated a quality that typifies much High Renaissance painting—that of tranquillity

—out of a personal psychological need. In his last great work, a series of cataclysmic drawings entitled *The Deluge*, Leonardo apparently transcended this vulnerability in facing his own bodily dissolution.

In his handling of the issue of trauma in Leonardo's life, Eissler followed his own sound methodological advice: He surveyed the artist's entire oeuvre longitudinally in order to obtain cues relevant to the latter's psychology. Perhaps the most important yield of this process was Eissler's conclusion that, contrary to Freud's view, Leonardo's scientific pursuits were synergistic with his artistic aims. The goals associated with these latter aims encompassed the depiction of transcendence through images that simultaneously depicted actual scenes in a seemingly naturalistic manner. Such an artistic quest reaches for a quasi-divine creative attainment that one might term "metaphysical magic." The realization of such an ambition requires extraordinary preparations and infinite patience in execution; Leonardo's scientific research, including his heroic feats as an anatomist, formed one aspect of this effort. It follows that neither Leonardo's failure to publish his results in didactic form nor his meager output as a painter can be construed as evidence of an inhibition. Freud's belief that such supposed self-restriction had a sexual basis has been undermined by evidence that Leonardo did not have any difficulty in including sexuality within the scope of his scientific work. Unfortunately, Eissler was not entirely consistent is espousing this view. Occasionally, he lapsed into Freud's early perspective; this resulted in paradoxical statements, such as the claim that Leonardo's ease in producing drawings was inconsistent with his hesitant approach to painting.

The overall thrust of Eissler's study of Leonardo was still toward describing a creative personality rather than elucidating the visual arts per se. He has restated his conclusions about creativity on several occasions (1963 [Appendix T], 1967, 1971) without modifying them in any substantive way. In brief, Eissler agrees with Phyllis Greenacre (1957) as to the probability that, as a child, the future artist's special endowment will make him an "exception" (cf. Freud, 1916). For both of them, this circumstance is likely to interfere with development, particularly with the resolution of the Oedipus complex. Eissler further believes that the creativity of a genius will actually be stimulated by unresolved oedipal conflict, even though traumatic repetitions of certain childhood vicissitudes may ultimately interfere with the capacity to create.

In outstandingly creative individuals, Eissler postulates the occurrence of special psychological constellations, including a tendency to undergo repeated developmental crises that will transform the genius over and over again throughout the life cycle. In this manner, the impending death of a genius may release capacities that permit the creation of works of supreme significance. Another aspect of the psychopathology of genius is the occurrence of personal crises that superficially resemble the illnesses of ordinary people but leave the great artist unscathed or even enriched for his task. To use a spatial metaphor, we might say that, for Eissler, the ordinary psychopathology of a creative personality surrounds his genius.

III

PERHAPS THE MOST ambitious effort to examine the creativity of one artist psychoanalytically is Eissler's 1963 study of Goethe. This monumental work of over 1500 pages is certainly the most detailed attempt ever to apply psychoanalytic tools to the investigation of an historical subject. The book is not marred by the polemical overtones of Eissler's work on Leonardo, and it is more closely reasoned as well. It might therefore serve as a prototype of those appropriate applications of psychoanalysis to the cultural realm of the past generation. On the other hand, its very prolixity is discouraging to the prospective student, especially as this massive work covers only a single decade of Goethe's creative life. Eissler's microscopic approach results in a most persuasive treatment of specifics, but it prevents the author from cross-correlating various themes in Goethe's life and oeuvre on a sufficiently inclusive basis. By confining his correlations to evidence pertaining to a single decade of Goethe's life and work, in other words, Eissler arrives at premature closures that must render suspect his conclusions in the study. From a methodological standpoint, Bernard Meyer's 1967 biography of Joseph Conrad actually meets the criteria Eissler has enunciated over the years more closely than Eissler's own intensive treatment of Goethe. Hence, it is Meyer's work that I shall review as the prototype of an adequate psychoanalytic biography of a creative artist.

Leaning on a wide array of biographical source materials, Meyer attempts to reconstruct Conrad's inner life from boyhood to death, and he tries, in addition, to assess the influence of certain emergent depth-psychological patterns on the thematic content of Conrad's literary production in its entirety. To give but one illustration of the illuminating results of this investigation, Meyer is able to link the theme of another self in Conrad's superb novella, "The Secret Sharer," with Conrad's own need to form a series of partnerships in which he could unconsciously feel merged with someone else. We shall have occasion to return to this central insight repeatedly in the course of our discussion. "The Secret Sharer," it should be noted, was in fact written in 1909, at the climax of Conrad's intimate relationship with his fellow author, Ford Madox Hueffer. In Meyer's judgment, Conrad was never again able to sustain the peak level of his creativity following his rupture with Hueffer around 1910: "Now Conrad resembled the captain of 'The Secret Sharer' when separated from [his double]: part of him was absent, and no reflection of himself appeared in the depths of a sombre and immense mirror" (p. 167), to use the image Conrad himself invoked in referring to the wellsprings of his inspiration. Following the break with Hueffer, the novelist's art became comparatively shallow; it was "the spiritual union of these two inhibited men [that had] len[t] Conrad a certain boldness in his willingness to search his inner self" (p. 167).

Meyer proceeds to trace the emergence of the theme of a double in Conrad's other writings, for example, in Marlow's self-recognition on encountering the regression of Kurtz in "Heart of Darkness" (1898–1899) and the protagonist's acknowledgment of his fatal flaws when confronted by a band of criminal marauders in Lord Jim (1900). He observes that it can hardly be a matter of coincidence that Conrad wrote "Heart of Darkness" and Lord Jim immediately after establishing his bonds with Hueffer and "The Secret Sharer" just before their rupture. Moreover, Meyer demonstrates that the need for an alter ego characterized Conrad throughout his life, from his tragic early years as a motherless child dependent on a severely depressed father to the ultimate depression of his later years that followed his elder son's abandonment of him through an elopement.

The motif of a secret sharer is only one of many themes that Meyer illuminates in the foregoing manner. To give only a partial listing of other motifs that were equally significant for Conrad's art: There is the theme of the relationship of a weak and passive man with an all-powerful, androgynous woman, a transaction tinged with incestuous overtones (best exemplified in The Arrow of Gold [1919]); the theme of betrayal, explicit in Under Western Eyes (1911) but implicit in many other works (e.g., the abandonment of the passengers of a sinking ship by its crew in Lord Jim); the theme of rescue or rehabilitation (e.g., "Amy Foster" [1901], "A Smile of Fortune" [1912], and "The Planter of Malata" [1913]); and the theme of neurotic exogamy (e.g., "Heart of Darkness" and An Outcast of the Islands [1896]). These and other aspects of Conrad's artistic subject matter are convincingly correlated with the major psychological issues of his private life. Meyer selected the issues he discussed as relevant to Conrad's subject matter by studying varied biographical sources, including the several volumes of Conrad's autobiographical writings.

But Meyer's focus is not restricted to the personal sources of Conrad's fiction. On a number of occasions, he proceeds in the opposite direction, making inferences about the author's personality on the basis of the thematic content of his work. Although Meyer pursues this strategy with discretion, his pathobiographical excursions are highly speculative nonetheless: Outside the context of the psychoanalytic treatment process, it is impossible to form a reliable estimate of the relative import of any particular mental content within the overall personality—not that this is easily accomplished in the course of psychoanalytic treatment, for that matter.

Meyer asserts, for example, that certain parallels between the protagonist of *An Outcast of the Islands* and its author make it likely that this "fictional love story illuminates the real one" Conrad was engaged in at the time he wrote the book (p. 116). Meyer's convincing interpretation of the story revolves around its portrayal of Conrad's fantasy about "the destructive and devouring nature of a woman's love." His conclusion that, in the early months of his marriage, Conrad behaved like "a trapped man constantly plotting his escape" (p. 119) is equally persuasive, but the implication that Conrad's inner turmoil at that time can be understood from the view of women presented in this novel simply does not follow. It is just as likely, for example, that the novelist's postmarital anxiety was caused by an intense fear of object loss (i.e., a fear of losing his new wife), given the fact that he had lost both parents through death in his childhood. Fortunately, Meyer does not rely on this kind of speculative inference very often in arriving at his estimation of Conrad's personality.

A more serious criticism that might be leveled at Meyer is his failure to extend his inquiry into the realm of aesthetics (i.e., to consider elements of Conrad's art beyond its narrative content) or, with the exception of the issue of a secret sharer, to extend it into the realm of the psychology of creativity (i.e., to consider the sources of the writer's productivity and artistic power).[2] Instead, Meyer is content merely to assert that Conrad's work declined in quality after his frightening brush with psychosis (during a febrile illness) in 1910. Although there can be no question about the supreme merit of many of the works that preceded this event (extending from *The Nigger of the Narcissus* of 1896 to "The Secret Sharer" of 1909), Meyer's contempt for Conrad's subsequent production is probably unjustified.[3]

It may well be true, as Meyer claims, that Conrad's terrifying experience with psychological illness caused him to recoil from the genre that had made him great—the psychological narrative. But we have no right to judge Conrad's late work according to the standard of what *we* would have preferred him to write: He knowingly chose to create romances, and this body of work must be judged by the aesthetic criteria relevant to that

2. A more recent work, Mary Gedo's *Picasso: Art as Autobiography* (1980a), tackles these very issues, and its methods and conclusions have informed my approach to the subject matter of this volume. Unfortunately, my relationship to the author precludes my use of her work as the illustrative example for this chapter.

3. At the very least, I would include *Under Western Eyes* among Conrad's major works, although this tale of betrayal may well reflect the author's reaction to the loss of Hueffer and thereby constitute an extension of their relationship. In this sense, it would not constitute an exception to Meyer's thesis. For a view concerning Conrad's late work that is contrary to Meyer's, see Karl (1979, especially pp. 683–686). In Karl's judgment, Conrad's decline in artistic power commenced after 1914.

genre. Meyer dismisses these tales simply because they deal repetitively with the theme of woman's primitive power—or, conversely, because their heroes are "well-meaning but unmanly creatures, tentative and inert" (p. 223)—and because only the plots of these narratives differ from one another. Meyer does acknowledge one exception to this judgment, the fine quasi-autobiographical novel of 1915, *The Shadow Line*. Curiously, Meyer feels that the production of this work does not weaken his argument, inasmuch as this story of life at sea does not deal with the relations between the sexes.

But Meyer's judgment that Conrad's misogyny and the peculiarity of the character types he portrayed in his late works necessarily reduces the quality of these works is unconvincing in any event. In taking such a position, Meyer places himself among those critics who are out of sympathy with the entire thrust of Western literature in our century. One wonders what he would make of the characters who people the works of Beckett, Camus, or Céline? The relevant point, at any rate, is that Meyer refuses to examine Conrad's late work on its own terms; instead, he is content to dissect the author's regressive behavior in private life during his waning years.

Despite these limitations, Meyer's achievement in tracing the autobiographical courses of Conrad's fiction is impressive. He succeeds in showing that every major character and incident therein can be directly derived from Conrad's personal experience (see pp. 267–290). Meyer caps this tour de force by tracing certain subtle fetishistic themes through the author's oeuvre, showing them to be most explicit in *The Arrow of Gold*. At the same time, he provides compelling evidence of the ubiquitous horror of the female genitals that also suffuses Conrad's writings—along with the castration anxiety that underlies such an attitude.

In his effort to correlate these literary preoccupations with elements of Conrad's actual behavior, Meyer arrives at a series of convincing conclusions about the novelist's personality organization: "The tenuousness of the sense of self and the reparative reliance on fetishism pervading Conrad's fiction was a projection of identical elements in his own personality" (p. 321). Furthermore, "Conrad employed . . . manifold defenses against the danger of genital mutilation and in a broader sense against total destruction [yet] in his actual behavior he often gave the appearance of openly encouraging these same dreaded eventualities . . . to relinquish both the adult and the masculine role, and to become the helpless plaything of a strong woman with whom he seeks to rediscover the boundless 'oneness' of mother and child" (pp. 333–335). Paralleling these regressive longings are Conrad's misogyny and paranoid fear of women, which testify to his fear of engulfment within a symbiotic union.

Rather than putting these brilliant results to work in the service of further illuminating Conrad's literary work, Meyer regrettably chose to conclude his study by engaging in the traditional psychoanalytic exercise of attempting to reconstruct the childhood antecedents of these adult constellations. In fact, Meyer's imaginative depiction of the young Polish aristocrat's "disorder and early sorrow" is superbly done, and it helps to round out his earlier insights about Conrad's personality. If Meyer has not entirely ruled out the plausibility of alternative reconstructions, he has at the very least succeeded in etching an unforgettable and internally consistent portrait of Josef Teodor Konrad Korzeniowski.

Only the last four pages of Meyer's book cause one to decry the biographer's choice of focus, for here Meyer finally provides a brief example of the kind of contribution to the study of aesthetics and creativity that might have issued from his work. He takes up the question of Conrad's use of English as his literary medium, astutely suggesting that the author needed to create psychological distance between the world of his creation and the origins of his literary imagination in his early experience by avoiding his mother tongue. In this way, Conrad was able to blunt an intensity of feeling that would have impaired his artistic capacity. Meyer also makes the acute observation that the last three novels Conrad began all dealt with French subject matter. If we recall that French was the second language of Conrad's childhood and that his family had numerous significant connections with France, we may conclude that this choice of content indicates the author's increasing loss of the necessary distance from his traumatic past; this, in turn, may account for certain of the weaknesses Meyer detects in these late works. Conrad's unfinished last work, *Suspense*, incorporated so much from the writings of a long dead Countess de Boigne that its publication by the author would have constituted plagiarism or, from a depth-psychological viewpoint, the final achievement of merger with a maternal figure. Yet even this enactment allowed Conrad to avoid his Polish origins and, presumably, the memory of his real mother, and opt instead for the repetition of a deeply satisfying relationship with a French governess at the age of 4.

But this exceptional excursion into the realm of aesthetics in Meyer's concluding pages merely serves as a reminder of the power of depth psychology to illuminate such problems; otherwise, his biography stays within the boundaries of an investigation of the sources of an author's literary themes in his personal life experience.[4]

---

4. Armstrong (1971) has taken issue with Meyer's emphasis on the primary role of Conrad's earliest ties to his mother in determining the themes of his fiction. He does not dispute the conclusion that these vicissitudes had the greatest impact on the formation of Conrad's personality, but he feels that "the active struggle with the father figure is at the heart of Conrad's most successful fiction" (p. 532). In arguing this point, Armstrong pays particular attention to *Lord Jim* and "Heart of Darkness" as one pair of variations on the theme, and *Under Western Eyes* and "The Secret Sharer" as another.

Although Armstrong's contention probably holds true for this reduced sample of Conrad's oeuvre, the fact that Armstrong is able to make a seemingly valid correlation for

IV

HOW CAN WE best summarize the nature of the evolutionary change illustrated by the sequence of works from the Sterbas' *Beethoven* to Meyer's *Joseph Conrad*? In my judgment, the most significant dimension of this shift is the steadily decreasing emphasis on problems relevant to the clinical theory of psychoanalysis in favor of issues that fall within the realm of aesthetics and the psychology of creativity. The Sterbas' illumination of Beethoven's troubled relationship with his nephew and the latter's mother as a regressive syndrome of late middle age in a childless person is an example of the earlier stress. In contrast, Meyer's demonstration that Conrad's ascendance (and possible decline) as a psychological novelist can be correlated with the availability of Hueffer as a secret sharer is a contribution to the study of creativity. This trend away from clinical concerns has continued since Meyer's work of 1967. Increasingly, scholars from other disciplines have turned to the conceptual tools of psychoanalysis for help in resolving questions in their respective fields.

Consider, for example, Mary Gedo's studies of Picasso (1979, 1980a, 1980b, 1981), which are sharply focused on the latter's artistic production. Because Picasso's body of work is largely autobiographical, as the artist himself proclaimed, the development of Picasso's psychological world contributed to the formation of both the narrative content and the stylistic vicissitudes of his artistic output. Hence, the meaning of Picasso's images can only be grasped fully by taking into account the extent to which these images constitute reflections of the artist's subjective universe; the historian is obliged to become a "psychoiconographer" who follows the course of this universe as it can be discerned on the basis of a variety of sources. This procedure is hardly equivalent to psychoanalytic personality diagnosis or, as Max Graf put it, to the writing of a case history. By way of contrast, the Sterbas (1954) used essentially similar biographical materials to construct the very kind of multifaceted, presumably objective view of Beethoven's behavior that the analyst attempts to form on the basis of clinical data.

---

the four works he discussed underscores the ease of constructing plausible formulations of this kind by selecting data that will buttress them. In my judgment, Armstrong has overlooked a persistent undertone even within the works that support his thesis, namely, the protagonist's identification with a nurturant mother who sustains the inadequate father. The underlying maternal identification suggests that even where the fiction manifestly highlights father–son relations, the latent (homosexual) theme stems directly from an earlier, pregenital source.

Furthermore, Armstrong's extensive paper deals exclusively with narrative content and (naively) assumes that the artist's adaptive style in everyday life might be impaired by his efforts to tackle anxiety-producing themes in his work. I believe that one of the most valuable features of Meyer's book is the demonstration that Conrad was able to handle such material only when his adaptation was at its best as a result of optimally favorable life circumstances.

Paralleling these salutary changes in the matter of relevance, the inter-disciplinary work of the past two decades has also mitigated the pitfall of reductionism, that is, the tendency to explain cultural phenomena entirely in terms of their putative sources in the psychological world of early childhood. We can grasp the nature of this change through another brief illustration. We recall that Freud traced the Mona Lisa smile to Leonardo's supposed childhood memories of his mother's facies—a highly speculative inference. Yet it is easy to formulate an alternative hypothesis: We can assume that this stylistic feature of Leonardo's art had its roots in memories from his adolescence in Verrocchio's studio. We can postulate that it was in his admired master's works, in other words, that Leonardo found the source of this striking feature of his art. Such an interpretation is no less psychoanalytic than Freud's reconstruction and, incidentally, does not even contradict the latter. Moreover, it does not reduce the artist's choice to a psychological automatism; in addition to highlighting the meaning of this stylistic identification as an indication of Verrocchio's role as a parental figure for his apprentice, the alternative hypothesis acknowledges the likelihood that Leonardo's creative solution was, at the same time, a conscious process of matching available stylistic alternatives to the creative problem involved in the work as a gestalt.

As I have already mentioned, Eissler's 1961 study of Leonardo certainly paid a fair amount of attention to considerations of this kind, but at that time his approach was still based on the assumption that the subject of a biography might be understood psychologically by means of inferences deductively derived from the psychoanalytic hypotheses of the day. This procedure constitutes another form of reductionism: Forcing all behavior into the preexisting categories of our theory not only stultifies the poten-tial expansion of psychoanalytic knowledge but pours the creative genius into the confining mold of a mental world familiar to us. By 1967, of course, Eissler himself explicitly postulated that much of the unusual behavior of creative personalities should not be confused with ordinary psychopathology. In the spirit of Eissler's injunction, Meyer's description of an artist's need for a double was the earliest appearance of such a syndrome in the analytic literature; the corresponding psychopathology of ordinary persons would only be delineated later (Kohut, 1968, 1971). But even Meyer's work stops short of the ambitious goal that Max Graf posed for applied analysis, that of developing a "theory of artistic creation."

V

THE VALIDITY of hypotheses about the psychology of the artist could, of course, best be tested with clinical data from the analytic treatment of personalities creative in various media (see Section II). But the problem of confidentiality that reduces the frequency of clinical reports about actual analyses is greatly compounded in the case of successful artists, and few such artists have probably sought analytic assistance in any event. Probably owing to these circumstances, the number of clinical reports dealing with successful artists has been surprisingly small.

In this respect, I once surveyed the entire psychoanalytic literature pertaining to the visual arts (Gedo, 1970b) and found that Pfister (1922) was the first analyst to describe the treatment of such a patient, an expressionist painter. In retrospect, this analysis probably came to grief because of Pfister's excessive interest in examining the distortions in his patient's drawings at the expense of exploring his crisis-ridden life. In the earlier literature, brief accounts of successfully treated analytic patients in whose lives painting played an important part include only one who could possibly be rated a professional artist with real talent (Heimann, 1942). Moreover, all we can learn about creativity from the account of this analysis is that the quality of the patient's artistic work allegedly improved during the analysis and deteriorated with exacerbations of his conflicts. The products of the amateur artists treated by other analysts seemed to deal with traumatic memories; that is, they were transient attempts to master certain overwhelming experiences. One receives a very different perspective on amateur productions from the autobiographical account of the amateur painter and psychoanalyst Marion Milner (1969). She explains her own creative efforts in terms of reparative impulsions in reaction to unconscious aggression. As I have stated elsewhere (Gedo, 1972b), great art necessarily differs from the symptomatic products created to master such conflicts, because it cannot be confined to such a schematic focus on a single psychological problem.

Because of the scarcity of published clinical data about creative people in general, an extensive report by Niederland (1967) assumes added significance. He described seven patients, including four painters, with a commendable refusal to generalize from his experience. All of his patients had sustained what Niederland designated as severe and permanent narcissistic injuries (often in the form of bodily defects); they subsequently used their creativeness in the service of reaching for unattainable perfection. More recently, Niederland (1976) has reaffirmed these hypotheses and has drawn on historical data in an effort to show that the artist's narcissistic vulnerability may result either from bodily imperfections or bereavements. Niederland has noted the disparity between his conclusions and those related by Greenacre (1957) in her account of the childhood of the artist. Unfortunately, we are not in a position to weigh this difference of opinion, because these authors are at opposite poles in terms of the way they have presented their data. Greenacre's concern about confidentiality led her to omit all personal facts about her patients, to the point of refusing to divulge even their sphere of artistic endeavor. In contrast,

Niederland (1967) published photographs of the paintings of one patient through which the latter's identity might well have become known to a certain number of people. Kleinschmidt (1967) has also reported on the treatment of an artist of "worldwide fame"; unless the data have been fictionalized, more than a few people will be able to identify his patient. Severe "narcissistic problems" were also found in this case, although here creation was seen by the analyst as an angry act that permitted the artist to maintain an illusion of omnipotent control over his environment. As far as I know, no psychoanalyst has to date equaled the breach of confidence perpetrated by the therapist of Jackson Pollock, who published interpretations of drawings that Pollock produced as part of the treatment efforts (Wysuph, 1970).

Perhaps the most interesting clinical report published thus far is Oremland's (1975) account of the analysis of a jazz musician. This talented performer, according to the analyst, used his wind instrument as a bond to his mother and expressed his grief about various losses and disappointments through the mournful music he selected to play. Analysis uncovered the fact that the instrument had previously belonged to a woman who had actually been his principal childhood caretaker; hence, it could continue to compensate him for his mother's general lack of availability. Since he unconsciously used the instrument as an auxiliary phallus, he developed an inhibition about performing in public at certain stages of the analysis, that is, when his musical activities acquired the significance in the transference relationship that his phallic masculinity had had in childhood in relation to his mother. Concurrently, he began to pay attention to his own spontaneous invention of melodies, although he was significantly conflicted about communicating them to his analyst. He eventually began to compose, and, significantly, his first completed composition was a trio, a form that symbolized the harmony he sought within his nuclear family. The patient's capacity to perform in public returned after Oremland had grasped the fact that, for him, playing the work of other composers was a compromise between his ambition to become original and autonomous and his symbiotic need to remain an extension of his mother. The analysis achieved a reasonably satisfactory therapeutic result, given the artist's numerous personal difficulties. He continued to be successful as a performer, although several years after termination he reported being unable to bring his compositions to a satisfactory closure.

One of the greatest merits of Oremland's paper is the candor of his exposition about the course of the analysis and its outcome. In my judgment, the analysis reached a partial stalemate over the issue of the patient's view of Oremland as a magical caretaker. In terms of his childhood experience, the patient had learned to sacrifice his autonomy in order to maintain this illusory protection. It is on the basis of the repetition of such a fantasy that his continuing creative inhibition could perhaps be explained. This is not the place to speculate about the probable reasons for this outcome; in general terms, however, Oremland may have focused his interpretations on the derivatives of the oedipal phase of development to the relative neglect of more archaic issues.

The various clinical reports I have cited demonstrate yet another difference in approach. Greenacre makes careful distinctions among amateurs, artisans, artists of moderate gifts, and artists of great talent. She points out that the psychology of the creative impulsions in these separate groups is probably quite distinct. Niederland, on the other hand, accepts any attempt at artistic production as creative. Dare one conclude that his patients lacked the special endowments Greenacre attributes to the future artist because they actually lacked major artistic talent? To be sure, such a question cannot be answered on the basis of worldly success; judging by the published photographs, however, it seems that at least one of Niederland's patients lacked the requisite talent. At any rate, the issue of relevance as it pertains to clinical evidence brought forward to buttress psychoanalytic propositions about creativity will remain insoluble until we can agree on criteria about just what constitutes significant artistic achievement. And until we reach such a consensus, we shall still need to leave the confines of the consulting room in order to investigate biographically the nature of creativity in the greatest of its exemplars.

Chapter Two

Studies of Aesthetics and Creativity

I

IN A PENETRATING review of psychoanalytic contributions to aesthetics, Louis Fraiberg (1956) observed that these efforts have concentrated on literature because it can be studied by means of the familiar symbolic notation of everyday language. He pointed out that the understanding of other art forms, notably music and the visual arts, requires mastery of their specific, often unfamiliar symbolic languages; without the requisite preparation, the investigator cannot hope to decipher their message. Aesthetic media that convey the artist's meaning in essentially wordless ways rely much less on subject matter or overt narrative content than does literature. Even the art of the writer depends on aesthetic form, however, so that its significance cannot be grasped by the study of content alone.

As a group, psychoanalysts are notorious for their investment in the word, and this predilection doubtless directed their attention to the literary arts. Even within this area, moreover, they have largely confined themselves to biographical studies,[1] as their actual area of expertise is the

---

1. The most natural extension of psychobiography has been in the field of fictional narrative where it has served as a key to the understanding of the motivations of characters. To the extent that an author has created his fictional universe with true psychological insight, such extrapolation presents relatively few problems for those naturalistic works in which each character presumably stands for a person one might encounter in actuality. But the application of depth psychology to literature (and to other forms of narrative, such as opera or motion pictures) is a most difficult enterprise because of uncertainties about the limits of naturalistic representation in great art (see Gedo, 1972a, 1978). We cannot invariably assume that every character in a story portrays one discrete human being. Authors often create characters as abstract symbols of particular human propensities, for example, as personifications of virtues or vices, humors, character traits, or various aspects of intrapsychic conflicts. Hence, it is often more sound to correlate fictional characters with

psychological examination of individual lives. By contrast, aestheticians have turned to depth psychology in the hope of elucidating the meaning of the abstract symbolism hidden within the nonrepresentational forms of any artistic statement. Such critics tend to value the aesthetic object to the degree that it serves to express a pattern of emotion symbolically. From this novel point of view, psychoanalysis could become an indispensable tool of art theory, one that underscores the primacy of form over narrative content in art. We must always remember that the affective impact of a work of art depends on its formal qualities; this impact is entirely absent in an unaesthetic presentation of its content.

With his Freud Lectures of 1963, Robert Waelder (1965) inaugurated an era of increased sophistication in the application of psychoanalysis to aesthetics. He provided a map of the various avenues to art (as he called them) made available by psychoanalytic theory by organizing his presentation in terms of the groups of conflicting mental functions depicted in Freud's final, structural model of the mind. According to Waelder, the id approach to art consisted of the identification of the potent latent meanings depicted by the artist; this was the traditional method of interpretation used in psychoanalytic studies of culture. Waelder stressed the uselessness of such decoding of the overt subject matter in adjudging the aesthetic merit of art. Those formal elements through which the artist conveys his central affective message to the audience were better investigated through an ego approach that considered either the economy of artistic solutions (as in Mies van der Rohe's aphorism "Less is more") or the power and grandeur embodied in the complexity of these solutions. Waelder placed the question of artistic meaning in the realm of a superego approach related to the aesthetic transcendence of nature, or, if you will, to the spiritualization accomplished through the relinquishment of illusions. From this standpoint, one of the main functions of art, as Stendhal reportedly observed, is "to purge the soul, as swiftly and durably as possible, of every taint of this world."

Waelder was aware of the limitations of a psychology of art that was confined to the tripartite model which Freud devised to portray the mind in conflict (see Gedo & Goldberg, 1973, Chapter 3). In recognition of

---

embodiments of the *generalizations* of psychoanalytic psychology about human nature than to treat such symbolic constructs as if they were meant to represent an actual person.

As one illustration of such a correlation with prototypes of human traits, already used by the pioneers of depth-psychological literary studies, one can cite Otto Rank's discussion of the Don Juan legend (1924): Rank interprets the figure of Leporello in Mozart's operatic version as a personification of the devalued conscience of Don Juan himself. Of course, it was relatively easy to arrive at this conclusion, as *Don Giovanni* explicitly abandoned naturalistic representation in a number of obvious ways. In cases where an author refrains from forewarning us of such departures in an analogous manner, we may mistakenly accept a pseudonaturalistic surface at face value.

this fact, he did provide an avenue for studying artistic phenomena that did not fit into this schema. Intent on providing a way to comprehend the patterns of tension and discharge created in the audience by the formal elements of the work, he labeled this extension of the model the "prestructural approach." Waelder's reservations about the ability of the structural theory to encompass aesthetic issues raise a crucial issue that will be addressed throughout this volume: Do artistic creation and aesthetic response belong in the realm of psychic conflict at all? We will consider this question in detail in Sections II and III; here, it suffices to note that even those mental operations that Waelder, for the sake of didactic convenience, associated with the id, ego, and superego approaches respectively, may ordinarily take place in a conflict-free manner, as he himself acknowledged (cf. Esman, 1979).

It is true that until recently psychoanalytic theory was content to assign all the impelling forces of the archaic self to the id, all the higher intellectual functions to the sphere of the ego, and the sum of man's ideals to the superego. Even in the clinical arena, however, these schematic conceptualizations left much to be desired. It would be more accurate to say that, *in case of conflict*, these functions seemed to approximate most closely those aspects of the personality that represented repudiated archaic aims, currently acceptable goals, and individual value systems respectively. In the absence of conflict, however, the personality cannot be meaningfully subdivided in this manner (see Gedo & Goldberg, 1973, Chapter 12; Gedo, 1979a, 1981a). Thus, the economy of an artistic solution, to take one example, is not only rooted in the activity of the ego. In fact, psychoanalytic theory assigns every behavior multiple functions— a principle enunciated long ago by Waelder himself (1930).

In a difficult and erudite essay entitled "On the Creation of Beauty and Thought," Joseph Coltrera (1965) was the first to articulate the demand that applied analysis attain adequacy both in historical scholarship and theoretical coherence. Coltrera convincingly demonstrated that formulations of the arts based on a focus on the unconscious, that is, formulations relying only on Freud's topographic theory of mental function of 1900, were seriously inadequate. Coltrera saw correlations of the subject matter of the arts with presumed unconscious sources in the artist as all too easy; he aptly derided such efforts as "a specie of psychoanalytic fauvism."

A more viable alternative to the approach criticized by Coltrera was suggested by D. W. Winnicott in 1967. He attributed artistic experience to that realm of mental life, beginning in infancy, which involved "transitional objects and phenomena." Winnicott was of course referring to the phase of psychological development that precedes the separation of the ego from the id—and even the differentiation of one's own person from the outside world. His attempt to derive artistic experience from this developmental phase is congruent with studies of Phyllis Greenacre (1957,

1958a, 1958b, 1960) that point to the status of art as a repository of vital aspects of the self that have been created through the use of drive energies that have not been sublimated—a finding that runs counter to Freud's assumptions about the relationship between sublimation and art. In Greenacre's view, the artistic product is an idealized object, tenuously distinguished from the self and therefore akin to an infantile fetish. A fetish, in this connection, refers to an object the young child endows with magical significance and uses to ward off anxiety; such fetishes are referable to a developmental level when Winnicott's "transitional objects" have normally been relinquished.

Rosen (1964) has found support for these hypotheses in a study of gifted adolescents who related to their playthings in a special manner comparable to the way primitive people deal with their religious fetishes. Similar formulations were put forward two decades earlier by the English critic Adrian Stokes (1945), who emphasized that the aesthetic object is an ideal object that is seen as lively, complete, and stable. Whatever its subject matter, the aesthetic object is capable of giving pleasure through the poignancy of its facture; in this way, archaic aspects of the inner world that are ordinarily unacceptable to many persons may be made public through externalization into a realm of illusion without conflict.[2] Donald Meltzer (in Stokes, 1963) has extended this notion into a definition of art as analogous to a sermon urging the acknowledgment of archaic conflicts, an enterprise that unavoidably arouses resistances. Although Meltzer's conception of art may be excessively narrow, its relevance to a large segment of recent culture will be demonstrated repeatedly in this book.

More recently, Modell (1970) and Weissman (1971) have independently seconded Winnicott's formulation by placing it into a developmental perspective. These authors view the objects created by the artist as more sophisticated versions of the transitional objects of the infant (i.e., cherished possessions with special meaning, such as a blanket or a teddy bear). From this point of view, artistic activity is in no sense regressive or pathological, as earlier psychoanalytic conceptualizations frequently implied. McDonald (1970), in this connection, has made explicit the notion of a developmental line for aesthetic capabilities. She has postulated that, in certain homes, infants are provided with musical experiences that make it possible for the child to create a "transitional activity" by way of

---

2. I shall not discuss *in extenso* the psychoanalytic theories of art put forward by Melanie Klein and her followers, because I regard the conceptualizations of this psychoanalytic school as radically in error from a scientific point of view. It is regrettable that the interdisciplinary work of a critic as distinguished as Stokes should have been marred by reliance on these unsound foundations. I have reviewed one of Stokes's major books (1963) in some detail elsewhere (Gedo, 1970b). Bychowski (1951) demonstrated long ago that Kleinian formulations on aesthetics are unacceptably reductionistic.

mastering a tune. She believes, in other words, that the child will simultaneously experience the creation of the melody as part of himself and as an independent event. By way of evidence for her hypothesis, McDonald quotes a number of musicians who were "imbued with the spirit of music from the cradle." Perhaps musical talent originates via the extension of such transitional phenomena from specific tunes to music as a whole.

II

THE INTENSE intellectual ferment surrounding the application of depth psychology to aesthetics perhaps culminated with the publication of Anton Ehrenzweig's posthumous work, *The Hidden Order of Art* (1967). This important book is marred by the uneasy use of psychoanalytic conceptualizations often characteristic of scholars lacking clinical experience. Ehrenzweig tends to concretize and reify psychoanalytic constructs; the resulting difficulty is compounded by his preference for the terminology of various British schools of psychoanalysis that is generally alien to American readers. But any temptation to dismiss Ehrenzweig's work on these grounds should be resisted; the particular analytic constructs he uses are by no means central to his thesis, which can, in any event, be easily translated into more meaningful analytic terminology.

Ehrenzweig had unusual credentials as an art educator: Familiar with music as well as the visual arts, he acquired expertise in the theories of both Gestalt psychology and psychoanalysis. As his earlier book on aesthetics (1953) deals with many of the same issues he would discuss with greater clarity in the posthumous volume, I shall refrain from commenting on the earlier expression of Ehrenzweig's views, beyond calling attention to several points that are more fully elaborated in the first book.

Ehrenzweig views art as a process of communication in which ambiguity plays a central role (cf. Kris, 1952, Chapter 10). He propounds the hypothesis (1967, pp. 21–31) that aesthetic feeling results whenever successful articulation has been attained between two distinct modes of perception: One mode is composed of gestalten, the other mode is gestalt-free. Ehrenzweig also offers a hypothesis concerning the developmental line of the perceptual functions that illuminates the existence of and interrelatedness between the two perceptual modes (pp. 3–20). He follows Freud in postulating that the child's initial mode of perceiving is global, syncretistic, and abstract. Freud had noted that the nature of such early percepts is inevitably falsified by attempts to describe them in words. Ehrenzweig believes that, in the visual sphere, the child acquires a new capacity for "analytic" vision at around the age of eight that enables him to compare the details of objects and to establish their gestalt. Parallel developments presumably take place in the other perceptual channels for, as Piaget (1923) has shown, the child's thinking in general is reorganized around the age of eight. For most people, the more archaic mode of perceiving is gradually crowded out of consciousness. Ehrenzweig attributes this process to the operation of repression; he seems to have been unfamiliar with the psychoanalytic concept of a hierarchy of alternative defense mechanisms (see Gedo & Goldberg, 1973, pp. 89–100). In my judgment, the particular mechanism most likely to be employed in the type of circumstances Ehrenzweig has in mind is that of disavowal.[3]

The most persuasive evidence for Ehrenzweig's general hypothesis about the two modes of perception comes from experiences in teaching people cured of blindness to see for the first time (1967, p. 13). These individuals find it extremely difficult to grasp the gestalten of objects; they have much greater success in perceiving people or things they care about in a syncretistic manner. Perhaps this point can be clarified through a clinical illustration from my practice: A grossly obese woman reported that her little daughter had frequently called her beautiful until the child reached the age of 6. At that time, she began to show distress on looking at her mother, complaining that the latter had "too much meat." This example underscores the fact that form perception is a relatively late achievement; prior to this time, objects are recognized in a global manner without regard to their actual details.

The coexistence of two modes of perception, only one of which is regularly available for subsequent cognitive activity, is an important depth-psychological discovery; it extends into the perceptual sphere our understanding of the lack of correspondence between consciousness and reality. People are generally quite reluctant to acknowledge the limitations of their self-knowledge. In light of this fact, Ehrenzweig recommends personal experimentation to convince oneself of the instability of one's own "reality constancy": He urges us to record, over time, our changing perceptions of new styles in art. As hitherto unperceived elements of the stimulus are gradually integrated by the new observer, Ehrenzweig theorizes, they gradually enter into the familiar language of artistic discourse, capable of verbal articulation. He credits Gombrich (1954) with observing that when the potential for such articulation is realized, the artistic mode in question turns into a "mere" symbol; innovators will at that point turn to new modes that supply the audience with fewer cues about how to read them.

---

3. Repression implies that an *idea* is kept out of consciousness; it is therefore unclear how repression could apply to the processing of a percept without producing a negative hallucination. With the defense of disavowal, it is the *significance* of mental contents that is not given proper weight.

According to Ehrenzweig (1953, pp. 22-44), the surface gestalt, which screens the gestalt-free elements that carry unconscious symbolism, is the main agent of beauty in the work of art. The hidden elements that serve as vehicles for deeper affects in musical performance, for example, are the interpretive variations (e.g., "primitive" vibrato or glissando) that are not to be found in the written score. Kris (1952, p. 57) believes that great art attracts a wider audience by offering the pleasure of its beauty in exchange for the acceptance of disturbing aspects of its message. But Ehrenzweig observes that an image possessing only the surface qualities of beautiful gestalt will be unable to convey the feeling that it is real, the quality he terms "plasticity." The conviction of truth conveyed either aurally or visually is the result of strong perceptual elements that do not explicitly enter consciousness. (The same principle must be valid for literature and particularly poetry.) Even the artist cannot at first detect this hidden fabric in his work. At length, this exciting aspect of the gestalt-free percept will be recognized; for a period of time, the art work incorporating the percept may be felt to be ugly, only to be ultimately enshrined as beautiful but passé—that is, as an example of an historical style.

Ehrenzweig's aesthetic theory also illuminates the genesis of artistic talent in the capacity to preserve the use of both modes of perception. For the ordinary person, fresh perception is impossible; our manner of seeing (and hearing) is always learned. Thus, conventional schemata or mannerisms always win acceptance as *the* valid representation of reality. It is instructive, in this connection, to compare the way Western art represents reality with the vastly different conventions of Far Eastern painting. Ehrenzweig observes that the illusionism characteristic of the Renaissance and its sequelae should not, in fact, be construed as the triumph of realism. In his work of 1953, he demonstrated that the achievement of this era in the history of art had been precisely the opposite: In the aftermath of the Renaissance, the artist no longer tried to create an image of perceived reality but offered, in its place, a rational schematization; that is, the discovery of perspective foreshortening amounts to the abandonment of the constancy of form. In actuality, it was the more "abstract" representational mode of pre-Renaissance painting that presented the percepts of things "objectively."

In fact, as Ehrenzweig (1967, pp. 178-192) shows, the history of Western painting since 1400 is a steady progression in the degree of subjectivity permitted the artist. Painters of the baroque era discovered the possibilities inherent in abandoning the constancy of tone, that is, in the use of chiaroscuro; the impressionists abandoned color constancy in their studies of atmospheric variation; finally, Cézanne gave up even the constancy of localization in his integration of peripheral perceptions in his images. In painting, each of these formal developments yielded an art form more lifelike, more plastic, and less stylized than its predecessor—

provided the viewer was willing to abandon the perceptual schemata he had been trained to understand and see instead the actual percepts he was being offered by the artist. It is fascinating to learn that the Chinese, when first exposed to Western painting in the 17th century, were quickly able to integrate foreshortening but could not accept the use of chiaroscuro. This evidence suggests that the sequence in which the various constancies of form were abandoned in Europe could not have been accidental. It would follow that the acquisition of the perceptual schemata corresponding to these various constancies must take place in the reverse order in individual development: first localization, then color, shading, and finally gestalt form.

Ehrenzweig's view of the structure of art implies that the task of the artist is deliberately to invite his audience to complete the perceptual–cognitive task of reading his work more or less as he intended; pleasure probably ensues from the mastery of this intellectual challenge (cf. Freud's related hypothesis about the power of jokes [1905c, pp. 95–96]). From this viewpoint, productions that do not involve intentionality on the part of their creator but rely entirely on the projections of the audience should not be defined as art. In recent years, the audience has adapted ever more rapidly to the successive disruptions of its traditional schemata: The novelty of avant-garde styles wears off faster and faster. When artists begin to use these styles consciously, they have become academic and decorative. When even the audience has gained the ability to perceive them consciously, these same "new" styles are experienced as calm and beautiful. We thus see Greek sculpture in terms of its Apollonian harmony, whereas the Hellenes themselves probably reacted to it with Dionysiac excitement. It follows that the qualities of a given style have no specific reality of their own.

For Ehrenzweig, it remains true nevertheless that much of the art of our own century is without precedent in requiring no response at all at the level of a gestalt; we are forced to focus entirely on its hidden order (1967, pp. 64–77). In making this claim, he means to suggest that such works are uniquely poor in intellectual content. Ehrenzweig believes that Cézanne was the last major painter to have worked within the tradition of rationalism; his successors espoused a return to the irrational, gestalt-free modes of primitive art. Traditional art had contained the same gestalt-free elements in its backgrounds; from the point of view of aesthetic impact, it was these inconspicuous elements that acquired crucial significance. Originality had consisted in varying details, not in changing styles and traditions altogether—a hallmark of the evolution of art in recent times.

Because the contemporary artist is unable to perceive consciously the image (or composition) he is about to create, his work may seem to be automatic, and he is often said to be in touch with his unconscious. Such claims seem absurd in terms of what psychoanalysis means by unconsciousness; Ehrenzweig's hypotheses provide us with a reasonable explanation of this phenomenon in terms of the archaic perceptual mode that continues to operate alongside the conscious one. We do not have to rely on magical notions about artistic creativity if we distinguish between the operation of these parallel perceptual processes and abide by Freud's basic discovery of the two kinds of thinking that typify preconscious mental activity: the "primary process" that is the language of subjectivity and the "secondary process" that is the language of rational thought.

Much of the psychoanalytic literature on aesthetics suffers from obscurity as a result of a failure to differentiate the issue of conscious versus gestalt-free perception from the issue of primary process versus secondary process thinking. Both Kohut (1957) and Noy (1968), for example, seem to regard evidence of the employment of mechanisms such as condensation and displacement within the structure of the aesthetic object as support for the conclusion that both artist and audience make use of primary process thinking. In fact, such evidence merely demonstrates an analogy between art and dreaming; it does not mean that the two activities are homologous. I believe that the resulting confusion would have been avoided if psychoanalysts, following Freud's example, had not characterized all mental operations involving condensation and displacement as primary processes *by definition.*

It would be more fruitful to differentiate primary process from secondary processes in terms of the appropriateness of the means of thought utilized for meaningful communication. Corbin (1974) shares my sense that many analytic authors have erred in equating the technical devices of art with primitive thought processes such as those found in dreaming. When the mechanisms of thinking found in dreams are consciously manipulated by the artist, Corbin plausibly construes them as tools of rational thought. Noy (1972) himself has offered a similar perspective in his more recent work; he asserts that mature artistic talent involves the capacity to handle a specific medium in optimal fashion in the service of conveying a message to an audience. Hence, Noy concludes, art is one channel for the communication of human experience, whereas dreaming and fantasy constitute alternative channels of transmission.

III

IF WE NOW RETURN to the problem of creativity, we might sum up the essence of Ehrenzweig's theoretical contribution by stating that creative thinking cannot be conceptualized as a return to the archaic, a "regression in the service of the ego" as Kris (1952, pp. 310–318) once put it. On the contrary, creativity must be based on inborn capacities that have an independent line of development and only come to fruition after a long process of maturation.[4] Of course, this conclusion was already implicit in Eissler's 1961 study of Leonardo. In proposing that the genius undergoes repeated personality alterations throughout his life cycle without permanently solving his conflicts (which may then serve as a spur to his creativity), Eissler stressed that in such exceptional individuals an ego of unusual strength permitted the use of mental operations from all developmental levels. This sophisticated formulation is not adequately encompassed by Kris's simple notion of regression in the service of the ego.

The depth psychology of perception developed by Ehrenzweig suggests that the artist is able to create through the simultaneous use of two types of perception. He must be able to divide his attention between them without letting this activity intrude on his awareness, that is, via a preconscious scanning that is simultaneously conjunctive and serial. The process is most easily illustrated with regard to musical composition because musical notation actually distributes these distinct elements in different spatial dimensions on the paper: The harmonic gestalt is noted vertically whereas the unfocused polyphony is entered horizontally. Very similar mental dispositions have been associated with virtuosity in mathematics, chess, the evenly hovering attention required of the psychoanalyst, and so forth. The integration of hidden substructures is most impressively exemplified by the creative activities of Bach and Mozart, composers able to imagine whole works in a time-free fashion, that is, to complete entire compositions synchronously.

These considerations led Ehrenzweig to conclude that creative work requires the capacity to tolerate imperfections in oneself as well as in one's product; it presupposes mastery, in other words, of archaic grandiose ambitions. Accordingly, Ehrenzweig suspected that neurotic inhibitions of creativity usually stemmed from "narcissistic" problems. In seeming paradox, overt psychosis does not necessarily prevent artists from producing art, even though cognitive disruptions of this magnitude may make it impossible to produce works in which good gestalt is preserved. Ehrenzweig therefore defined artistic work as "psychotic" whenever it lacked inner coherence and, consequently, aesthetic merit. We may restate this position by claiming that great art needs affective contributions from all developmental levels; severe pathology in the artist cuts off potential access to the depths. In contrast, the productions of children lack aesthetic value because of their concreteness, that is, because of the absence of a contribution from more developmentally advanced sectors of the personality. The creation of great art may give rise to profound anxiety

---

4. Nass (1975) attributes the hyperacuity of musicians to sounds and rhythms to early vicissitudes within the mother–child unit that organize the cognitive functions around the auditory sphere.

precisely because it obliges the artist to become aware of the earliest levels of his affectivity, even those preceding the unification of his self-organization (see Gedo, 1979a, 1981a). Ehrenzweig believes that artists often concretize their awareness of subjective experience originating in the era preceding unification of the self through typical fantasies symbolizing the dissolution of psychic integrity.

Noy (1969) has made use of Ehrenzweig's viewpoint in an important reevaluation of the psychoanalytic theory of thinking. In agreement with a number of authors who have followed the lead of Jean Piaget, he proposes that primary and secondary processes must have independent developmental lines, that is, that both modes of thought continue to coexist throughout life. Thus, Noy no longer believes that the language of rational thought grows out of a prior language expressive of subjectivity. Clearly, artistic activities depend on the creative use of both primary and secondary process thinking as well as on the integration of both modes of perception.[5]

Nass (1971) may have been the first author to spell out the implications of this perspective for a specific creative activity, that of musical composition. Beginning with Suzanne Langer's assumption that music is a symbolic form (i.e., a nonverbal language) which articulates human feeling states that cannot be rendered discursively, he postulated that individuals with a cognitive style centered around the auditory sphere are able simultaneously to use early and later perceptual modes to handle this highly rational medium in a nonregressive fashion. Noy (1968), in his own writings on music, also stressed that earlier psychoanalytic authors had erred in their discussions of music by confusing its subject matter, which Noy equates with the full gamut of human emotions, with its aesthetic, which is organized in a highly sophisticated manner. Noy cogently observed that the assumption that music is universally accessible as a language is simply false: Its comprehension requires training within a specific tradition and is perhaps facilitated by the possession of special gifts.

Noy (1966) has also made perceptive contributions to our understanding of the development of artistic talent. He defines such talent as a special ability to structure the product by means of both primary and

---

5. As I have discussed in greater detail elsewhere (Gedo, 1972a), Eissler (1971) has attempted to conceptualize the unusual capacity of the great creator to make optimal use in his work of both primary and secondary thought processes as a special ego function (for which he proposes the term "doxatheleic"). But this semantic solution provides no specific explanation of the nature of this function. More germanely, Rothenberg (1971) has postulated that a variety of specific ways of thinking may be involved in this capacity, the most important of which he characterizes as "Janusian thought." By this, Rothenberg refers to the simultaneous conception of mutually contradictory alternatives as one new gestalt. It is difficult to grasp how this idea differs from the viewpoint of Ehrenzweig.

secondary process thinking. Such talent may well be confined to a specific medium of communication. If Noy is correct, it would also follow that talents in various fields of artistic endeavor may originate at various junctures in development. This finding would imply that conclusions about the creativity of one group of artists cannot be legitimately applied to other groups. Noy argues that because the artist has to relate to his medium in a twofold manner—as both a set of concrete objects and events organized in accord with the primary process and as a rationally organized set of communicative signs, symbols, and signals—the genesis of artistic talent must occur at the very time that the specific perceptual modality implicated in a specific medium undergoes its transition from primary to secondary process functioning. In making this claim, Noy seems to fall into the confusion that has characterized the literature in general: He fails to distinguish the issue of different perceptual modalities from the subsequent controlled processing of these modalities via the full gamut of cognitive operations. Talent, in other words, must consist in the optimal development of both modes of perception whereby they may be used simultaneously and subjected to the widest possible array of cognitive transformations.

I would agree with Noy's more specific claim that the acquisition of the particular capacities that lead to poetic talent must occur when the consensual meaning of words is being added to the infant's paleological verbalizations somewhere around the end of the second year of life. It is generally agreed that the nonverbal arts probably rely on talents that must be consolidated even earlier, but we do not yet possess any reasonable schema to indicate the sequence in which they might arise. Perhaps Ehrenzweig's listing of the component structures of music and of the visual arts may serve as a program for future investigation of these problems. We might attempt to study, for example, what in the childhood experience of painters who are great colorists differs from the childhood experience of painters who are great draftsmen.

It should also be stressed that the hypothesis that talents arise at very early stages of development implies neither that their genesis is purely experiential (i.e., independent of constitutional variables), nor that their presence in the adult is irreversibly determined in infancy. On the contrary, the epigenetic theory of development intrinsic to psychoanalytic psychology obliges us to view any mental quality in the adult as the product of cumulative vicissitudes in the maturational sequence. It follows that artistic talent is equally influenced by experiences at the various stages of childhood and adolescence and, in the case of certain talents that mature later in life—the ability to perform successful clinical psychoanalyses may be one such talent—even by experiences of adulthood. In short, the anlagen of talents established in earliest childhood must undergo growth by means of a developmental process. This is yet another way of reiterating that the association of creativity with regression is not only unsatisfactory but downright misleading. In fact, Noy (1969) is probably correct in claiming that the autonomous functions involved in creation must actually undergo *unusual* growth in order to become available volitionally.

IV

THE MOST RECENT effort to apply the tools of depth psychology to the twin problems of aesthetics and creativity is the analyst Gilbert Rose's *The Power of Form* (1980). Rose correctly attributes the paucity of analytic studies in this field to the neglect of problems of perceptual organization, which has led, in turn, to a reductionistic focus on the artist's motivations. As I have observed, analysts have traditionally assumed that the artist's motivations are most clearly reflected in the narrative content of his work—an assumption, by the way, that Rose is unwilling to grant (see pp. 7–8). In his view, man actively creates his external world and, in this evolving process, great art permanently alters community perceptions by providing new organizing principles that we term "forms." Hence, Rose is unwilling to accept the usual dichotomy between art and science; quite reasonably, he defines scientific creativity as artistic activity in the medium of pure thought (pp. 28–30). From this perspective, art (in the narrow sense) is understood as deepening our vision about the categories of time, space, and personhood.

Rose concurs with the critics of Kris's understanding of artistic creation as a regression in the service of the ego, perceptively pointing out that this notion confuses the artist's creative capacities, which must be autonomous and developmentally advanced, with certain personal motivations for undertaking the creative task (pp. 76–77). (In Chapter 7 I shall discuss two distinct sets of such motivations.) As an example of such motivations, Rose considers the effort to achieve a form of perfection through creativity, presumably because such perfection was desired but never attained in the course of the artist's first creative endeavor, the organization of his self in early childhood (pp. 33–47). Rose calls self-creation "the creativity of everyday life" (pp. 114–115). If the artist's motivation for his work is to attain perfection, its reparative function is conceivable only if the work is never completely differentiated from the creator's own person. To this extent, Rose sees artistic activity as the restoration of a state in which the self is expanded through a fantasy of fusion with an external object—an idea similar to Winnicott's concept of "transitional phenomena."

Because artistic activity may involve such archaic fantasies, much of the subject matter of contemporary art has been the quasi-autobiographical depiction of these primitive states of being. In works such as Samuel Beckett's *Molloy* (which Rose discusses with great sensitivity), literary art comes close to paralleling psychoanalytic interpretive activity (pp. 79–90). In this respect, even works with such primitive subject matter must be seen as expressions of mastery rather than signs of psychopathology.

Rose emphasizes the fact that all artistic creativity makes use of bodily activity; in this sense, the most fundamental component of every art is movement (pp. 97–109). This assertion is most obviously valid with respect to the dance and musical performance as well as the execution of work in the plastic arts; if we conceptualize poetry in terms of the spoken word, it would apply to this form of creative expression as well. It is less clear what kind of motor activity might be involved in musical composition, the conceptualization of works in the visual arts, or the creation of various types of narratives. For Rose, at any rate, the earliest signs of artistic talent are probably to be sought in the child's motor organization.

Rose agrees with previous authors who have stated that aesthetic form harmonizes logically irreconcilable dualities. He also believes that the artist must consciously use a combination (or continuum) of primary and secondary thought processes in a flexible manner if he is to achieve this end (pp. 130–143). In essence, then, Rose agrees with Ehrenzweig's viewpoint, but he is not absolutely consistent in clarifying that the various artistic media do not differ as to *subject matter* but only in terms of the kind of *percepts* they utilize. He correctly observes that visual art involves the manipulation of spatial percepts, whereas poetry proffers words simultaneously as carriers of ideas and as sounds arranged in a metrical fashion. In certain contexts, however, Rose writes as if poetry could not describe a landscape or an interior in spatial terms, or as if painting were always merely the equivalent of an architectural blueprint. Obviously, Rose knows better.

He demonstrates his understanding in a masterful analysis of the orchestration of time in William Faulkner's novel *Light in August* (pp. 168–192). Rose is well aware, in other words, that, *as part of their subject matter*, music, the visual arts, and literature may all deal in the most profound manner with problems of time, space, or person. In terms of forms, however, music is the medium involved with the "plasticity of time" in the same way as architecture and sculpture make use of transforming space, painting of transmitting color, dancing of regulating movement, and so forth. In this sense, Rose does not sufficiently emphasize the fact that literature differs fundamentally from other media because it is necessarily encoded in one particular language that is also a vernacular.[6]

---

6. The enormous complexity of the aesthetics of literature may be gleaned by comparing the quartets of formal components Ehrenzweig (1953) compiled for music (pp. 153–167) and painting (pp. 143–152) with a similar list Rose took from a work on poetics by John Ciardi (1960). He mentions rhythm, diction, rhyme, grammatical structure, line length, imagery, vowel quantity, and consonantal sequence (in Rose, 1980, p. 142). Obviously, the language in which the poem is written should be added to this list.

Rose postulates that the appreciation of a work of art requires a "temporary lifting of the boundaries between self and object" (p. 203), that is, between the self and whatever the artist has offered. In this way, the audience accepts a message akin to an analytic interpretation; its formal qualities are apprehended simultaneously as aspects of "an *idealized* representation of the workings of one's own mind" (p. 203), thus replenishing self-esteem. In my judgment, it is Rose's consistent stress on the nature of artistic activity as dialogue that constitutes the decisive contribution of his work to the psychoanalytic study of aesthetics.

If we view Rose's work as the most recent manifestation of the new psychoanalytic approaches to aesthetics and creativity that have become increasingly prominent over the past two decades, it may serve as an appropriate illustration of the fact that an avant-garde within psychoanalysis has begun to satisfy Spector's (1973, p. 145) demand "that students building on Freud's insights . . . bridge the gaps toward the formal, perceptual aspects of art." The works of Ehrenzweig, Rose, and other recent contributors (e.g., M. Gedo, 1980a, 1980b) constitute an auspicious start in this direction. Much remains to be done to forge a fully satisfactory psychoanalytic theory of aesthetics, but we should take heart at the progress of the past 20 years; it has opened the way for depth-psychological studies of creativity free of the deficiencies of earlier psychoanalytic efforts in this field. The remainder of this volume represents my own contribution to the contemporary psychoanalytic understanding of the creative process.

Section II

Clinical Studies

AS I HAVE TRIED to demonstrate in Section I, psychoanalysis as a
conceptual system has the power to illuminate problems of biography,
aesthetics, creativity, and the significance of works of art. But however
meaningful the conclusions of such studies may be, they cannot be
validated within the boundaries of nonclinical applications of the psychoanalytic method. Correspondingly, propositions developed in the course
of studying cultural materials psychoanalytically can be submitted to the
test of scientific validation in the course of certain relevant psychoanalytic
treatments. And the resulting conclusions can subsequently be reapplied
to further historical data.

It should be noted that clinical validation studies cannot be arranged in
advance. The opportunity to test given propositions can only be grasped
in retrospect, once the natural experiment of a therapeutic analysis has
yielded results and the analyst, now turned investigator, realizes that
these results are relevant to the resolution of certain scientific questions.
This is tantamount to acknowledging that the only legitimate function of
a psychoanalytic treatment is the gain in the analysand's self-knowledge
it optimally yields; any tendentious interest on the part of the analyst,
including the desire to carry out a piece of scientific research, risks being
experienced by the analysand as outrageous exploitation. In fact, it may
severely prejudice the outcome of treatment if it happens to repeat certain
traumatic aspects of the patient's childhood past, that is, if the parents also
exploited the child for their own private ends. Hence, it is incumbent on
the analyst to defer scientific interest in a given case until the therapeutic
task has been completed.

With appropriate safeguards of this kind, the analytic situation, that is,
the unfolding of free associations in the presence of an empathic witness,
remains the royal road to the attainment of new depth-psychological

insights. In this section, I shall report on my opportunities to study creativity and its disturbances *in vivo* in the clinical setting. Despite the fact that few of the creative individuals who have sought my assistance have attained the stature of the historical figures studied by biographers, my clinical data remain illuminating because they bring to light relevant information about the artist's childhood seldom available on the basis of historical research.

In this regard, I have been surprised to discover, as a result of widespread albeit unsystematic inquiries, that my clientele is decidedly atypical when compared to that of most colleagues in my community. The only analyst whose writings convey a sense of continuous exposure to creative people of the kind I have experienced is Phyllis Greenacre (1971). Other analysts have reported intensive clinical exposure to more limited segments of the creative community, such as the world of the New York theater (cf. Weissman, 1965). The Hollywood movie industry has also produced its share of celebrated patients, but the problem of confidentiality with such people is so unmanageable that these clinical encounters have thus far gone unreported.

The sampling issue is of some importance, because it influences the course of the psychoanalytic treatment process in the clinical encounters on which I base my conclusions: I believe that an unusually large number of individuals with creative ambitions are referred to me because the colleagues who make these referrals sense, if only preconsciously, that I am both comfortable and relatively successful in assisting people whose gifts can render them somewhat intimidating. It is even conceivable that certain of these patients who were affirmed in their creative pursuits as an outcome of analytic work with me might have followed a different route to healthy adaptation (by no means less desirable from their personal point of view) had they been treated by an analyst with different predilections and sensibilities.

The foregoing observation is particularly cogent with respect to a few analysands who began their work with me as students, before they had begun to make effective use of their talents. In other words, my enthusiasm for the results of most creative activities may well have pulled these patients in the direction of exploiting their gifts. Lest this remark be construed as an advertisement for my services, I hasten to add that one cannot beat the law of averages: A relative advantage in one particular area simultaneously constitutes a handicap in another. In over 25 years of private practice, for example, I have never analyzed a single business executive—although this occupational group forms the backbone of the clientele of many of my colleagues in Chicago. I infer that those analysts in a position to commend me to prospective analysands have arrived at certain negative conclusions about my potential impact on this group. Of course, I trust that I have been underestimated in this regard!

The unique advantage of the psychoanalytic situation as an investigative tool is the opportunity it provides for systematic observations of the unfolding transference. These observations permit delineation of many intricate patterns of childhood transactions that are relived in the context of the analytic relationship. Consequently, as the transferences develop, we are able to reconstruct a significant subjective history of the analysand's early years. Reconstructions of this kind cannot be made on the basis of selected samples of material such as those generally available outside the clinical setting. Largely because of this fact, the hypotheses of applied analysis require validation within the analytic situation proper. In line with the general rules of scientific inference, real progress is made whenever a hypothesis has been *disproved*; evidence in support of most propositions is, unfortunately, all too easy to obtain.

Whatever the nature of the evidence for its conclusions, the essence of psychoanalysis remains the attempt to understand the human condition. This fact has been frequently overlooked as a result of the natural if regrettable public demand for immediate benefits from the practical applications of pure science. In this country, these pressures have been aggravated by the predominantly medical orientation of the psychoanalytic profession. Moreover, this pragmatic bias has subtly diverted psychoanalysts from using their difficult introspective method to *study* mental life, either in the clinical setting or outside it. In its place, the various psychoanalytic theories have been routinely invoked as deductive explanatory instruments. This process makes psychoanalytic propositions into arbitrary formulas, at best plausible, and at worst little more than magical clichés. The derivative and intellectually unsatisfying results of these unsound procedures may have brought psychoanalysis, or at least this degraded version of it, into some disrepute. An appropriate use of introspection and empathy in the service of illuminating man and his creations necessarily avoids all such preconceptions about the specific meanings of any body of psychological material.

The conclusions I shall report in this section were derived inductively from clinical applications of the psychoanalytic method that were free, to the best of my ability, from theoretical preconceptions. In the course of the two decades of analytic work described here, I have developed a controversial viewpoint within psychoanalysis—idiosyncratic or innovative, depending on one's perspective—based on this agnostic approach to the clinical encounter. I elaborated this position first in collaboration with Arnold Goldberg in *Models of the Mind* (1973) and subsequently in *Beyond Interpretation* (1979a) and *Advances in Clinical Psychoanalysis* (1981a). Readers interested in the clinical aspects of my work can approach it most conveniently through the most recent of these volumes; those who wish to pursue the theoretical implications of my clinical orientation will find it more helpful to refer to the two earlier works.

I have organized my clinical conclusions about creativity under four separate headings. In Chapter 3, I discuss disturbances in the ability to create in all fields of endeavor; the great variety of psychological issues relevant to such difficulties are arranged in terms of the hierarchical conceptual model developed in my collaborative work with Goldberg (1973). Chapter 4 is devoted to the special problems encountered by creative women, psychological obstacles that appear to obstruct their creative pursuits more frequently than their male counterparts. By contrast, male homosexuals seem to retain their creative capacities, even if their personality problems are relatively severe in other respects; I discuss the complex relationship between homosexuality and creativity in Chapter 5. Finally, in Chapter 6 I examine the psychology of genius, that is, the psychology of personalities whose creativity seems able to transcend every obstacle.

The clinical conclusions about creativity spelled out in these chapters will subsequently be brought to bear on the historical materials considered in Sections III and IV.

Chapter Three

Creative Paralysis: The Captivity of Idleness

I

SOME YEARS AGO, a young sculptor on the verge of critical acclaim was nearing the end of his analysis when he was suddenly overtaken by a wave of unprecedented bodily symptoms. His general malaise suggested the possibility of somatic illness, but he described his sensations so graphically (he was a man often able to use language almost as effectively as his pencil), in terms suggesting he was being drawn and quartered, that I urged him to explore the psychological context of his experience. His associations led to a phone call he just received from a collector who had recently purchased one of his large wooden constructions. The caller requested a slight modification of the manner in which this assemblage was put together in order to facilitate its installation in his home; at certain junctions where components of the piece were rigidly joined by metal plates, he requested the substitution of hinges that would allow for greater maneuverability. As the patient became aware that he experienced the prospect of separating various parts of his construction as if his own body were about to be dismembered, his painful somatic state abruptly disappeared.

From the vantage point of clinical psychoanalysis, this incident is practically banal, for such "conversion symptoms," that is, the concretizing of ideas through the medium of the body substrate, were first decoded a century ago (see Breuer & Freud, 1895). To be sure, we might consider the interesting question of whether the psychological states generally grouped under the rubric of hysteria may actually be regarded as artistic products in their own right, but I will defer discussion of this issue until the Epilogue. Here, my intention in introducing this clinical material is only to demonstrate that literally every aspect of creative activity can be unconsciously related to the artist's subjectivity. The relationship between creative activity and subjectivity goes beyond the ostensible subject matter of art—the particular aspect most frequently studied from the psychological viewpoint. It further transcends the issue of formal expression, for the proposed change in my patient's sculpture would not have altered the perceptual gestalt of the piece in any way. In fact, this clinical episode points to the fact that the relationship between creativity and subjectivity can encompass the very stuff from which the artist creates his work.

Obviously, the individual I am describing here was unusually sensitive to encroachments on his autonomy; other artists have been known to modify major finished works on demand. We know, for example, that Balthus eliminated an offensive part of the image from his early magnum opus *The Street* (1933) at the request of its first private owner, who was unwilling to hang in his living room a representation of a man fingering a young girl's vulva. In contrast, my patient ruined his chance to be represented in the collection of a major museum by indignantly rejecting the suggestion of the interested curator that he have the sculpture in question cast in a certain material—not because he felt the proposed medium was unsuitable but in order to rid himself of the threat of external control.

Should such a psychological trait be construed as an obstacle to creativity? In the case of this patient, it certainly made for difficulties in getting along within the byzantine world of the current art scene! But it is extremely difficult to posit psychological impediments to the creative process in an *a priori* way; the very pattern of behavior that seems to be disadvantageous from one point of view may turn out to be absolutely essential to the artist's ability to work when approached from another. Thus, the sculptor I was analyzing had sought psychological assistance precisely because of a creative paralysis that came about, in part, because he allowed his wife, a woman of solid common sense and discerning aesthetic judgment, to influence many decisions impinging on his work. At times when his wife's influence supervened, he described his sensations as those of a person drowning in a pit of tar.

Because of the complexities inherent in the creative process, we can only be certain that we have identified a psychological trait that interferes with creativity when, in the course of analytic treatment, a shift in the relative influence of a specific psychic pattern produces an immediate liberation of the individual's creative potential. Fortunately, illustrations of such therapeutic changes are not difficult to find in clinical psychoanalytic practice.

II

IT MAY SEEM difficult to understand that the psychological issue most frequently found to underlie various inhibitions in analytic patients, namely, the irrational fear of retaliatory hostility on the part of potential rivals (usually termed "castration anxiety"; see Freud, 1926), does not appear to be the most frequent source of such problems in persons who seek analysis for disturbances of creativity. I shall nonetheless provide a few examples that fit the traditional pattern in my consideration of the special problems of creative women in Chapter 4. Here, I merely wish to note that, though this syndrome may not be the most common, its effects are devastating when it is present. In creative persons, however, we are just as likely to encounter the expectation, generally based on the encouragement of competitive activities in childhood by their fathers, that they will receive help and support if they demonstrate creative excellence. I believe this circumstance explains the relative infrequency with which we find anxieties about great achievements in creative people.

It may be easiest to illustrate this point by returning to the case of the young sculptor I have already cited. This man had older brothers who both excelled in athletics and served with distinction in the Korean war, where they had glamorous roles in the armed services. Their father was rightfully proud of his sons' achievements and made my patient feel that he would naturally follow in his brothers' footsteps. He did indeed become a successful basketball player in high school, and he subsequently volunteered for military service during the early stages of the Vietnam conflict. The first public demonstration of his artistic skill followed his assignment to redecorate an army mess hall; when he did so by producing some striking murals, both his superiors and fellow soldiers were enthusiastic, and this success led to his decision to devote himself to an artistic career upon his discharge. As a result of this background, the patient was perpetually puzzled and surprised by the bitchiness of many fellow artists. Competitive issues, however, never made him anxious.

I can provide another example from the analysis of a distinguished scientist who was equally unconcerned about professional rivalries. His father had been a successful executive and an older brother had comparable achievements in another professional field. The patient had always felt—correctly, I believe—that he could rely on the unconditional support of both men because they were truly secure about the worth of their respective vocational accomplishments. It is noteworthy that the analysis of this man uncovered certain inhibitions in the sexual sphere deriving from competitive rivalries but demonstrated that the resulting anxieties had never been displaced onto the sphere of his work. Perhaps the spread of castration anxiety to nonsexual spheres will only take place in families where the specific nonsexual activity in question has been a chronic source of conflict by virtue of its meaning for one or both parents.

Although fears of retaliation for creative success appear, in my experience, relatively uncommon among those who possess the requisite talent to achieve such success, unconscious conflict about high accomplishments is not at all unusual. In my own practice, I have often encountered strong irrational guilt about potential competitive triumphs that would involve the exercise of creativity. Whenever the individual is unaware of this aspect of his own psychology (a circumstance not at all uncommon in our culture), a dangerous tendency exists to expiate past "sins" and/or forestall future ones by avoiding the success in question.

By way of illustration, I can cite the case of a respected social scientist who was married to an eminent colleague in her own field. She was always careful to adapt the direction and pace of her own career to the requirements of her husband's, ostensibly because the latter was likely to make the greater intellectual contribution to their discipline. Insofar as these constraints retarded her academic advancement and even forced her, during certain periods, to withdraw from the job market altogether, she cheerfully busied herself with a number of avocations in addition to the care of her family. One of the projects she completed under these circumstances was a work of fiction that she published under a pseudonym; the book had an entirely unexpected critical success. Needless to say, this demonstration of excellence greatly enhanced her bargaining power in the academic world. Unfortunately, however, the recognition associated with this success coincided with a troubled period in the career of her husband. The shift in their relative degrees of public esteem was very difficult for him to accommodate, and he developed a significant illness of psychosomatic origin. Under these circumstances, my patient responded with a severe work inhibition that was relieved only when analysis uncovered her lifelong propensity to sacrifice her own interests in order to avoid hurting others.

In order to understand the way in which this behavioral disposition was motivated by unconscious guilt, we also had to uncover the psychological world of the patient's early childhood. We eventually grasped that the crucial event of her formative years was the *de facto* separation of her parents when she was 3 years old. The mother had taken a prestigious academic(!) position in California, far from the Midwestern city where her husband was a senior civil servant. Although the dissolution of the marriage was never acknowledged by the adults, the patient, who was an only child, soon realized that her father was lapsing into alcoholism because he felt abandoned. The patient concluded, probably with some justification, that the mother had deserted him for the sake of an exclusive relationship with her, and she became progressively overwhelmed with remorse as her father continued to deteriorate. In late adolescence, she made an heroic effort to rescue her father from his foreseeable doom, an endeavor that was brought to a tragic climax when, in a drunken furor, he made a serious attempt to murder her. Clearly, the father shared the child's assessment that he had lost his wife to this female Oedipus. It is unnecessary, in this context, to belabor the parallels between these circumstances of early childhood and the ones that brought on the patient's creative paralysis during adulthood.

It would be seriously misleading to leave the discussion of creative inhibitions based on competitive conflicts without mentioning the fact that, in terms of childhood antecedents, the act of creation per se is most frequently equated not with masculine accomplishments but with feminine procreative powers. Another way of putting this insight is to note that the creative achievement that small children are able to grasp earlier than any other is the production of a live baby. The birth of a younger sibling appears to fill with the greatest awe and admiration precisely those children who possess the most inquisitive and perceptive minds and who respond to their environment with the most differentiated affects and most insightful questions.

Male children of precocious intelligence seem particularly vulnerable to a sense of chronic humiliation on realizing that, in comparison with the procreative potential of an adult woman, their own efforts to produce something from within themselves are paltry, inanimate, and meaningless. These issues are particularly likely to remain problematic if the mother aggravates the child's mortification either by ridiculing his naive endeavors to compete with her or by responding to these endeavors with other forms of hostility generally covered over with a veneer of rationalization. For example, one scientist revealed in analysis that his mother mocked as inhuman activities his boyhood interests in simple gadgeteering, hobbies that were to lead in a straight line to his brilliant involvement with high technology. In her eyes, he was a little robot rather than a child.

Another distinguished academic reported that his mother fancied herself a literary lioness and looked on all other endeavors with open contempt. This man was exceedingly fearful about the humiliation that would ensue if he made his work public in an imperfect state. We gradually discovered that he experienced his creations as lifeless fecal lumps; all he could do to compensate for their insignificance was to ensure that they would be the most unusual turds ever produced. Hence, he wrote papers more than 50 times longer than the customary contributions to his field, triumphantly imagining that he was giving anal birth to these monstrosities.

Such fantasies of humiliation, whether they stem from competing with maternal procreativeness or from other childhood issues, may stop creative efforts altogether. One instance in my practice in which a total inhibition about revealing artistic efforts was traced back to just this source concerned a man who believed himself to be the world's greatest unpublished poet. He was a trickster whose primary aim was ostensibly to confuse people about his identity and merits; he derived his self-esteem from accomplishments such as his success in provoking a major novelist to refer to him in one of her books, by actual name, as the most loathsome character she had ever known.

This transaction turned out to echo the patient's childhood relationship with his mother, a pious, smug, and rigid woman whom he was able to scandalize through various misbehaviors. The patient was her only son, born after she had had several girls; the birth of a younger sister when he was nearly 3 appears to have set off his hostile *peccadilloes*. For much of his childhood, he and his mother were engaged in a struggle over flushing the toilet, the point of which seemed to be the patient's desire to confuse her about whether or not he had had a bowel movement; he was most triumphant if she failed to realize that his feces would confront her when she raised the lid of the toilet. He subsequently flaunted his great unpublished poems, as he had triumphantly exhibited his childhood turds. He behaved as if the poems merited the closest attention, half believing in his own propaganda and mortally afraid that his adult pretensions were as empty as his childhood ones had been. When, in the analysis, he finally succeeded in mastering his fear of humiliation at the hands of superior females, he was able to submit his poetry for publication for the first time. He eventually proved himself a capable artist.

III

COMMON AS THE neurotic conflicts I have thus far adduced to explain disturbances of creativity may be, they probably constitute less frequent obstacles for my patients than an entirely different set of problems. From the observer's vantage point, the issues to which I am now referring might well be characterized as disturbances in the potential artist's relationship to the traditions of his craft (see Gay, 1976). Compared to problems involving the patient's intrapsychic world, problems in this area can be conceptualized in terms of the persistence of illusions, either about the discipline to which the artist adheres (including the qualities of its practitioners), his own stature and aptitude for that discipline, or both.

The clearest example I can provide concerns a well-to-do young man who was attending a graduate school of business at the insistence of his family following a short and abortive attempt to launch himself as a writer. He was bitterly disappointed with himself for having been unable to take advantage of the leisure provided by his solid financial backing to produce anything whatsoever in the way of fiction. Having "wasted" a number of years following graduation from an excellent college of liberal arts, he suspected himself of being a fraud and an impostor. In actuality, he had joined a circle of glamorous writers and intellectuals in New York in a desperate effort to make the transition from student to "modern novelist." Needless to say, he succeeded only in learning about the latest fashions of the prosperous bohemia of the upper East Side. Realizing that he still needed the discipline of an organized program, he proceeded to enroll in a graduate course in literature, only to be overwhelmed by the achievements of the predecessors he most admired. As he studied the great psychological novelists—Dostoevski, Tolstoy, Flaubert, Proust— he became convinced that he had nothing to say and might as well yield to "common sense" and prepare to join the family business.

In contending that such a collapse in self-confidence amounts to a disorder in the artist's relation to his craft, I mean that this man was unable to realize that virtually every major novelist has to go through a painstaking period of apprenticeship. He was perfectly aware, of course, that Flaubert had worked on *Madame Bovary* for 17 years and Proust had candidly described his decades of seemingly aimless participation in Parisian high society as necessary preparation for the creation of *A la recherche du temps perdu*. But Flaubert and Proust were certified culture heroes, so the constraints within which they worked seemed—like the labors of Hercules—to have been so many obstacles miraculously overcome. The patient's own travails as a beginner, on the other hand, only proved to him that his hopes and ambitions were unrealistic. He knew that by his own standards he was likely to produce "garbage," and he was keenly aware of the fact that he would be too humiliated to persevere unless he could match Dostoevski in producing a masterpiece through his initial effort.

The genesis of such syndromes in childhood illusions is more readily seen in cases that involve problems pertaining to either idealization of others or unrealistic self-aggrandizement, rather than the mixture of both issues seen in the foregoing instance. To be sure, the behavior of this aspiring novelist was outwardly humble; it was only the fact that he invited comparison with the greatest practitioners of his art that betrayed his immoderate ambition. Even the outward form of his existence matched the corresponding events in the life of Flaubert, who was forced to study the law by parental pressure. Under his surface modesty, in other words, this man had to contend with a grandiose self-concept, the demands of which could never be satisfied in actual performance; it was the discrepancy between his accurate sense of what he was capable of accomplishing and the necessity to be a Flaubert that crushed his self-confidence.

Creative individuals who do not idealize great predecessors often betray their grandiose ambitions much more openly. They tend to have an equally disturbed relationship to their craft, however, as they are usually unable to accept any master and often rebel against all tradition. One man who demonstrated these characteristics entered analysis because of difficulties in carrying out his clinical responsibilities as a physician. The son of an eminent scientist, he had always assumed he would be able to surpass the achievements of his father. Although he had, in fact, shown outstanding aptitude for laboratory investigation, he had chosen to specialize in clinical medicine because of his contempt for the tradition of academic research. As a schoolboy, he excelled in mathematics to the degree that he was almost tempted into this field. He rejected this alternative, however, precisely because it would not have presented him with much of a challenge. His actual problems with medical work stemmed from a tendency to lapse into an unthinking reliance on the magic of fantasied occult healing powers in lieu of the accepted methods of the craft.

These grandiose illusions had been more or less overt throughout the patient's life. In early childhood he had developed specific therapeutic ambitions modeled on his view of his mother as a magical healer, but he certainly never doubted his essential greatness in general. He recalled that he had always been supported in this estimation of his exceptional worth by his mother, a woman of superficially masochistic demeanor who subtly dominated the household. As her eldest son, the patient was expected to fight his father on her behalf; in return, she protected him from retaliation and inflated his pride. It took several years of analytic work to uncover the fact that this mutual admiration society was a relatively late development in the patient's childhood and served to disavow a traumatic disruption of the initial bond to his mother late in the second year of his life.

The crisis took place—and was aggravated by virtue of the fact that it did so—before the child had acquired the capacity to communicate through language. His language development was, as it happens, extremely slow— an eventuality we shall also encounter in Chapter 10 when we consider the childhood of Friedrich Nietzsche. The patient's mother was at the time pregnant with her next child, so that the occurrence of the ensuing crisis overstrained her resources. The boy developed a foul-smelling diarrhea of several weeks' duration; his earliest memory concerned his mother's tearful efforts to force him to eat bananas, a diet generally prescribed for sprue. The patient's later vulnerability to the slightest insult suggested that his mother, in her frustration and rage, may have wanted to turn away from him entirely. Be that as it may, as the outcome of these difficult circumstances, the mother and child gradually built a myth of mutual perfection and concord based on their esoteric skills as healers. Obviously, only those who do not possess such magical powers need turn to scientific research to develop effective therapeutic tools. It followed that this man held the exercise of his actual creative gifts in contempt and was thereby condemned to the career of a mediocre physician—or of an apprentice sorcerer!

It is more difficult to find illustrative clinical material in which illusions about others, uncontaminated by personal grandiosity, interfere with the exercise of creative potential. I believe this last constellation may have obtained in the case of a journalist who only stayed in analysis for a relatively brief period, but I cannot rule out the possibility that further investigation might also have revealed the role of subject-centered grandiosity in her difficulties. The woman in question worked as a publicist for a religious organization she had joined in late adolescence when she was beginning to feel disappointed in her mother and the latter's fervently held belief system. But her current organizational activities exposed her to certain disillusioning aspects of her own faith, at least in the version upheld by many of her coreligionists. Instead of criticizing these individuals, all of whom were male, she regarded herself as a presumptuous sinner unable to curb her own "heretical" disagreement with these spiritual brethren. It was the turmoil surrounding this conflict, both internal and interpersonal, that impelled her to seek psychological assistance.

The analysis revealed that this woman was committed to the propagation of certain moral principles and seemed to have the language skills to do so in a charismatic manner. Her disagreements with aspects of the dogma of her church struck me as products of her originality; had she felt free to assume a prophetic stance, she might well have followed in the footsteps of Jung (see Chapters 13 and 14) as the founder of a modern system of religious belief. As it turned out, her treatment did not alter this aspect of her personality before she chose to settle for certain improvements that relieved her acute conflict. Specifically, she was content to continue as an orthodox believer but with greater tolerance for human imperfections, including her own, and she diverted her creative energy into private activities as a painter. I have absolutely no information about the extent of her talent in this area, but she had no training in art (in contrast to her professional status as a writer) and was beyond the age that generally permits the amateur to shed the status of a "naive."

But what is pertinent here is the manner in which this patient's need to idealize the authority of her church blocked her capacity to be creative in the moral sphere. Her need to submit to—and, with great conflict, to rebel against—the leadership of idealized males was the legacy of an endless series of cruel rebuffs from her father, whom her mother had left when the patient was 3. Much later, she realized that he was a psychotic man who abused his other children in ways even more damaging than his refusal to acknowledge the patient as his own child. This circumstance had actually spared her from exposure to most of his bizarre behaviors. Simultaneously, it had permitted her to compensate for her disappointing life with her mother by weaving a web of illusions around the father's person. In their original version, these childhood fantasies gradually lost their power, but they were revived in a more sophisticated and culturally sanctioned form in her veneration of the leaders of her church. For this patient, some fathers always had to know best.

IV

OCCASIONALLY, CERTAIN psychological issues which originate even earlier in childhood than the oedipal issues that result in neurotic conflicts, or the preoedipal issues that eventuate in persisting illusions, also contribute to the paralysis of creative functioning. But such primitive psychological dispositions generally underlie the formation of every form of psychopathology and, to that degree, are almost never found "in pure culture" (Gedo, 1979a, 1981a, 1981b). Thus, the very fact that an individual has difficulty with the legacy of such early developmental phases in adult life makes it overwhelmingly likely that the same individual will suffer from a variety of infantile illusions and/or intrapsychic conflicts as well. It is nonetheless possible to single out some unusual cases in which a disposition of archaic origin appeared to play the decisive role in preventing creative success. Doubtless, instances in which such a disposition is but one of a variety of factors that interfere with creativity are much more numerous.

One attribute of very early psychic life that may persist into adulthood is the inability to coordinate one coherent hierarchy of personal aims. Thus, some people appear to fail in their various enterprises because they keep too many irons in the fire and, when the inevitable crunch supervenes, are unable to order their priorities on behalf of salvaging their most important projects. One young man of great promise scattered his efforts in such a bewildering way that he could not even keep track of his manifold commitments. He was allegedly working toward a degree at a prestigious university, promoting the career of a female pop singer involved in the drug scene, investigating certain intellectual problems pertaining to the epistemology of the social sciences (but irrelevant to the degree program he was pursuing), mastering the use of computers for the full-time job that occupied him from midnight to morning, participating in rancorous campus political battles, reading avidly in *belles lettres* and the fine arts—but I cannot complete the list, for I am certain I did not hear about a host of other activities that captured him only fleetingly. The resulting chaos continued well into his analysis, until his other aims faded into the background as a result of his eventual decision to give priority to our collaborative effort. Needless to say, this decision entailed a greater emphasis on the remunerative work that enabled him to finance the analysis. Thus, he could no longer afford to take leaves of absence to help out friends who might be producing an underground movie.

Our therapeutic success enabled this man to defer less urgent tasks for the sake of a coherent program of action. Interestingly, he was then able to achieve most of his original goals in sequence: He completed his degree, married a promising scholar whose intellectual work he could encourage and support, carried his epistemological research forward in an organized manner in the context of pursuing a doctorate, became a well-paid expert in computerized data processing and, in general, a very cultivated person. He also carried out a plan undreamt of at the start of the analysis: He devotedly saw his father through the latter's terminal illness, thereby overcoming the bitter family problems that had formerly propelled him into a series of rash political involvements. Of course, in the foregoing, I have condensed the results of more than a dozen years of analytic adherence to the voice of reason (Freud's characterization of the outcome of a successful psychoanalysis) into a series of achievements that might be found in the curriculum vitae of any scholarly person in his mid-30s. The crux of the matter actually lies in the reasons why this brilliant student was unable to live his life in accord with simple common sense without the experience of a lengthy analysis.

The reasons were sufficiently complex to defy categorization in simple terms here (but see Gedo, 1979a, Chapters 4 and 5, where this analysis is described and discussed *in extenso*; see also the Epilogue to this volume where I return to this example). One way to approach the nexus of factors involved is to characterize this patient's principal psychological requirements as a need for external assistance that would enable him to organize his behavior without impinging on his personal autonomy. After a series of disruptive events that occurred when the patient was 3 years old, his mother took over the role of combating his disorganization, without ever teaching him to manage this task for himself. She intervened on every possible occasion to correct his mistakes, in other words, but she never imparted the advice that would help him avoid such errors in the first place. Moreover, because of certain features of the mother's own personality, her helpfulness generally overstepped the boundaries of the child's needs, so that he came to experience her assistance as unsolicited interference with his personal autonomy. As he became older, he tended to fight off his mother's influence, and this legitimate wish for personal initiative came to encompass not only her active interventions in his personal affairs but her entire philosophy of life—especially her explicit espousal of pragmatism and common sense.

Another, if somewhat attenuated, example of the disruptive effects on creativity of problems in the organization of the self (as I prefer to call these archaic syndromes) concerns a successful academic in a scientific field who managed to fulfill the day-to-day requirements of his job but seldom got around to his research activities. Instead, he was involved in the turmoil of an unsatisfactory marriage to a childish woman who did not measure up to his standards in most areas of living. His own estimation of the situation, which was probably quite false, was that he could not in good conscience abandon this fragile person to her fate. He found solace for the frustration of spending so much time propping up a seeming psychological invalid in the musical activities to which he devoted his spare time. He was a clarinetist of sufficient skill to be one of the strongest members of a community orchestra of high standards, but his scientific interests and obligations "prevented" him from becoming a performer of professional caliber.

In this case, as in that of the student I formerly described, the pattern of running off madly in several directions was largely determined by the need to safeguard a fragile sense of autonomy from the influence of very impressive parental figures. Both parents were not only quite successful in their respective professional fields but had many other outstanding personal qualities, especially those conspicuously lacking in the patient's wife. He had carefully chosen an area of study utterly unfamiliar to either parent, and his dedication to music was also without precedent in the family. In fact, his need to reject parental values went so far as to exclude most facets of their upper-class existence in favor of the "counterculture" of the 1960s.

Paradoxically, the patient had remained close to his mother, whose company he continued to prefer to that of anyone else until her death. In the analysis, it became clear that his aversion to any externally observable identification with her screened a pattern of organization based on that very rejection of what she stood for. Without her input, he felt confused; her death finally impelled him to seek analytic assistance. We found that his negativistic mode of personality organization was established late in the second year of his life when, following the birth of his sister, he was separated from his mother for a significant period of time because of certain postpartum obstetrical complications. In his unfortunate marriage, the patient reenacted the mitigation of his disrupted infantile state that followed the return of his mother by mothering, in his turn, a person he regarded as helpless. In comparison to these issues of life and death, he regarded the creative activities that constituted his professional work as esoteric, so that his career paled into insignificance in his eyes.

In addition to such problems of self-definition (see Gedo & Goldberg, 1973), the earliest phases of personality development in infancy may leave residues that interfere with creative activities by way of impairing the capacity to regulate tension.[1] Creative success tends to be extremely stimulating over long spans of time—probably more so than sexual or competitive triumphs, the effects of which tend to wear off relatively quickly. In order to avoid overstimulation (which is characterized by a variety of undesirable somatic consequences; see Chapter 6 for some examples), the individual must have at his disposal effective behavioral measures to reduce tension. The general frequency of self-soothing by means of alcohol or pharmacological agents makes it evident that many persons are unable to achieve optimal tension levels through their own resources. But the resort to medication or alcohol quickly interferes with the mental acuity requisite for creative work; in this way, alcoholism and addiction to certain drugs (those popularly termed "downers") are the most common paths by which these archaic psychological dispositions destroy the artist's creative potential.

Tragic examples of this kind are probably familiar to everyone—perhaps one of the best known cases concerns the pathologically excitable Vincent van Gogh. For van Gogh, this personality attribute was probably caused by a neurological deficit that also resulted in his psychomotor epilepsy. I shall discuss van Gogh's difficulties in some detail in Chapter 8; here I would only mention that before his celebrated disintegration in Arles during Paul Gauguin's fateful visit, Vincent tried to sedate himself by excessive drinking and recorded his own concern about the ultimate consequences of this habit in letters to his brother Theo. I resort to this illustration from nonclinical, biographical sources because, in general, problems of this kind cannot be handled adequately in the ordinary psychoanalytic setting, and I have, in fact, never been responsible for the care of such a person.

I have encountered creative individuals who experienced traumatic episodes of overstimulation in the course of their work and were so frightened by these phenomena, the nature of which they did not understand, that they were literally afraid to resume the activities that led to them. The sculptor whose reactions to the threat of external influence I described at the beginning of this chapter initially entered treatment because of such a sequence of events. To be more precise, he did not quite realize that he was phobic about his artistic work; he merely found himself unable to resist various distractions that pulled him in other directions. On one occasion, for instance, he spent the better part of a year remodeling an old house, ostensibly to set up an appropriate studio. Although this undertaking proved viable from a financial standpoint, it interrupted and damaged his artistic development. Nor did it lead to the

1. The problem of overstimulation versus tension "discharge" has been relatively neglected in recent psychoanalytic discourse, although Freud gave close attention to it in his work of the 1890s. From 1900 through the mid-1960s, such "psychoeconomic" issues were overshadowed by the exciting discoveries of psychoanalysis about the meaning of hitherto unconscious psychic contents. My own recent clinical contributions (1979a, 1981a) have returned to the problem of tension regulation.

abatement of his anxiety about the potential recurrence of tension states once he resumed his creative work; he found ever new distractions—some of them a great deal less constructive than renovating buildings—until he decided that the problem required analytic help.

Well into the analysis, whenever his artistic progress brought him measurably closer to his own ideals, this man experienced nightmares—*prima facie* evidence of being overstimulated—the content of which amounted to variations on the theme of suffering unbearable dizzy spells if he dared to climb any higher. Although the dreams contained clear allusions to the conflicts about autonomy I have mentioned earlier in describing this person—to climb higher inevitably involved leaving behind people toward whom his loyalty constituted the tar pit he was struggling to escape—the reference to dizziness actually recalled his initial episode of overstimulation through artistic success. This incident occurred during his army service when he went on leave immediately after his decision to become an artist. He had gone to Paris and climbed the tower of Notre Dame where he experienced severe vertigo for the first time (cf. Freud, 1936). Every artistic achievement threatened to make him dizzy with success once again.

V

WHATEVER THE psychological sources of work inhibitions may be, their presence generally constitutes a devastating problem for the creative person, whether he or she has already embarked on an artistic career or is still poised at its threshold. But the statement can also be reversed: The possession of a creative gift opens compensatory channels that render life bearable even under the most trying circumstances. To illustrate, when Sigmund Freud lost a daughter and a favorite grandchild in rapid succession in his mid-60s, he owed his stoical response to the sustaining power of his intellectual work (Jones, 1957, pp. 19–20, 92). An even more striking example concerns Giuseppe Tomasi, Prince of Lampedusa, who overcame his inconsolable grief over the destruction of his ancestral palazzo by aerial bombardment in 1943 through writing; the outcome of his effort was the posthumous novel, *The Leopard*, which he had begun at the age of 58 (Colquhoun, 1968).

Conversely, for the artist, the disruption of creative activities is characteristically a loss even more bitter than that of a beloved person, of an irreplaceable possession, or of bodily integrity, because it tends to rob him of the central goals that characterize his being (cf. Gedo, 1979a). Hence even a temporary lapse into an artistic hiatus is generally experienced as a catastrophic threat, equivalent to castration anxiety in the sexual sphere. If the inability to produce proves enduring, it will undermine the self-esteem of all but the rare spirits who have already achieved more than they ever thought possible. I shall discuss the special vulnerability of persons of genius in Chapter 6; here, I wish to note that whereas most people do not require outstanding achievements to maintain their self-esteem, they do need to be able to live up to their customary standards well into the twilight of their existence.

Psychoanalytic treatment may restore or establish creative possibilities by overcoming specific obstacles of the kind I have surveyed in this chapter. At the same time, it may also help to overcome creative paralyses in a more nonspecific manner by providing (sometimes for the first time) a secret sharer of the kind Joseph Conrad apparently required to realize his artistic potential (see Chapter 1). It is by no means unusual to witness the flowering of a creative career in the context of a treatment that can only be rated a failure in terms of the usual criteria used to assess the psychoanalytic process. Although such an analysand may gain little or no insight into his inner psychological world, the therapeutic relationship may enable him to consolidate certain successful working methods that can later be maintained without external psychological assistance.[2]

Of course, in my experience, it is much more common to encounter these specific and nonspecific therapeutic effects of analysis acting synergistically. In the very act of formulating valid interpretations of the analysand's inner world of conflicts, illusions, disparate aims, and tension states, the analyst provides him with a living model of creative struggle. If the patient in question is striving to achieve his own artistic goals, the analyst's work, with its successes and failures, will inevitably mirror the patient's own creative difficulties. And the analyst's perseverance, conscientiousness, and humility in his service will incline the patient toward meeting the preconditions of productive performance.

2. I have previously described an analysis in which I observed this combination of circumstances; for the clinical details, see Gedo (1981a, pp. 68–77).

Chapter Four

Barefoot and Pregnant: The Dilemma of the Woman Artist

I

IN THIS ERA of feminism, the question of creativity and gender has become politicized. Perhaps no psychoanalytic hypothesis has aroused as much scorn and hatred among dogmatic egalitarians as the proposition, most clearly articulated by Phyllis Greenacre in her work on women artists (1960), that major creativity is the correlate of childlessness. Greenacre meant this in the sense that the impulse to create is always, at least in part, an effort to compensate for the frustration of that most powerful and archaic human wish based on the universal identification with the mother of early childhood: the wish to give birth to a child of one's own. Although in the course of childhood development such wishes are, of course, repressed with the vast majority of males and with a certain number of females as well, the frequency with which artists consciously or unconsciously look upon their products as the children of their fancy lends powerful support to Greenacre's idea.

It is too early at this time to predict the effects of those novel childrearing practices that propose to replace the biological mother as principal care-taker by some combination of figures, at least one of whom, presumably the child's father, will be male. It is by no means inconceivable that such a revolution in gender roles may bring about corresponding changes in the way children view motherhood, and the seeming miracle of creating new life may actually lose its glamour for all. Yet one suspects that the dedifferentiation of the roles of men and women in caring for the next generation may exert its greatest impact by impelling boys to cling more tenaciously to their procreative wishes than they were able to do in the past when sexual roles were more definite. As I tried to show in Chapter 3, one source of interference with the creativity of certain males may well be the fact that such creativity, at least in specific instances and to a certain extent, is based on identification with the mother of procreation or, to put it differently, that such creativity finds too little support in identifications with the creative activities of paternal figures. Identifications with the activities of males are necessarily acquired in later childhood or even in adolescence. If novel childrearing practices, in addition to facilitating boys' identification with their mothers, make it more difficult to idealize male role models, these social reforms will probably create fresh obstacles to the creativity of men. At the same time, it is difficult to see how such efforts in social engineering could eliminate obstacles to the creativity of women.

At any rate, for the time being we must assess Greenacre's hypothesis on the basis of past history. In terms of information in the public domain, her contention is plausible without being conclusively proven: The great majority of women of genius have, indeed, been childless, although this fact may or may not be causally related to their accomplishments. In Western societies, for example, for more than a millenium women found the best opportunities for the expression of their creativity in the religious sphere, a vocational choice that essentially precluded family life for them. Would the formidable activities of a Joan of Arc or St. Catherine of Siena have been conceivable if they had been married and borne children? Although one might guess that nothing short of obstetrical disasters could have totally stopped these indomitable figures, it is fair to assert that motherhood would have precluded their assumption of roles that entailed rallying large constituencies to their banners. After all, the French still call their heroine "the Maiden"—*la Pucelle.* We have even less basis for speculating whether the greatest of women artists, writers such as Jane Austen and George Eliot or the painter Artemisia Gentileschi, would have been diverted from their paths by motherhood.

Psychoanalytic experience contributes no clear answers to this puzzle because we are unable to differentiate the subsequent effects of child-bearing from the effects of the mother's caretaking responsibilities— considerable even in families that adopt special measures to mitigate these burdens. It requires no depth-psychological insight to realize that most mothers who currently succeed in creative endeavors tend to do so after their children are well launched in life. From the point of view of their career goals, moreover, the loss of a crucial decade (generally that between the ages of 25 and 35) can never be totally overcome.[1]

What the psychoanalyst can bring to this aspect of the discussion is evidence about the corrosive effects on creativity of the guilt many career women experience, frequently consciously but equally often outside

1. The performing arts may constitute a partial exception to these claims.

awareness, concerning the deprivations they have been impelled to impose on their children in order to pursue their work. This phenomenon is probably only the obverse of the common observation that many of the most successful women of our age have been notoriously adamant about minimizing their family obligations. To cite only several instances widely reported in the press, eminent public figures such as Indira Gandhi and Golda Meir as well as the great sculptor Louise Nevelson deliberately gave priority to their career goals. Although young women of the current generation tend to disavow the difficulties inherent in failing to choose between primary commitments to work and children, they are seldom able, on trying to do justice to both spheres, to deal with their sense of inadequacy and resulting guilt without resorting to expiatory self-punishment. All too often, such self-punishment takes the form of arranging to derive no benefit from any of their activities; they condemn themselves, in other words, to creative failure.

One more psychoanalytic finding may be worth reporting here: A certain group of women seek assistance for low self-esteem that turns out, on close scrutiny, to be the consequence of an inability, for whatever reasons, to make effective use of creative talents. Syndromes of this kind tend to be quite refractory to treatment unless the obstacles to the individual's productivity happen to disappear; it is indeed true that no bitterness is so profound as that caused by the necessity to remain fallow. My clinical experience suggests that if such a woman has a child before she can become creative in other ways, her frustrated ambitions will not disappear; on the other hand, the cases with which I am familiar point to the fact that giving birth can substantially diminish the desperate quality of the dissatisfaction that brings these women into analysis.

II

LEAVING ASIDE the question of motherhood and its diverse effects on creativity, is the feminist movement justified in asserting that the rarity of genius in women is the consequence of their social oppression? Although it would be cavalier to dismiss altogether the influence of hormonal and chromosomal differences between the sexes on these matters, I am inclined on the basis of my clinical experience to endorse the feminist viewpoint in this regard, with the added proviso that I do not find it a self-sufficient explanation. Moreover, insofar as this viewpoint is valid, the social oppression in question cannot be altered by human action. In other words, I do not believe that true genius has ever been deterred from successful creativity by mere institutional constraints without some contribution from personal motives: In Victorian England, George Eliot may have found it expedient to adopt a male pseudonym, but from Sappho through Lady Murasaki, from the Marquise de Sévigné to Anna Akhmatova, great female writers have overcome the handicaps of social forms designed to keep them barefoot and pregnant—if necessary, by ruses such as Eliot's.

I am well aware, of course, that the production of increments to culture presupposes the attainment of a high cultural level, for example, that it cannot be achieved by the peasantry in a single generation. But the fact that the cultural achievements of the children depend on the previous status of the family has no bearing on the status of *women*. In no historical period have they been prevented from reaching whatever desired degree of cultivation their families could provide. Hence I believe that examination of the dilemma of the woman artist calls for the closest attention to the determining role of familial influences.

My own psychoanalytic observations with creative women have pointed in several directions with regard to the nature of the so-called oppression these individuals experience as little girls. Perhaps the possibility that dovetails most closely with feminist preconceptions is the effect the discovery of the child's talent may have on her relationship with her father. I do not mean to imply, of course, that the pattern I am about to describe is invariable or even the most frequent eventuality; it is merely the one that is found most intimidating by many girls who encounter it. The response I wish to highlight is the exact opposite of the pattern found by Helson and her associates (1971) in families whose daughters achieved creative success: In the latter group, the father encouraged the girl to identify with his own intellectual pursuits and took pleasure in her "masculine" qualities. In short, this study suggested that, at the expense of the desirable erotic undertones of a father–daughter relationship, a girl's creativity could be enhanced by gaining a special position with her father by sharing his values. Helson's study seems to imply that the creative potential of talented girls might best be realized by promoting their idealization of fathers who provide inspiring professional role models.

In a contrasting group of women who have needed analytic assistance to realize their creative potentials, the father responded to the child's promise by feeling personally threatened by its implications. In the most flagrant cases, this reaction resulted in a campaign of persecution—belittlement, ridicule, false accusations of hostility, and worse. In one instance, this type of response was motivated by the fact that the father's own creative ambitions, generated by his considerable talents, had never been realized. In another, the father became violently jealous because his own father, who had never paid much attention to him, was openly captivated by his granddaughter's sparkling intellect. Perhaps the most common source of these mirror images of a negative oedipal constellation is a pathological reaction on the part of the child's mother, who arouses her husband's jealous hatred by abandoning him emotionally in favor of a symbiotic relationship with this particular daughter, probably chosen because the mother wishes to share in her future promise. A particularly insidious form of the destructive paternal response is one in which its hostile nature is masked by a surface attitude of flirtatiousness or other seductive behavior, pushing the child away from her intellectual interests in favor of a pseudo-oedipal involvement.

Depending on the nature of the child's comprehension of her father's attitude, the consequences of such a dilemma may be diverse. Least damaging, in a certain sense, is the possibility that the girl may conclude that her father is a selfish monster, the male chauvinist pig of feminist rhetoric. This alternative generally leads to embroilment in guerrilla warfare that all too readily coalesces into a chronic attitude of hostility toward men. With fathers of the kind I am describing, it is generally too dangerous for the child to show counterhostility openly; in the erotized form of the syndrome, which endows the father with a romantic aura, it is particularly difficult for the girl to justify her anger. In adult life, then, these women appear to be inhibited about their aggression at the same time as they seem to be patently castrating—a combination of personality traits that has disastrous consequences in terms of getting along in the world. Since it was the very creative potential of these women that seemed so castrating to their fathers in the first place, they remain forever terrified about exercising their gifts to the full.

Needless to say, I cannot discuss in this context the full range of a child's possible responses to a father's ambivalence. But the spectrum of potentialities may be best suggested by focusing on the alternative farthest from the one I have just described: The child, perhaps overwhelmed with guilt, will often conclude that she is, indeed, the disruptive influence she is accused of being. In that eventuality, inhibited hostility is supplanted by an identification with parental aggression: The individual will live her life in the shadow of a series of baseless self-accusations and anxious efforts to expiate imaginary sins—including the sin of wanting to become a creative person. Grotesque compromise formations may also take place whereby the adult woman both justifies her father's hostility and reasserts her right to success; a common form is the enactment of the role of a *femme fatale*, that is, one who succeeds in her destructiveness.

Instead of discussing additional patterns of response, I must direct my attention to a more pivotal issue: In what way do these unfortunate contingencies in the childhood of talented females differ from the corresponding circumstances in the lives of their brothers? After all, Oedipus was to be exposed on the mountainside because the oracle had told Laius that his son would overcome him; in this sense, the Theban myth is prototypical of the dangers of creativity. This theme is even more explicit in the myth of Marsyas, whom Apollo flayed alive for his artistic activities. And King Oedipus rightly accuses Apollo of persecuting him because his wisdom rivals that of the god's oracles at Delphi. Psychoanalytic experience is rife with instances of males whose creativity is inhibited by the fear of retaliation for achieving their ambitions. But if Oedipus could grow up to kill his father—and ultimately to achieve sacred status at Colonus in the face of Apollo's hatred—why are his daughters content to devote their lives to the service of their incestuous parent?

III

IN ATTEMPTING to answer the foregoing question, I shall simultaneously address a different set of psychological issues that has its own bearing on the attainment of creative potentials—issues, in other words, that may interfere with creative work as much as insoluble conflict about oedipal competition. Let me begin, therefore, by stating the answer without the many qualifications its complexity actually requires: Girls are affected by competition with their fathers more adversely than boys because such a circumstance constitutes a derailment of their optimal course of emotional development; for boys the same circumstance is, within reasonable limits, an expectable maturational challenge.

We can restate this verdict in different terms by stating that the boy, in order to become an effective person, must have the opportunity to test himself against his father at the same time as he transforms his relationship to his mother into one characterized by an active, autonomous stance. The corresponding maturational requirements for the girl are more difficult to achieve: She must overcome the relative passivity of earliest childhood in order to arrive at the capacity to compete with her mother, developments generally made possible by the increasing importance of the girl's affectionate bond to her father. In other words, however anxious the boy may become as a result of his oedipal competitiveness, the experience prepares him for adulthood; the girl needs the very same opportunity vis-à-vis her *mother* and cannot afford to be additionally burdened by major hostile developments involving her father.[2]

2. Obviously, some boys also experience this phase of development in less favorable ways: In many instances, they end up competing with their mothers for masculine favor. For various complex reasons that have no relevance to a chapter focused on the special problems of women, the foregoing combination of circumstances, otherwise quite unfavorable in its implications, does not seem to interfere with the future creativity of these individuals, especially if they happen to find favor with some admirable masculine mentor. (This eventuality is discussed in Chapter 5.)

I would not go so far, however, as to agree with those propagandists for homosexuality who claim that an aversion for women actually enhances creativity. The point here is simply the empirical observation that, *in both men and women*, one requirement for creative success seems to be the reversal of infantile passivity vis-à-vis the primary caretaker into an active attitude congruent with independent initiative.

To look at the matter from a purely developmental perspective (see Gedo & Goldberg, 1973; Gedo, 1979a), we might say that most families have "oppressed" their daughters—and will inevitably continue to do so—because they have no predictable ways of emancipating them from their close bonds to the mother; in contrast, boys achieve some degree of independence and sense of separateness automatically, by virtue of their gender. Incidentally, it is at this point that I would invoke biological differences to explain the contrasting developmental patterns of the sexes (see Parens, 1979). The fact is that boys have a higher activity level from birth, that they tend to range further from their caretakers than girls as soon as they acquire the means of independent locomotion, and that they have a more urgent need to assert their own volition. As Freud put it, anatomy is destiny—although today we would probably be more interested in the crucial role of the glands of internal secretion than in the perception of manifest differences in genital equipment to which he referred.

In connection with the issue of the girl's identification with her mother, it is quite pertinent to note that no change in childrearing arrangements is likely to alter children's perceptions of who "mother" and "father" actually are. The children of families in which the biological mother played a minimal role in raising the child, whether because of the customary upper-class mores or the mother's career, have long constituted a high proportion of the clientele of psychoanalysts. My clinical experience with such patients points to the conclusion that however many early caretakers these children may have had, and however faithful and reliable some of them may have been, the children invariably had the same attitudes toward their biological parents as the children of more traditional families.

Perhaps the clearest illustration I can provide concerns a talented woman who was raised by a devoted nursemaid from birth until well into her third year. The departure of this primary caretaker proved to be devastating for her. As we discovered through the unfolding analytic transference, however, the impact of the departure did not result from the loss of the nursemaid's *person*. Rather, it was her efficacy in countering the corrosive effect on the child's self-esteem of her mother's predominant commitment to a career that made the nursemaid (and later the *analyst*) indispensable. The devotion of other members of the family—or, in adult life, the devotion of her husband—could never compensate this woman for having been deprived of the esteem of her mother. As Bruno Bettelheim put it in the title of his celebrated book, "Love is not enough"! Instead of ordinary loving devotion, that is, this woman needed to have her worth continuously reconfirmed through the willingness of someone to care for her, no matter how helpless or troublesome she acted, in *preference* to that caretaker's other pursuits.

It was particularly important in this regard that the success of her analysis bring me no prestige whatsoever, in contrast to the vocational success that had brought her mother much public recognition. Whenever it appeared that my effective clinical work with her might become known to other people, the patient began to experience me as the rejecting mother. When the anonymity of our collaboration seemed assured, on the other hand, I became a reincarnation of the faithful nursemaid. At such times, she was able to trust my assessment of her value as a human being—that is, as a person on whose behalf it was natural to make efforts that brought no immediate rewards—but she experienced us as jointly isolated from the rest of the world where, she felt, our values were depreciated. After all, a nursemaid is only hired help. Need I add that this woman entered analysis with a fervent commitment to ambitious career goals—and a fear of having children lest she abandon them as she herself had been abandoned?

IV

WHY SHOULD the persistence of patterns of human relatedness modeled on the tie to the mother of earliest childhood interfere with creative endeavors? This question is difficult to answer on a conceptual basis, although abundant empirical evidence obtained in the psychoanalytic setting substantiates the fact that such fixations do, indeed, severely limit the exercise of individual talents. Perhaps a few illustrative examples will therefore facilitate discussion of this issue.

One young woman began her analysis with the angry claim that her life was largely ruined because her father had prevented her from pursuing her true vocation, ballet. He had allegedly forced her into an academic program in college that made it impossible for her to continue her dancing. She then lost confidence in her own talent and accepted the family ethos that only intellectual endeavors were worthwhile. In the course of treatment, she did resume dancing on an amateur basis, and her talent, after a decade of inactivity, was judged by competent authorities to be superior. It also became clear, however, that, far from being intrusively controlling, her father had merely expressed the opinion that his adolescent daughter might be wise to rely on her considerable intellect rather than pursue the risky course of a ballet dancer. The patient had reacted to this rather hesitant advice as if it were a command because of her lifelong tendency to assume a posture of automatic obedience vis-à-vis self-appointed leaders. It should come as no surprise that we discovered her primary caretaker had been quite rigid and, correspondingly, that when she became old enough to play without adult supervision, the patient offered herself as the masochistic victim to older children who would torture her. In order for this girl puppet to use her talents, she needed to find an impresario who would *make* her dance! She was a Petrushka in search of her Diaghilev.

Another instance of creative paralysis as a result of excessive attachment to the mother—one that involved a less extreme form of archaic pathology—came to my attention during the analysis of a mature woman who had chosen an intellectual occupation for which she was quite well suited. Although everyone connected with the institutions within which she functioned looked upon her as a scholar of great promise, she had, in fact, failed to produce anything of scholarly value before the age of 40. It was widely understood that difficulties in her personal life—a stormy marriage, a bitter divorce, endless struggles over the custody of her child, unfortunate romantic entanglements—had prevented her from achieving her creative goals. Our analytic work led to the discovery that she was diverted from these goals by the need to enact an identification with an aspect of her mother's life that the patient had been the only person to witness. Specifically, when she was in her oedipal years, she had accompanied her mother on the latter's secret trysts with her physician; she was subsequently the sole support for her mother when the latter was grief-stricken after the affair had come to its abortive end. The child proceeded to repress totally the memories of these events; she was condemned, instead, to repeat them endlessly, albeit with herself in the role of the thwarted protagonist. This pattern continued until she gained conscious awareness into this aspect of her past.

It goes without saying that not every child would have reacted in this manner to the witnessing of a mother's secret romance. The fact that my patient identified with the mother's faithlessness and with the need to expiate it was determined by her relative immaturity at the time she was exposed to these overwhelming impressions. More specifically, this child was forced to accompany her mother even on such clandestine affairs because she had been raised, systematically, to remain the mother's symbiotic partner. It was only in adolescence that she finally rebelled against this servitude, tearing herself away from home in order to begin intellectual training at a distinguished university.

I shall adduce one more example to illustrate that the problem at hand is not simply related to the girl's identification with her mother's inattentiveness to intellectual pursuits. In this case, the patient had, in fact, followed her father into a scientific vocation but had always admired her mother's genuine superiority in the cultural realm. The mother's intellectual merit transcended her respectable career as a high school teacher before the birth of her daughter. The patient's own work history was satisfactory but devoid of creative accomplishments before an analysis undertaken as a result of difficulties ostensibly unrelated to vocational issues. The patient's scientific productivity was a surprising by-product of analytic progress in overcoming her lifelong reliance on assistance from a hidden collaborator—originally the mother who actively intruded into the patient's childhood endeavors, including much of her schoolwork.

It is not irrelevant to this case that the mother was similarly enmeshed in her husband's activities, to the point that the patient scarcely thought of her two parents as separate individuals. Hence, in identifying with her father in this professional role, she was at the same time confirming her symbiotic bond to her mother. We discovered that the patient had been energetically opposed in her strivings to establish her own autonomy in the second and third years of life and richly rewarded (not to say bribed or corrupted) for allowing her mother to use her as an extension of the former's own person. In adult life, the patient had to establish similar symbiotic bonds with new partners in order to perpetuate this adaptation, and this ongoing requirement often led to real difficulties rather than enhancing her level of performance as the mother's covert participation had done. Even when she found a willing secret sharer, moreover, the passivity that pervaded her character prevented this woman from accomplishing any creative task.

Although we might legitimately formulate the unfavorable effects of archaic fixations on the exercise of creative talents in terms of the perpetuation of passive character traits and a general lack of initiative, as the first and third of these illustrative case vignettes seem to imply, such fixations are surely not the only factors at work; in point of fact, the pattern of passivity was not a significant issue in the second of my three examples. Another insight we may extract from these clinical vignettes concerns the implications of the commitment these women made to the emotional well-being of their mothers: This commitment proved as major a career obstacle as the analogous commitment to raise a child. At some level, the nurture these individuals provided for their symbiotic partners actually had a higher priority in their hierarchy of personal goals than creative activities. But granting this point, I should add that I do not believe it to be of decisive significance; such as symbiosis, after all, need not be disrupted by the success of either partner in other enterprises.

Perhaps a more fundamental answer might be found by considering the effects of early fixations on the child's subsequent encounters with new contingencies. Because constraints on psychological development generally leave children poorly equipped to deal with the expectable challenges of various age levels, children subjected to such constraints will tend to avoid these challenges as much as possible, becoming progressively more handicapped in comparison with their peers. A policy of chronically avoiding novel situations may then become structured as a character trait in these personalities. If we conceive of creative endeavors as successful quests for hitherto unknown configurations, we can readily understand that excessive attachment to the relationships of earliest childhood would exert a powerful restraining influence on such quests.

V

IT WOULD BE grossly misleading to imply that the kind of archaic fixations I have been describing are found exclusively in women or are less likely to interfere with the creativity of males than of females. It is my impression, however, that these circumstances arise with greater frequency among girls—at least, this has been my personal clinical experience in private practice. I do not know whether this finding reflects a general preference on the part of mothers with symbiotic needs to satisfy these needs through their daughters, but I suspect this is often the case. I have had a number of male patients whose mothers had placed similar demands upon them without succeeding in enmeshing them in the symbiosis. To be sure, the consequences of such attempts for the personality development of these boys were often catastrophic, but this was the case precisely because the boys tended negativistically to fight off even benign external influence. Parenthetically, the older brother of the last woman I described in this chapter appears to have been victorious in a bitter struggle to emancipate himself from the mother before my patient was born. I must acknowledge, on the other side of the coin, that I have occasionally treated men who failed to fight off such enmeshment, and these patients were just as unable to use their talents effectively as my women patients with symbiotic adjustments.

We should further recall that unresolved oedipal conflicts, especially in relation to the father, will also cause grave difficulties for a potentially creative child and that the excessive intimacy of the kind of mother-daughter relationships I have highlighted tends to exacerbate father-daughter rivalries. By the same token, boys who may be initially entrapped in the maternal symbiosis have an opportunity to emancipate themselves if they are able to identify with an admirable (oedipal) father, a task little girls probably find infinitely more difficult to accomplish, especially in families that overtly value their femininity. Even the less favorable solution of a flight from women—either into homosexuality (see Chapter 5) or into a celibate life-style (witness the case of Nietzsche, described in Chapter 10)—may succeed in preserving a boy's potential for creativity. Women do not have equally accessible and effective pathways for detaching themselves from their mothers.

Of course, I should reiterate that the clinical material I have cited concerns instances of unequivocal pathology stimulated by unusually unfavorable family dynamics. Most girls are probably raised without being subjected to such extremes, although the incidence of psycho-pathology in general far exceeds the estimates of laymen. But creativity is the most fragile of functional capacities, so that negative influences of even the most subtle kind may have far-reaching effects on the frequency of its emergence in large populations. Perhaps, after all, the psychology of even the more fortunate women does predispose them to vital conservative roles in our society because of their natural tendency to identify with the mother of procreation.

But I do not wish to leave this topic on an entirely pessimistic note, for the prospects of creative women may well be improved if their families become a source of encouragement, rather than the setting for the type of destructive transactions I have described. The kind of cultural changes advocated by the feminist movement may be the basis for some slight hope in this regard, for it is presently undeniable that most families use a standard for evaluating the behavior of their daughters that differs from the one they apply to their sons. Concerning the depreciation of children who are "different" precisely because they possess the seeds of future talent (an issue I have discussed in Chapter 3), I have the impression that girls are more easily robbed of self-confidence than boys of comparable ability.

One example I can describe concerns a young woman who proved to be unusually gifted with languages and mathematics and who possessed unusual administrative skills. She was the child of working-class parents who, after a lifetime of struggle, made their small business a success. The one male child of this couple showed outstanding quantitative gifts and found it natural to obtain an engineering degree at one of the elite technological institutes in the area. One sister, favored in childhood because of her grace and attractiveness, married straight out of high school and bore as many children as her mother; another sister, the youngest child, though a good student, contented herself with training in a semiprofessional service occupation. My patient had effortlessly obtained top grades in every school she attended but was sent nonetheless to a state college of mediocre standards where she obtained a teaching certificate. Armed with these flimsy credentials, she had a responsible and well-paying job in educational publishing within five years of graduation; in addition, she functioned effectively as a freelance publicist within the communications industry. But her mother continued to view her as a complete failure because her breasts were somewhat pendulous—the fact that many men found the girl attractive made no difference whatsoever as far as the mother was concerned. Although the father did not share these grotesque attitudes, his own past experiences had, in a variety of ways, been so very difficult that he could only think of his daughter's future in terms of security; her adventuresome career simply made him too anxious to be of any use in countering the mother's influence.

Even in early childhood, this girl's efforts to impress her parents with her intellectual abilities elicited only negative feedback: The father sermonized about the dangers of attracting excessive attention through showing off while the mother counseled against stepping into the spotlight when such rashness could reveal the imperfections of one's figure. Neither parent ever commented approvingly on the patient's mastery of any skill irrelevant to a future as a suburban housewife; she was, after all, clearly unqualified for the destiny her mother coveted for all her daughters —that of the Hollywood sex-kitten. It stands to reason, then, that this patient sought analysis because she was overweight and felt unable to form a relationship with a reasonable prospect of marriage. What requires special emphasis, however, is the fact that my gifted patient was singled out among her siblings for this kind of maltreatment: Her brother went quietly about his business without threatening the father through his success, whereas her sisters were seen as average girls on the proper path in life. It was the patient, on the other hand, who had always seemed out of place in this family—in need of correction in some undefinable manner, an anomaly, perhaps a bad seed, ever in mischief, full of dangerous ideas.

The very fact that families who encourage their daughters to attend ranking colleges and universities do not often behave in these ways betokens positive social change. We might compare this heartening possibility to the startling mitigation of the double standard with respect to sexual behavior in the past generation. Yet shifts of this kind are also evanescent: The Victorian era, after all, succeeded a century with its share of libertinage. Even now, many members of the social elite of metropolitan America refuse to participate in the rush to send their daughters into the job market, and this so-called age of feminism may well eventuate in a general loss of status for most women. So the future attitude toward creative careers for women is extremely difficult to predict. But it is certain, I believe, that it will not be determined by economic factors alone: The kind of discrimination I described in my last vignette is by no means confined to the lower middle class.

I will underscore this point by offering one final example of the overwhelming importance of unconscious parental preconceptions about gender roles on the creative potential of a little girl. The child in question grew up to have outstanding ability to think abstractly. Early in life, her powerful intellect manifested itself in acute observations about her environment that were often at sharp variance with her parents' perceptions of the same matters. The family lived in material comfort; the patient's father, though uneducated, was quite successful in business. My patient's younger brother attended an excellent university as a matter of course and became a respected scientist and academic. My patient's education, by contrast, was left entirely to her own devices: She was able to scrounge together enough money to obtain a degree in a semivocational subject from a local college of small reputation; there was no question of receiving enough support from her family to pay the dormitory fees of even the local state university. While she was trying to make her college arrangements toward the end of her high school years, her father placed strong pressure on her to "date" older men on the fringes of the underworld—ostensibly because their financial support would secure her future. This story may have made a charming film as *Gigi*, but this girl saw it, with her usual clarity of vision, as an expression of her father's lifelong need to prove, preferably in action, that all women are whores.

Social changes are unlikely to alter psychological needs of this kind.

Chapter Five

Spared by the Fire
from Heaven

I

FAR FROM BEING regarded as an obstacle to creativity, overt homosexuality in both men and women has long been associated in the public
mind with the artistic temperament. From Sappho through Donatello,
Michelangelo, Tchaikowsky, Proust, and Rauschenberg, a distinguished
succession of major creative figures has been rumored to be homosexual.
Whether the personality disturbances that generally underlie sexual inversion interfered in some way with the working capacity of these artists
remains an open question, but there can be little doubt that the sexual
abnormality per se did not do so. On the contemporary scene, moreover,
the homosexual community certainly appears to be heavily represented in
most creative endeavors—and even more so among the consumers of high
culture.

In startling contrast to the position of women with creative ambitions,
especially those who lead conventional family lives, it would seem at first
glance that homosexuals actually enjoy unusually favorable circumstances
for realizing their creative potential. To be sure, these circumstances may
to some degree simply result from the relative lack of interest in our
philistine culture for activities that yield little profit or prestige and may
therefore just as well be ceded to disadvantaged groups as their special
preserves; women are probably unable to take full advantage of the
opportunities of being allowed to succeed in the arts because that is not
where the power elite competes, for the psychological reasons I have
discussed in the previous chapter. On the other hand, I would not give
too much weight to this type of sociological explanation; the cultural
commitments of homosexuals, after all, are scarcely paralleled by those of

other male groups of relatively low status. In light of this fact, it may be more illuminating to turn to individual case studies to determine the specific motivations that simultaneously turn a given person toward homosexuality and toward the arts.

No psychoanalyst can hope to work with either a significant number of creative persons or a significant number of overt homosexuals—much less with a combination of both—even in the course of a lifetime of full-time clinical practice. As I have noted elsewhere (Gedo, 1979b), the completion of 60 to 80 analyses at most is probably the outer possible limit in our profession. My personal analytic experience of the past quarter century has included only two male homosexuals, and I believe this paucity of interest in my services on the part of the homosexual community is entirely typical. (Needless to say, in the current atmosphere of "sexual politics," lesbians are not likely to consult a male analyst, and I have never had the opportunity to work with one.) If, despite this very limited exposure, I proceed to offer some impressions derived from my clinical activities, I do so because both of my analysands had an appreciable measure of creative talent and seemed to be fairly representative of the cultivated homosexual circles of a contemporary American metropolis.

II

SOME YEARS AGO, I was consulted by a young physician who wished to overcome his distressing and unwelcomed homosexual activities. He had engaged in these activities overtly since before puberty, although he had never completely resigned himself to the identity of a "gay" person. In particular, he resolved to turn over a new leaf when, following his graduation from medical school, he was inducted into military service and thereby removed from the milieu in which his homosexuality was common knowledge. While serving with some distinction in combat conditions in Viet Nam, he decided to shed his despised, effeminate persona. He hoped to effect this change by getting married and, to this end, he entered into correspondence with a girl from his home town who had openly shown an interest in him when they were in high school. They were married on his return. Although the patient experienced little difficulty in their sexual relations, he found his new wife to be conventional, rigid, and dull. His increasing disappointment in their relationship led him into renewed homosexual adventures that entailed a not inconsiderable risk to the professional career he wished to carve out for himself in a highly conservative suburban community.

In the course of the ensuing analysis, I was surprised to learn that medicine, a profession that was opening a path into the upper middle class for this small-town boy of decidedly modest origins, had never been the patient's first choice as a vocation. In fact, he bewailed his lack of courage in pursuing this sensible but down-to-earth profession, rather than becoming the great concert pianist he had dreamed of being as a child. Through high school, he had been the only serious musician in his community, so superior in this sphere that his prestige equaled that of the outstanding local athletes who otherwise dominated the teen-age scene. He maintained his immersion in music at the excellent church-affiliated small college he attended, but the quality of instruction available to him there clearly did not suffice as professional preparation. He was unable to tear himself away from the security of this setting, however, largely because he was afraid of determining whether his talent made it feasible for him to risk all on a concert career. As time went on, it became clear that he could easily gain admission to medical school, and he abandoned his music altogether in favor of concentrating on scientific studies.

The patient's conviction that he had made a grave error in giving up his musical ambitions seemed to be contradicted by his loss of courage at that crucial juncture. Consequently, at an appropriate moment, I told him that he would forever be tortured by these doubts and regrets unless he obtained a reliable estimate, even at this late date, of the actual extent of his musical talent. Challenged by this idea, he eventually resumed piano practice and submitted himself to a series of auditions before judges of progressively greater stature. Their verdicts were entirely consistent: The patient possessed "musicality" of the highest order, but his piano technique was too deficient to be remedied without years of concentrated effort. In other words, the patient was essentially correct in judging that he had missed his true vocation.

By this time, being well-established in his medical practice, the patient realized he could earn a sufficient income on a limited schedule that would enable him to resume serious musical studies. Moreover, the fact that his secure financial position freed him from the need to earn a living through music meant that he could joyfully compromise on a program to become a serious amateur performer. Although the analysis had proceeded reasonably well to this point, the patient had overcome neither his dissatisfaction with his wife nor his occasional homosexual activities—the latter becoming increasingly concentrated during periods when our work was for some reason temporarily interrupted. We were therefore completely unprepared for one of the consequences of his new routine of several hours of daily piano practice: Never again did he feel the need for sexual relations with men!

To characterize this development differently, we observed that musical performance and homosexuality could interchangeably serve some of the same functions for this patient. He now realized that this had probably always been the case, so that his abandonment of the piano in college had seriously aggravated his homosexual needs. In view of the fact that his frantic sexual activities in adolescence had never interfered with his commitment to music, however, it was quite clear that they had not prevented the development of his creativity. This could not be said for other of his psychological problems, such as the grandiose ambitions that impelled him to avoid the risk of competitive defeats.

Before we embark on an examination of the manner in which a sexual inversion and a creative vocation had come to serve some of the same functions in this man's mental life, it may be fruitful to compare the foregoing data with corresponding facts from the analysis of the second patient whose history is relevant in this connection. The latter entered analysis in his late 30s when he sensed he would no longer be able to derive most of his satisfaction in life from being the highly sought-after object of male lovers eager to compete for his favors. At the same time, this fading Ganymede realized that he had ruined a promising academic career in the humanities by his cavalier disregard of the need to publish scholarly research; this failure resulted in large measure from the masochistic relationship he had established with the chairman of his department. This relationship took the form of a continuing struggle in which the patient was generally humiliated but felt vindicated because he could blame his persecutor for his difficulties. But he also knew that he had allowed these circumstances to develop in order to punish his wife, a clinging and immature person who did not in his judgment deserve a tenured professor as a husband. Thus his academic career faltered at the very time he was about to lose his position as a star of the steambaths.

Although the patient was able to secure a modest teaching job in his own field after he left the prestigious university where he had enacted this drama, he continued his chaotic way of life well into the second year of his analysis. The only island of calm and decency in his existence was an ongoing relationship with a male lover. Unlike the patient's wife, this paramour was able to respect his autonomy and privacy, and the time spent with him invariably restored the patient's equilibrium. In contrast, his wife's intrusiveness and insensitivity generally infuriated and disrupted him, often leading to dangerous and frenetic sexual escapades.

As was the case with the first patient, this man had married in a futile effort to transcend a well-established homosexual adaptation, also on the occasion of a move to a community where his history was unknown. Needless to say, his choice of a spouse was based entirely on considerations of immediate prestige: A beautiful and socially acceptable young woman too naive to detect his homosexuality, she predictably turned out to be an immature person. Ironically, the patient's lover had all the qualities of empathy and loving concern lacking in his wife but possessed neither the education nor the social position that would have made him acceptable to the patient as an openly acknowledged companion.

The complexities of this double life, interspersed with episodes of wild promiscuity, scarcely left the patient enough time or energy to do the scholarly work required to repair his derailed career. Eventually he faced the fact that his masochistic attitude in the marriage paralleled his attitude toward his departmental chairman at the university, and he decided to seek a way out of his impasse by obtaining a divorce. Somewhat to his surprise, his wife readily agreed to an amicable parting when he approached her shouldering the blame for the failure of their relationship. Nor did his homosexual affair take on added importance as a result of the divorce; on the contrary, as he seemed less troubled by the continual disappointments of the marriage, he had less and less need for what his lover had formerly offered him. Instead, he became progressively more interested in his work, assuming greater teaching and administrative responsibilities. Gradually he restored his academic reputation, although he still failed to undertake scholarly writing for a long time. I shall not go into the details of the manifold ways in which the analysis assisted this man in overcoming some of the psychological handicaps that had hindered his work; suffice it to say that he made steady progress in these matters for a number of years without any major change in his sexual adaptation. The only significant shift in this regard was the fact that his promiscuous escapades now occurred only when he was disappointed within the analytic relationship, mostly in connection with interruptions in our schedule.

Ultimately, the patient's general progress at work enabled him to obtain a better position, one in an academic setting but with greatly reduced teaching responsibilities. In line with the opportunities provided by this new appointment, he took charge of certain extracurricular programs, both as the planner who conceived them and the administrator who carried them out. (I regret that the need to conceal the patient's identity precludes a description of the specifics involved in his work; this would render my account much more convincing.) Because the patient enjoyed the practical aspects of his work much more than he liked teaching or research, he gradually realized that his decision to become a college professor had been a betrayal of his own natural preferences, largely in the service of seeking the kind of status that would have impressed certain members of his family. Again, I must omit the fascinating details of how these emotional needs had come into operation; what is relevant for our purposes here is that the patient was now able to reconsider his vocational goals. As he clarified his program of action in this respect, the analytic focus of interest gradually shifted once again to the question of his sexual aims. It was at this time that he spontaneously and definitively decided to leave his homosexuality behind. He ended the relationship with his lover with deep regret over the latter's pain at this decision, but, despite some guilt about having exploited a loyal person, he was able to cease his other homosexual activities at the same time. He continued to display increasing creativity at work, eventually even attempting some scholarly writing, and he found no real difficulty in establishing a heterosexual adaptation.

Like the first patient I discussed, this man was the product of an isolated small town, although his family was much more prosperous and possessed much higher social status. His maternal grandmother, in particular, had the pretensions of a grande dame, and she probably stimulated the patient's intense boyhood interest in the humanities. Because of his early intellectuality, he felt himself to be decisively different from everyone else in town, especially after the death of the grandmother, which occurred as he was entering puberty. Like the would-be pianist in *his* community, this youthful devotee of high culture also believed he was the sole adherent of homoerotism in his milieu. At the same time, both boys were convinced that their homosexual activities were startling inventions entirely original with them—their first and greatest creative achievements. In view of the fact that during their analyses both men were able to fend off "disorder and early sorrow" by emergency resort to homosexual behavior, it is by no means unreasonable to look upon these childhood adaptive solutions as more or less effective home remedies created without external assistance.

III

ANALYTIC RECONSTRUCTION of the early childhood ambiance in which these homosexual patients were raised filled me with amazement at the fact that the community in which they had chosen to live prefers to call itself "gay." Their inner landscape was in actuality chronically bleak and, at least in childhood, generally unrelieved by the availability of satisfying alternatives to the family relationships that were failing them. The future pianist discovered around the age of four that he could master his dysphoric states by concentrating on individual notes he struck on the largely unused family piano; his subsequent music lessons were arranged because he was spending more and more time on his own initiative with the instrument. The would-be humanist obtained similar results by means of occasionally sharing in his mother's religious exaltation. She would allow him to join her in fervent prayer to a deity conceived in the most exalted terms as the source of comfort and salvation; at such moments, the boy was able to transcend his own narcissistic universe and feel himself part of the City of God. In neither case, however, were these avenues of self-healing available during the crucial earliest years of life. In childhood, musical performance and spiritual participation, capacities these individuals happened to possess to an unusual degree, came to serve as antidotes for inner disorder, but they were not the only means through which these children learned to maintain their equilibrium. Among other regulatory measures, sexual activities clearly came to take pride of place.

Both boys desperately longed to be rescued from their subjective distress by fathers they falsely idealized, but neither father was in the least responsive to these overtures. This was partly because each father was frightened and revolted by his son's effeminacy. In addition, the father of the first patient seemed to be hostile to him, probably because he correctly sensed that his son's abilities were superior to his own; in the second case, the father was severely alcoholic and often disgraced himself in painfully disillusioning ways. In both families, there were also younger daughters who pleased the fathers effortlessly, to the endless chagrin of my patients. This circumstance only served, naturally enough, to reinforce the boy's feminine longings.

What each boy needed to be rescued *from* was perhaps clearer in the second of my illustrative cases. This patient was the second of three children in a household manipulated by the maternal grandmother. His mother was very much under the thumb of this tyrannical matriarch and, furthermore, was caught in the cross fire between her mother and her husband—mortal antagonists to be sure. By the time the patient was born, each of these rivals was trying to claim the mother by acting sicker and more helplessly demanding than the other. Although the patient's mother was sweet and loving (albeit a bit fey and deficient in common sense), she was overwhelmed by these competing claims and the needs of her children; she solved her dilemma by appeasing the adults at the expense of the children. The children's care was thus largely entrusted to domestics. Significantly, the patient's older brother identified with these servants; he became a country bumpkin well able to fend for himself. He also became the first of the sadistic tormentors to whom the patient submitted with a feeling of triumphant superiority.

In the family warfare, the older brother allied himself with the father; more or less willy-nilly, the patient was therefore forced into alliance with his grandmother. He identified with her arrogance, malice, manipulativeness, vanity, and preciosity—if you will, with that caricature of femininity (cf. Stoller, 1975) now often termed "gay." At the same time, he hated her, hated himself, and longed for a reversal of alliances. But his father's rebuffs, teamed with his grandmother's blatant bribery (including encouragement to share her bed), precluded any escape from her. Of course, he also tried to look to his mother for succor, but he lost hope in that possibility at the age of five when his sister was born. He was at that time flooded with hatred as he saw his mother nursing the baby, and he sealed his own fate by decisively rejecting his mother's religious values. This rejection actually took the form of a conscious pact with the Devil—

a living presence in this house! At times, when he was able to persuade himself that even his mother was wicked, the patient switched sides, feeling himself to be the Archangel Michael divinely charged with the punishment of his entire family. The repeated public disgrace he brought upon himself, both through his homosexual activities and the periodic failures in all his subsequent enterprises, satisfied the requirements of both these fantasy systems. Predictably, the fate of the analytic effort hinged on the clarification of these issues as they emerged in the transference.

If the predisposing factors for my first patient's feminine identification or, to stress the other side of the same coin, for his fear and hatred of women, are more difficult to relate, this is because his early years were entirely uneventful. Indeed, the personality traits in question came into being in the context of an uninterrupted and seemingly close attachment to his mother. In this case, too, the birth of the younger sister created a reversal in the boy's feelings, based on a bottomless sense of betrayal by the person who had raised him to look upon himself as part of her. The patient's mother certainly continued to make use of her son as an extension of herself, especially in the sphere of narcissistic gratifications; whenever he lent himself to such exploitation, the patient experienced himself as his mother's fantasied phallus. If he tried to assert his autonomy, his mother was cleverly able to undermine him by depreciating his independent activities in a seemingly objective manner. His public successes, whether in music or in medicine, were rapidly appropriated by the mother as her own, and the patient regarded her as too pitiful to be punished by depriving her of these gratifications.

Because they did not get the masculine assistance that might have pulled them out of these tar pits of regressive, symbiotic relations with women, both boys were thrown back on their own resources.[1] As I have stated already, both devised the same homosexual remedy for this dilemma, based on fantasies of incorporating masculine qualities through concrete acts of swallowing a penis or engulfing it rectally. By means of quasi-feminine seductiveness, they found their way into an exclusively masculine world, safe from the intrusiveness of predatory women. Here finally was one area of endeavor that could not be coopted for anyone else's narcissistic gain—in both cases, the boy's homosexuality, although blatant, was entirely denied by the woman from whom it was originally designed to escape.

Moreover, the wives who were betrayed and dishonored by the promiscuity of these men also managed to deny completely the evidence

---

1. The childhood of the analysand who felt so betrayed by the birth of his sister might profitably be compared with that of Pablo Picasso (see M. Gedo, 1980a, as well as Chapter 7), whose beginnings were apparently similar. But Picasso's father devoted himself to rescuing his traumatized child, and the latter grew up to have a most unusual capacity to make use of constructive partnerships with men.

for it, or, at the very least, to disavow its significance. To be sure, they were overtly frustrated by their husband's aloofness and contempt, particularly as these attitudes focused on their femininity. Via the justifiable disaffection of these women, we can see that the price both patients paid for maintaining the homosexual adaptation was the sacrifice of intimacy in adult relations with women. The regressive pull of the symbiotic propensities these men had failed to overcome in early childhood found its outlet in their homosexual acts—to be more precise, in the fantasies of magically merging into the being of idealized males that frequently (though not invariably) accompanied fellatio or intercourse. In the course of their analyses, after they had gained insight into this aspect of their homosexuality, these patients were able to experience similar feelings within the transference relationship without the need to concretize the sense of union through bodily contact.

Perhaps the best way to summarize the advantages of the turn of sexual inversion for these men is to emphasize that it removed them, once and for all, from the symbiotic orbit in which they had been reduced to instruments of a woman's narcissistic strivings. In neither instance was this assertion of autonomy accomplished without conflict; the patients' self-hatred for being homosexual reflected their identification with the disapproval they expected for overthrowing the influence of their primary caretakers. From this viewpoint, the success of each treatment was contingent on demonstrating that homosexuality had represented a valuable developmental achievement for these boys. Of course, in cases where this kind of conflict over the homosexual choice is lacking, the motivation to seek help to overcome the sexual inversion will probably be absent as well.[2]

Be that as it may, these men were able to pursue creative endeavors as long as their homosexual adaptations permitted them to retain a sense of autonomous functioning that was more or less intact; they ran into major difficulties in this regard only after their rash marriages to women who demanded as much of a symbiotic commitment from them as the primary caretakers who had originally entrapped them. Modell (1965) has attrib-

---

2. Needless to say, homosexuals may seek analysis even in the absence of such motivation for a variety of other reasons. Moreover, they may conceal their reluctance to overcome the inversion if they suspect that the analyst might reject them if the truth were revealed. Clearly, it is imperative *not* to have any agenda if one wishes to work with such persons. The psychoanalyst's only legitimate activity is to attempt to learn the truth; the analysand alone has the prerogative to decide what to do with it.

I have been involved as a consultant with one analysis undertaken in such circumstances; interestingly enough, the patient in question was quite similar in most respects to the two individuals I have described here, although the positive aspect of his relationship to his icy but intrusive mother was less meaningful than the corresponding feelings of my patients. Nonetheless, after careful analysis of its adaptive functions, homosexuality proved to be no more difficult to relinquish in this case than in the two I have recounted.

uted the compliance adult patients show to such demands to the presence of "separation guilt." Indeed, both of my patients felt extremely guilty because, unlike the original symbiotic partners of childhood, their wives had never betrayed the terms on which the symbiotic relationships had been founded; the patients thereupon felt much more reprehensible in being untrue to them than in fleeing the primary caretakers. The compromise they effected was devastating to the patients' creative enterprises: They behaved in a manner that yielded profit or pleasure neither to themselves nor to their spouses, even when the latter were kept at bay. When the spouses were not so fended off, the patients proved utterly incapable of all independent initiative.

IV

IT WOULD SEEM that Marcel Proust was certainly justified in claiming, in the epigraph that introduces *Sodome et Gomorrhe*, that the fire from heaven had actually spared some of the inhabitants of the Cities of the Plain. Homosexuals who have come to the attention of objective observers have generally given the impression of suffering impaired adaptation, but their psychic scars, frequently covering the wounds sustained in a battle against a primary identification with the mother, may leave them with enhanced creative abilities owing to their driving need to differentiate themselves from the surrounding matrix—often not only the maternal milieu but also the entire cultural ambiance. This was certainly the case for the two patients I have described.

In both of these clinical examples, the mother came to represent the prevailing culture of small-town America that both patients left behind. The "small-town" appellation should not be read in a pejorative sense: That culture held many attractions for both these men, particularly in the religious sphere, and their mothers stood for the best it had to offer. In contrast, the patients' fathers were boorish and mediocre despite their middle-class status. From this viewpoint, one of the attractions of the homosexual circles my patients encountered in the wider world was the social sanction they offered for *males* to be seriously committed to high culture. In their adolescence, these men had been regarded as "sissies" not because their furtive homosexual exploits were publicly known but simply because of their overt interest in the life of the mind. As adults, they did not retreat from their intellectual aspirations. Instead, they left their mothers behind by attempting to become members of the avant-garde.

It is difficult to decide how far the inferences I have drawn from my limited clinical sample might be generalized. Clearly, there are homosexuals whose feminine identification is even more pervasive than that of my patients or, emphasizing the issue I actually believe to be central for creative activity, whose efforts to overcome enmeshment in a symbiotic life-style are less successful. Could these be the people whom the gay community despises as "faggots"? I am not sure, but I would assume in any event that my conclusions would not apply to such individuals; they would tend to slide into a morass of sadomasochistic struggles in their homosexual relationships, with results paralleling the loss of initiative suffered by my patients in reaction to their marriages. For many homosexuals, in other words, all human relations are potentially impregnated with the poison of paralyzing fear and hatred generated vis-à-vis their mothers.

Of course, this problem could also be approached from the vantage point of the psychology of the successful homosexual artist. To date, however, there are few satisfactory biographical works focusing on the interplay between homosexuality and creativity, despite the fact that the lives of such famous artists as Michelangelo Buonarroti and Oscar Wilde have been studied in great detail. Perhaps the outstanding exception to this statement is Jean Delay's (1956-1958) closely documented biography of the young André Gide. As it happens, judging on the basis of that study, Gide appears to have been rather similar in his personality organization to the homosexual patients I have seen. His inversion helped him to escape the constraints of his Huguenot upbringing, especially the influence of his widowed mother. His unconsummated marriage to a reluctant *cousine* exemplifies both the risk and the attraction of returning to the bondage from which homosexuality had freed him. His work was largely concerned with the conflicts of young men torn between obligations to society and family on the one hand and the need for self-assertion beyond the bounds of morality on the other. But Gide's own position in these matters was always close to the individualism promulgated by Nietzsche. It was the latter's claim to be "the Immoralist," after all, that Gide adopted as the title of an autobiographical novel about the onset of his homosexuality.

It may not be too fanciful to recall in this connection that in his late magnum opus *Doctor Faustus*, Thomas Mann, another great writer of homosexual inclination, characterized commitment to the creative life as a pact with the devil. Mann's prototypical hero, Adrian Leverkühn, is loosely modeled on Friedrich Nietzsche himself (see Chapter 10). Perhaps our age is one in which all artists must be immoralists in league with the powers of darkness. It follows that their *via crucis* will parallel that of the sexual invert who is compelled to repudiate his own *Magna Mater*.

Chapter Six

The Psychology of Genius
Revisited

I

A DECADE AGO, I wrote an essay on the psychology of genius (Gedo, 1972b) based on clinical experience in analyzing a creative person universally acknowledged as supreme in his field. I ended my paper by posing a series of questions that my study had been unable to resolve: I did not know to what extent the conclusions drawn from analytic observation of one man of genius could be generalized, and I was puzzled by the methodological dilemma posed by the problem of establishing a workable typology of personalities geared to outstanding achievement. In an exhaustive search of the psychoanalytic literature, I found that such individuals rarely seem to seek analytic assistance. This statement is particularly true if we accept the definition of genius offered by Eissler (1963). He restricts the term to "persons . . . capable of recreating the human cosmos, or part of it, in a way that [is] significant and not comparable to any previous recreation" (p. 1353). If, on occasion, one of these exceptional people does in fact become a psychoanalytic patient, disclosure of the conclusions of the clinical work presents such insuperable problems of confidentiality that literally no reports of this kind had appeared prior to my report of 1972.

I attempted to circumvent the possibility of inadvertently revealing the identity of my patient by confining my discussion to a number of outstanding problems that had gained attention over the years in the

A previous version of this material appeared in *The Annual of Psychoanalysis*, 7:269–283, 1979.

psychoanalytic literature on creativity. Specifically, I followed Eissler's suggestion (1967), made on the strength of his extensive experience as a psychobiographer (see Chapter 1), that the seemingly pathological behaviors of a genius might be fruitfully teased apart into a number of categories. First, he noted phenomena related to ordinary psychic conflicts that bore no special connection to the creative functions, although they might secondarily come to interfere with them. (I have attempted to illustrate problems of this kind in the preceding three chapters.) Second, Eissler pinpointed age-appropriate developmental crises that might, he believed, possess certain special features in the outstandingly gifted. Finally, he listed behaviors that form an integral part of the creative activity itself; these were defined as part of the "psychopathology of creativity." By focusing exclusively on the second and third of these categories, I thought I could present my clinical findings without risking any indiscretions.

Although my conclusions were generally congruent with those previously made from the studies of psychobiographers, I saw the publication of a case study as an important complement to and validation of the extensive literature on creativity derived from the application of psychoanalysis to biographical materials. Instead of making comparisons between the subjects of the numerous and rather disparate analytic biographies of men of genius and the man I analyzed,[1] I decided to focus my study on the psychological similarities and differences between my patient and a group of talented and creative people of both sexes who had availed themselves of my analytic services but did not quite meet Eissler's stringent criteria of genius.

In the intervening years, my practice has continued to provide me with the opportunity to work with creative personalities from a variety of fields—writers and scholars, artists and scientists, thinkers and doers. Among these patients, at least one other has impressed me as a genius, although (for reasons I shall spell out below) he had not gained the kind of public acclaim that would conclusively confirm my opinion. Perhaps I should add that a number of talented young people whom I have treated also had great promise but were engaged in enterprises that take many years to come to fruition. With the passage of time, in other words, they too may emerge as major contributors to their respective fields. For the time being, however, I cannot affirm that they will prove themselves to be equal to the two individuals I am singling out in this chapter. I make this point because I am convinced that the natural history of major accomplishments in various occupations differs markedly: Psychoanaly-

1. Alas, there are no such biographies about women, a fact that raises a host of disturbing questions, some of which I have tried to answer in Chapter 4.

sis, for instance, is notorious for the slow maturation of its practitioners—Freud's accomplishment in making his greatest discoveries before the age of 50 has absolutely no parallel, even on a smaller scale, within the field.

At any rate, I now find myself in the fortunate position of having analytic data from my own practice with which to test my conclusions of 1972 about the psychology of genius. In this chapter therefore, I plan to review the ground I covered in my earlier report, amplifying my remarks with illustrative material drawn from both case histories. I shall also take the opportunity to revise some of the conceptualizations I put forward initially in the light of the evolution of my psychoanalytic thinking in the intervening years. Specifically, I shall attend to the clinical data from the standpoint of the self-organization, the unconscious hierarchy of personal goals and values that I have postulated as the framework of our depth psychology (see Gedo, 1979a, 1981a).

II

THE TWO MEN I shall describe sought help in the course of the fourth decade of their lives for problems of real gravity. These problems seemed to have little or no connection with their creative activities, however, except for the fact that, for one of them, the crisis had severely interfered with his work opportunities, and this circumstance had caused, secondarily, an ominous depressive reaction with suicidal ideation. Both men had solid but unspectacular bourgeois backgrounds and came from families that had settled for generations in out-of-the-way, conservative communities. In each instance, both parents had shown impressive talents in fields of endeavor completely unrelated to the area in which the son turned out to have spectacular gifts.

The analytic work with these men was unusually successful, perhaps more so than one might have expected on the basis of the presenting picture; in both cases, the treatment was terminated by mutual consent after a relatively brief course (13 months in one case; approximately 3 years in the other). As one might expect for analyses in which such uncomplicated progress takes place, the central problem was discovered to be a set of intrapsychic conflicts in the context of a well-organized personality structure. My experience with these individuals therefore flatly contradicts a conclusion K. R. Eissler has reached in his biographical studies, namely, that creative efforts of the highest quality require the renunciation of sexual intimacy with a beloved person. To the contrary, the capacity of my patients for intimacy with their sexual partners improved markedly as a result of their analyses, and one by-product of this change turned out to be heightened creative output. I thus find myself in agreement with the implications of van Gogh's recognition that many artists, including his friend Gauguin, were, unlike himself, capable of combining intense relationships with women and artistic activity (1959c, pp. 466, 509). In certain types of genius, creativity may actually suffer as a result of loneliness![2]

With these men of genius, the analytic process had certain special qualities that I attributed to their unusual mental capacities. For example, both men showed great aptitude for the apprehension of psychological configurations, so that the necessity for interpretive interventions on my part was strikingly reduced in terms of both frequency and degree of necessary detail. Even more unusual was their integrative capacity, as demonstrated, for example, in their dreaming. The manifest content of their dreams was in general strikingly simple and brief, but this imagery always contained exceptionally overdetermined multiple meanings that were represented in highly ingenious ways. In terms of Freud's (1900) description of "dream work," these persons might be described as virtuosi of "secondary revision," that is, they constructed a smooth and coherent gestalt out of the perceptual elements of the dream. (Note the similarity of this process to Ehrenzweig's [1967] requirements for artistic creativity as reviewed in Chapter 2.) Another genius whose dreams are accessible to us in some detail, Sigmund Freud himself, accomplished similar feats of condensation. As demonstrated in *The Interpretation of Dreams* (1900), he too teased apart the multiple strands of meaning combined in the dream imagery. Eissler (1963) has reported intellectual achievements of an even more complex type from Goethe's dream life, which allegedly included freshly created, complete lyric poems.

Both of my analysands experienced certain "symptoms" directly related to their creative activities; although some of these phenomena have acquired secondary meanings as convenient carriers of one or another legacy of childhood conflict, they did not disappear when we had resolved the relevant psychological issues through the treatment. In other words, these phenomena, at their core, turned out to constitute separate entitites, actual by-products of the patients' work. One of these men required almost complete perceptual isolation in order to concentrate on his task from a purely abstract vantage point; for example, he could not reach the requisite state of total concentration on his thoughts if he tried to make notes on yellow paper instead of plain white paper, and he worked best in a darkened room. He could maintain a state of withdrawal from other stimuli for up to 72 hours in order to arrive at a solution to an abstract

---

2. As a result, entering psychological treatment may have a nonspecific beneficial effect on disturbances of creativity simply because it mitigates the disruptive effects of personal isolation.

problem.[3] The patient's vigils were regularly followed by a syndrome of intense stimulus hunger, particularly in the visual sphere, and he was compelled to seek perceptual experiences in various voyeuristic activities. The specific content of the percepts he sought out changed, in accord with the progress of his analytic insight, from rather infantile preoccupations with need-gratifications, through a period of intense sexual curiosity, to an ultimate commitment to mature aesthetic interests.

In line with the markedly different demands of his field of activity, the second patient showed a different response to his work. When called upon to exercise his gifts on a new problem, he had always experienced states of excited enthusiasm; as he gradually allowed himself greater scope for originality, partly as one favorable outcome of our analytic effort, his exaltation in the actual process of creation would fill his whole being to the extent that he would eventually lose track of the environment. He was able to continue his work despite this change in consciousness; he might then recover self-awareness after an interval of several hours, typically awakening from a sleep of exhaustion. Any threatened emergence of unusual psychic states had always been extremely frightening for this man, so much so that he tended to shy away from the very work that excited him most or to undertake it only when he had dulled his potential reactions through some medication that generally interfered with the requisite mental acuity. One of the results of the analysis for which he felt most grateful was the elimination of this anxiety through his simple discovery of the fact that his behavior was no less rational and well-organized during such altered states of consciousness than at other times.

It is interesting to note that, as a child, this man had been a sleepwalker. Although this behavior seemed to have been a regressive response to certain acute stresses of unusual intensity, in the course of his sleepwalking the patient had indulged in the only overt expression of highly significant aspects of his true self. Specifically, it was only during these altered states of consciousness that he was able to experience his hatred of a sadistic stepmother. We might say, in Freud's original terminology, that the patient experienced a "return of the repressed," but without registration in consciousness. Clearly, the automatically produced results of the patient's adult creativity were analogous externalizations.[4]

---

3. As I have noted previously (Gedo, 1972b), this patient was cognizant of the effectiveness of this unique procedure. Consequently, he had concealed his working methods from everyone in order to retain an advantage over potential competitors. As the fantasy that he needed to conceal a mere gimmick reveals, he was unable to acknowledge the fact that he possessed a most unusual biological gift: The ability to remain in focus for an astonishingly long period of reflection. Instead, he preferred to believe that he had invented his ingenious trick when he decided, as a young child, that the secret of success was to work harder than anyone else!

III

PHYLLIS GREENACRE (1957) has postulated that children destined for major creative accomplishments have special hereditary endowments that first become discernible around the age of 3. Although my analysands had no conception, even in adulthood, of the rarity of their childhood capacities, they did in fact remember unique performances dating back to the earliest period of their lives. I have already mentioned that one of them realized, probably around the age of 4, that he could put forth more effort than anyone else he knew; the other, among his unusual accomplishments, taught himself to read at the age of 3. In both cases, these achievements proved quite frightening because they stimulated fantasies of greatness in the child—not in the realm in which the individual was, in fact, destined to excel but in the realm of those phase-appropriate ambitions (e.g., oedipal ambitions) that most young children experience at various stages of development.

Like ordinary children, my two patients experienced the expectable need to disavow the sense of being special; their burial of all archaic ambitions was therefore at the root of their subsequently impaired ability to use their exceptional gifts to full advantage. But the sense of greatness unconsciously active within these personalities was radically different from the hidden megalomania so often found in the course of analyzing persons who have suffered severe early childhood traumatization. As a child, the genius perceives his special capacities but can make no realistic assessment of their purport. He may be tempted to imagine that he faces a life of limitless possibilities, but this fantasy is not essential to his continued integration, as the bizarre grandiose ideas of the traumatized child seem to be for his.

In the psychic life of these analysands, the conviction of being special did indeed have truth-value in the spheres in which their individual capacities and performances were far beyond those of ordinary persons. When analysis had freed them of their fears about being extraordinary, their self-assessments in these areas became completely matter of fact. In this regard, we would do well to recall that Paul Cézanne was stating a

---

4. This clinical material suggests a hitherto undiscovered explanation for organized behaviors in the absence of consciousness, including some forms of sleepwalking: They may be a regressive return to a state of psychological organization characteristic of children before they achieve subjective self-awareness (perhaps some time in the first part of the second year of life). In such a state, various subsets of personal goals may temporarily determine the child's activity, without regard for subsets of equal importance, that is, without coordination or foresight. (See Gedo, 1979a, 1981a, for more detailed discussions of various archaic states of psychic organization.) In the adult, the capacity to return to such a state of organization may permit the expression of otherwise inaccessible mental contents in the creative act.

literal truth when he remarked (see Lindsay, 1969, p. 322) that a talent such as his appeared only once every 200 years—I interpret his remark to apply to the history of French painting, in which his only true predecessor in depicting three-dimensional space via color had been Nicolas Poussin, who died in 1665. In every other respect, Cézanne happened to be a man suffering from a pathetic deficiency in self-esteem.[5] To put the same point in still another way, genius does not seem to preclude expectable psychological development. Both of my patients had achieved reasonably satisfactory patterns of personality organization, impaired only by specific conflicts related to interpersonal vicissitudes within their families of origin.

To be sure, the foregoing statement does not consider the continuing influence of one disavowed aspect of the self, that which encompasses the ambition to achieve great things by means of dimly sensed special gifts. Such ambitions are generally warded off defensively, except for those rare occasions, such as that involving Mozart, in which the caretakers correctly recognize the nature and the specific value of the child's capacities.[6] We have to assume that extraordinary nurturance of this kind is a prerequisite for the early unfolding of genius, which is therefore the rarest of events.

Left to his own devices, the child with extraordinary gifts will inevitably evaluate these gifts from the standpoint of his naive outlook upon the world. He will be unable to grasp the actual uses to which his capabilities may eventually be put; in their childhood guise, his potentialities may well be lacking any specific function. Thus, one of my patients was long preoccupied in childhood with certain solitary games in which he privately solved spatial problems posed by his surroundings, for example, turning three-dimensional percepts into flat images or vice versa. It should scarcely

5. The most dramatic illustration of this deficiency occurred at a party organized by Monet to honor Cézanne on one of the latter's periodic trips to Paris in the late 1880s (cf. Lindsay, 1969, p. 253). When the 50-year-old genius realized that the distinguished company had gathered to pay him homage, he had a paranoid reaction and fled Monet's house, allegedly to escape being mocked!

6. Recent reports (quoted in Hildesheimer, 1982, p. 184) that Mozart impoverished himself through gambling—specifically by playing billiards for money—raise the possibility that early childhood recognition of his genius had not, in fact, come soon enough (or had not been accurate enough) to save him from these intractable problems of self-esteem. Such difficulties, in other words, probably crystallized as a result of transactions that antedated the recognition of his supreme talent. (It should be recalled that he was thought to be destined for a career as a performing virtuoso and that his sister was expected to match him in this respect.) On the other hand, it is also conceivable that Mozart's pathology resulted from never having experienced the realistic limits of whatever his capacities would permit him to achieve; in this sense, his reputed gambling losses, incurred through repeated proof of his personal limitations as a player, may actually have served to reduce the threat of megalomanic fantasies. On balance, however, I believe it is more likely that even Mozart was underestimated by his family.

come as a surprise that children will accept their parents' responses to such activities as the only proper judgment to be made about them.

Creative personalities who have sought my analytic assistance, including the two I am describing here in detail, have generally recalled that caretakers responded to the early manifestations of their special gifts in grossly inappropriate ways. These reactions often went beyond the envy and hostility routinely found in many families that signal ambivalence toward their children. More damaging than devaluation motivated by competitiveness were the reactions to the fear these children inspired in their parents by being different. Out of this fear, their assets were frequently misread as signs of being not-quite-human, "masculine" girls, "feminine" boys, homosexual, and so on. In the cases I am highlighting here, the children were taught that their inclination to pursue activities related to their extraordinary gifts was useless and, by extension, selfish or wicked. Hence, it became impossible for these boys to integrate the ambitions deriving from their talents into the hierarchy of their acceptable goals and thereby to value realistically their own achievements.

Very occasionally, I have encountered instances of positive parental responses to a child's budding talent, generally on the part of a parent who had shown similar inclinations in his or her early life. Under such circumstances, the future artist (or scientist) tends to respond with intense gratitude and loyalty, however disappointing the parent in question may prove to be in other respects, and these ecstatic transactions will then be remembered, justifiably, as the early experiences that called the person into his vocation. The most moving story of this kind, possibly apocryphal, is the alleged childhood recollection of the astronomer Johannes Kepler, who had been entrusted to his grandparents while his mother followed his soldier-father on endless campaigns. Kepler apparently recalled that, on one of her rare visits, his mother awakened him to share her awe of the appearance of a comet. I have made no attempt to check the historical accuracy of this anecdote: *Si non è vero, è ben' trovato!*

To return to my clinical material, in neither case did parents or educators become aware of the child's outstanding talents prior to late adolescence. In fact, during this part of their lives, the performances of these boys on the standard tasks expected of them were no better than those of other people of superior intelligence, such as their siblings. In both patients, the specific capabilities through which their extraordinary creativity would gain expression first manifested themselves in the subtlest ways; these boys would have been more difficult to pick out as outstanding than many talented individuals whose areas of competence are easily detectable at an early age.[7]

7. I do not mean to imply that it is impossible to find children of potential genius if one looks for them. One of my former analysands, whose gifts may yet prove to be on the same plane as those of the men I am describing here, was singled out as such a child during the earliest school years through a statewide screening program.

As a consequence, both patients viewed their recurrent fantasies of possessing superior knowledge about some aspect of the cosmos as dangerous ideas, possibly as delusions. Both were also convinced that the other men in their families possessed greater potential, even if they had failed to exercise it. It was only during their college years that both patients were "discovered" by perceptive faculty members; one literally had to be dragged, even then, into the field of study that prepared him for his destiny. The sense of being mad rather than original persisted for both men in the guise of endless doubts about the meaningfulness of their contributions—and this despite ample recognition from the necessarily narrow circles qualified to judge their work. Greenacre (1958a) has already drawn attention to the genesis of such difficulties in the feelings of inferiority generated in the child of potential genius.

By contrast, Tartakoff (1966) has described certain "normal personalities" whose gifts are recognized in early childhood and lead to the formation of a syndrome the author calls the "Nobel Prize complex." In many ways, the developments Tartakoff calls to our attention form the converse of those that typify the individuals I have here singled out as possessing genius. As she stated, "The effect of silent adoration or verbal acclaim in the face of precocious development must, at a very early age, affirm the growing child's fantasy that he is 'the center of the world' . . . confirming his own feelings that a special destiny awaits him" (p. 246). Perhaps, after all, the contingencies discussed by Tartakoff may be even more damaging to future creativity than the transactions I have found in the childhood histories of my patients.[8]

I have found a poetic exposition of these dilemmas of the artist in the Cervantes novella, *The Man of Glass* (1613). Cervantes himself began his literary efforts in adolescence but did not achieve excellence until late middle age—a stellar example of the practitioner of a genre in which life experience is a prerequisite for success. In the interval, Cervantes had sought glory on the battlefield, successfully, through actions of outstanding heroism. *The Man of Glass* reveals the reason for this 20-year excursion into a field capable of yielding immediate grandeur. In the story, a performer who has lost his audience cannot tolerate the lack of public response to his efforts and joins the army. The sense of having infinite riches to display for his readers is represented in the story by the performer's delusion that he *is* a glass-fronted cabinet. The tragedy of the adolescent who senses his future greatness but cannot yet demonstrate it to his public is embodied in the plot of the novella: People are eager to

---

8. For one thing, parental attitudes of this sort eventually come to be experienced as a form of pressure to excel. Such exploitation for the parents' narcissistic ends may lead to an automatic refusal to perform. For another, the standards implicitly conveyed to the child through such parental attitudes are generally impossible to live up to—a circumstance likely to undermine self-esteem once the child grows up and faces the challenges of adult life.

gape at the performer if he is exhibited as a bizarre madman, but they walk away if he claims to be sane and serious.

Greenacre (1958a) has also postulated that gifted children are likely to respond to such a state of affairs with compensatory fantasies of exalted parentage. Daydreams of being an adopted (or kidnapped) child are hardly uncommon under any circumstances. In one of the two patients under discussion, such fantasies were more or less in accord with the actualities, inasmuch as he really had the most wicked of stepmothers, a psychotic woman who savagely persecuted him, and inasmuch as he could in fact regard the excellent grandmother who had raised him for a number of years in his earlier childhood as his true parent. The other patient did indeed develop childhood fantasies of divine parentage (and an actual identification with Jesus) that soon clashed with his sense of reality and were repressed before the age of 7. In spite of this successful defense against grandiose ideation, the boy continued to experience his position in his family as that of a cuckoo in a nest of sparrows.

In both analyses, one of the crucial determinants of the fortunate outcome was the manner in which we dealt with the patient's despair about the possibility of receiving a fair assessment of his actual gifts. To promote realistic self-acceptance, that is, it was essential to demonstrate that the patients were, in effect, unresponsive to the contemporary appreciation of their achievements which, as I have noted, was indeed forthcoming. Like Vincent van Gogh, who killed himself at the very threshold of major public acceptance, these men resonated emotionally only to unappreciative attitudes, such as those of their childhood caretakers. Thus, one of these analysands was able to throw off the system of values of his peculiar mother only after he had, in the analysis, relived his conviction that she was justified in failing to appreciate him because his aptitudes and interests, including his gender, were different from hers. In this case, the past was reexperienced in the manner most customary in analysis, through repeating the archaic pattern in question within a transference relationship. In other words, the patient became convinced that, in exact analogy to the circumstances of his childhood, I regarded all endeavors outside of psychoanalysis as essentially unworthy, and that my ignorance of his field was the result of my contemptuous disinterest, rather than the extremely specialized nature of the subject matter involved.

In the analysis of my other patient, it was necessary to uncover the guiding ideals he had acquired from the beloved grandmother of early childhood; these ideals had been disavowed under the impact of the later pressure placed on the child to accept a utilitarian value system before the time he was able to value his own work. The archaic ideals handed down by the grandmother did not interfere with his creative activities as flagrantly as the subsequent injunctions to be constantly useful in some concrete and pragmatic way, but they did preclude any effort on the patient's part to seek public recognition or financial reward for his work.[9] Before he started analysis, the patient had solved this dilemma by arranging to function in a setting that preserved his anonymity, even though the groups with which he was associated did become celebrated. He had avoided the specific type of creative activity about which he was most enthusiastic, however, because even moderate success in such an endeavor would have made him widely known. He could pursue these preferred creative activities anonymously, as van Gogh pursued his art, only if he received outside financial support, so that it would be unnecessary to market the work to make a living.

All in all, my analytic work with the second man has confirmed the impression I gained in analyzing his predecessor: The incapacity of the caretakers to apprehend those particular childhood attributes that eventually made his creative accomplishments possible did not, in fact, represent some unusual limitation on their part. We cannot expect the average parent to have the perspicacity of Leopold Mozart or Pablo Picasso's father (see Chapter 7). More often, they are bewildered innocents, like the parents of Friedrich Nietzsche—a story I shall tell in Chapter 10.[10]

9. The specific reasons for this circumstance are not strictly relevant to my exposition, but they are of intrinsic interest. The patient's grandmother had been a highly creative person in the religious sphere—a genre of creative activity to which I shall return in my consideration of Jung in Chapters 13 and 14. This woman had developed a beautiful private belief system based on Far Eastern prototypes. She had made no attempt to indoctrinate anyone, but her charismatic personality had inspired several members of her family to adopt many of her ideals. Because the patient had been separated from her at the age of 6, his version of her beliefs still had the literalness and absolutism characteristic of childhood thought. Part of this naive identification concerned her refusal to promote her belief system and accept any status beyond that of an ordinary housewife. I should add that the patient ostensibly retained this aspect of his identification with her despite the successful termination of the analysis, the expansion of his creativity, and his periodic reports of continuing well-being; he has thus far made no effort to make his work public, and he keeps house while his wife holds a remunerative job.

10. It is illuminating, in this connection, to consider a relevant incident from the life of Sigmund Freud. From his autobiographical revelations in *The Interpretation of Dreams* (1900, pp. 216ff., 428, 447, 468-469), we learn that one of his crucial childhood memories concerned an incident from his seventh or eighth years: His father emphatically declared that young Sigmund would never amount to anything because the latter had urinated before his parents in the chamberpot in their bedroom. Freud recalled this incident as a spur to his ambitiousness, which he therefore labeled "urethral." One may surmise that his father intended his cutting remark to serve in precisely this manner in the first place.

In this instance, the overt underestimation of a gifted child actually increased his determination to excel. But we gain some insight into the traumatic potential of such parental behavior from the fact that Freud reported this memory in assocation to a dream he had shortly after his father died—a dream laden with murderous hostility toward the latter. Oedipal rivalries, to be sure, are difficult enough to transcend without having to absorb unjustified derogation in the process. And the dreams of the mature Freud, engaged in creating his magnum opus, often portrayed his triumphs via the image of an irresistible stream of urine poured forth by a figure like Hercules or Gargantua!

For both my patients, the puzzling oddities of boyhood did not undergo metamorphosis into dazzling capacities until late in adolescence. At that time, significant numbers of supportive friends and teachers confirmed them in their vocations despite the continuing incomprehension of their families. The parents' failure to participate in this process led to another psychological complication. Until the recognition of their giftedness by strangers, both of my analysands managed to maintain overidealized views of their families, except for a few members, like one patient's dreadful stepmother, about whom no favorable opinion was possible.[11] These attitudes could not be sustained when it became apparent that other people could supply these adolescents with confirmation about the worth of their actual capabilities which they had needed throughout childhood but could not—and would never be able to—obtain from the parents.

In fact, the idealization of the parents was quite shallow in both instances. In the first place, these children (who sensed such potential greatness in themselves) needed figures of heroic qualities to admire; only the lost grandmother of one patient's early childhood might have filled this need. Moreover, both patients were able to perceive certain actual limitations of their parents much earlier than children of lesser endowment would have done. As a result of this combination of circumstances, premature disillusionment in the parents could not be avoided. Although as children both patients managed to disavow these traumatic reactions and erect compensatory overidealizations of their families, the threat of reexperiencing the devastating loss of faith in the caretakers of early childhood was ever present. In both cases, the recognition of the patients' true worth in adolescence by persons outside their families brought about a repetition of the earlier traumatic disillusionment and led to severe life crises.[12]

IV

THE DRAMATIC EVENTS that marked the late adolescence of these two patients were superficially similar to those described by Eissler

11. For a discussion of the need for such idealizations and the unrealistic ways in which they are maintained in case of disillusionment, see Gedo (1981a, Chapter 4).

12. In one instance, this took the form of a syndrome of exhaustion that was misdiagnosed as an endocrine disease but which, in retrospect, must have been a depressive illness. In the other case, the adolescent crisis involved the loss of the patient's religious faith, that is, his abandonment of the fervently held beliefs of the family, the affective concomitants of which were correctly identified as an emotional emergency. For this second patient, the consequences of this adolescent disillusionment were minimized by excellent psychotherapeutic intervention—a happy result that also prepared him to seek analysis later.

(1961, 1963) in his biographies of Leonardo and of Goethe. In my judgment, however, these events did not amount to the kind of dissolution of defensive structures that Eissler postulated to explain the crises that seemed to characterize the adolescence of a budding genius. Nor would it be legitimate to assume, in the spirit of Eissler's work, that renunciation of the idealization of the family is traumatic for every adolescent destined for greatness. In two biographical papers on the adolescence of Sigmund Freud (Gedo & Wolf, 1970, 1973), I have attempted to trace the history of such issues in the mental life of that genius. Freud's parents, like those of my patients, did not possess the stature to remain serviceable as idealized figures beyond their son's middle childhood, and, throughout his life, Freud continued to suffer from an unusual vulnerability to the imperfections of people who became important to him (see Gedo & Pollock, 1976).

Freud had a relatively tranquil adolescence nonetheless, probably owing to his ability to find satisfactory replacements for the idealized parents in the form of historical figures of poetic greatness—ideal models such as Goethe, Shakespeare, Cervantes, and Horace (see Chapter 11). In this regard, Freud seems to have belonged to a group of creative personalities described by Greenacre (1957)—those who are protected against disappointments by a "love affair with the world."[13] This attitude is probably established in earliest childhood; in Greenacre's terms, the future creator has the capacity to erect "collective alternates" for the mothering person.[14]

At any rate, the adolescent reorganization of my patients into personalities whose creative activities earned them the designation of genius occurred with the resolution of crises precipitated by the discovery of the

13. Eissler (1978) has continued to insist that Freud's adolescence was only superficially untroubled. He regards a transient episode of infatuation in mid-adolescence as a traumatic event precisely because it had no sequel: Freud turned away from women until he met his wife-to-be almost a decade later. Eissler's argument is both excessively tortured and implausible. Freud's shyness with girls is not likely to have begun at so late a date. It was, in fact, a lifelong character trait, and his so-called love for Gisela Fluss in adolescence had the quality of an abortive experiment with becoming a ladies' man rather than of a breakthrough of sexual passion. Eissler assumes that Freud fled into the study of science because his love of literature threatened to activate his sexual conflicts—a totally arbitrary idea given the frequency of asceticism among writers (cf. Freud's contemporary, Henry James). It would seem much more plausible simply to postulate that Freud, like one of the men I am describing here, was compelled to avoid the very activities he found most exciting.

14. Greenacre did not specify whether this capacity is an outgrowth of the child's unusual constitutional endowments, of the specifics of its early infantile experiences, or of a combination of nature and nurture. Winnicott (1967) was the first to offer a hypothesis that places the development of such alternatives, as they pertain to the relationship with the mother, into the framework of expectable emotional maturation (see Chapter 2). With my colleagues, I have hypothesized that the essence of the adolescent process in general is the transformation of the self-schema necessitated by disillusionment with the parents and the vicissitudes of the subsequent need to find new ideals (see Wolf, Gedo, & Terman, 1972).

magnitude of their talents. The fallible persons they had formerly idealized were subsequently replaced in their emotional lives by secure idealizations of their newly chosen spheres of creative endeavor. In a manner I see as completely analogous, the 18-year-old Freud had become inspired to pursue a scientific career on hearing a reading of the *Essay on Nature* then attributed to Goethe; he dropped his former ambitions for legal or political success and committed himself to a decade of intensive effort in preparation for the fulfillment of his new ideals. My patients demonstrated the same enthusiastic immersion into their new disciplines—and, in their respective cases, this immersion involved no retreat from sexuality. From that time on, their creative activities were always able to protect them against other blows to their self-esteem, for they could repeatedly reconfirm their worth without resorting to unrealistic fantasies. On the other hand, the interruption of one patient's opportunity to work, shortly before seeking my assistance, had rapidly led him into severe depression and a sense of aimlessness.

As this ominous decompensation showed, the continuous confirmation of worth through creative work does not in and of itself lead to enduring self-esteem. For both patients, a permanent deficit had resulted from the disavowal and/or repression of those childhood interactions that had left them with conceptions of themselves as odd and troublesome. In other words, these men were unable to connect their highly valued adult creativity with the "shameful" childhood characteristics that had been its precursors, and they continued to accept the unfavorable judgments of the early environment about their overall worth. As Vincent van Gogh put it years before reaching his full stature as an artist, "The history of great men is tragic. . . . For a long time during their lives they are under a kind of depression because of the opposition and difficulties of struggling through life" (van Gogh, 1959b, p. 67).

Paradoxically, then, the creativity of these individuals was spurred by the fact that their great accomplishments could temporarily compensate for their chronic lack of self-esteem; the latter, in turn, was largely a product of the inability of their childhood caretakers to bear accurate witness to their future potentialities. For both men, the creative act had become an emotional necessity.[15] It was the relentlessness of this need that

15. This explanation of the reparative functions of creative work partially overlaps with the position of the British school of psychoanalysis founded by Melanie Klein (cf. Segal, 1957). According to Kleinian theory, however, the depression warded off by creativity is caused by turning innate destructiveness against one's own person; this destructiveness mainly takes the form of envy directed toward those who have "more to give." My patients had their share of aggressiveness, but it was invariably evoked by interference with their vital interests rather than embodying this Kleinian version of Original Sin. Observers of early childhood have convincingly demonstrated that toddlers do not turn their aggression against themselves in ordinary circumstances (see Parens, 1979).

imbued their work with the daemonic flavor that distinguished it from the productive activity of people of lesser talent. The genius, it would seem, is a phoenix able to rise from its own ashes.

To recapitulate: In my experience, the key to the psychology of men of genius is the inevitable underestimation that typifies their formative years. This circumstance gives rise both to their daemonic efforts to create and to their fragile sense of worth. Specific personality configurations will then be determined by other aspects of their childhood experience. Among these, the availability of a warmly supportive parent appears to have particular importance for creativity in adult life. The oddities of children destined for greatness often represent serious threats to the parents' self-esteem, a point I shall try to illustrate at length in the next chapter. Furthermore, I have already recorded my impression that, in our society, parents tend to be less tolerant of the eccentricities of their gifted daughters than of their gifted sons.

Historical Studies

For THE PSYCHOANALYTIC clinician, the application of insights gained in the consulting room to other fields of endeavor, "beyond the bounds of the basic rule" of free association, as Heinz Kohut (1960) once put it, is always an enterprise fraught with pitfalls (see Gedo, 1978). The most dangerous among these is that of dilettantism—the naive meddling in disciplines whose problems can only be profitably tackled after many years of conscientious scholarship. As Walter Kaufmann (1980a, pp. 54, 133–134) wittily observed, humanistic studies may be generally enriched by the use of the "third ear," but this instrument can never supplant our other two ears! The dilemma is inescapable: The absorbing clinical commitments that alone yield fresh psychoanalytic insights are too demanding to permit the psychoanalytic practitioner to immerse himself in another discipline.

If analysts nonetheless venture regularly into the interdisciplinary arena, their motivation probably originates in part in private concerns that lie beyond the boundaries of their putative scholarly aims. Over a decade ago, I characterized such efforts as *formes frustes* of attempted introspective insights, hazily objectified by externalization upon an alter ego (Gedo, 1970b). Since then, the intellectual climate has shifted in the direction of acknowledging the subjectivity of every creative endeavor; it is now frequently observed that every biography is, simultaneously, a chapter in its author's autobiography.

What, then, is the significance of my choice of historical figures to illustrate my hypotheses about creativity? What are the links between Nietzsche, Freud, and Jung; between van Gogh, Gauguin, Picasso, and Caravaggio? I could easily claim that I have selected these men as subjects for obvious "external" reasons: the relevance of the first trio to the birth of my own profession and the centrality of most of the others to the history of modern painting, the academic specialty of my wife. Moreover, these seminal figures of our culture have been studied in sufficient detail—even from a depth-psychological perspective—to allow the nonspecialist to deal with their lives and work by using (and comparing) the copious and readily accessible secondary sources.

Although the foregoing considerations are certainly relevant to my choice of subjects, they have played only a subsidiary role in my work. I have been interested in these particular individuals for decades; they have meant more to me than other creators of comparable stature, say Manet, Gropius, or Mondrian—the subjects of Peter Gay's *Art and Act* (1976). It was the work of Erich Heller (1976) that ultimately alerted me to the rationale for my unexamined preferences. Heller has described the evolution of the arts in the past four centuries as a "journey into the interior"—one suspects Heller views this journey as the heart of darkness—the unfolding of ever deeper layers of the artist's subjectivity. Whatever their other merits, the creative figures to whom the psychoanalyst necessarily responds most profoundly are those who have contributed most directly to the progress of the collective psychological journey Heller described. In this sense, the artist is the prophet of man's fate, and his creativity must be fed by his personal capacity for insight. Clearly, there are major contributors in every creative sphere who do not belong in this tradition—there are those, to begin with, whom Heller would characterize as classicists. But there are also important artists whose work defies categorization in Heller's terms: Witness Mondrian, whose artistic achievements have been persuasively described as resulting from a flight from subjectivity (Gay, 1976), but who are utterly lacking in the vital relation to society that Heller sees as the cardinal characteristic of classicism.

In spite of the fact that my sample of historically significant creators reflects the idiosyncratic personal interests of a clinical psychoanalyst, I believe my clinical orientation makes this collection of biographical studies sufficiently representative from a point of view that is also central to the study of creativity. The chapters in this section have been organized to demonstrate serially various facets of the complex, dialectical relationship between the creative process and psychopathology within the artist's personality. Clearly, many of these issues have already been elucidated in the preceding clinical section. To this extent, the historical studies that follow may be seen as demonstrating the power of psychoanalytic insights gained in the consulting room to illuminate certain cultural problems—the creativity of major artists in this specific instance—despite the fact that few, if any, of my patients can match the stature of the supreme creators generally studied by the historian.

There can be no question about the fact that Nietzsche, the poet-philosopher, and all the painters I shall discuss, suffered from a severe psychopathology. I therefore feel constrained to reiterate once again that, however disturbed great creative figures may be, I do not regard the correlation between creativity and significant psychopathology as an invariable one. In this section it will undoubtedly seem ubiquitous because I am trying to describe how these processes may influence each other when they do in fact coexist. In the last section of this volume, largely devoted to a more detailed study of the creative career of C. G. Jung, I shall also include material about a man of genius whose adaptation was largely satisfactory: Sigmund Freud. Although my primary reason for introducing Freud will be to contrast Jung's approach to the field of psychotherapy with the approach of the founder of psychoanalysis, I trust that even my tangential discussion of Freud's personality will suffice to counterbalance the false impression I may be engendering by devoting the other historical chapters to such seriously disturbed individuals.[1]

At any rate, in this section I shall approach my material from a consistent vantage point: In each essay, I shall discuss the manner in which a major creator struggled to overcome his personal distress through the act of making art while simultaneously attempting to protect his creativity by keeping his psychopathology isolated from the sphere of his work. We shall see, furthermore, how the creative artist frequently depicts himself and often his sickness through his creative productions and at the same time falls victim, to varying degrees, to psychological illness, as a consequence of the overwhelming burdens of the creative life. These burdens often fall upon the individuals who serve as the artist's caretakers: In the last chapter of this section, I shall look at the early life of Nietzsche to demonstrate the manner in which the special capacities and peculiar developmental progression of a gifted child can overstrain his family, in turn producing those vulnerabilities in the personality configuration of the future artist that often lead to psychopathology in adult life.

1. The reader whose curiosity about Freud's creative life is whetted by this sampling may be interested in my previous studies on creativity, which are almost exclusively concentrated on Freud and his circle. Most of these studies have been collected in *Freud: The Fusion of Science and Humanism* (Gedo & Pollock, 1976). This volume also reprints a paper in which I explore the career of Miguel de Cervantes, another great artist who mastered his inner conflicts by gaining a "victory over himself," in the words of the protagonist of his *Don Quixote* (Gedo & Wolf, 1973). Elsewhere, I have tried to portray the personality of another well-adapted genius, the philosopher Michel de Montaigne (Wolf & Gedo, 1975).

Chapter Seven

On van Gogh, Picasso, and the Dynamics of Creativity

I

WE ARE TOLD that in extreme old age Pablo Picasso was strongly preoccupied with the fate of Vincent van Gogh (Hess, 1971). Yet, characteristically, the great Dutch expatriate did not appear undisguised among the personae who populate Picasso's late works, nor did Picasso use van Gogh's oeuvre as a source of subject matter as he used those of Delacroix, Manet, and, above all, Velázquez. If Picasso's life work is overwhelmingly autobiographical, as the artist himself proclaimed (Brassaï, 1966, p. 100), much of the subject matter of his last years amounts to retrospective meditations on the creative life. Reportedly, he was consciously brooding about the contrast between his achievement of international fame before the age of 30—a celebrity that was to endure and grow uninterruptedly for almost seven decades—and Vincent's lonely, tragic existence and untimely death (Parmelin, n.d., pp. 106–107).

It would seem that, despite their numerous and major differences as artists and human beings, Picasso looked upon van Gogh as the standard-bearer against whom he was destined to measure himself. Perhaps it was in his occasional portrayals of Rembrandt, Holland's master painter who was Vincent's supreme model and predecessor, that Picasso made allusion to van Gogh. The Spanish master's preoccupation with Rembrandt was evident as early as the 1930s in the series of etchings known as the Vollard Suite (Figure 3). By the same token, the numerous depictions of Velázquez in Picasso's late work should probably be understood as the last of a long series of self-depictions via alter egos—secret sharers, to use Conrad's poetic phraseology (see Chapter 1).

Figure 3. Pablo Picasso, *Paris, January 31, 1934*. Combined technique (Vollard Suite, 35). Private collection.

In any case, the contrast between Velázquez and Rembrandt, one a courtier of Philip IV and the other a recluse in the ghetto of Amsterdam, illustrates radically different creative possibilities. Perhaps the first Mme. Picasso had a contrast of this sort in mind when she taunted her husband with postcards of Rembrandt's works bearing messages such as, "If you were like him, you would be a great artist!" (Gilot & Lake, 1964, p. 154).

Because of Picasso's extraordinary life span of 93 years and van Gogh's premature demise at 37, it is now easy to overlook the fact that they were men of nearly the same generation who arrived in Paris only 15 years apart. Widely regarded as the most powerful artists to have gravitated to France in the modern era, they are perhaps the greatest humanist painters since the age of Goya. Hence Picasso was on solid ground in comparing the vicissitudes of his own creativity with the vicissitudes of Vincent's. Judging by the bitter tone and self-mockery of the aged artist's self-portrayals, I would infer that, in Picasso's view, it was van Gogh who had lived in accord with the highest artistic ideals. Be that as it may, it is the distinctive patterns embodied in their respective creative activities that deserve more extensive scrutiny in the context of our concern with the psychology of creativity.

II

WE MIGHT APPROACH the task of comparing Picasso and van Gogh by noting that both men suffered from the effects of severe personal vulnerabilities that rendered them essentially incapable of functioning effectively in ordinary human contexts when left to their own devices. The story of Vincent's so-called failures has become the stuff of popular legend. He found himself unable to manage as a clerk at the art dealer Goupil's; as a schoolteacher in England; as a student preparing for admission to a school of theology in Amsterdam; as an evangelist among the miners of the Borinage in the Belgian coal country; and even as an art student at the academy in Antwerp. In addition to these vocational disasters, Vincent suffered a series of humiliations while courting a number of unsuitable women, among them a widowed cousin still engaged in deep mourning. Under the oppressive weight of these circumstances, van Gogh's biographers have probably underestimated the seeming miracle of Vincent's success in producing an outpouring of masterful works during his decade of activity as an artist (see Rewald, 1962; Tralbaut, 1969).

To be sure, this success was in one sense simply the result of Vincent's finding his proper métier. There is reason to believe, however, that his productivity was contingent on his oft-expressed fantasy that the work was not his alone but the fruit of a joint effort with his brother Theo. From this standpoint, van Gogh's suicide following his realization of the gravity of Theo's eventually fatal illness may have been the only response he could devise to the imminent termination of a symbiosis on which his creativity depended. Had Theo's contribution been primarily financial, Vincent would hardly have consented to exchange works he rightly considered worthy of the Louvre (cf. Tralbaut, 1969, p. 243) for the modest sums his brother sent him. As he put it, "If you can give me nothing more than financial help, you may keep that too" (van Gogh, 1959a, p. 199). In terms of their content, Vincent's letters to Theo achieve literary distinction largely because of the unparalleled manner in which they express the symbiotic nature of van Gogh's creativity.

Pablo Picasso has also become the hero of a popular myth. Despite his unusual candor in revealing his lifelong emotional difficulties both through the content of his works and in explicit personal reminiscences, the public, including most of his biographers and critics, insists on viewing him as the patricidal minotaur–rapist of his most wishful fantasies. As Mary Gedo's researches of the past decade have revealed (1980a, 1980b, 1981), the actualities could not be more different. Like van Gogh, Picasso needed a partner to enable him to create, and, again paralleling the case of van Gogh, the first of these vital relationships developed within his family of origin: As a boy, Picasso was dependent on the empathic assistance of his father.

After his move to Paris, Picasso was able to use a variety of men and women to the same end; depending on the particulars of each partnership, there were dramatic consequences for the style, content, and volume of his work. Given the number of individuals who sustained Picasso through the creative achievements of a lifetime, we can see that he was needlessly self-critical about having outlived van Gogh. The latter's inability to enlist anyone but Theo as a secret sharer in the service of his personal needs was the most tragic aspect of his psychopathology; it is impossible to adjudge the sole reliance on Theo a virtue. But stressing Vincent's exclusive use of his brother for assistance still leaves out of account his self-destructive need to repeat the experience of being unjustly rejected and despised—most dramatically enacted in his legendary encounter with Paul Gauguin in Arles (see Chapter 8 for a discussion of this event). Vincent was, like Nietzsche (see Chapter 10), compelled to recreate the disasters of his childhood over and over again.

Picasso survived the rupture with his father that marked the end of his adolescence, but his creative life was characterized by a series of disruptions whenever his human milieu failed to live up to his stringent requirements. The most celebrated of these so-called dry spells followed the birth of his daughter Maya in 1935, when Picasso was equally estranged from his wife and from the mother of the newborn child, his mistress

Marie-Thérèse Walter. A number of briefer episodes of the same kind occurred throughout the artist's career. Probably the earliest was in 1898, when he made a first and unsuccessful effort to manage on his own by enrolling in the Madrid art school. Another major crisis took place in the dark days of 1915, when Picasso's beloved Eva was dying of tuberculosis and the sustaining friends of his prewar years in Paris, Georges Braque and Guillaume Apollinaire, were serving in the French army. Yet another episode of this kind supervened during the gradual deterioration of the painter's relationship with Françoise Gilot in the early 1950s. In the midst of some of these stressful events, Picasso was unable to work altogether; during other disruptive interludes, he turned to productive activities markedly less successful than his creative best, such as his minor literary efforts of the mid-1930s or the ceramics he produced in Vallauris at the time of his difficulties with Gilot.

In contrast to van Gogh, about whose earliest years we know practically nothing of significance, some crucial vicissitudes of Picasso's childhood are now reasonably well understood. Mary Gedo (1980a) has with great plausibility reconstructed that, at the age of 3, Picasso reacted to the birth of his sister Lola by radically turning away from his mother. The catastrophic Málaga earthquake of 1884 that coincided with these familial events came to represent them in Picasso's recollections. The child apparently underwent a severe regression as a result of these traumata; for many years thereafter he remained confused and disorganized whenever separated from his family. It was in these grave circumstances that Picasso's father successfully rescued him by lending himself to the child as an organizer of his behavior.

The most significant of the activities that grew out of this collaboration was Pablo's incessant drawing. This early activity seemingly permitted the integration of the child's perceptual world through expressive action in the visual sphere—an achievement Picasso was to utilize when he traversed this route in reverse in inventing the cubist style (M. Gedo, 1980b). In the relationship to his father, artistic creation became the guarantor of Picasso's psychological integrity, presumably because of his astonishingly precocious talents as a draftsman. At the same time, the benign presence of a soothing and understanding witness became a prerequisite for his ability to perform creative work.

As we have observed in Chapter 1, clinical studies of individuals with great creative gifts (e.g., Greenacre, 1971) suggest that during childhood such individuals often show peculiarities associated with unusual perceptual and cognitive organization. Later, I shall recount the story of Nietzsche's development in some detail (Chapter 10) to illustrate that the families of such odd youngsters tend, not unnaturally, to misconstrue such behaviors as signs of some deficit rather than precursors of genius. Picasso was no exception: His hyperacuity in the sphere of visual perception rendered him incapable of taking an abstract attitude toward numerals, for example, so that he was incapacitated in the act of learning arithmetic (M. Gedo, 1980a, p. 15). It would seem that his father, like Mozart's, was exceptionally attuned to the boy's promise and maximally supportive of his artistic aspirations, although his vision of a successful career for his son, like that of Leopold Mozart for his son, fell far short of the dazzling reality that was to come.

I would assume that this felicitous childhood experience with his father later enabled Picasso to find a series of similarly enthusiastic collaborators. Mary Gedo has shown that Apollinaire and Braque were the most significant and most successful of these partners, but on a more mundane level other artists such as Max Jacob, Jean Cocteau, and Paul Eluard also played some role in sustaining Picasso. Moreover, a number of adolescent friends remained permanently faithful to Picasso either as good genies or in other helpful capacities: Manuel Pallarés, Jaime Sabartés, and Julio González might be mentioned as the most prominent among them. Mary Gedo has also demonstrated that Picasso's increasing stature and fame made it progressively more difficult for him to find male collaborators worthy of inheriting the mantle of a paternal surrogate. Matisse, in his last years, may have served, if only in a limited way, as the last of these paternal figures. These circumstances may have condemned Picasso to the gradual decline of artistic power that most observers detect in the work of his last three decades.

To the extent that Picasso could only be sustained by the availability of an idealizable male who at the same time promoted his art, he proves both strikingly similar to and crucially different from Joseph Conrad. As we have seen in Chapter 1, Meyer (1967) has shown that Conrad needed an available double to mobilize fully his own creative powers; it is very likely, moreover, that this kind of relationship echoed the novelist's childhood attachment to his father. But here the similarity ends. Because Conrad's father was severely depressed during this period—and because the period only came to a tragic end when he died of this condition—the adult writer could not allow himself to relive such an intense relationship, except for the single experience with Ford Madox Hueffer. As Meyer has also demonstrated, Conrad was severely traumatized by the disruption of the symbiosis in this latter episode. Unlike Picasso, in other words, Conrad did not possess a highly developed capacity to utilize the right people for his own artistic ends.

Whenever living partners of the right kind were unavailable, Picasso had the further ability to draw inspiration from certain great predecessors. During the period of relative isolation imposed on him by World War I, for example, he adopted Ingres as his imaginary artistic collaborator; the choice was based on their common admiration for Raphael, whom Picasso had determined to surpass as a draftsman. In later life, as I have mentioned, he became more explicit about the actual paternity of his art in turning directly to Velázquez (or to the latter's 19th-century disciple, Manet) for much of his subject matter. The preoccupation with van Gogh, we may assume, played a similarly restitutive function. Yet, Picasso was unable to make do on an indefinite basis with fantasies of creative partnership with historical figures. On both of the occasions I have singled out, he soon contracted a marriage that would provide the dominant tone to his art and life for many years thereafter.

Pursuing these biographical considerations further, Mary Gedo (1980a, p. 80) has concluded that Picasso had a remarkable imaginative capacity, as measured by the subject matter of his art, to create fantasies in which various individuals, including the artist himself, might assume a variety of masculine and feminine roles. It should not surprise us, therefore, that in adult life Picasso was often able to form relationships with persons of either sex that could sustain his artistic productivity just as his early relationship with his father had sustained him in childhood. To put this in the conventional manner of the Greeks, we may say that Picasso was able to use many women as muses of his art. Unlike Nietzsche, whose one attempt of this kind ended in a disastrous embroilment with Lou Salomé, a woman utterly unwilling to assist him, Picasso had a number of mistresses who both inspired great bursts of creativity and gave him devoted support in everyday life for long periods. The most celebrated relationship of this sort was Picasso's affair with Marie-Thérèse Walter. The relationship is recorded in a flood of masterpieces between c. 1927 and the late 1930s, many of which have as their explicit theme the relationship between an artist and his muse (Figure 4). But Picasso's greatest love was probably Eva, whom he celebrated as *"ma jolie"* in many of the masterpieces of his high cubist period; her joyous influence may be responsible for the gaiety of his art shortly before the outbreak of World War I (Figure 5). In addition, Mary Gedo (1980a, pp. 60–75) gives partial credit for the hopeful romanticism of the artist's rose period to the auspicious start of his first great affair—the relationship with Fernande Olivier—after Picasso settled in Paris in 1905. Still other examples could be cited from later stages of the artist's long career.

However resourceful Picasso was in making others satisfy the requirements of his creative productivity, it should be noted that whenever his principal partner was a woman, he was always in danger of a recurrence of the early childhood difficulties with his mother, that is, of having a "transference reaction," to use psychoanalytic parlance. It was in these circumstances that he underwent crises similar to the one that overwhelmed Conrad when his collaborative intimacy with Ford Madox Hueffer was overshadowed by the latter's marriage. One possible outcome for Picasso was creative paralysis, echoing the disorganization he had undergone at the age of 3. Short of such a drastic interruption of his

Figure 4. Pablo Picasso, *Paris, January 31, 1934*. Etching (Vollard Suite, 36). Private collection.

capacity to work, in difficult but less traumatizing circumstances involving his relations with women, Picasso would focus his art on the very personal travails that beset him. His subject matter at such times would concentrate on the psychopathology of women (Figure 6) or the predicament of a person trapped in a stifling relationship with a female monster.

During his first marriage, Picasso was able to retain a separate studio and a number of important friendships that counterbalanced the destructive influence of his insufferable wife sufficiently and allowed him to transform his personal suffering into an art of grandeur and ferocity. When, in his eighth decade, he resigned himself to the tutelage of his second wife, Jacqueline Rocque, Picasso soon became the prisoner of an atmosphere of uncritical adulation from which dissenting voices were systematically excluded. In this manner, Picasso's old age actually became an echo of his earliest years when he had been surrounded by a bevy of admiring women who praised him for his physical beauty! It was to fatuous misunderstandings of this kind that Nietzsche responded with his last, despairing cry, "Above all, do not mistake me for someone else!" (1888, p. 217). From the perspective of his life in Mougins with Jacqueline, Picasso must have regarded van Gogh's refusal of public acclaim as a precondition of artistic integrity. He was full of self-contempt for lending himself to the travesty of acting the part of international celebrity to please the queen of his heart. This situation progressively undermined the quality of Picasso's work—after all, did the fatuous queen really deserve the best from her *premier peintre?*

III

ACCORDING TO Parmelin (n.d., pp. 106–107), "For [Picasso], van Gogh's was the exemplary life of a painter. And that includes his death." We are accustomed to thinking of Vincent's suicide as an act of despair in the face of illness, destitution, and solitude. It would seem that Picasso was able to view it with superior empathy, as a defiant affirmation of uncompromising adherence to the single goal of creating a sublime art. In this sense, van Gogh differed from Picasso in refusing to use his creative powers to overcome his own emotional vulnerabilities. Far from being self-protective in this regard, van Gogh did not deem himself worthy of survival unless he could produce a body of work of universal import. We may choose to stress the profound depressive pathology embodied in such an attitude, but Picasso's startling insight on this score may in fact have greater relevance.

In my judgment, Vincent's compact with his brother Theo succeeded in postponing his suicide by making it possible for him to unite his artistic capacities and evangelical fervor in the production of a great religious

Figure 5. Pablo Picasso, *Man with a Pipe*, 1915. Oil on canvas. Collection of The Art Institute of Chicago, gift of Mary L. Block in memory of Albert D. Lasker.

THE DYNAMICS OF CREATIVITY

statement. Accordingly, I do not believe it a mere coincidence that van
Gogh killed himself exactly 10 years after he and Theo arrived at their
understanding in July 1880. Of course, we know nothing about the
nature of their agreement. The crucial interchange took place when Theo
stopped to visit his brother in Belgium on his way back to Paris from the
family home in Holland; it was never recorded in their correspondence.
We therefore have no hint about how much time Vincent planned to
allow himself to carry out his chosen task, although we do know he was
convinced that he would not live long as an artist (van Gogh, 1959b, p.
105).

But let us explore those clues we do have about the nature of the
compact between the two brothers: Van Gogh invited Theo's collaboration to free him through fraternal love from what he called "the captivity
of idleness." He made this request in the context of asking whether he,
Vincent, could do anything for Theo: "In the event that I could render
you some service, ask it of me" (1959a, p. 199). We may reasonably
assume that Theo subsequently asked Vincent, at the time of his stopover
in the Borinage, to undertake his artistic endeavors, probably to forestall
Vincent's predictable suicide. Vincent must have had Theo's intent in
mind when he wrote his brother: "But you know, don't you, that I
consider you to have saved my life" (1959b, p. 233).[1]

The point I want to emphasize here is the significance of the pact with
Theo for Vincent's creativity: Apparently, on his own, Vincent had been
unable to accept his artistic vocation as a personal goal. I assume he could
not do so because he was unable to move toward the greatness he must
have known he could attain; it will be recalled that an obstacle of just this
sort stood in the way of one of the patients whose analysis I discussed in
Chapter 6, compelling this very gifted person to engage in activities that
would ensure his anonymity. In the symbiotic partnership undertaken at
Theo's initiative, Vincent apparently overcame a prohibition comparable
to this.

We possess one crucial piece of evidence bearing on the conflict I have
just described. Theo's widow has reported that, at around the age of
eight, Vincent destroyed some of his own drawings and other works
when, for the first time, they elicited serious praise from his family (van

1. It is much more difficult to document the probability that Theo felt compelled to attempt
to save Vincent because his own survival was contingent on the availability of his older
brother. It may be recalled in this connection that Vincent had played a protective role
toward Theo through much of the latter's childhood and that several of the younger
children in the family eventually collapsed into psychosis. Vincent recorded his own insight
into Theo's psychology in a letter to their mother shortly before his suicide: "And after
Father was no more and I came to Theo in Paris, then he became so attached to me that I
understood how much he had loved Father" (van Gogh, 1959c, p. 239). Theo's reaction to
Vincent's suicide is discussed in Chapter 8.

Figure 6. Pablo Picasso, *Seated Bather*, 1930. Oil on canvas, 64¼ ″ × 51 ″. Collection, The Museum of Modern Art, New York, Mrs. Simon Guggenheim Fund.

Gogh-Bonger, 1959, p. xx). On the one hand, we might conceptualize this reaction as the child's rivalry with his own product, ever destined to be infinitely better appreciated than Vincent would be as a person. But this observation hardly accounts for the fact that, on reaching the age of 11, Vincent avoided serious exercise of his supreme talent, with a few minor exceptions, for about 15 years—even in private.

The psychology of genius, as we have already seen, is usually conducive to the opposite result: As in the case of Picasso, the exercise of a great gift typically produces a confirmation of self-esteem so intense as to override all other considerations. This is the final pathway of the creator's daemonic commitment to his work. Indeed, as soon as van Gogh had circumvented his self-imposed prohibition through the compact with Theo, his absorption in his work became so absolute that, in the pursuit of his art, he often neglected even his physical needs. In this respect, the two analysands I described in Chapter 6 resembled him very much. Given the liberating effect of the agreement with Theo, we must assume that Vincent's previous avoidance of his creative destiny was necessitated by adherence to certain categorical imperatives that defined his existence even more centrally than did his artistic genius. In the remaining portion of this chapter, we shall see that these imperatives resided in van Gogh's identity as a religious prophet. As Vincent once put it, "Well, well, there are moments when I am twisted by enthusiasm or madness or prophecy, like a Greek oracle on the tripod" (1959c, p. 134).

To date, no detailed attention has been given to van Gogh as a religious thinker, although Lubin's (1972) valuable psychological biography has made a start in this direction. Yet, without an understanding of Vincent's religious convictions, as reflected both in his writings and his visual art, it is extremely difficult to assess the impact of his religiosity on his creative activities. Even a superficial reading of the correspondence reveals van Gogh's maximally serious involvement with cosmological issues; consider, for example, his penetrating statement in the fall of 1888, just three months before his psychotic episode, that he was continuously in danger of losing himself in the contemplation of Eternity (van Gogh, 1959c, p. 90).

We know that in his late adolescence Vincent's religious preoccupations were still channeled into the Calvinist orthodoxy in which he had been raised. At this time, his originality in the religious sphere was foreshadowed only by the strange intensity of sermonizing letters that were more reminiscent of the world of Rembrandt's Mennonite friends than the pallid religiosity of van Gogh's own father. Vincent presumably came to the realization that the Dutch Reformed Church did not represent his own version of Truth while he was in Amsterdam attempting to prepare for theological training. Van Gogh later declared that the obstacle that defeated him in his effort to master classical languages must have been created by a need to abort his impending career as a minister. In view of Vincent's brilliance in adopting both French and English as alternatives to his mother tongue, it is indeed clear that his language difficulties in Amsterdam must have derived from a reluctance to devote himself to the Reformed Church. His subsequent service as an evangelist in the Borinage was still performed under Christian auspices, but his disaffection with Calvinism was by that time unmistakable. The subsequent collapse of his mission among the miners was, therefore, no simple vocational crisis: It also signified Vincent's acknowledgment that he could no longer maintain membership in any Christian community.

This verdict was so crucial for the future development of van Gogh's art that it requires some further elaboration. On his arrival in the Borinage, at Christmas time of 1878, Vincent still expressed his faith in entirely conventional terms in writing to his brother: "Jesus Christ is the Master who can comfort and strengthen a man . . . because He is the Great Man of Sorrows Who . . . worked for 30 years in a humble carpenter's shop to fulfill God's will. And God wills that in imitation of Christ man should live humbly and go through life not reaching for the sky . . . learning from the Gospel to be meek and simple of heart" (van Gogh, 1959a, p. 184). Yet, after this recitation of a Christian ethos, van Gogh never again used the language of Christian faith in his correspondence.

We have only five relatively brief letters from van Gogh spanning the 18 months that followed this final expression of Christian sentiment. This is the period van Gogh characterized as a "molting time" from which he hoped to "emerge renewed" (1959a, p. 194). In the most revealing of these letters, Vincent confessed to his brother in July 1880 that he was "often homesick for the land of pictures." But he made clear that he still considered himself an evangelist, even though he spent all of his time studying, and much of his time pondering the literature that spoke to his heart: the Bible, Shakespeare, Dickens, Aeschylus. Like Jesus excoriating the Pharisees, van Gogh went on to assail those who, misusing religion for selfish ends, had excluded him from the work of evangelism because of his fervent beliefs. At the same time, he had begun to realize that art and religion have parallel aims: "There is something of Rembrandt in the Gospel, or something of the Gospel in Rembrandt" (1959a, p. 196). He would echo this sentiment near the end of his life in these words: "If I had had the strength to continue, I should have made portraits of saints and holy women from life who would have seemed to belong to another age, and they would be middle-class women of the present day, and yet they would have had something in common with the very primitive Christians" (1959c, p. 211).

Vincent was struggling with the very problem which, we shall see, was destined to beset C. G. Jung, that of finding the proper medium for the delivery of his message (see Section IV). Consider van Gogh's plaint to his brother in the letter of July 1880: "I am rather faithful in my unfaithfulness and, though changed, I am the same; my only anxiety is, How can I be of use in the world?" (1959a, p. 197). I believe these words should be understood not only as a general affirmation of van Gogh's personal credo but also as a specific affirmation of his religious faith. Thus, at the same time as van Gogh expressed awareness that his chronic depression resulted from an inability to "participate in certain work" (presumably his missionary activities), he avowed his continuing religious quest by describing feelings that echo the laments of a Job abandoned by Jehovah: "How long, my God!" But even in his misery Vincent continued to trust that people would come to "warm themselves" by the "great fire" in his soul, and he counseled himself to be patient: "Let him who believes in God wait for the hour that will come sooner or later."

In this same letter to Theo, van Gogh rejected his family's verdict that his religious beliefs were "impossible," and he went on to explicate them in terms of an explicitly pantheistic creed: "I think that everything which is really good and beautiful—of inner moral, spiritual, and sublime beauty in men and their works—comes from God, and all which is bad and wrong in men and their works is not of God, and God does not approve of it." He continued: "I always think that the best way to know God is to love many things. Love a friend, a wife, something . . . you will be on the way to knowing more about Him. . . . To try to understand the real significance of what the great artists, the serious masters, tell us in their masterpieces, *that* leads to God" (1959a, pp. 197–198). Vincent was to become the most serious of great masters in the service of this program.

At the same time, Vincent was sufficiently self-critical to know that he had been unable to convey his religious message in words because he was "too visionary"; he knew that it was therefore essential for him to find an alternative means of communication: "A man who has seemed good-for-nothing and incapable of any employment, any function, ends in finding one and becoming active and capable of action" (1959a, p. 198). He explained that he had seemed idle because he had lacked the productive means to convey to others what was in him; in this sense, he compared himself to a caged bird, melancholy at the season of migration. But deliverance was to come through Theo's affection. Vincent, we have already noted, invited such deliverance by offering his services *to* his brother: "If I can do anything for you, be of some use to you, know that I am at your disposal" (1959a, p. 199). It was apparently in response to the plentiful cues contained in this letter that Theo entered into the fraternal arrangement that was to permit Vincent to devote himself to his art.

Another way of characterizing Vincent's emergence from the chrysalis is to say that he found his own original belief system in the course of choosing the proper medium for its transmission. Was van Gogh daunted by the burden of becoming a prophet? For us, the passage of 100 years

has dimmed the enormity of such a commitment. We may remind ourselves of what might have lain in store for a Jesus in the Low Countries of
van Gogh's day by paying serious heed to the bitter parody that constitutes James Ensor's greatest canvas, *The Entry of Christ into Brussels in
1888*. (Figure 7 illustrates Ensor's etching of the same theme.) In 1880,
when Vincent embarked on his career, Nietzsche had not yet proclaimed
the death of the Christian deity, and many who had lost their traditional
faith were still crudely and determinedly antireligious. Even a generation
later, C. G. Jung, the founder of a non-Christian religious movement, felt
constrained to characterize his true vocation as an *arrheton*—a "thing
never to be named" (Jung, 1963, p. 102).

Perhaps, then, van Gogh's fantasy of sharing his enterprise with Theo
was needed both as moral sanction for his momentous task and as a source
of strength in discharging it. Similarly, Picasso and Braque needed to feel
roped together, like mountaineers, in order to undertake the development
of a radically novel style of painting—an effort for which, at the time, no
one had as yet been martyred (see M. Gedo, 1980a, p. 85). We might also
hearken back to Meyer's judgment that Conrad needed the encouragement of his secret sharer, Hueffer, in order to embark on the introspective
journeys of his great psychological novels.

It should come as no surprise, then, that van Gogh thought of himself
as a martyr and predicted, correctly, that he would live no more than 6 to
10 years while engaged on this Calvary (1959b, p. 105). Had he decided
to commit suicide at a specific time as he set out on his *via dolorosa*? Or was
his presentiment simply based on an identification with Jesus? Although
Vincent had ceased to be a Christian, as his letter of July 1880 indicates,
he still conceived of his religious quest in terms of an *imitation of Christ*.
Paul Gauguin was probably the first to perceive Vincent's identification
with Jesus, an insight he recorded in a marvelous religious canvas, the
Agony in the Garden (Figure 8: W. 326²), painted shortly after leaving van
Gogh in Arles. With characteristic arrogance, Gauguin portrayed himself
as the Christ, but he acknowledged the fact that Vincent actually fitted
the role better by giving the Savior van Gogh's fiery red hair.

In his two versions of Delacroix's *Pietà* (F. 630, [Figure 9], F. 757), one
of the rare biblical themes in his work, van Gogh affirmed this identification with Jesus in the same manner. These two works provide a very rare
hint of Vincent's underlying attitude, for he seems to have shared the
humility of the great religious figures of his Christian heritage. His
refusal to seek public acclaim, despite his secure conviction of artistic

2. The works of Gauguin are conventionally identified by the numbers assigned to them in
Wildenstein's *catalogue raisonné*, usually abbreviated as "W. #"; similarly, van Gogh's oeuvre
is assigned catalogue numbers "F. #" after the catalogue of de la Faille.

Figure 7. James Ensor, *The Entry of Christ into Brussels in 1888*, 1898. Etching. Private collection.

Figure 8. Paul Gauguin, *Agony in the Garden*, 1889. Oil on canvas. Norton Gallery and School of Art, West Palm Beach, Florida.

Figure 9. Vincent van Gogh, *Pietà (after Delacroix)*, 1889. Oil on canvas. Collection National Museum Vincent van Gogh, Amsterdam.

greatness, was part and parcel of his system of beliefs. In this respect, he seemed to follow his great Dutch predecessor, Thomas à Kempis, author of the *Imitatio Christi*, on the path of self-abnegation. This attitude is most clearly discernible in Vincent's response to the first laudatory article on his work, Albert Aurier's piece in *Le Mercure de France* early in 1890. The review appeared at the very time van Gogh's paintings were also being shown for the first time at the prestigious exhibit of *Les Vingt* in Brussels. In a private reply to Aurier, Vincent insisted on being seen as only one link in the great artistic tradition, a quasi-anonymous member of the collective he had attempted to bring into being (van Gogh, 1959c, pp. 256–258).

Despite Gauguin's overt reluctance to engage in such a transcendent partnership, Vincent apparently experienced his presence in Arles in 1888 as an expansion of the symbiotic system with Theo. In circumstances of this kind, struggles for dominance within the collective are unavoidable. Their occurrence here is most clearly revealed in van Gogh's temporary acceptance of Gauguin's method of working from the imagination, and Vincent indeed produced several paintings heavily influenced by the French artist's style (Figures 10 and 11: W. 300 and F. 496). We may infer that the symbiotic pull was equally strong in the opposite direction from the crudity of Gauguin's later boast that at Arles he had taught van Gogh the most valuable aspects of his art. We may further surmise that Vincent's argumentativeness in his actual dealings with Gauguin was the unavoidable reaction to this threat to his autonomy. Gauguin, it appears, was certainly justified in choosing to sever so dangerous a connection. But we may glimpse the profound significance of van Gogh's merger fantasies at the time if we think of his self-mutilation in response to Gauguin's determination to leave him as a symbolic expression of his feeling that he was about to lose a part of himself.

Lubin (1972, pp. 168, 179) is undoubtedly correct in relating the specific nature of Vincent's self-mutilation—the cutting off of one ear—to the story of the betrayal of Christ in the garden of Gethsemane and in proposing, in this connection, that Vincent viewed Gauguin as a Judas Iscariot. Perhaps the paintings of Gethsemane that van Gogh created and destroyed just before Gauguin's arrival in July and September of 1888 betray his awareness that, in inviting the calculating Gauguin to become an apostle, he was inviting betrayal. In the delirium that followed his self-mutilation, van Gogh's delusions reportedly consisted of what he termed "perverted and frightful ideas about religion" (van Gogh, 1959c, p. 214). But this hardly comes as a surprise. By now, I trust I have provided sufficient detail to document that every aspect of Vincent's life was suffused with the transcendental. Indeed, his was a holy spirit, although

Figure 10. Paul Gauguin, *Old Women of Arles*, 1888. Oil on canvas. Collection of The Art Institute of Chicago, Mr. and Mrs. Lewis Coburn Collection.

Figure 11. Vincent van Gogh, *Souvenir of the Garden at Etten*, 1888. Oil on canvas. The Hermitage Museum, Leningrad.

he was able to affirm this openly only in his delirium: "*Je suis Saint Esprit. Je suis sain d'esprit*" (Lubin, 1972, p. 98).[3]

In the final analysis, Vincent's art expresses a faith intended, in his own words, to "comfort us so that we might stop feeling guilty and wretched and could go on just as we are without losing ourselves in solitude and nothingness" (1959c, p. 57). Lubin has rightly observed that, in creating this art, van Gogh was following the precepts of his contemporary Ernest Renan: "Man is not on earth only to be happy. . . . He is there to realize great things for humanity, to attain nobility, and to surmount the vulgarity of nearly every individual" (quoted in Lubin, 1972, p. 104). But Lubin's conclusion that Vincent made use of his identification with Christ to achieve a more successful adaptation as an artist strikes me as lame. I believe that van Gogh's work is not religious merely in its approach to subject matter, that, as Lubin believes, it amounts merely to a presentation in pictorial form of a doctrine of nature worship. Vincent did produce visual parables, to be sure, but the role of religion in his work is even more fundamental.

To put the matter as simply as possible: Contrary to those who understand van Gogh's religious fervor as a defensive reaction to his repeated disappointments in love relationships, I regard it as the central motivation throughout his life. It is a motivation that presumably goes back to the dawn of his consciousness, though Vincent obviously only acquired the capacity to conceptualize his experiences in religious terms much later. It is precisely the child's inability to grasp the nature of subjective mystical states and strivings for perfection that results in his provisional acceptance of whatever religious doctrine he is taught. Thus Vincent falsely believed himself to be a Calvinist into his mid-20s. Throughout his life, however, it was the capacity for ecstatic communion that ruled his entire universe, including his dealings with his family and friends.

I assume that van Gogh's repetitive disappointments in human relationships, beginning in early childhood with difficulties involving his mother, resulted in large part from the unusual demands that Vincent's search for perfection in human affairs placed on his companions. There can be no question, of course, that the child's self-esteem was undermined by his failure to establish harmony with those he loved and that his lifelong loneliness and depression were consequences of this failure. By the same token, he always felt better if someone accepted his love or care, even if the compulsion to repeat invariably caused him to become involved with people who did not appreciate his efforts.

---

3. Literally translated: "I am the Holy Spirit. I have a healthy mind." Because van Gogh had *written* this on the wall of his house, it became a visual pun. The two sentences are pronounced in absolutely identical fashion.

At any rate, I would surmise that van Gogh's genius was prefigured in early childhood by puzzling experiential states that alienated him from his mother. These ways of perceiving the world gradually crystallized into a complex set of aims that governed Vincent's entire existence—goals and values generally classified as religious. His life, like the life of Jesus, was a model for mankind; his art expressed these beliefs. Pablo Picasso understood that van Gogh's personal behavior, his psychological organization, and his created products formed an inseparable whole. Vincent was not reconstituted by creating images as Picasso was: Like a comet, he burnt himself up in blazing a trail through the darkness. Conversely, unlike the great Spaniard, van Gogh was compelled to repeat early childhood experiences that, in human terms, always ended disastrously. At times of maximal stress, Picasso too betrayed an identification with Jesus (see M. Gedo, 1980a, pp. 142, 149, 189), but his salvation usually lay in his unique capacity to attract to himself a variety of individuals able to render the human assistance he needed.

Chapter Eight

Creativity and Psychopathology: van Gogh and Gauguin as Prototypes

I

IF VINCENT VAN GOGH'S life represents the ideal course for a serious artist, as Pablo Picasso came to believe, it is, in a different sense, prototypical of various kinds of pathology that may beset the creative person. Nor is this vantage point less illuminating than the one that focuses on van Gogh's ability to use his talents adaptively to fulfill his personal goals; it complements the latter perspective in a crucial way, throwing light not so much on Vincent's work as on his tragic personal destiny. Insofar as the artist's biography and the subjective meanings of his work are interrelated in complex ways (see M. Gedo, 1980a, 1980b, 1981) a psychobiographical approach to the life of the creator that takes into account his personal problems becomes a necessary tool of cultural history. I shall therefore proceed to review van Gogh's life from this point of view, gaining my entry point through the existing historical and psychological literature. For purposes of comparison, I have chosen Vincent's temporary partner in artistic brotherhood, Paul Gauguin, a man whose psychopathology had equally devastating effects on his adaptation.

Before we consider van Gogh's psychological problems, it must be noted that he probably suffered from epilepsy and that his epilepsy most likely took the form of psychomotor seizures. Moreover, his febrile illness at the time of his breakdown, his history of alcoholism and addiction to absinthe, and the fact that his physicians rashly tried to sedate him with a highly toxic medication (potassium bromide) all make it cavalier to attribute the artist's deterioration to emotional problems alone.

Although there can be no question about van Gogh's severe depressive propensities, any approach to explicating his psychological difficulties must incorporate the possibility that his psychotic episodes may well have been the product of a combination of acute toxic episodes and a chronic brain syndrome, possibly even one based on constitutional factors. If this hypothesis is valid, we must even consider the possibility that the progressive aggravation of van Gogh's despair, culminating in his suicide, may have been partly caused by the irremediable mortification of his cerebral illness per se; it was not, in other words, entirely attributable to serious interpersonal difficulties as previous authors have assumed.

Most biographers (e.g., Nagera, 1967) portray Vincent as desperately dependent on his brother, Theo. In point of fact, it was Theo who became overtly psychotic after Vincent's death, presumably because of his absolute need for the symbiotic relationship the brothers had established between themselves (see Rewald, 1962, p. 414). A grave systemic disease may well have contributed to Theo's collapse although, in point of fact, the available descriptions of his terminal illness do not permit us to make a reliable judgment about whether his psychosis led to the physical complications or vice versa. In any case, it is more consistent with the view of Vincent's character I have elaborated in the previous chapter to suppose that his desperate wish to cater to his younger brother's symbiotic needs imparted meaning to his own existence than to imagine that a severely traumatized person like Vincent van Gogh would actually permit himself to become emotionally dependent on another human being. In my clinical experience, patients of his character type would never permit themselves to enter interpersonal situations they rightly regarded as maximally dangerous. Moreover, there is historical evidence pointing to the former possibility: Vincent formed a series of relationships with overtly needy individuals like Sien, the pregnant prostitute he tried to rescue in 1885.

Another common misconception about van Gogh's personality concerns his inability to accept public acclaim. Nagera (1967), for example, interprets Vincent's conflicts about exhibiting or selling his work as expressing an inhibition about achieving success, that is, the kind of neurotic fears psychoanalysts encounter in patients in conflict over oedipal issues. It would seem more accurate to consider Vincent's problems in this regard as manifesting unresolved disturbances of self-esteem, disturbances possibly related to unconscious grandiose wishes. It seems even less plausible to explain Vincent's suicide in terms of the dynamics of a garden variety neurosis—an eventuality never encountered in clinical practice—but this is in fact Nagera's point of view.

An adequate formulation of van Gogh's psychopathology should provide us with insight into his "sickness unto death," as Kierkegaard, echoing Jesus, characterized his own illness. The most ambitious effort to date in this direction is Albert J. Lubin's *Stranger on the Earth* (1972), a study that arrives at many convincing insights about Vincent's character. Lubin wisely begins his portrait by noting van Gogh's extreme loneliness along with its counterpart, his need for solitude. He locates the cause of this seeming paradox in Vincent's inability to form relationships in which both individuals could function independently. As a result of this inability, van Gogh was often dangerously angry, although he generally managed to deflect his rage from those who had disappointed him. At the same time, he idealized suffering, including his own, and he identified with the oppressed. Lubin gives proper weight to van Gogh's deep religiosity, a commitment for which, as I tried to show in the preceding chapter, his art came to serve as the principal vehicle. He points out, in this connection, that Vincent unconsciously identified with Christ as the Man of Sorrows: Witness van Gogh setting out on his artistic career around the age of 30, the age at which Jesus began his mission. Vincent's conviction that he would soon die in the service of his art may have been one consequence of this identification. Its presence is also suggested by the special significance Christmas seems to have had for van Gogh, as well as certain aspects of his drama with Paul Gauguin (his Judas) and the prostitute Sien (his Mary Magdalene).

After renouncing his ambition to become a minister, van Gogh accurately sensed that he could become a great mystical and introspective preacher through his art, an enterprise in which the interpersonal difficulties that had undermined his missionary work would not create an insuperable handicap. In this new effort, his brother Theo could serve as a link to the world of humanity—an arrangement that proved workable most of the time. In fact, it was marred only by a few episodes of suspiciousness about Theo's motives, probably caused by transactions in which Theo failed to treat Vincent with the requisite empathy.

Vincent's scrupulous reluctance to burden his brother has obscured the latter's failures to pay sufficient attention to the painter's human needs. Theo, for example, came to Arles in 1888 at the time of his brother's initial psychotic episode. Setting out in response to Gauguin's urgent summons of December 24 (van Gogh, 1959c, p. 110), Theo could not have arrived in Arles before Christmas Day, but he left his brother no later than December 31—well before the course of Vincent's acute illness could be predicted. Vincent was subsequently able to express his disappointment in *Gauguin* for abandoning him in this crisis (p. 122) but, strangely, commentators have overlooked the significance of the fact that Gauguin actually returned to Paris in Theo's company (p. 110). Moreover, no financial provisions were made to cover the expenses associated with Vincent's illness. Theo rushed off to Holland to celebrate his engagement and was a week late in sending Vincent the next installment of his stipend. As a result, for Vincent, "the time between [was] a most rigorous fast, the most painful because [he could not] recover under such conditions" from the loss of blood he had suffered (p. 118). I would hardly rate Theo's performance in this instance an adequate demonstration of family loyalty.

The financial arrangement between the brothers could only have been based on van Gogh's conviction of his own greatness as an artist, that is, the fantasy that he would repay Theo with immortality—as he in fact did. Vincent protected his creativity with fierce determination, and the need to place the ability to create ahead of other considerations prevented him from ever being indoctrinated by artistic authorities. On the other hand, Vincent also had a sober appreciation of his own flaws as a human being, of his seeming insubstantiality as a person in comparison with the vitality and strength of his work. His suicide may have been precipitated by his moral aversion to the possibility that his progressive illness would cause him to become a real burden to a brother newly weighed down with family responsibilities and showing signs of illness himself.

Commendably, Lubin's reconstructions of van Gogh's subjective world in childhood refrain from speculation. He confines himself to the hypothesis that Vincent was able to turn to nature, particularly to the countryside, as an "alternate parent," so that he found his own internal states reflected in his physical environment. The capacity to turn mystically to earth and sky was retained throughout van Gogh's life and enabled him to portray his internal states by painting landscapes. In fact, Lubin proceeds on the assumption that the totality of Vincent's subject matter adds up to a self-portrait. He believes, for example, that van Gogh projected his rough and shaggy appearance into the texture of his works, even going so far as to suggest that some of van Gogh's unique coloristic effects may have been based on the unusual orange and blue of his own hair and eyes and that his swirling lines may have depicted the vertigo from which he suffered. Lubin further sees van Gogh's numerous overt self-portraits as successful measures of the artist's struggle to avoid losing his sense of being a cohesive person.

These are original thoughts, giving fertile hints of possible connections between a painter's self-image and formal aspects of his work; it is hypotheses of just this kind that justify the clinician's forays into interdisciplinary work. Previous authors, it should be noted, have offered comparable suggestions about van Gogh. Schnier (1950), for example, assumed that Vincent's favorite color, chrome yellow, represented the sun, a body with which van Gogh identified. Westermann-Holstijn (1951), on the other hand, noted that for van Gogh sunflowers explicitly represented love. It has thus been stated more than once that Vincent anthropomorphized nature, so that formal elements of his nature studies came to reflect indirectly various physical and psychological aspects of his person.

Lubin also observes how van Gogh originally idealized his father and the latter's vocation as minister. He points out that Vincent became bitterly disillusioned with both his father and the Reformed Church because he viewed their concern with respectability as a compromise with evil. When he rejected Calvinism with its emphasis on guilt in favor of a creed of mystical union with a loving God, the metamorphosis was accompanied by rejection of his mother tongue; French supplanted Dutch as his primary language. But van Gogh's abandonment of father and church did not have a primarily regressive significance; he retained his capacity for idealization and was able fruitfully to adopt great artist-predecessors as revered models.

Reconstructing Vincent's relationship with his mother, Lubin assumes that the repetitive choice of unresponsive women in adult life must have recreated the emotional conditions of his early upbringing. Presumably, an important factor in the derailment of the mother–child relationship was the fact that Vincent was a replacement for a namesake, a brother who was stillborn the year preceding his own birth. As a further consequence of such tragic beginnings, Lubin points to van Gogh's tendency to feel empty or ghostlike when his adult relationships were failing. He also implies that Vincent must have had profound empathy for his mother's grief because she was still in mourning at the time of his birth. Based on this latter supposition, he persuasively propounds the hypothesis that van Gogh's first masterpiece, *The Potato Eaters* of 1885 (Figure 12: F. 82), reflects his reaction to his mother's mourning after the death of the Reverend van Gogh.

In contrast to Nagera, Lubin rejects psychosexual explanations of the van Gogh–Gauguin episode as unconvincing; he claims only that the rupture of this relationship caused Vincent's self-mutilation. Cutting off his own ear may have been the condensed representation of a series of fantasies that van Gogh had: Lubin discusses his preoccupation with Jack the Ripper, with bullfights, and, most cogently, with Christ's vigil on the Mount of Olives culminating in the episode in which Peter severed the ear of Malchus. In any case, van Gogh's primary need in the relationship with Gauguin was to be helpful to a great artist in distress. As in his choice of women, Vincent ensured the failure of this effort by selecting an unsuitable partner. But then Vincent's entire career is testimony to his horror of success—presumably deriving from a psychological need to repeat the catastrophes of his early childhood.

Perhaps I have said enough to demonstrate that Lubin has drawn a sensitive portrait of his subject with thorough and reliable scholarship. On this score, I would raise but one question: Lubin consistently omits consideration of the influence of Theo van Gogh's psychopathology on the symbiosis between the two brothers. He entirely fails to mention that Vincent may in fact have agreed to become an artist for Theo's sake, that

Figure 12. Vincent van Gogh, *The Potato Eaters*, 1885. Oil on canvas. Collection National Museum Vincent van Gogh, Amsterdam.

is, with the explicit understanding that his work would be a joint enterprise for which Theo would bear equal responsibility. Like Nagera,
Lubin also fails to discuss Theo's mental collapse after Vincent's death. I
have already alluded to the seriousness of this omission: Even if organic
factors played some role in Theo's illness (which is by no means the most
likely possibility), the timing of his collapse raises the likelihood that
Vincent had secured his brother's integration throughout their relationship.

Apart from these omissions, my difficulties with Lubin's work generally pertain to certain psychological inferences he makes on the basis of
psychoanalytic hypotheses that may once have had wide currency but
which I believe to be either invalid or at least inapplicable to the case of
van Gogh. Thus, Lubin infers that Vincent's need to erect defenses
against murderous hostility was a ubiquitous feature of his life and art and
that Vincent tried to expiate guilt occasioned by this hostility through
masochism and self-deprivation or to forestall it through overcompen-
satory expressions of compassionate saintliness. Along similar lines, Lubin
claims that van Gogh needed to provoke persecution in order to rationalize
his chronic rage.

I do not mean to minimize van Gogh's chronic irascibility, especially in
the face of what he perceived as attacks on his ideals or depreciation of his
mission. But I am calling into question the assumption that depressive
illness results from turning such hostility against oneself. Here is an
example of the psychological biographer applying an outworn psychoanalytic proposition rather than developing formulations on the basis of
existing documentary evidence: Judging from his correspondence and the
reports of intimates, nobody could be *less* conflicted about his hostility
than van Gogh seems to have been.

In general, Lubin tends to attribute many of Vincent's character traits
to conflicts involving putatively infantile wishes. In most of these instances, I see instead a lifelong commitment to certain ideals pursued with
perfectionistic zeal. Thus, I understand van Gogh's avoidance of successful and eminent people as a corollary of his absolute renunciation of all
personal ambition and resulting distaste for the worshippers of Moloch. If
we are to understand van Gogh's life, in other words, I believe it
imperative *not* to presuppose that his primary goal of sainthood was part
of his psychopathology.

In fact, Vincent's repetitive depressive episodes seem to have resulted
from his inability to live up to his towering ideals; indeed, I regard the
need to achieve the impossible in order to maintain self-esteem as the core
of van Gogh's psychopathology. As the greatest of Christian saints,
Francis of Assisi, emphasized, the emulation of Jesus should never be
pushed into presumptuous efforts to equal his achievements. Lubin's
assertion that Vincent's emulation of Jesus was a rationalization for his

Figure 13. Vincent van Gogh, *Portrait of the Artist's Mother*, 1888. Oil on canvas. Norton Simon, Inc., Foundation.

eccentricities strikes me as equally depreciatory toward both figures. For me, an attitude of this kind raises questions about the discretion of a biographer with a bias about religious innovation who chooses to study the life of a saint.

Finally, Lubin's book is marred by his unacknowledged adoption of the viewpoint of the van Gogh family in singling out Vincent as the truly disturbed member. As a result of his decision to absolve the family of responsibility for the artist's tragedy, Lubin makes the unwarranted assumption that the mother's failure with van Gogh was principally the result of her mourning the death of his predecessor, her firstborn Vincent. It would seem more probable that this woman, four of whose six children grew up to have severe psychological disturbances, was incapacitated as a parent by a character defect. Vincent's only portrayal of her (Figure 13: F. 477), contemporaneous with a self-portrait he sent Gauguin as a gift (Figure 14: F. 476), depicts a green-faced old woman staring at the viewer with a cold glare. The self-portrait, in which Vincent presents himself as a Buddhist monk, has a green background that echoes the color he gave his mother's face. Was van Gogh expressing in these related images the idea that his monkish character was an outgrowth of his mother's granitelike inaccessibility?

Lubin does acknowledge that van Gogh saw himself as a victim of mistreatment by his family, but he consistently underplays the monstrous failure on the part of the van Goghs to acknowledge Vincent's greatness. The most outrageous instance of this attitude was his mother's wanton abandonment of much of the work Vincent left at the parental home when, following his father's death, he departed for the last time. But Lubin's tendency to tilt the scales against Vincent is even more apparent in his depiction of the artist's relationship with Theo. To be sure, this latter bias is characteristic of the entire literature on the van Goghs. It was Theo's widow, after all, who published the relevant documents, and all van Gogh biographers to date have been beholden to Theo's gracious son for personal assistance with their efforts. Under these circumstances, would it have been an affront to suggest that Vincent may have been even more supportive of Theo than vice versa; that Theo's helpfulness and empathy may sometimes have left something to be desired; that, in their supposedly equal partnership, Vincent was actually forced to undertake a disproportionate share of the risks and sacrifices; or that, far from being too demanding and difficult, Vincent may have been excessively considerate of the needs of his brother?

Of course, the very way I frame these questions reveals my own bias in favor of the claims of the genius on those around him, and this viewpoint may be every bit as illegitimate as I believe Lubin's to be. But my point is precisely that an adequate study of Vincent's psychology cannot omit

Figure 14. Vincent van Gogh, *Self-Portrait*, 1888. Oil on canvas. Courtesy of the Fogg Art Museum, Harvard University, Bequest—Collection of Maurice Wertheim, Class of 1906.

consideration of such issues; a *psychoanalytic* biography, in other words, must include just such an examination of the biographer's attitude toward his subject (see Meyer, in Gedo, 1972c).

II

.IN A MAJOR biographical work, Wayne Andersen (1971) has shown that the traditional perspective on Paul Gauguin's life, assiduously culti-vated by the artist himself, constitutes a "personal myth" (see Kris, 1956).[1] In other words, in the service of disavowing the significance of certain pathological aspects of his own character, Gauguin espoused a romantic idealization of primitivism. But far from resembling the passively suffering Christ who was a victim of society, as Gauguin often seemed to claim, he was a hard and offensive person. Generally nasty even toward his helpers and admirers, he was arrogantly overconfident about his actual commercial prospects as an artist. When the inevitable disappoint-ments overtook him, he would rage at the world in a paranoid manner, that is, without acknowledging his own responsibility. He often provoked rejection, especially at the hands of his wife, and at such times he would ostentatiously play the role of the painfilled pariah. He abandoned his artistic allies in order to assert his uniqueness, and he consistently dis-owned his teachers for the same reason. On the other hand, his daring stylistic innovation—the creation of an original pictorial world out of the painter's own fantasies of form—was also contingent on his assurance that he possessed extraordinary powers.

Andersen wisely endorses van Gogh's insight that his kinship with Gauguin was based on their shared identity, that of the "mad artist." He is, in fact, judicious in his assessment of the relationship between the two painters, taking pains to describe Gauguin's exploitativeness and truculent refusal to extend himself on behalf of van Gogh. One contemporary called Gauguin's self-centeredness the legitimate ferocity of a productive egoism; Andersen himself withholds such an endorsement of Gauguin's

1. There have been even fewer efforts to correlate the psychology of an artist with his oeuvre from the side of art history than from that of psychoanalysis. Andersen's biography of Gauguin is one of the few major studies in the former category. As one would expect, Andersen always uses psychology in the service of illuminating Gauguin's art, and his consideration of the aesthetic and historical problems posed by that body of work is notably more sophisticated than the discussions of psychoanalytic biographers who have under-taken similar studies. Andersen had the benefit of consultation with a number of analysts, and his approach is seldom lacking in depth-psychological expertise. He tends to express his psychological insights obliquely, however, perhaps in an effort to avoid offending the community of art historians. As a result, his portrait of Gauguin emerges somewhat unfocused, as if the biographer had refrained from putting the various elements of his interpretation into one cohesive gestalt.

sense of entitlement to ruthlessness without guilt. In justifying his position, he might well have borrowed another of van Gogh's brilliant psychological observations, namely, his conclusion that Gauguin was lacking in foresight about the endlessness of troubles.[2]

The heart of Andersen's thesis is his assertion that Gauguin's work centers on the theme of a woman's life cycle, portrayed in mythic terms as the story of Eve before and after the Fall. From this perspective, the crucial event during a woman's life-span is her loss of virginity. Because this event is the prerequisite for the creation of new life, Gauguin apparently equated it with the Crucifixion. Andersen's iconographic analysis follows from a closely reasoned examination of the mythic themes he attributes to Gauguin—an achievement dependent on Andersen's imposing knowledge of the history of culture. It follows that the work of a painter as intellectual as Gauguin can only be interpreted from the psychological viewpoint after we have decoded its esoteric pictorial symbolism into discursive language. But this preliminary step on the road to interpretation is almost as difficult as articulating the meaning of pictorial forms in words. Given its enormous difficulty, Andersen confines his analysis to Gauguin's overt subject matter; his book thereby foregoes consideration of the equally important problems of style, form, and technique.

Unfortunately, such a truncated approach has its shortcomings, and these may be highlighted by contrasting it with the most extensive study to date correlating an artist's biography with his created products, namely, Mary Gedo's *Picasso: Art as Autobiography* (1980a). This work demonstrates that the psychological vicissitudes of Picasso's life were often reflected in his art not through changes in overt subject matter but in formal innovations and even technical inventions. The most outstanding

---

2. In passing, Andersen gives a profound interpretation of the actual significance of van Gogh's two paintings of the chairs he had prepared for Gauguin and himself in the yellow house he occupied at Arles (see Figures 1 and 2, pp. 4 and 6). Andersen sees these as a *momento mori* for a dying union. He convincingly relates the iconography of these works to Gauguin's excellence as a magician of the imagination, in contrast to Vincent's own need to anchor himself in the concreteness of an actual model lest he slip into contemplation of eternity. In these paintings, van Gogh represented Gauguin's conceptual approach to art through phallic symbolism; Andersen thereby demonstrates that the sexual elements of the paintings were conscious and overt rather than expressions of unconscious forces.

Andersen's analysis of this pair of paintings is significant, as Blum (1956) and Nagera (1967), detecting the phallic imagery described by Andersen, formerly interpreted these very same works as carriers of unconscious homosexual symbolism. The point is, of course, whether or not the painter knew what he was painting. Andersen's interpretation is convincing because he demonstrates that the conscious use of phallic symbols was integral to the narrative point corresponding with van Gogh's overall conception of the two related works.

example of such a formal shift was the development of Cubism as a style. These findings, it should be noted, depended on consideration of the artist's entire output; Andersen, by contrast, discusses only a fraction of Gauguin's work: 88 pieces altogether and only 58 of well over 600 paintings. Hence Andersen can at best illustrate his thesis; his argument is inconclusive because we cannot gauge the range of its applicability.

But certain biographical considerations would suggest that Andersen's thesis is limited indeed. Even a cursory glance at Gauguin's *catalogue raisonné* shows that the artist essentially remained a landscapist (like most of the impressionists), at least until 1888. Human figures do not begin to loom larger in his foregrounds until shortly before he joined van Gogh in Arles. Andersen's attempts to find the very mythic themes in Gauguin's earlier works that apparently preoccupied him thereafter are consequently short of convincing. As a matter of fact, the first paintings in which Gauguin unequivocally focused on women as the protagonists of human misery were made under the impact of his encounter with Vincent (W. 301, 304).

Despite the limited scope of his inquiry, Andersen does succeed in several instances in correlating the subject matter of specific works with the actualities of Gauguin's daily life. Immediately prior to his first trip to Tahiti, for example, the painter created a portrait of his dead mother (W. 385) after a photograph; at this same time, he painted an exotic, nude Eve at the moment of the Fall (W. 389), giving her the head of this youthful mother. Hence the mythic woman was Gauguin's mother, and his repetitive tropical quest was an unconscious effort to find her once again in Eden. Andersen's interpretation here is persuasive, especially when we recall that the adolescent Gauguin had learned of his mother's death while working as a sailor in the tropics. This interpretation is reinforced by the discovery that Gauguin's first explicit depiction of a suffering Eve was derived from the image of a Peruvian mummy exhibited in Paris in 1889; he used this image in a canvas entitled *Life and Death* (W. 335). Gauguin's mother, it turns out, had been a member of a prominent Peruvian family, and several years of the artist's early child-hood were spent in Lima. To be sure, the past could not be recaptured, but Gauguin would succeed in creating an acceptable image of mother-hood in Tahiti. His work there was full of echoes of the Christian theme of the sin of Eve redeemed by the sacrifice of Mary; in his great *We Hail Thee, Mary* of 1891 (Figure 15: W. 428), moreover, Gauguin found his own place as a radiant Christ child on the shoulders of his mother.

Although he is less than explicit in his remarks on this subject, Andersen seems to understand the deeper wishes that underlay Gauguin's ultimate representation of motherhood. For one thing, he pays proper attention to the work the artist chose as a marker for his own grave in the Marquesas: *Oviri*, a stoneware sculpture of a savage, cannibal mother–goddess

Figure 15. Paul Gauguin, *We Hail Thee, Mary*, 1891. Oil on canvas. The Metropolitan Museum of Art, bequest of Samuel A. Lewisohn, 1951.

(Figure 16 illustrates Gauguin's woodcut after this carving). Given his attentiveness to the sentiments embodied in this striking piece of sculpture, it is indeed surprising that Andersen fails to note that Gauguin's romanticized account of his golden years with his mother in Peru must have been part of the same personal myth the artist promulgated to conceal the actualities of his inner life. Nor does Andersen ask whether the beloved child of a devoted mother, the image of his early years Gauguin would have us accept, would have accused his inoffensive wife of driving him to his death, as Gauguin seems to have done in certain works. Yet it is Andersen's original detective work that deciphers for us the iconography of a jewel casket Gauguin carved for his wife; the accusation implicit therein, Andersen tells us, reveals the artist's paranoid fear of women.

Another canvas that Andersen succeeds in fitting into the particulars of the painter's life is the *Tahitian with Ax* of 1891 (Figure 17: W. 430). He believes this painting to be a commemoration of a climactic event during Gauguin's first sojourn on the island. According to the artist's memoir, *Noa Noa*, he went into the forest with a young native and was almost overcome by homosexual impulses toward the boy. After mastering these feelings, as well as the wish to murder the boy who had aroused them, Gauguin claimed to have vented his fury by cutting down a tree. Andersen takes this story at face value and assumes that the painting of the ax-wielding youth represents Gauguin's fantasy of having been reborn from these experiences as a Maori. In my opinion, however, Andersen is overestimating the factual accuracy of Gauguin's so-called autobiographical writings; there is no reason to look upon *Noa Noa* as a documentary record rather than a work of art.

Preparatory work for the *Tahitian with Ax* probably took place at the very beginning of Gauguin's stay in Tahiti (Rewald, 1954), a fact that would in itself invalidate any correlation of this image with the account in *Noa Noa*, whether fantasied or real. Nonetheless, Andersen may have put his finger on one key to the psychology of Gauguin's work in Tahiti, for this effigy of the man wielding an ax is one of very few representations of a male protagonist in his depiction of native life there. Hence, it is probably valid to relate the painting in a general way to Gauguin's avowal of homosexual impulses in *Noa Noa*. By the same token, *Tahitian with Ax* may also allude to Gauguin's accusation that van Gogh threatened him with a razor before he left Arles—a connection Andersen does not make. But it should be recalled that Gauguin added this charge about Vincent's menacing behavior to his initial testimony many years later. Actually, Gauguin's supposed confession in *Noa Noa* suggests that murderous hostility as a defense against homosexual temptations was part of *Gauguin's* psychology and that he arbitrarily attributed the same problem to van Gogh.

Figure 16. Paul Gauguin, *Oviri*, 1895. Woodcut. Collection of The Art Institute of Chicago.

These conjectures notwithstanding, the fact is that the bearing of the material about a Tahitian boy on the painting depicting the man with the ax cannot be determined without a precise chronology of the artist's production. Andersen does not attempt to link specific works with actual events in the artist's life, so that his correlations of subject matter with the artist's psychology must remain confined to general trends. This methodological limitation causes him to miss a number of insights inherent in his material.

To mention only one fascinating example, Andersen reports that the peculiar slanted eyes of the fox-devil about to ravish a naked girl in Gauguin's 1890 painting *Loss of Innocence* (Figure 18: W. 412) are derived from van Gogh's great self-portrait as a Buddhist monk (Figure 14: F. 476). Vincent had presented this canvas to Gauguin in 1888. It would seem that this borrowing is an effort to depict van Gogh as an evil seducer; by implication, I would conclude that the maiden whose life history so preoccupied Gauguin—the mythic Eve that Andersen sees in a number of major works depicting women—must also represent one key aspect of Gauguin himself: his identification with his mother. Andersen is not oblivious to Gauguin's feminine identification; he deals with it most expicitly in connection with the painter's alleged attempt to commit suicide in 1898. But it would have been even more germane, in this respect, to re-examine the catastrophe in Arles as a consequence of Gauguin's panic over his homosexual attraction to van Gogh. Andersen, after all, does understand some aspects of Gauguin's Tahitian experience in just such terms; specifically, he interprets the female figures drinking at sacred fountains in two paintings of 1893, *Mysterious Water* (Figure 19: watercolor version of W. 498) and *The Moon and the Earth* (Figure 20: W. 499), as expressions of Gauguin's fantasies of fellatio. He further assumes that the numerous depictions of Polynesian male deities in Gauguin's work represent the artist's unconscious longing for the paternal authority he had never experienced because of his father's death when he was 15 months of age.

III

I BELIEVE the foregoing surveys of the personality problems of van Gogh and Gauguin, based on the best existing assessments in the literature, provide a sufficient framework for reconsidering the relationship between creativity and psychopathology. To recapitulate our principal conclusions about these two great artists: Vincent suffered from a severe disorder in self-esteem regulation; he needed to achieve perfection (especially in the moral sphere) to avoid feeling wretched, but he repetitively reenacted failures in the sphere of interpersonal relations—failures that caused him to feel unbearable pain, humiliation, and a sense of human

Figure 17. Paul Gauguin, *Tahitian with Ax*, 1891. Collection of Mr. and Mrs. Alexander Lewyt, New York.

inadequacy. In contrast, Gauguin emerges as a personality vainly struggling to fend off the consequences of the feminine identification he made as a fatherless child. In part, this defensive effort took the form of the provocative and rebellious behavior that eventuated in the artist's tragic decline as an "outcast of the islands."

At the most concrete level, the maladaptive personality of each painter brought his productive period to a premature end. Vincent, we recall, practiced his art for exactly 10 years before his suicide, and his period of creative maturity lasted for barely 4 or 5 years. Gauguin, for his part, acquired a number of disabling physical illnesses through his rash behavior. These illnesses led to his demise in his mid-50s and interfered with his capacity to work for a number of years before this period. Gauguin had scarcely a decade of unimpeded creative activity between the time he committed himself to painting as a full-time occupation and the effectively incapacitating compound leg fracture he suffered (in a fight he could have avoided) when he returned to France for the last time in 1894. Of course, van Gogh and Gauguin are the prototypical *artistes maudits* and to stress their self-destructiveness may only underscore the obvious. But I believe their psychopathology also interfered with their creative work in more subtle ways.

As I have recounted in the preceding chapter, van Gogh could not bear to engage in an activity that would confer greatness upon him unless he could function in anonymity—hence his inability even to begin an artistic career until his brother relieved him of the responsibility for its results. Vincent's suicidal despair in the spring of 1890 could only supervene as a result of his refusal to acknowledge the ultimate significance of his work as the greatest artistic statement of his people since that of Rembrandt. It is conceivable, in fact, that van Gogh ended his life because he could no longer continue to maintain—as he had done in his response to the critic Aurier—that he was no better an artist than predecessors like the estimable Millet or the eccentric Monticelli. In any event, Vincent's artistic productivity was drastically limited by his need for humility.

In a comparable way, Gauguin's characterological need to involve himself in endless provocative disputes with colonial authorities and the clergy in Tahiti and the Marquesas certainly diverted him from painting. The reduced output of his final years was partly due to his absorption in these fruitless activities. It is true that upon his death a portion of his late work may have been destroyed as "obscene" by the vengeful priests he had opposed, so that we have no accurate count of his production. But *à la guerre comme à la guerre*: Gauguin was certainly more interested in guerrilla warfare than in safeguarding his work. Nor was the problem confined to one particular period of his life; in the course of his career, Gauguin's restlessness often led to lengthy travels in the course of which he could not paint. Thus, his very first tropical misadventure, an 1887 journey to

Figure 18. Paul Gauguin, *Loss of Innocence*, 1890. The Chrysler Museum, Norfolk, Virginia, gift of Walter P. Chrysler, Jr.

Panama and Martinique, yielded perhaps a dozen paintings over a period of seven months—a rate of production markedly lower than his customary output.

In addition to the absolute limits on their productivity imposed by the characterological attributes of these artists, their psychopathology also defeated their efforts to create works on certain themes. I have already alluded to van Gogh's occasional attempts to deal with New Testament subjects in his paintings and his overt identification with Jesus in these works. At the same time, he was able to complete only biblical paintings based on previous versions by Delacroix and Rembrandt: Vincent's compositions of *Agony in the Garden* apparently defeated him to the extent that he destroyed them. These facts lend powerful support to Meyer's hypothesis, cited in Chapter 1, that the artist has to avoid subject matter too close to his active conflicts in order to do his best work. Vincent was too self-critical to produce mediocre paintings; consequently, his biographers have found very few clues to his adaptational difficulties by studying his art. As a matter of fact, it has been a commonplace of van Gogh criticism to stress the noble, vibrant, and affirmative qualities with which he endowed the entirety of his subject matter.[3]

Perhaps the point can be made even more emphatically with regard to Gauguin's work, the narrative content of which is more easily correlated with the painter's personal life than is the content of van Gogh's work.[4] We may begin to illustrate the manner in which Gauguin's psychopathology entered his art by comparing the overall subject matter of his paintings with the subject matter of his ceramics and woodcarvings—that is, with his work in media that most critics consider as less indicative of his artistic stature. Needless to say, I am not proposing an exhaustive survey of either genre here; I only seek to highlight certain startling dissimilarities in iconography between the works in these media and Gauguin's paintings. Moreover, I will immediately add as a disclaimer

3. In the visual arts, the clearest example of a body of work containing a substantial number of paintings generally considered to be less successful than the artist's best, presumably because the subject matter made him excessively anxious, is the oeuvre of Paul Cézanne. I discuss his work in Chapter 9.

4. It is noteworthy that the most remarkable exception to this statement is the canvas in which Vincent was most clearly influenced by his association with Gauguin, his *Souvenir of the Garden at Etten* (Figure 11: F. 496). Among the 16 paintings ascribed to Gauguin during his two-month stay in Arles with Vincent, a scene of two Arlésiennes promenading in the public garden (Figure 10: W. 300) is probably the most successful. Van Gogh's version of this composition (F. 496) ostensibly depicts a memory of the garden of his father's parsonage; the women he portrays in the painting are his mother and (probably) his cousin Kee, the two individuals whose rejecting attitudes had caused him the deepest pain. I take the presence of these women in this work to be another indication that Vincent foresaw the tragic end of his effort to woo Gauguin. The canvas may well hint at this perception that he was in the process of enacting a repetition of his most pathological relationships.

Figure 19. Paul Gauguin, *Mysterious Water*, 1891–1893. Watercolor on paper. Collection of The Art Institute of Chicago, gift of Mrs. Emily Crane Chadbourne.

that I am not implying Gauguin's efforts in three-dimensional media are aesthetically inferior. I do believe, however, that painting was universally seen as the summit of the visual arts during Gauguin's lifetime and that this attitude perforce determined Gauguin's approach to his work in every genre.

Andersen (1971) has discussed the iconography of many of Gauguin's small sculptures in persuasive detail. Perhaps most striking from the standpoint of my focus is the stoneware sculpture *Oviri* that represents a female death-spirit standing over a dead wolf while holding a cub in her arms (Figure 16). Gauguin made this work in the spring of 1895, after being betrayed by the mulatto girl in whose defense he sustained the crippling injury that would fill the last eight years of his life with pain and physical disability. *Oviri* portrays a savage, cannibal goddess; Gauguin called her "a cruel enigma" and "*la Tueuse*" (the killer). Andersen articulates the enigma of the goddess by observing that "she kills what she nurtures" (p. 261); he also quotes Gauguin's proud boast that *he* was a wolf—a description first applied to his character by Degas.

Oviri, we have already had occasion to note, was the marker Gauguin wished to erect over his own grave in the Marquesas; the autobiographical significance of this image is therefore inescapable. The artist's quasi-paranoid fear of depending on a woman is presented openly. This admission, in turn, provides a clue for his repetitive choice of very young adolescents as his mistresses—a strategy through which he must have tried to escape this anxiety. The same problem emerges in the iconography of a jewel box Gauguin carved in wood for his wife (Andersen, 1971, pp. 33–34): A grotesque female on the lid represents a goddess of destruction like the Hindu Kali; the dead figure of her husband–son at the bottom of the box must stand for the artist himself. The theme receives even more explicit presentation in a statuette of 1889 called *Black Venus*. This stoneware sculpture shows a kneeling half-breed from Martinique with a grotesque severed head bearing Gauguin's features at her knees.

Instead of multiplying these illustrative examples, let us turn to Gauguin's paintings to ascertain how these issues may have emerged within the narrative content of these works. It so happens that in 1898 the artist created a painting, *"The Evil Demon Is Present"* (W. 570), depicting an idol—a Marquesan goddess of evil—against a mountain backdrop. Here the image of the cult statue stands alone, without the animal symbols of man's fate that betray the autobiographic significance of *Oviri*. A number of additional paintings contain images of Gauguin's sculptural works that refer indirectly to the theme of female destructiveness. Two canvases of 1902 (W. 629, 630), for example, show collections of dead birds on a white tablecloth; behind the table stands a small terracotta idol of Gauguin's making that depicts a female deity. Two earlier still lifes

Figure 20. Paul Gauguin, *The Moon and the Earth*, 1893. Oil on burlap, 45″ × 24 1/2″. Collection, The Museum of Modern Art, New York, Lillie P. Bliss Collection.

(W. 375, 405) include a ceramic of a man's head that probably bears the artist's features: In this instance, all direct references to women have been deleted. A similar sculpture of a severed head forms the main feature of an 1892 canvas, *The End of Royalty* (W. 453). This work commemorates the demise of the last native king of Tahiti; two female mourners are depicted in attitudes that Andersen (1971, p. 210) interprets as a reference to regeneration.

To summarize: In his paintings, Gauguin treated the themes I view as most proximate to his psychopathology in a manner so indirect that we must use sources of information extrinsic to these works in order to decipher the allusions. In the examples cited, these clues are provided by the iconographically transparent small sculptures that are ostensibly included in the paintings as elements of still life. Neither these nor other derivatives of Gauguin's principal conflicts enter the subject matter of his paintings more directly in any other way. As Andersen has shown at some length, the artist was probably portraying his own feminine identification in the cycle of works dealing with the myth of Eve, but there is nothing in these images that explicitly links their female protagonists with Gauguin himself. On the contrary, the painter boastfully laid claim to the role of the serpent in a caricatured self-portrait of 1889 (W. 323) and gave his late mother's features to his *Exotic Eve* of 1890 (W. 389). The barbaric deities that recur in Gauguin's scenes of Tahiti, moreover, cast their evil spell on women rather than on men.[5]

Having said this much, I should add that the theme of Gauguin's masochism might be read into his occasional treatment of Christian subject matter, particularly the 1896 self-portrait (W. 534) inscribed "*Près du Golgotha*" (Nearing Golgotha). It will be recalled that the painter had previously portrayed himself as Christ in *Agony in the Garden* (Figure 8: W. 326) that seemed to commemorate his betrayal of van Gogh. Of course, Gauguin probably felt entitled to abandon others because his own father had forsaken him in his infancy. It cannot be coincidental, therefore, that he also painted his only two renditions of the Crucifixion (W. 327 [Figure 21], 328)—once again, at one remove from actuality, as scenes of Breton peasants worshipping at sculpted monuments depicting the Passion—under the impact of his drama with Vincent.[6] As if to underscore the fact that he felt like a martyr abandoned to his fate, he made a self-portrait at the same time (W. 324) in which his own *Yellow Christ* (W. 327) serves as the background. But in all these paintings the

5. See W. 457, 458, 459, 460, 499, 513, 514, 561, 568, 579.

6. I would infer that this emergence of Christian iconography in the work of the irreligious Gauguin was a sign of his identification with van Gogh's religious fervor after fleeing from their relationship. In other words, Gauguin had good reason to dread that he might be excessively subject to van Gogh's influence if their association were to continue.

Figure 21. Paul Gauguin, *The Yellow Christ*, 1889. Albright-Knox Art Gallery, Buffalo, New York, General Purchase Funds, 1946.

personal difficulty is divorced from its actual source in Gauguin's history: his problematic relationship with his mother.

If anything, Gauguin's occasional works that might be interpreted as references to childhood appear to present an idealized or otherwise distorted version of the biographical actualities. This is most obviously the case in the great *We Hail Thee, Mary* of 1891 (Figure 15: W. 428) in which the Holy Mother and Child exist in a Tahitian Garden of Eden. We might say the same of Gauguin's two renditions of the Nativity in 1896 (W. 540, 541), except for the fact that we know that the child his native girl bore him at the time was stillborn. The only other work relevant in this context is Gauguin's most impressive sculpture, the sardonically titled 1889 wood relief, *Be in Love, You Will Be Happy* (Figure 22). Here, as Andersen (1971, pp. 12–13, 112–116) has convincingly demonstrated, the artist portrayed himself as an infant–monster, the source of Original Sin, while the maternal figure was depicted as a submissive victim of oral aggression. The devil appears in this scene in the shape of a fox, carrying a younger woman off to hell, but the work also contains a number of subsidiary figures derived from the imagery of the damned in various celebrated representations of the Last Judgment. Once again, Gauguin came closest to revealing one of his central conflicts in a carving, but even here the basic mistrust of the woman is turned into boasting about his own primary wickedness.

The paintings that approach most openly the other pole of Gauguin's insoluble personal dilemma, that of his unacceptable passivity toward men, generally represent this temptation in the guise of the same bestial spirit. I have already alluded to the initial appearance of this theme in Gauguin's painting in *Loss of Innocence* (Figure 18: W. 412); I further interpreted the allusion in this work to van Gogh's self-portrait of 1888 as Gauguin's avowal that he had experienced Vincent as an evil seducer.[7]

7. The matter is, in fact, even more complex: Gauguin first used the image of the bestial, slanted eyes as part of the visage of a girl in the background of a still life of 1888 (W. 288). Andersen (1971, p. 86) astutely interprets this as a representation of Eve tempted by the apple, that is, by sexual knowledge. Are we justified in assuming that Gauguin was also alluding to his greedy acquiescence to the tempting offer of a subsidy from the van Gogh brothers? If so, this work must have been executed around the middle of October, just after Gauguin received Vincent's self-portrait as a Buddhist monk with Oriental eyes. This interpretation is supported by evidence from one of the last canvases Gauguin completed before he joined Vincent in Arles at the end of the month, a *Still Life with Puppies* (W. 293). In this mocking reminiscence of the Last Supper, Sugana (1972) interprets the three puppies eating from the same dish as the "convivial fraternity that united Gauguin, van Gogh, and the young painter [Emile Bernard]" (p. 94; my translation).

According to Andersen (1971, p. 106), Gauguin replicated the female "dreaming of forbidden pleasures" as the protagonist of *Human Misery* (W. 304), one of the crucial works of the period spent with Vincent in Arles. Thus, it was only after the rupture with van Gogh that Gauguin reversed the significance of his presentation: Henceforth evil was not attributed to the figure we can construe as a symbolic self-representation but to the figure that stood for another man.

Figure 22. Paul Gauguin, *Be in Love, You Will Be Happy*, 1889. Painted wood. Bequest of W. G. Russell Allen, Courtesy, Museum of Fine Arts, Boston, Arthur Tracy Cabot Fund.

The same implicit accusation was subsequently directed at the very next person upon whom Gauguin depended for assistance, the *Dutch*-Jewish artist Jacob Meyer de Haan. It is entirely understandable that de Haan became a substitute for Vincent in Gauguin's psychological world: Not only did the French painter depend on both Dutchmen for financial support but, more germanely, Gauguin was introduced to de Haan by Theo van Gogh. In fact, before moving to Brittany where Gauguin joined him, de Haan actually stayed with Theo in the latter's Paris apartment (see van Gogh, 1959c, pp. 88, 133, 250, 283n., 534, 543). Gauguin painted de Haan as a devil–figure on three occasions (W. 317, 320, 625). In two of these works, *Nirvana* of 1889 (Figure 23) and *Barbaric Tales* of 1902 (Figure 24), de Haan's satanic figure dominates several yielding, nubile women; in the second canvas, painted in the Marquesas, de Haan's foot is explicitly represented as the paw of a beast of prey: the fox (cf. Andersen, 1971, pp. 107–108)! It seems that the hunchbacked de Haan had actually bested Gauguin in winning the favors of a woman in Brittany—but one suspects that the second female in each of these paintings stands for Gauguin himself, unmanned.[8] The third de Haan portrait also dates from 1889; here, the sinister little figure rests his chin on an animal's paw. The theme of diabolism is underscored by the titles of the books on the table in front of him: *Paradise Lost* and Carlyle's *Sartor Resartus* (with its angelic–demonic hero, Herr Teufels-dröckh—devil's dung).

A scholar more intimately familiar with the details of Gauguin's life history might well be able to survey the visual record of his oeuvre and detect additional, subtler correlations between various paintings and the artist's inner life. On the basis of my familiarity with the standard biographical materials, however, I would venture the judgment that the works I have discussed thus far are the only ones that link up with Gauguin's major psychological problems. These paintings successfully avoid any *direct* confrontation of Gauguin's fears of passivity in relation to both men and women: Handled at this remove, that is, externalized, projected, or reversed into their opposites, these conflictual issues did not defeat the artist in his creative quest. We can reiterate this point by inverting the foregoing statement: Gauguin succeeded in creating a superb body of work on the theme of human helplessness by directing his attention away from his *own* helplessness to that of women in primitive societies, namely, Breton peasants, Blacks from Martinique, and the people of Tahiti.

---

8. Is there some significance attached to the flaming red hair of one of the Polynesian beauties in *Barbaric Tales*? Are we in the presence of a reprise of Gauguin as a red-haired Christ in the Garden of Olives? The fact that one of the female figures echoes the pose of Buddha in a Javanese temple frieze suggests that the answer may be yes.

Figure 23. Paul Gauguin, *Nirvana—Portrait of Jacob Meyer de Haan*, 1889. Oil on canvas. Courtesy Wadsworth Atheneum, Hartford, Connecticut, Ella Gallup Sumner and Mary Catlin Sumner Collection.

Figure 24. Paul Gauguin, *Barbaric Tales*, 1902. Oil on canvas. Museum Folkwang, Essen.

Should these findings turn out to be generalizable—that is, if the successful isolation of conflictual issues within the artist's everyday life should regularly permit the creation of a body of work free from the creator's undesirable traits—we would have taken a step toward explaining the paradox that great humanist art is frequently produced by individuals whose personal conduct may strike many of us as shocking in its wickedness.

Chapter Nine

Terribilità: The Paranoid Monster as Creative Genius

I

THE DEVELOPMENT of secular high culture creates novel opportunities and obligations for the individuals whose performances constitute the summit of its achievements. Notoriety during one's lifetime and posthumous fame, with all the ambiguous perquisites that accompany them, may be the highest rewards earned by our greatest artists. On the other side of the ledger, one of the most difficult obligations with which the great artist is automatically burdened is that of fulfilling the public role of culture hero—recipient of general adulation, object of merciless scrutiny, and obligatory embodiment of many ideals of his civilization. Although such a role may be congenial to certain public figures and artists—Thomas Jefferson and Peter Paul Rubens come most readily to mind as examples—the personal lives of creative men can more often be made to conform to public requirements only by a process of mythification.

In an important essay initially published in German in the mid-1930s, Ernst Kris (1952, Chapter 2) called attention to the distorting effects of tradition on the standard biographies of the artist, citing numerous examples of the application of idealizing formulas that conceal the actual facts. It was Editha and Richard Sterba (1954) who brought to our attention one of the most striking illustrations of this process—the usual portrayal of Beethoven as a character reflecting the nobility of his greatest compositions. As I reviewed in Chapter 1, the Sterbas' psychoanalytic investigation brought to light a very different—and much more fascinating—state of affairs. Far from having been an admirable individual in private life, Beethoven's personal conduct was often characterized by delinquency (in financial matters), imposture (in passing himself off as a member of the nobility), and in ruthless exploitativeness (especially in his dealings with his supposedly beloved nephew, Karl). The Sterbas' book thus raised a crucial question for the understanding of the creative process: How is it possible for the most fallible of mortals to produce masterpieces of humanism?

This issue would be significant as a matter of principle even if the case of Beethoven were highly unusual. It becomes even more important in view of the fact that the great composer's personality flaws are by no means unique among men of genius. To name only a few others who impress one as monsters of one kind or another: In music, Richard Wagner's virulent anti-Semitism is in itself sufficient to justify his inclusion on such a list; in literature, Jean-Jacques Rousseau's practice of forcing his mistress to abandon their numerous children perhaps earns him pride of place on this roster; in the visual arts, Michelangelo Buonarroti's misanthropy and propensity for outbursts of rage—his legendary terribilità—probably qualify him as a paranoid personality. Instead of multiplying instances here, I should like to focus on a proto-typical illustration that represents the most extreme form of this paradox: the coincidence of personal wickedness and the creation of great art full of ethical meaning. I find this paradox embodied in the person of the most influential painter of the early 17th century, Michelangelo Merisi, called Caravaggio.

II

THE LIFE OF Caravaggio, like that of his exact contemporary, William Shakespeare, is poorly documented; legends still surround him, although recent archival discoveries have begun to dispel some of the mythic aura about his person (see Cinotti, dell'Acqua, & Rossi, 1973, pp. 23–43, for a concise summary of all existing documents). Michelangelo Merisi was the oldest child of Fermo Merisi and Lucia Aratori, residents of Milan. Fermo had been a widower whose oldest child, a daughter, was born in 1565; it is assumed that he remarried by 1569 and that Michelangelo was born at the end of 1570 or early in 1571. At any rate, his brother Giovanni Battista was less than two years his junior, and another brother and a sister were born before Fermo died, presumably in the plague of 1577. Traditionally, Fermo Merisi was thought to be an architect in the employ of the Marquis of Caravaggio, but recent knowledge of his continuing residence in Milan has put that story in doubt. The family owned land around the town of Caravaggio and had relatives in the priesthood and connections with Milanese tradespeople. In all probability, they enjoyed a certain degree of prosperity in spite of the early death of the paterfamilias.

Michelangelo was apprenticed to the Milanese painter Peterzano at the age of 14 and stayed in his studio for the next four years. During this interval, the family apparently moved to Caravaggio. By the time of the move, Michelangelo's younger brother, Giovanni Pietro, had already died. Later, his sister, Caterina, married and his remaining brother, Giovanni Battista, entered the priesthood. In 1589, when Michelangelo completed his training, he evidently rejoined his family; deeds of sale for some of their land attest to the fact that the family had by then fallen upon hard times. Some time between 1590 and 1592, the mother died. In May 1592, the three surviving children divided their inheritance, and the 22-year-old artist evidently used his share to finance his move to Rome, the artistic capital of the age.

Caravaggio survived for a number of years by working in the studios of other painters or by selling his works on the popular market. At the age of 25, he acquired his first important patron, the Cardinal del Monte. Henceforth, Caravaggio's work was in increasing demand, especially by the most discriminating of the Roman collectors. In 1599, he received his first truly important commission, the decoration of the Contarelli chapel in the church of S. Luigi dei Francesi. From that time on, his entire output dealt with religious themes, almost always Christian, with a very small representation of classical mythology. Caravaggio died in highly dramatic circumstances in 1610 before he reached the age of 40—but more of this later.

Scholars of baroque painting generally agree that Caravaggio's art marked a turning point in the history of taste (see Venturi, 1952). He introduced an unprecedented degree of subjectivity in every facet of his work, and in this sense he can be regarded as the first of the modern masters. Richard Spear (1971) has stressed that the painter's mature work betokens a change in his inner being, presumably from youthful preoccupations with personal concerns to a tender, steadfast faith presented in the contemporary spirit of those exemplars of Counter-Reformation piety, St. Philip Neri and St. Charles Borromeo (see Friedlaender, 1955, Chapter 6). As Rudolf Wittkower (1965) puts it, Caravaggio's art corresponds to the pleas of these great visionaries for a direct gnosis of the divine. Lionello Venturi (1952) was alluding to this same issue when he averred that the truest value of Caravaggio's art lies in the painter's humility. Many of Caravaggio's contemporaries were scandalized by his presentation of sacred themes in terms of figures culled from the streets of Rome; today, we are impressed by his successful use of these common folk to portray the subjectivity of religious ecstasy. Caravaggio's greatest achievement was his success in representing mystical visions through irrational lighting effects alone, that is, without concretely showing the imagery perceived by the mystic (Wittkower, 1965). Hence, modern

Figure 25. Michelangelo Merisi da Caravaggio, *The Conversion of the Magdalen* (The Alzaga Caravaggio), 1597–1598. Oil on canvas. Courtesy of the Detroit Institute of Arts, the Kresge Foundation, and Mr. and Ms. Edsel B. Ford.

critics no longer classify him as a realist. In his own day, however, Caravaggio stunned his audience with the immediacy of his representations of what they perceived as actualities. As Röttgen (1974) has observed, he may have further shocked his audience because his own faith was lacking in Christian *spes*—hope—a quality we no longer require in our age of skepticism. These aspects of Caravaggio's unconventionality notwithstanding, the impact of his work perfused the art of Europe in the first quarter of the 17th century and was subsequently absorbed and expanded in the work of Velázquez, Georges de la Tour, and Rembrandt (see Kitson, 1969).

In order to appreciate the magnitude of the internal changes these critics discern in the painter, we have to review the evolution of Caravaggio's oeuvre, especially that of his early works. Although the surviving paintings that preceded the Contarelli St. Matthew cycle of 1598–1602 include an ever increasing proportion of religious works, we are obliged to accept Wittkower's judgment that, during the first several years of the artist's activity, his religious works were more theatrical in spirit than expressive of the profound faith characteristic of his later output. He favored scenes of decapitation (e.g., *Judith and Holofernes*, the *Medusa*, *The Sacrifice of Isaac*) or the portrayal of beautiful, self-absorbed young people (such as *Narcissus*, *The Penitent Magdalen*, or *St. Catherine*). Perhaps the Detroit *Conversion of the Magdalen* (Figure 25) represents a transitional stage in Caravaggio's development, as it combines one figure representing the humility of the faithful with another preparing to desist contemplating her beautiful image in a mirror: It is the moment of the Magdalen's conversion (Salerno, 1974).

Aside from a few indifferent portraits and a strikingly beautiful still life, the core of Caravaggio's youthful production consists of paintings that have been widely interpreted as autobiographical (cf. M. Gedo, 1983). Many of the androgynous figures depicted in these works were probably actual self-portraits; others may have been idealized self-representations involving alter egos, probably members of a small band of Caravaggio's boon companions. Several of these genre scenes deal with criminal activities, usually depicting cardsharpers or prostitute/fortune-tellers victimizing gullible thrill seekers.

A second category of Caravaggio's early canvases depicts late adolescents, generally as single, half-length figures; in the case of *The Musicians* (Figure 26), such figures are in a group. These paintings are widely interpreted as possessing strong homosexual overtones. Michael Kitson (1969, p. 87) has therefore concluded that Caravaggio must have been working for a homosexual circle of ecclesiastical patrons, and he shares the impression of many (e.g., Frommel, 1971; Posner, 1971) that the artist himself may have been homosexual. Other scholars (Battisti,

Figure 26. Michelangelo Merisi da Caravaggio, *The Musicians*, c. 1596. Oil on canvas. The Metropolitan Museum of Art, Rogers Fund, 1952.

1960; Salerno, Kinkead, & Wilson, 1966), it should be noted, have stressed the allegorical nature of these commissioned works. Röttgen (1974), who views Caravaggio's first patron, the Cardinal del Monte, as a discreet politician interested in covering over his homosexual inclinations with a veneer of allegory, believes that Caravaggio succeeded in fulfilling the intentions of his patrons at the same time as he imparted a rich vein of private meaning to these works. Be that as it may, the tone of some of these works (e.g., the Leningrad *Lute Player* [Figure 27] or *The Musicians*) is reminiscent of Shakespeare's contemporaneous sonnets, presumably addressed to patrons of a similar sort by a polymorphous genius about to find his destiny.

In *The Lute Player*, Caravaggio's female impersonation is so convincing that the figure has often been mistaken for a girl. No such error is possible concerning the *Adolescent Bacchus* in the Uffizi (Figure 28); here, the mythological trappings can scarcely be taken at face value because of the indecency of the protagonist's androgynous appeal. Close scrutiny, for example, reveals that Bacchus is wearing a wig only appropriate for a girl.[1] Contemporary documents prove that the last painting of this type that Caravaggio produced, the *Victorious Love* commissioned by the Marchese Giustiniani (Figure 29), was created no later than the St. Matthew cycle. Kitson (1969, p. 96) has aptly called this "a painting of enormous vitality and charm . . . and of outrageous erotic appeal." Yet, the *Victorious Love* is, in fact, only marginally more brazen than some of the ostensibly religious works Caravaggio painted only a few years earlier. These include his representations of a provocatively nude youth who, as John the Baptist, embraces a ram as a symbol of Christ. Clearly, in the sexually charged atmosphere created by the Roman *cognoscenti*, the ideal of Platonic homoerotism could pass muster as a form of religious expression. If the Lamb of God had reached maturity, it was apparently not blasphemous to allude to this fact. Perhaps, then, Caravaggio's renditions of Bacchus and Eros should not be dismissed out-of-hand as variants of a single conception of Divine Love in a mythological guise. By taking the homoerotism in such works seriously, we are forced to conclude that Caravaggio's transformation into a serious religious painter was a gradual process indeed.

In fact, after 1602 the artist never reverted to the presentation of erotic material in his work. Thus, his later versions of the youthful John the Baptist (e.g., Figure 30) are solemn and stark in their sobriety; the only mythological subject he painted in his last years was a *Sleeping Cupid*, tenderly portrayed as a child of about 2 years. It seems likely that

1. I came to this conclusion independently in front of the canvas in June 1980. By good fortune, my observation was immediately confirmed by the eminent Caravaggio scholar, Alfred Moir, in a personal conversation at the church of S. Trinità.

Figure 27. Michelangelo Merisi da Caravaggio, *The Lute Player*, c. 1596. Oil on canvas. The Hermitage Museum, Leningrad.

Caravaggio's strengthened religious faith began to satisfy certain idealizing needs that had formerly found expression only in homoerotic fantasies and/or behavior. It is quite conceivable that his homoerotic activities were held in abeyance for certain periods. Toward the end of his residence in Rome, for example, he appears to have had a regular relationship with a female prostitute (see Friedlaender, 1955, p. 284).

Although no critic has ventured to speculate about the causes of the reorganization of Caravaggio's personality in his late 20s, there is general agreement that the shift in style and subject matter that typifies his middle period, the "austere seriousness penetrat[ing] the monumental creations of his 'maniera magnifica'" (Friedlaender, p. 117), could occur only on the basis of such a development. The available biographical evidence tends to confirm that Caravaggio underwent a major character change around 1600, although the nature of the shift, as best one can infer from these sources, was highly equivocal. The only biographer to have known Caravaggio personally, the painter Giovanni Baglione, bore a deep and justified grudge against him and was therefore unlikely to focus on favorable aspects of his antagonist's development.

III

WALTER FRIEDLAENDER (1955, p. 119) has astutely noted that the astonishing succession of violent acts associated with Caravaggio all occurred after 1600; there is no record of any misbehavior on his part before that date, although one 17th-century biographer, Pietro Bellori, recounts an unsubstantiated story that the painter committed a murder as a youth in Milan. However apocryphal the tale may be, its circulation only half a century after Caravaggio's death testifies to the awe his black character must have inspired among his contemporaries.

Another unverified defamatory anecdote, less implausible than the story of a homicide in adolescence, is described in Giulio Mancini's *Trattato* (quoted in Friedlaender, 1955, pp. 255–258), published in 1620 when many eyewitnesses of these events were still living. According to Mancini, when Caravaggio's brother, the priest Giovanni Battista, heard of his artistic success, he went to Rome and sought him out at the Palazzo del Monte. In response to inquiries from the cardinal, the painter denied that he had any brothers and adamantly maintained the denial when confronted by his sibling. The biographer reports this story to illustrate Caravaggio's "extravagant" behavior and eccentricity. We now have documentary evidence that Giovanni Battista Merisi was indeed in Rome in 1596, but we have no clues about the brothers' relationship. True or false, Mancini's account suggests that Caravaggio was believed to be deficient in human feelings, although one suspects that the knowledge of

Figure 28. Michelangelo Merisi da Caravaggio, *Adolescent Bacchus*, c. 1596. Oil on canvas. Galleria Uffizi, Florence.

Figure 29. Michelangelo Merisi da Caravaggio, *Victorious Love*, c. 1602. Oil on canvas. Staatliche Museen Preussicher Kulturbesitz, Gemäldegalerie, Berlin (West).

his later misdeeds may have led biographers to depict the artist's insouciant youth in excessively dark colors.

It so happens that we possess a dispassionate summary of Caravaggio's mode of life around the turn of the century. It was published in 1604 by the Dutch art reporter Karel van Mander: "There is beside the grain the chaff, to wit that he does not pursue his studies steadfastly so that after a fortnight's work he will swagger about for a month or two with his sword at his side and with a servant following him, from one ball-court to the next, ever ready to engage in a fight or argument, with the result that it is most awkward to get along with him" (quoted in Friedlaender, 1955, p. 260). Van Mander's informant, a Netherlander who met Caravaggio as a fellow worker in the studio of his first major employer, the Cavaliere d'Arpino, was all too accurate: The Rome police records attest to the steadily increasing seriousness of Caravaggio's misconduct from 1600 to 1606, when he capped his exploits with manslaughter after a quarrel involving a ball game. Because these documents are precisely dated, it is now possible to correlate the major untoward events of the painter's personal life with his progress as an artist.

Caravaggio's name first appears on the police blotter on October 25, 1600, as a witness to a street brawl. On November 19 he was cited as an actual participant in such an affair, and on February 7, 1601, he was directed to make peace with a soldier he had wounded in a swordfight. Be it noted that the painter completed *The Calling* and *The Martyrdom of St. Matthew* (Figure 31) for the side walls of the Contarelli Chapel by July 4, 1600, when he received payment for these works. On September 25 of the same year, he signed the contract for his next great commission, the paintings of *The Conversion of St. Paul* and *The Crucifixion of St. Peter* in the Cerasi Chapel of Sta. Maria del Popolo. It would seem that the decisive triumph he enjoyed with his first paintings created for a public space, rapidly followed by the recognition entailed in receiving another important opportunity in a church associated with Raphael and Bramante, must have thrown this brittle personality into a state of unmanageable tension and excitement. Under such circumstances, irritability and quarrelsomeness are common, and physical violence may serve as a desperate safety valve in the attempted mitigation of a quasi-hypomanic state.[2] I believe that van Mander's informant has provided us with an

2. In a discussion that followed the initial presentation of this material before the Michigan Association for Psychoanalysis as the Fifth Sterba Lecture (January 9, 1982), Seymour Baxter raised the intriguing possibility that there may have been nothing "quasi" about Caravaggio's hypomania: The onset of cyclothymic mood swings often takes place around the age of 30. Another diagnostic possibility mentioned by Baxter (and seconded by Alexander Grinstein) was that of psychomotor epilepsy (the very syndrome that was probably responsible for van Gogh's chronic overexcited state). This second hypothesis is even more plausible than the one of manic–depressive illness, given the fact that exacerba-

excellent description of this clinical syndrome. But, significantly, it is during the very fall of 1600 when Caravaggio entered the police blotter for his violent behavior that he seems to have made the revisions in *The Martyrdom of St. Matthew* that elevate this painting to its present grandeur; the alterpiece was installed in December 1600.

The original version of *The Martyrdom of St. Matthew* has been convincingly reconstructed on the basis of radiographic studies. In this composition, the elderly apostle stands in front of an imposing backdrop of classical architecture, his right hand raised in a dignified gesture to ward off the armed men about to assault him. In its definitive form, we witness a version of the scene without precedent in Roman art (cf. Röttgen, 1974, p. 232): The assassin is a nearly naked youth and St. Matthew, lying upon a platform almost at ground level, tries ineffectually to prevent the fatal blow as various onlookers demonstrate intense personal reactions to an event that has now been robbed of all its idealizing aspects. One of the witnesses, facing the spectator from the furthest recesses of the murky background, is Caravaggio himself, wearing a facial expression of unmistakable horror.

It is tempting to conclude that the painter chose to portray his own reaction to the disturbing developments in his private life in this allegorical manner. The accelerating disintegration of his self-control, culminating in the acts of violence documented in the Rome police records, is depicted in the imagery of the mature apostle of Christ about to be murdered by a barbaric adolescent (see also M. Gedo, 1983).

It should also be noted, in this connection, that Caravaggio left the household of the Cardinal del Monte sometime between 1600 and 1603. Whether this move resulted from del Monte's disappointment with the misconduct of his protégé, from a breach caused by the cardinal's behavior, or simply as a consequence of the expansion of Caravaggio's circle of patrons is an important question we are at present unable to answer. It does seem likely, however, that the unique relationship with del Monte had a calming and restraining influence on the painter that was never again duplicated in his later career.

The next episode of delinquency for which documentary evidence exists was perhaps less serious in its psychopathological implications but turned out to have graver long-term consequences for Caravaggio's reputation. His opponent in that quarrel was Giovanni Baglione, the

---

tions of the latter would be less likely to correlate closely with real life events. Such correlation, as I will proceed to show, does indeed typify the case of Caravaggio. Epileptic attacks, on the other hand, are known to be precipitated by emotional stress, so that this diagnosis in no way conflicts with the psychological conclusions of my study. It should be noted, moreover, that psychomotor seizures often result from previous head injuries, so that Caravaggio's deterioration in self-control could well have been a consequence of such an injury sustained in an earlier brawl.

Figure 30. Michelangelo Merisi da Caravaggio, *St. John the Baptist*, 1602–1604. Oil on canvas. Nelson Gallery, Atkins Museum, Kansas City, Missouri (Nelson Fund).

future author of a series of brief biographies (1642) that would be one of the principal sources of information about his antagonist. Richard Spear had noted with great psychological perspicacity that Baglione was the first artist "known to have emulated [Caravaggio's] style. . . . It is possible that Caravaggio himself considered [some of Baglione's] pictures to be the first conscious imitations of his art and that his hostility towards Baglione was immediately kindled" (1971, pp. 25–26). After Caravaggio created the *Victorious Love* for the learned collector Vincenzo Giustiniani, Baglione painted several versions of *Divine Love* for the latter's brother, Cardinal Giustiniani, sometime in the period 1602–1603. Although Baglione's activity undoubtedly had a competitive aspect, Caravaggio would certainly have realized that his own career had reached a new stage by virtue of the fact that a reputable painter was trying to emulate his style.

Subsequent events suggest that Caravaggio warded off a second bout of disruptive excitement by savagely depreciating Baglione, thereby de-valuing the significance of the latter's adherence to his standard. Caravaggio drew his usual cronies, as well as certain artists who had been offended by Baglione, into this game. They mocked poor Baglione by writing scurril-ous, defamatory verses about him that they proceeded to circulate within the Roman artistic community. Inevitably, the matter came to Baglione's attention, and in August 1603 he brought suit for slander against Caravaggio and some of his accessories.

Caravaggio was arrested, but he denied everything in court and managed to obtain his release through the intercession of the French ambassador. Further insulted by Caravaggio's depreciating statements on the witness stand ("I know nothing about there being any painter who will praise Giovanni Baglione as a good painter" [in Friedlaender, 1955, p. 227]), the embittered Baglione understandably changed his artistic direction. Under the circumstances, his approach to Caravaggio's work in the book he wrote in old age is impressively generous; he reserved his condemnation for Caravaggio's personal character, calling him "a satirical and haughty man" who spoke ill of others (Friedlaender, 1955, p. 235). Rather!

For the remainder of his years in Rome, Caravaggio was spared the task of accepting the homage of any followers. Spear has concluded that "Caravaggio's absence from Rome actually may have stimulated Caravaggesque painting after 1605," (1971, p. 25), adding that this circumstance must have come about because Caravaggio actively dis-couraged potential followers (pp. 25–26). The youthful Bartolomeo Manfredi, more than 15 years Caravaggio's junior and a member of the artistic circle around the Giustinianis, was probably the first recruit to the school of Caravaggio after the latter's flight from Rome in May 1606.

Figure 31. Michelangelo Merisi da Caravaggio, *The Martyrdom of St. Matthew*, 1600. Oil on canvas. Church of S. Luigi dei Francesi, Rome.

After the Baglione affair, Caravaggio had a number of minor brushes with the police during 1604 and 1605, always as a result of losing his temper when he felt he was treated with insufficient deference. On one occasion, for example, he assaulted a disrespectful waiter, yelling, "If I am not mistaken, you damned cuckold, you think you are serving some bum" (in Friedlaender, 1955, p. 280). On July 29, 1605, there was an outburst of a more serious kind, a murderous assault on someone with whom Caravaggio had a dispute over a girl, perhaps a model or a prostitute. This incident was grave enough to impel the painter temporarily to flee to Genoa, but he returned to face the charges within a fortnight. He was able to clear himself by making a public apology to his opponent, whose injuries turned out to be less serious than they first appeared. But the next quarrel of May 29, 1606, culminated in the murder of Caravaggio's antagonist and the painter's definitive flight from Rome.[3]

In my judgment, this succession of events suggests that Caravaggio's self-control became progressively more tenuous until the episode of July 1605. Perhaps sobered by this experience, the artist held himself in better check for 10 months, only to disintegrate into homicidal rage in the end. In view of Caravaggio's descent into a chronic paranoid state, it is truly astonishing to review the stream of masterpieces he created in this period. To mention only well-documented paintings of the greatest importance, Caravaggio's *peccadilloes* in 1604 took place while he was probably completing *The Entombment of Christ*. Not only was this tragic canvas considered to be the artist's best work by his contemporaries; it may have had special significance for Caravaggio because it was destined for the Chiesa Nuova, the church of St. Philip Neri himself, on commission from the revered ecclesiastic's good friend, Pietro Vittrice.

On the heels of this confirmation of his stature as the greatest religious artist of his age, the 34-year-old painter began work on *The Madonna of the Pilgrims*, still the altarpiece in the Cavaletti Chapel of S. Agostino. It is known that Caravaggio's tender homage to popular faith was installed before March 1606; if a slightly romanticized account in an early source,

---

3. It is by no means certain, of course, that Caravaggio's violent behavior was confined to the incidents that found their way into the written records thus far unearthed. On the contrary, it is much more likely that most of his *peccadilloes* never came to the attention of the authorities. Moreover, further evidence about his misbehavior continues to surface. The 1973 summary of Caravaggesque documentation (Cinotti, dell'Acqua, & Rossi, 1973) contains an account of October 24, 1605 that was formerly unreported: a notary's interrogation of Caravaggio concerning certain wounds the painter had sustained around his head. Caravaggio obstinately and preposterously maintained that he had accidentally fallen on his own sword, and the circumstances of this particular sword fight never did come to light. Who knows how many other similar incidents there may have been?

Figure 32. Michelangelo Merisi da Caravaggio, *David with the Head of Goliath*, c. 1606. Oil on canvas. Galleria Borghese, Rome.

Passeri, is to be trusted, the artist's outburst of violence in July 1605 was, in fact, connected with the completion of this work (see Kitson, 1969, p. 99). Nor was this grand commission the only reason for Caravaggio's head to be turned that summer. He was also creating *The Madonna of the Serpent* for the confraternity of the Palafrenieri of the Vatican; the work would decorate their chapel in St. Peter's Basilica. We know that Caravaggio was working on this canvas in October 1605 and received final payment for it in April 1606. Regrettably the Palafrenieri lost their chapel within the basilica because of the reconstruction of St. Peter's, and Caravaggio's altarpiece was installed in the Old Sacristy instead.

But this was only a minor disappointment in the course of the artist's intoxicating progress during his final year in Rome. Sometime in 1605, Caravaggio acquired a new patron able to assure him primacy of place among the painters of Rome. This was Cardinal Scipione Borghese, nephew of the new pope, Paul V Borghese. The cardinal began energetically to collect Caravaggio's works, rapidly forming that unrivaled nucleus of his oeuvre that is still the glory of the Borghese Gallery. He also arranged for Caravaggio to paint a portrait of the pope. The canvas now in the possession of the Borghese family leaves the modern viewer cold, but (assuming it is indeed *Caravaggio's* portrait of Paul V) it reportedly pleased the sitter.

Another Borghese commission, *David with the Head of Goliath* (Figure 32), indubitably belongs on the list of Caravaggio's masterpieces. It has always been recognized that the artist gave Goliath his own features, and Friedlaender (1955, p. 203) has called attention to the fact that this choice signifies Caravaggio's awareness of the psychological implications of this identification with "the victim of a superior and innocent power." It has remained for Mary Gedo (1983) to point out that, in positing such an identification, Caravaggio was predicting his own destruction by the daemonic forces within his personality, that is, that David also represented Caravaggio in his former guise as a youth of infinite promise. I believe the observation is valid even if this painting was created after the artist fled Rome, as most authorities now believe.

The last major work Caravaggio executed in Rome was *The Death of the Virgin* (Figure 33). Unfortunately, the installation of this altarpiece in the church of Sta. Maria della Scala cannot be dated with precision. It is quite tempting to conjecture, however, that Caravaggio's blowup in the summer of 1606 was in reaction to the decision of the Carmelite clergy in charge of the church to replace his painting with a more "decorous" substitute. Baglione reported that they objected to the representation of the deceased "swollen up and with bare legs"; other sources maintain that Caravaggio's use of a prostitute as the model for the Virgin had given offense (Kitson, 1969, p. 101). One cannot imagine that Caravaggio suffered such fools gladly, nor would it have consoled him that the

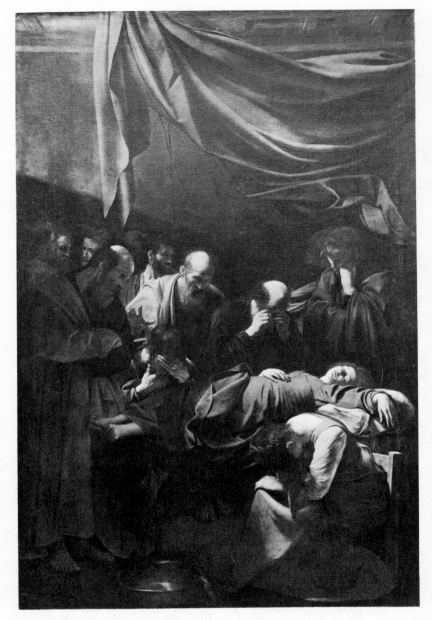

Figure 33. Michelangelo Merisi da Caravaggio, *The Death of the Virgin*, c. 1606. Oil on canvas. Musée du Louvre, Paris.

original patron, Laerzio Cherubini, retained the painting in his private collection.

It so happens that Caravaggio was triumphantly vindicated in February 1607 when the agent of the Gonzaga Dukes of Mantua, Peter Paul Rubens, bought this masterpiece for his employers. But by this time Caravaggio was in exile. Nor did he need this fresh evidence of the spread of his influence to Northern Italy and Flanders to realize that his success would not be confined to Rome. Some time before August 1605, agents of the Este Dukes of Modena had approached Caravaggio to create an altarpiece for that city; their reports to the duke (in Friedlaender, 1955, pp. 310–314) reveal that they did not lose hope of getting a work from the painter, for which he received an advance, until the summer of 1607.

IV

ONE HISTORIAN (Skira-Venturi, 1952, p. 31) has been bold enough to diagnose Caravaggio's mental state as a "persecution mania." It would seem, however, that he was generally able to provoke sufficient opposition to make it unnecessary for him to form *delusions* of persecution. As a fugitive from Roman justice, his need to suffer was apparently satisfied to a degree sufficient to reduce his level of tension. At least, he seems to have avoided further difficulties during the next two years, when he was first sheltered by Prince Colonna in the Sabine Hills and subsequently stayed in Naples. Because of the uncertainties of his situation, he worked mostly on paintings smaller than his great Roman works. Nonetheless, he did complete several ambitious projects in Naples, albeit in a hurried manner that could not always approximate his finest work. From the psychological viewpoint, the most interesting of the works of this period is *A Penitent St. Francis* in which Röttgen (1974) discerns Caravaggio's self-portrait. He plausibly concludes that the subject matter of this painting is the painter's guilt over the homicide he had recently committed.

Unable to obtain a pardon from the pope, Caravaggio moved on to Malta in the winter of 1607–1608. Cordially welcomed by the Knights of Malta, then completing the great building program that followed their glorious defense of the island against the Turks in 1565, the painter settled down to execute a series of important commissions. Among these, *The Beheading of John the Baptist* (Figure 34) in the cathedral at La Valletta marks one of the peaks of Caravaggio's oeuvre and the crystallization of his late style. As Spear puts it "Caravaggio's late figures, placed on a shallow middle ground stage, act out their tragic roles in constrained pantomime, engulfed by the darkness of night" (1971, p. 12). *The Beheading* is Caravaggio's most classical composition, but it tells the same story as his self-portrait in the guise of Goliath: Caravaggio signed his

Figure 34. Michelangelo Merisi da Caravaggio, *The Beheading of John the Baptist*, 1608. Oil on canvas. Cathedral of S. Giovanni, La Valletta, Malta.

immense canvas, cursively, in the form of the stream of blood issuing from the neck of the victim. One critic, Roberto Longhi, has called this work the painting of the century.

Alof de Wignacourt, Grand Master of the Knights of St. John, became the last of Caravaggio's major patrons. He was greatly pleased by the artist's work for the order, including two portraits of de Wignacourt himself. Neither the painter nor his new protector understood the implications of Caravaggio's personal history; hence, in July 1608, the artist was knighted and received into the order at his own request as a "Cavaliere di Grazia." This restoration to high favor immediately threw Caravaggio into a new paranoid crisis, although he was reportedly delighted with the luxurious perquisites of his new station. Within a few weeks, he was imprisoned, probably because he quarreled with one of his superiors in the hierarchy. He then sealed his fate by breaking out of jail and escaping to Sicily in a most daring manner—a capital offense in this military order. In December 1608, a criminal commission formally expelled him, but agents of the Knights of St. John probably continued to pursue him for the next year.

A fugitive once more, Caravaggio moved from town to town in Sicily, leaving behind him a trail of hastily created masterpieces on the themes of birth, death, and resurrection. In October 1609, he returned to Naples, where some *bravi* finally caught up with him, cut him up, and left him for dead. Had this punishment been meted out by the order of knights he had offended? Or had the painter provoked yet another quarrel with strangers? Röttgen (1974), for one, suspects that his fears of vengeance from the knights may have been delusional. In any event, the offshoot of this incident was the report of October 24, 1609 in the Duke of Urbino's dispatches from Rome: "Word has been received from Naples that Caravaggio, the famous painter, has been murdered. Others say disfigured" (in Friedlaender, 1955, p. 292).

It is appropriate to pause at this point and note the amazing number of untoward incidents in Caravaggio's life that all occurred in the month of October. His debut in the police annals, it will be recalled, involved a violent incident of October 25, 1600—one in which he was allegedly only a bystander. On October 19–20, 1604, Caravaggio was in prison in connection with an episode of disorderly conduct involving the police. On October 24, 1605, he was questioned about the mysterious wounds he claimed to have sustained by accident. Caravaggio's escape from his Maltese prison took place on October 6, 1608—perhaps a bit early to commemorate the usual anniversary of his criminal entanglements, but the painter may have had to seize his chance when opportunity presented itself. The fact that Caravaggio's last sword fight took place shortly before October 24, 1609, certainly calls into question the likelihood that he was cut up by the agents of de Wignacourt.

If these dates are not coincidental—and it defies the imagination to think that they are—we must look for the traumatic event they commemorate. The only clue we have in this connection is the fact that Caravaggio's brother was ordained a priest on October 26, 1596. This event hardly contains traumatic implications, unless the date of Giovanni Battista's ordination was intended to mark the anniversary of a prior event. As it happens, we know that Giovanni Battista was christened on November 4, 1572, so that it seems quite probable that he was born in October. Caravaggio's recurrent difficulties in that month may therefore have been determined, in part, by anniversary reactions to the birth of his next sibling.[4]

In any event, the artist spent 10 months convalescing in Naples after the attack on him. From a psychological perspective, it makes sense to assign his Neapolitan chef d'oeuvre, *The Flagellation of Christ* in the church of S. Domenico Maggiore, to this second stay in the city (as some recent scholarship has done on other grounds), for the painter infused the theme of suffering and humiliation with unprecedented pathos in this canvas. During this same time, he probably painted two versions of *Salome with the Head of John the Baptist* as well. Bellori, writing in the late 17th century, claimed that one of these works was sent to Malta as a present to appease de Wignacourt (in Friedlaender, 1955, p. 251), presumably before Caravaggio was assaulted.

In the summer of 1610, after four years of exile, Caravaggio's efforts to obtain a papal pardon finally began to bear fruit. In July, he took ship for Porto Ercole to await permission to return to the Eternal City at the very border of papal sovereignty. On landing at Porto Ercole, he was temporarily detained by the police and apparently suffered another paranoid episode. Although his arrest turned out to be a mistake, on being released he formed the delusion that the ship had sailed off with his possessions; he set off in pursuit of the vessel on foot. When he reached the next village, he collapsed with a high fever and died on July 31, 1610 (Kitson, 1969, p. 84). One final time, it seems, Caravaggio responded to prospects of good fortune with dangerous overexcitement and to relatively minor injuries to his self-esteem with uncontrolled rage and delusional thinking.

V

IT IS DIFFICULT to identify a creative person of similar stature whose personality incorporated Caravaggio's propensity for violence and malice. Perhaps psychotic characters with unusual talent tend to gravitate to

4. The foregoing hypothesis gains plausibility if we recall that Caravaggio returned repeatedly to the portrayal of John the Baptist in his work. It is particularly noteworthy that his depiction of the beheading of this saint in La Valletta, probably Caravaggio's supreme

public affairs rather than the arts and letters: If Michelangelo Merisi had become a *condottiere* instead of a painter, we might well compare his life with that of Alexander of Macedon. The adolescent conqueror appears to have possessed a vision impregnated with the civilized values of his Hellenic education, but this pupil of Aristotle was equally capable of murdering his loyal friend Kleitos, who failed to render the kind of homage he expected. Moreover, Alexander's incessant state of excitement drove him into exhaustion and a febrile illness that proved fatal at an age even younger than Caravaggio's at his death.

Comparisons aside, how can we comprehend Caravaggio's capacity to produce art of the highest order throughout his turbulent career while he simultaneously disintegrated over and over again into delusional states, self-destructive impulsiveness, and homicidal rages? It would seem that such a combination of behaviors could only typify an individual who was vulnerable to acute regressive episodes under stress but who was also capable of rapidly reversing these psychological catastrophes. Caravaggio's bouts of regressive behavior always supervened when his star was on the ascendant; I have postulated that his allergy to success is best understood as an inability to manage the excitement that inevitably accompanied such triumphs. It is equally possible that unconscious guilt played a part in wrecking the painter, in the manner Freud (1916) described in his celebrated analysis of the character of Lady Macbeth. But neither the biographical data bearing on Caravaggio's actual behavior nor the thematic content of his work suggests that he had an unconscious need to expiate guilt; to the contrary, Michelangelo Merisi seems to have regarded himself as a veritable Archangel Michael, entitled to mete out divine justice to his fellow men. Although John the Baptist and Goliath lost their heads, in other words, they did not lose them because they deserved punishment. I am therefore inclined to conclude that the prospect of continuing success produced excessive stress for Caravaggio simply by virtue of his inability to regulate tension states.

It is much more difficult to comprehend Caravaggio's inexhaustible capacity, once he found his feet as an independent artist in Rome, to reintegrate after his psychotic episodes so promptly that there are no discernible gaps in his productivity. Perhaps, after all, the disastrous consequences of his repeated misconduct were usually sufficient to sober him, reduce his excitement, and thus permit him to regain the ability to work. Nonetheless, it is certainly very unusual for psychotic patients to go directly from the most archaic to the most advanced modes of behavioral regulation (cf. Gedo & Goldberg, 1973; Gedo, 1979a). In

---

achievement, is unprecedently grisly: The executioner severs the last strands of flesh holding the Baptist's head in place with a hand knife. In this context, the painter's signature, "Michelangelo," written in the victim's blood, seems to acknowledge his murderous intent vis-à-vis his brother.

treatment settings, at any rate, people recovering from incidents of dis-integration generally need intensive human contact to help them organize their activities, even in terms of ordinary routines. Vincent van Gogh's decision to seek asylum in the hospital at St. Rémy (see Chapter 8) is a good illustration of the customary requirements of such a convalescence, even in a person whose disorganization was probably based on epilepsy. Caravaggio's ability to return to his highest level of functioning without such assistance also speaks for the likelihood that *his* disorganization usually resulted from the self-limiting circumstances of episodic incre-ments in tension levels, rather than from permanent intrapsychic disposi-tions, such as those produced by neurotic conflicts of various kinds or, for that matter, by hypomanic states.

This is not to deny that, along with his inability to regulate tension states adequately, the artist was apparently addicted to a life filled with painful difficulties. The compulsion to repeat (Freud, 1920) often obliges the individual to bring about actual events that are bound to reproduce the affective tone of his early childhood. In other words, I would infer that Caravaggio's earliest years were filled with rage and humiliation, suffering and disappointed hopes. But we know nothing of the actual circumstances of his early years. One can reasonably assume, however, the artistic activities became his best avenue for adaptation—as they were for Pablo Picasso (see Chapter 7). If this conjecture is valid, perhaps Caravaggio's astonishing recoveries from his psychotic episodes were facilitated by his continuing opportunities to practice his art.

Judging by Caravaggio's example, a paranoid monster may also func-tion as a creative genius if his psychotic episodes occur only under special circumstances of stress or, to put it differently, if his lapses into violence or sadistic malevolence are not the predominant mode of his behavioral organization. Perhaps, in this sense, Caravaggio is easier to understand than other gifted creators whose paranoid attitudes were more persistent. Yet, a Richard Wagner, who probably fits this alternative pattern, was able to effect a better overall adaptation than Caravaggio by focusing his paranoid hatred quite narrowly on a single issue, which subsequently gained expression in his genocidal fantasies about the Jews. Whatever the roots of this delusional system in the composer's earlier experience, it was apparently walled off from the rest of his mental life. As Peter Gay (1978) has noted, Wagner was able to fulminate against the Jewish menace, especially as it threatened "German" music, at the same time as he engaged a Jewish conductor, Hermann Levi, to oversee the premiere of *Parsifal*—only savagely to assault the man with anti-Semitic slurs throughout the enterprise.

Such internal incoherence betokens the individual's unwillingness to consider the totality of his personal aims; at any specific time, one portion or another of his mutually incompatible goals must be disavowed.

Defenses of this kind lead to what is often called "splitting" of the mind—
a metaphor that vividly conveys the price paid for failing to reconcile
conflicting mental dispositions. I assume that chronic paranoid attitudes
may occasionally be maintained in isolation through the use of massive
disavowal, thereby safeguarding creative functions from contamination
by psychotic ideation. More frequently, "the disavowed" continuously
threatens to permeate the individual's entire psychic life, and additional
precautions must be taken to avoid such catastrophic eventualities.

The fact that such defenses are essential to the preservation of the
artist's aesthetic power was conclusively demonstrated over four decades
ago by Ernst Kris (in 1952, Chapter 3). Although he conceded the
possibility of a continuum of transitional forms, he insisted that psychotic
ideation always contains a core of impenetrable meaning and therefore
fails in the crucial communicative dimension of art. Kris illustrated his
thesis with the example of a minor 18-century sculptor, F. X. Messerschmidt (1952, Chapter 4) who partially recovered in his mid-30s from a
psychotic illness characterized by confusion. He was not only able to
resume work despite the persistence of chronic paranoid delusions but
retained his considerable skill as a portraitist; the public works he produced always maintained a high artistic level. After his illness, however,
Messerschmidt turned increasingly to the production of grimacing self-
portrait busts with a bizarre private meaning. In the majority of these
works, as Kris has observed, "a comprehensible expression has not been
achieved" (p. 136). These images were apparently part of the sculptor's
delusional world. Moreover, Kris points out that the private meanings of
these works were not integrated with their overall structure in any
coherent manner.

VI

IN CONCLUSION, I would like to allude briefly to the work of a
very great painter—one fully comparable to Caravaggio in stature—who
was able to achieve the utmost in his art in the face of chronic paranoia by
limiting his subject matter to themes that did not touch upon his "complexes." I am referring to Paul Cézanne,[5] whose bizarre personal difficulties have been amply documented by his biographers (e.g., Lindsay,

5. It would take us too far afield to attempt to justify fully the claim that Cézanne was
chronically paranoid in his adult life. For purposes of my argument, I trust the reader will
take this clinical judgment on faith. But lest an assertion that may sound pejorative to the
layman deter readers from bearing with me in the following discussion, I offer the following
highlights from the available evidence. Consider the account of Cézanne's character by his
childhood friend, Emile Zola: "The painter was about as illogical in his ideas and behavior
as one could be. . . . The stubbornest of men . . . age and experience have not changed

1969). Although Cézanne struggled to solve artistic problems of the most difficult kind, his productivity was extraordinary—despite the fact that he allowed many of his works to be destroyed, we possess over 800 of his paintings alone. We might fruitfully contrast this uninterrupted stream of creativity with the inability of a very similar personality, Michelangelo Buonarroti, to complete any of the sculptural projects of his maturity, probably because the very process of carving in marble awakened his megalomanic propensities (Sterba & Sterba, 1956).

Cézanne's early work was undoubtedly powerful, but it was frequently clumsy and charged with raw violence, often in a sexual context. From the first, however, his landscapes and still lifes, as well as his portraits of familiars (people who presumably did not make him too anxious) were better resolved or, if you will, more successful. Judging by Cézanne's panic when confronted by a nude female model, his anxieties about the loss of impulse control were very great. Apparently the task of figure painting called forth similar sadistic propensities; yet Cézanne was obsessively drawn to such themes as perverse orgies, rapes, and murders (Figure 35). Around the age of 32, the artist came into contact with Camille Pissarro, a slightly older painter of gentle and modest disposition who was a superb teacher. Pissarro managed to avoid provoking Cézanne's usual paranoid response to those who tried to help him; the older man proceeded to give him sound advice about his techniques and firmly guided him into an area where his skill was the greatest: compositions done directly in front of his motif in its physical actuality (Figures 36 and 37).

Pissarro, in other words, succeeded in teaching Cézanne to avoid the subject matter of his own bizarre fantasy life. In the long series of *Bathers* executed throughout his later career, Cézanne treated the human figure almost as an abstract element of the landscape (Figure 38); after his mid-30s, he never undertook compositions with violent or overtly sexual

---

him at all. . . . Sensitive and easily offended, touchy and hot tempered, he ha[d] to be handled with extreme care" (in Niess, 1968, p. 93).

To cite but one illustration of Cézanne's *idées fixes*, when Zola published his immensely popular novel, *Nana*, in 1880, the painter feared the book would be ignored by the press as a result of an organized conspiracy (see Lindsay, 1969, p. 203). An even clearer instance of Cézanne's tendency to respond in a paranoid manner is the account of a luncheon Monet generously organized in his honor in 1894. In the presence of Renoir, Sisley, and other close friends, Monet toasted him by expressing personal affection and admiration for his work: "Paul stared at him in consternation and answered in a voice shaken with regrets and reproaches, 'You too are making fun of me,' snatched his overcoat, and rushed off" (in Lindsay, 1969, p. 253).

I believe Cézanne's conviction that his father was a man of tyrannical character may have been delusional as well; Paul was "afraid" to ask him for money although Cézanne *père* had legally given him his inheritance and merely served as the painter's banker in handling the estate (Lindsay, 1969, p. 178).

Figure 35. Paul Cézanne, *A Modern Olympia*, c. 1872. Oil on canvas. Musée d'Orsay, Paris.

Figure 36. Paul Cézanne, *Village Panorama*, 1873–1875. Oil on canvas. Collection of The Art Institute of Chicago.

Figure 37. Paul Cézanne, *Madame Cézanne in a Yellow Rocking Chair*, 1890–1894. Oil on canvas. Collection of The Art Institute of Chicago, Wilson L. Mead Fund.

Figure 38. Paul Cézanne, *The Bathers*, 1900–1905. Oil on canvas. Collection of The Art Institute of Chicago, gift of Colonel R. R. McCormick.

content. To put this in a different way, the emotional power that had characterized Cézanne's early subject matter became focused in his mature work on the formal aspects of his compositions. If the human figures in these paintings seem reduced to the role of architectonic elements, Cézanne's trees, hills, houses, or kitchen paraphernalia became vibrant symbols of an anthropomorphic universe. Cézanne's change of direction in mid-life turned him from an interesting eccentric into the seminal painter of our age. Insightfully, he came to boast that he painted with his balls, but we have ample reason to suspect that this amazing feat was contingent on the absence of sexual stimulation with the attendant risk of psychotic outbursts.

To recapitulate: A paranoid monster may create works of genius provided his psychosis can be localized—either isolated temporally, as in Caravaggio's case, or organized into a discrete delusional system, as in Wagner's. In still other instances—one thinks of Gauguin, Cézanne, and perhaps the first Michelangelo—a chronically paranoid artist can execute works of the highest order when neither the medium nor the subject matter impinges on his delusional world.

Chapter Ten

On the Lamentations of Doctor Faustus

I

IN HIS RETROSPECTIVE account of a creative lifetime, the elderly Thomas Mann condensed his own story with the biographies of the most eminent artists and thinkers of his people, conceived as one figure, the composer Adrian Leverkühn. Mann represents the creative gifts of genius through the symbol of Leverkühn's Faustian bargain with the forces of darkness. At the same time, he borrows from mythology the theme of the destruction of the would-be artist by the poisoned arrows of jealous Apollo. More concretely, he characterizes the consequence of commitment to the creative act as inevitable frustration of the need for human intimacy. This fate leads the great creator to concentrate on the subject of emotional suffering in his most significant works. Hence Mann entitles Leverkühn's supreme composition, *The Lamentations of Doctor Faustus*.

As I have observed in Chapter 1, psychoanalytic studies of genius have tended to focus on the biographies of manifestly depressive personalities such as Beethoven or van Gogh or on those of others, like Leonardo da Vinci and Goethe, who had significant difficulties in their personal relationships. Thus, these studies collectively suggest that Mann's portrayal of the creative personality might well serve as a general prototype. Such a conclusion has been made explicit by K. R. Eissler (1967), who assumes that genius and psychosis necessarily bear many common features—homologies particularly likely to surface during adolescence and whenever the great creator is deprived of the opportunity to exercise his gifts.

A previous version of this material appeared in *American Imago*, 35:77–91, 1978.

I have strong reservations about the universality of Eissler's characterization of greatness because I believe the hypothesis he propounds is based on circular reasoning; he and other proponents of this viewpoint deliberately choose overtly disturbed personalities as the subjects of their pathobiographical investigations and then, disregarding their original (legitimate) rationale for these choices, take their results as a meaningful commentary about genius in general. Ironically, the psychobiographies most solidly grounded in reliable data, those devoted to the life of Freud (e.g., Jones, 1953, 1955, 1957; Eissler, 1971; Schur, 1972; Gedo & Pollock, 1976), have had minimal impact in tempering this sampling error.

As I have outlined in Chapter 6, my clinical work has led to the conclusion that the lamentations of a Doctor Faustus may be evoked by the need in adult life to repeat certain crucial childhood transactions with the caretakers—traumatic repetitions of derailed dialogues within the mother–child dyad. These early misfortunes appear to result from the difficulties inherent in responding appropriately to the peculiarities of a highly gifted child, whatever adventitious factors may also be involved. In Thomas Mann's terms, Apollo's fatal arrows are propelled from the maternal bow. And the most striking example of this etiology is the life of Friedrich Nietzsche, generally conceded to be one of the principal models for the figure of Mann's Leverkühn.

Although a number of excellent biographies of Nietzsche are available in English (e.g., Jaspers, 1935; Hollingdale, 1965; Kaufmann, 1968, 1980a), these works focus, without exception, on the philosopher's intellectual progress. Scattered insights about one or another of Nietzsche's personal traits are offered by most of the scholars who write about him, but no coherent portrait of Nietzsche has been attempted that rivals Thomas Mann's literary depiction. Moreover, the standard biographies do not even summarize the scanty information about Nietzsche's childhood and adolescence that can be gleaned from his autobiographical writings and his sister's unreliable account of his life (Förster-Nietzsche, 1912, 1914). If I am in a position to offer a reinterpretation of the biographical evidence in line with insights I have reached in clinical work with personalities I take to be essentially similar to Nietzsche, I owe this good fortune to an opportunity I had to serve as consultant for an interdisciplinary project involving a psychoanalytic colleague and a historian (see Pletsch, 1977; Moraitis, 1979). This project focused on the latter's dissertation research into Nietzsche's psychology.

Unless otherwise noted, the historical data in this chapter have been taken from Pletsch's unpublished dissertation, although my view of the psychological significance of these data is substantially different from that of Pletsch. As I understand these data, Nietzsche's psychological development exemplifies the organization of a vulnerable personality that has experienced unfortunate transactions with the caretakers of early child-hood. As a result of these transactions, Nietzsche became a person poorly suited for interpersonal intimacy; in adult life, he was prone to suffer deeply because of his loneliness. In sum, his case illuminates the inter-connections between genius and the genesis of psychopathology in a particularly lucid manner.

II

FRIEDRICH WILHELM NIETZSCHE'S adult life began with star-tling suddenness when, at the age of 24, he was appointed Professor of Classical Philology at the University of Basel in 1869. It ended abruptly 20 years later, when the productive, mature philosopher lapsed into irreversible psychosis, almost certainly as a consequence of cerebral dam-age. In the interval, Nietzsche led an increasingly lonely existence, main-taining contact with a few loyal friends and disciples, mostly by corre-spondence.[1] A profound rift had developed between Nietzsche and the members of his family as a result of their refusal to believe that his interest in Lou Salomé, a beautiful and seductive young woman, was entirely proper—that is, Platonic in the original sense of a shared enthusiasm for philosophy. As Binion has shown (1968), Fräulein Salomé also ruined her relationship with Nietzsche by bursting out with open accusations that he intended to exploit her sexually—slanders probably based on the projection of her lifelong propensity to misuse men. At any rate, in the face of Lou's recurrent erotomanic delusions, Nietzsche felt compelled to withdraw from the woman who had cost him the goodwill of his mother and younger sister Elisabeth. The last seven years of his creative life were spent in complete emotional isolation, except for occasional expressions of interest in Nietzsche's work on the part of a very small number of discerning readers. In his poetry, Nietzsche was able to describe the consequences of this situation in the most moving manner:

> Ten years have passed—not a drop of water has reached me,
> no moist wind, no dew of love—a *rainless* land . . .

---

1. Most important in this regard was the church historian Franz Overbeck, with whom Nietzsche shared a house for a number of years in Basel. Jaspers (1935, p. 79) has astutely noted that this friendship endured because Overbeck remained personally reliable and kind to Nietzsche, but the men meant nothing more to each other. The other person whose loyalty endured was Nietzsche's amanuensis, Peter Gast, a resident of Venice who made himself available to the philosopher practically on demand. Jaspers (p. 58) correctly points out that Nietzsche enveloped this untalented man in illusion, believing him a composer superior to Wagner, in order to provide himself with a surrogate for everything of which he had been deprived.

ON THE LAMENTATIONS OF DOCTOR FAUSTUS

Now I ask my wisdom not to grow niggardly in this aridity:
you yourself must overflow, you yourself must shower down dew,
you yourself must be rain for this yellowed wilderness!

(translated in Hollingdale, 1965, p. 278)

As this statement shows, Nietzsche was keenly aware of his loneliness and suffering. Yet in his spiritual autobiography of 1888 he alluded to this aspect of his existence only indirectly by choosing a title that referred to the Passion of Christ: *Ecce Homo*. His correspondence reveals that he was in any case determined to persist in his withdrawal from human intimacy in order to safeguard his productivity. Overexposure to people who were important to Nietzsche severely aggravated his chronic migraine[2]—a fact he first discovered in the context of his relationship with Richard Wagner. Throughout the 1870s, Wagner's espousal of the nationalism of imperial Germany and promotion of a cult around his own person became increasingly intolerable to the young philosopher, and Nietzsche ended up attacking the great composer in print as the representative of a hopeless culture (see Jaspers, 1935, p. 66).

His disappointment in Wagner deprived Nietzsche of his only direct contact with a creative genius of his own stature, a person who might have been able to empathize with the awesome frustrations of the undiscovered and unappreciated artist in Nietzsche because of analogous experiences in his own past. However, Nietzsche made no direct reference to the personal meaning of his loss in subsequent polemics against everything Wagner had come to represent. We must therefore turn to a parallel instance, such as Vincent van Gogh's fervent hope for artistic brotherhood with Paul Gauguin, to gain some impression of the nature of Nietzsche's needs toward Wagner and to begin to grasp how deeply their rupture must have wounded him. Although Nietzsche did not enact this drama through self-mutilation and a portrayal of himself tragically swathed in bandages—as van Gogh would do exactly 10 years later—he did express his reactions in poetry of great, concentrated power:

Not long will you thirst,
burnt out heart!

2. The significance of Nietzsche's incapacitating headaches has been assessed in various ways by his biographers. Walter Kaufmann (1980a, p. 79) understood them as somatized reflections of the psychic pain caused by the insights Nietzsche achieved in his work. Karl Jaspers (1935, p. 95), himself a psychiatrist, also questioned the diagnosis of migraine. Nonetheless, I am inclined to favor the diagnosis on the basis of Nietzsche's report that periods of intense work brought on his attacks (see Hollingdale, 1965, p. 144). My clinical experience has led me to the conclusion that vascular headaches such as migraines are triggered by overstimulation and can be avoided if the patient carefully monitors his or her tension levels and makes appropriate behavioral adjustments to control them.

A promise is in the air,
from unknown lips it blows at me
—the great chill comes.
(translated in Kaufmann, 1962, p. 155)

Faustus, it would seem, is condemned to an icy hell!

To be sure, Nietzsche had no illusions about his vulnerability. Shortly after his rupture with Lou Salomé, when he felt himself on the verge of insanity, he was able to preserve his integration by consciously avoiding further encounters pregnant with false promises. When his progressive brain disease led to a sudden and total fragmentation of his personality, Nietzsche developed a series of megalomanic delusions, a characteristic reaction to such catastrophic losses of mental capacity (see Ferenczi & Hollós, 1922). The last vestige of Nietzsche's blasted hopes for human closeness was the pathetic message he subsequently sent to Wagner's widow, Cosima: "Ariadne, I love you—Dionysus."[3]

Nietzsche's resignation about his isolation from his fellow men merely confirmed him in a condition of which he was quite aware even as a schoolboy. Morgan (1941, p. 9) has stressed that, by the time he was 7, Nietzsche knew "that never a human word would reach me." Despite his self-conscious reticence, Nietzsche was able to conceal his isolation from those who did not share his intellectual preoccupations through a show of affability. This mask of social ease had been especially prominent in the months between Nietzsche's discharge from the Prussian army, following a severe riding accident, and his university appointment at Basel. Perhaps this unusually sunny interval reflected Nietzsche's joy at having finally found his vocation during the months of enforced idleness when

3. This avowal has generally been interpreted (e.g., Kaufmann, 1968, pp. 33–34; Pletsch, 1977) as a failure of repression that permitted Nietzsche's oedipal love for Cosima to resurface. I suspect that such a view is both too simple and too optimistic about the nature of Nietzsche's eccentricity. Kaufmann reports (1968, p. 32) that when Nietzsche was hospitalized, he stated, "My wife Cosima Wagner brought me here" (March 27, 1889). I would interpret this remark as revealing Nietzsche's delusion at the time that he was Richard Wagner (presumably not the despised figure the composer had become in Bayreuth but the idealized alter ego of the years of their intimacy). As for Nietzsche's megalomania, he at that point saw himself as the "successor to the dead God" (Jaspers, 1935, p. 88): He was not only Dionysus but "the Crucified" as well, a combination of the entities he had described as struggling for world dominance in the last line of *Ecce Homo*. Thus, the personal qualities Nietzsche had tried to overcome in repudiating his Christian origins ultimately returned from repression to coexist in chaotic internal contradiction with the person he had tried to become. In this way, the letter to Cosima expresses Nietzsche's frustrated hope that Wagner would become a modern Dionysus, not his erotic feeling for his widow. (It is also relevant that Wagner had made Cosima his mistress while she was still married to another man: Was it her first husband, von Bülow, whom Nietzsche equates with Theseus, Ariadne's mortal spouse?) It should also be borne in mind that, as a child, Nietzsche had idealized his dead father but resented his mother (cf. Kaufmann, 1968, p. 33). The implications of these attitudes are discussed below.

he was convalescing from his injuries. Immobilized by his injury so that his activities were confined to his own thinking, he had discovered his extraordinary capability for productive thought about philosophical matters. Of course, Nietzsche's happiness may also have resulted from the profound respect his professors and fellow students showed at the time for his dazzling capacities as a classicist. This positive response is exemplified by the fact that, for Nietzsche, the University of Leipzig waived the usual requirement of writing a dissertation to obtain the doctorate. Thus, it is clear that, at a later stage, in turning away from his academic specialty in order to pursue his original creative aims, Nietzsche was quite willing to forego not only human closeness but the enthusiastic acceptance of a significant public as well.

A few years earlier, when Nietzsche was a first-year student of theology at the University of Bonn, his attempts to avoid isolation by erecting a facade of ordinariness still possessed a clumsy and forced quality. He went through the motions of joining a fraternity and participating in its empty-headed carousing. Little wonder that he left Bonn at the end of the year to embark on his brief and intense academic career elsewhere. Although it has occasionally been assumed that Nietzsche contracted syphilis during this period of student debauchery, this diagnosis is based on insufficient evidence: inconclusive statements Nietzsche made after his mental collapse and records of his receiving antiluetic treatment as a student.

Although the possibility of central nervous system lues cannot be ruled out, of course, it is also possible that Nietzsche's brain disease was degenerative and familial. It should be recalled in this connection that his father had died of cerebral atrophy at the age of 35. On the basis of my understanding of Nietzsche's personality, I am also inclined to lend credence to the anecdote Thomas Mann incorporated into *Doctor Faustus* about the adolescent Nietzsche: When he blundered into the parlor of a bordello, the boy was apparently paralyzed by that strange world; he was able to flee after coming to his senses upon striking a familiar chord on the obligatory piano! The source of this story, Nietzsche's schoolmate Paul Deussen, was convinced that the future philosopher had never engaged in sexual relations.

Indeed, poor Nietzsche must have been a very strange schoolboy. His posturing as a roué was paralleled by his enrollment as a student of theology, a choice clearly dictated by family tradition rather than a personal belief in Christianity. And his next commitment, the study of classical philology at Leipzig, amounted to no more than a temporizing extension of his years at Schulpforta, the outstanding humanistic preparatory school where Nietzsche had spent his middle adolescence.

It is highly significant that the greatest intellectual influence Nietzsche encountered as a university student was the work of Arthur Schopenhauer,

which he discovered entirely on his own. Pletsch (1977) has explained
the effect of Nietzsche's self-styled discipleship toward Schopenhauer as
a revision in his system of ideals. I believe Pletsch's argument is a correct
extension of a model I once proposed to characterize Freud's adolescence
(see Gedo & Wolf, 1970, 1973; Wolf, Gedo, & Terman, 1972): Pletsch
views Nietzsche's enthusiasm for Schopenhauer as an idealization that
eventually led to an identification with his professional aims without
permanent acceptance of any of his substantive positions. Kaufmann
(1980a, p. 9) also believes that in Schopenhauer Nietzsche had seen his
own ideal self.

It must have been the capacity to live up to Schopenhauer's philosophical ideals that Nietzsche discovered in himself when his military service
temporarily suspended his philological labors. And it was the shared
idealization of Schopenhauer that led Nietzsche into his most meaningful
and mutual friendship, his relationship with his colleague Erwin Rohde.
Although at one point the friends described themselves as the Dioscuri,
the twins Castor and Pollux, this intimacy also proved to be impermanent
—Nietzsche could not reconcile himself to Rohde's disapproval of his
later work (see Jaspers, 1935, pp. 59–60).

But the fact is that the crystallization of Nietzsche's identity as an
original thinker, based on the example of a great predecessor, seems to
have enabled him to bear the dreadful costs of his creative endeavors. We
should keep in mind, moreover, that Schopenhauer had died in 1860—
just a few years before Nietzsche was inspired by his example; that he
was primarily concerned with moral and psychological issues—as
Nietzsche would be; and that he had no friends, never married, and was
estranged from his formidable mother. Did Nietzsche's identification
with this man shape his subsequent destiny, or was it based on an
intuitive understanding of their common personal characteristics?

In certain autobiographical comments dating back to his adolescence,
Nietzsche stressed his need for paternal guidance, a need that had only
been met, prior to his discovery of a professional progenitor in Schopenhauer, by the impersonal authority of his school. He received a scholarship
to Schulpforta at the age of 14; despite the fact that the institution was
within walking distance of his family's domicile in Naumburg, Nietzsche
suffered from severe homesickness during the first two years of his
attendance. He made incessant demands on his mother in urgent and
imperious tones, requesting visits, letters, and material supplies. He was
still more aggressive in pressuring two childhood friends, Wilhelm Pinder
and Gustav Krug, for contacts that would perpetuate their relationship as
it existed before Nietzsche's departure for boarding school. His biographers generally describe the future genius at this time of his life as old
for his years—*altklug*—and schoolmasterish; his teachers and fellow students later remembered him as too serious and introverted. He was never

interested in girls, nor did he engage in an "affectionate" relationship with any schoolmate. Despite his loneliness and discomfort, Nietzsche greatly appreciated the discipline and intellectual rigor of the school.

In his 17th year, Nietzsche seems to have made a unique effort to shed his own character, thus to revolt against his natural destiny. He briefly joined a number of students in rebellion against the exacting discipline of Schulpforta, going as far as to get intoxicated in public. This episode of rebellion lasted less than two months. Paul Deussen, the classmate at school who knew Nietzsche best, had the impression that the studious introvert derived no satisfaction from such pranks and soon returned to his scholarly proclivities. We might view the fragment of a projected novel, the only survivor of Nietzsche's extensive output of fiction during adolescence, in a similar light. Entitled *Euphorion*, after the son of Faust and Helen of Troy in Goethe's drama, the piece seems calculated to shock, dealing as it does with themes of brother–sister incest, murder, sacrilege, and so on. But beyond the gothic details, presumably included *pour épater les bourgeois*, one is most impressed with the fact the Euphorion, in gaining knowledge, grows "tired of himself"! The lamentations of Faustus are already to be heard: The protagonist's subjective experience is unbearable.

The only part of his past that Nietzsche actually shed during adolescence was his Christian faith, a change that occurred after his confirmation at the age of 17. From a contemporary perspective—largely molded by Nietzsche's own philosophy of radical individualism—it may be easy to underestimate the magnitude of this act of independence. But the conclusion of a profoundly religious person like Nietzsche that God is dead must be seen in the context of his familial circumstances (cf. Morgan, 1941, p. 36): His father and maternal grandfather were both Lutheran ministers, a traditional vocation in the Nietzsche family. Moreover, the 5-year-old Nietzsche had responded to the death of his father with a massive identification with the latter that earned him the nickname "the little pastor." He often recited scriptural passages and religious hymns with intense feeling, and in middle childhood he wrote stories and composed music on religious themes.

Nietzsche's family and friends were by no means oblivious to the peculiarities of the child—indeed, his boyhood companion Wilhelm Pinder perceived Friedrich's melancholy character when they were both 14 years of age! His grandfather, Pastor Oehler, worried about the boy who was being raised by a household of women: mother, sister, paternal grandmother, and aunts. Friedrich's mother, totally devoted to the care of her children, was quite concerned with his excessive seriousness, his preference for solitude, and his perfectionistic adherence to standards he had adopted even in the face of ridicule—in short, she was concerned for the lack of boyish playfulness in the child. In the autobiography he wrote at 14, Nietzsche himself attributed these character traits to the effect of the loss of his father. Whatever their source, Franziska Nietzsche saw her son's difference from other children as a defect, and she experienced his perfectionism as a sign of willfulness. Fortunately, in this dilemma she turned to her own father for guidance, and Pastor Oehler wisely counseled her to allow this unique personality to develop without interference. According to Nietzsche's sister, the grandfather explicitly recognized that Friedrich's peculiarities were harbingers of his genius. Although Elisabeth Nietzsche is notoriously unreliable as a witness, her claim in this regard may have some validity. She reports that during the summers spent at Pastor Oehler's, Friedrich would take long walks with his grandfather when they would engage in serious conversations on adult topics (cited in Pletsch, 1977). In his adolescent autobiography, moreover, Nietzsche himself reported: "Most of all I liked to hole up in grandfather's study and prowl around in the old books and papers; that was my greatest pleasure" (quoted in Pletsch, 1977, Chapter 3, pp. 8–9).

Actually, the boy's isolation was not complete; beginning with his second year of school, when he was transferred to a small private institution of high standards, he gained the loyalty of Wilhelm Pinder and Gustav Krug, and he led these two companions in joint creative endeavors and elaborate games of his invention. Admittedly, Pinder and Krug later reported that, on Nietzsche's side, the friendship was based less on spontaneous feeling than on an ideal. For his own part, Pinder regarded Nietzsche as a model in all things. When they were 16, the three boys formed a literary and musical fraternity, the Germania, by formally swearing allegiance to each other. Parenthetically, this is one significant respect in which the adolescent Nietzsche prefigures the adolescent Freud who founded the secret "Academia Castellana" with similar aims (see Gedo & Wolf, 1973).

This *Brüderschaft* was a rather clear predecessor of the intellectual trios Nietzsche was to form, first with Richard and Cosima Wagner, then with Lou Salomé and Paul Rée. On the other hand, it was preceded by an even more important relationship that retained its vitality well into Nietzsche's adulthood: his assumption of intellectual authority over his sister as her educator, her *Erzieher*. To what degree this educational role involved taking over functions previously performed by their father, we do not know. At any rate, Elisabeth's eager compliance must have been a sign of the profound needs fulfilled by her brother's activities. It is scarcely surprising, then, that she proved unable to tolerate being supplanted by Lou Salomé and that rupture with her brother should curdle her personality permanently. From Nietzsche's vantage point, both Elisabeth and his friends Wilhelm and Gustav must have served the vital function of an appreciative audience, much as brother Theo was to do for Vincent van Gogh.

This interpretation is confirmed by Elisabeth's account of the role she had been assigned in their favorite game, called "the domain of king squirrel." Although she was expected to assist in manipulating the props, her main function in this miniaturized theater was to serve as part of the public at the cultural events staged by Friedrich at the king's court. Concerts of his music, performances of his plays, exhibits of his paintings —Nietzsche executed all these things before his admiring sister in settings of his own design. Could the young boy have been aware of Goethe's activities 75 years earlier in Weimar, only 20 miles away? We do not know the answer, but it is certainly tempting to conclude that, given Friedrich's early proclivities, Franziska Nietzsche had been eminently correct in overcoming her own inclinations and moving with her late husband's people from the *Gemütlichkeit* of her father's country parsonage to the stimulating ambience of Naumburg.

We possess one piece of evidence about Nietzsche's emotional reaction to his father's death, a dream he recorded in his autobiography almost a decade later. To the accompaniment of funeral music, his father's grave opened, the dead man climbed out, entered the church, and returned with a child under his arm. He then descended into the grave, which closed over him as the dreamer awakened. Nietzsche allegedly never forgot this dream because it immediately preceded the sudden death of his little brother Joseph and was thereby regarded as a premonition fulfilled: The toddler was literally buried in the arms of his father. Whether the dream actually antedated Joseph's death or was stimulated by this event, one of its multiple meanings must surely have been Friedrich's wish to be reunited with his father—a wish unconsciously gratified by the child's pronounced identification with the dead man. Moreover, whatever the original form of the dream when Nietzche was 5, the written transcription of it at age 14 was surely informed by the boy's familiarity with Goethe's *Erlkönig*—perhaps even in Schubert's setting—with its mood of intense grief about the death of a child and longing for reunion.

In my judgment, then, we are justified in accepting Nietzsche's statements about his character having been shaped principally by the loss of his father, and we may also assume that unconsciously Ludwig Nietzsche had been his first idealized *Erzieher*. In Nietzsche's life, phallic competitiveness forever took the form of intellectual striving, specifically, efforts at moral persuasion through sermons, poetry, and music. Friedrich's basic ideal, eventually personified in his fictive *Doppelgänger* Zarathustra, was that of the prophet.[4] We should recall that in the psychotic state to

4. Kaufmann (1980a, p. 128) attempts to deny that Nietzsche was in actuality a prophet on the grounds that his philosophy is utterly devoid of dogma. But Kaufmann seems alone in this judgment. Jaspers (1935, p. 21) best resolves the question Kaufmann raises by pointing out that Nietzsche is the prophet who, unlike all other prophets, refers the seeker to his own inner being: "Psychological analysis becomes the medium of his philosophizing"

which he finally succumbed, he felt reincarnated as Dionysus. One of his last correspondents, August Strindberg, empathically grasped the import of Nietzsche's delusions, first responding as if these claims of omnipotence had been put forth with irony by signing his own message, *Deus optimus, maximus* [the supreme, almighty God]. When Nietzsche replied by escalating his divine pretensions, as if in competition with this rival god, Strindberg urged moderation by quoting Horace: "To live wisely, shun the deep sea"—and then, recognizing Nietzsche's definitive loss of self-mastery, broke off with the Greek verse: "In the meantime, let us enjoy being mad together!"

It would seem, then, that Nietzsche's incapacity to form lasting and close relationships in adult life was merely an extension of the personality organization that crystallized around the time of his father's death—a mode of organization which froze, as it were, as a result of a lack of external assistance. In the language of contemporary developmental psychology, we might say that, although Nietzsche was 5 years old when his development became arrested, he does not appear to have reached the expectable mode of the oedipal phase at the time. He was nonetheless able to adapt more or less successfully because he managed to turn his manner of reacting to his father into its opposite in all subsequent human contacts: From being symbiotically dependent on an *Erzieher*, he became the obligatory *Erzieher* of others.

We know very little about the possible antecedents that may have skewed Nietzsche's early object relations, although the frequency of similar dependence on a benign father is startling in the biographies of great men—so much so that it may well be one expectable path for their development. I have already discussed the fact that Pablo Picasso was quite unable to function without his father during his years as a schoolboy and scarcely overcame this symbiotic need until his late adolescence (see Chapter 7 and M. Gedo, 1980a). In this sense, Nietzsche may have fared as badly as he did because nobody was able to serve as a suitable replacement for his father. He seemed compelled to repeat this loss over and over again throughout his life, from his premature departures from the universities at Leipzig and Basel to his ruptures with Wagner, Lou Salomé, Elisabeth, and his mother. Doubtless, it was in part introspective effort that led Nietzsche to his concept of the "eternal recurrence."

(1935, p. 34). Jaspers stresses that Nietzsche's philosophical position would be traduced were he to acquire followers who "believed"; he quotes Nietzsche's disclaimer, "I am terribly afraid that some day I may be canonized" (1935, p. 22). At the very least, one must concur with Stern (1978, p. 100) who points out that Nietzsche consciously explicated the possibilities of "prophetic utterance." Personally, however, I agree with Morgan (1941, pp. 4–5) who sets Nietzsche apart from "minor prophets" who lack his "amplitude"—he was a major prophet indeed.

We can at present only conjecture on how Nietzsche's symbiotic needs become focused on his father. However, it is highly plausible to surmise that his seeming lack of erotic interest in women as an adolescent and an adult signified that he had turned away from his mother with a degree of finality seldom found in children, even those who experience the birth of two siblings within the first four years of life.[5] There is nothing in the descriptions of Franziska Nietzsche by any of her contemporaries, including Friedrich, that would lead one to predict such a derailment of her relationship to her son. It is highly unlikely that her relative failure as a primary caretaker would have occurred with an ordinary child. As it happens, we do know about the extraordinary burdens the young Nietzsche placed upon her and about the manner in which she attempted to meet them.

In her biography of Nietzsche, Elisabeth reports that the philosopher was slow in learning to talk—a circumstance confirmed in Nietzsche's adolescent autobiography. When he was about $2^{1}/_{2}$ years old, the family consulted their physician who concluded that the child was not motivated to put his wishes into words because his caretakers were ready to meet them in any case. A policy of frustrating the child unless he named the desired objects presented to him was instituted. Allegedly, the *first* word Friedrich proceeded to articulate was "Omamma," by way of asking for a *picture* of his grandmother. The contrast between the lack of verbalization and the advanced cognitive development implicit in recognizing a pictorial gestalt is indeed striking.[6]

5. It is difficult to assess the significance of the report (see Kaufmann, 1968, p. 34) that, after his collapse, Nietzsche asked for women when he was in the asylum. Whether such psychotic verbalizations reflected an actual sexual impulse, a delusional fantasy of the conduct to be expected from a Dionysus, or something even more bizarre can hardly be determined at this remove. Earlier biographers assumed that Nietzsche was sexually interested in the alluring Lou Salomé, but Binion (1968) has demonstrated that this view of the relationship was a fabrication put forth by Lou: She even spread the tale that Nietzsche asked Paul Rée to propose marriage to her on his behalf (also see Kaufmann, 1980a, p. 146). Significantly, Thomas Mann attributed Leverkühn's need to seek out prostitutes to an actual, if probably unconscious, wish to be infected with syphilis rather than to sexual desire. As Kaufmann points out (1968, p. 24), the very name Leverkühn, "he who lives audaciously," is an allusion to Nietzsche's philosophy. In this connection, Jaspers (1935, p. 74) reminds us that Nietzsche called himself a modern Philoctetes. This snake-bitten pariah, who was shunned for a decade by the Greeks besieging Troy, was a victim of Apollo. At the same time, he was also a sacred figure without whom the Trojan war could not be won. It is by no means beyond belief that Nietzsche, a passionate student of Greek mythology, could have enacted his identification with Philoctetes in the manner postulated by Thomas Mann.

6. It may not be superfluous to point out that the physician's diagnosis was preposterous. Language development is scarcely influenced by psychological dynamics of the kind he postulated: Human faculties hardly ever originate for utilitarian reasons. It should also be noted that the acquisition of language runs parallel with the comprehension of languages,

Pletsch (1977) has correctly inferred that the frustrating regime at the hands of his mother in his third year must have led Nietzsche to become an obstinate child—*starrköpfig* in family parlance. It may well have caused the boy to be disappointed in his formerly indulgent mother gravely enough to turn decisively toward his father. The fact that his sister Elisabeth was a young baby at the time, obviously requiring much of the mother's attention, would doubtless have facilitated such a change. Whatever the developmental actualities, one can hardly disagree with Jaspers' verdict: "One senses occasionally, like a shadow over [Nietzsche's] life, that his mother meant little to him in his heart" (1935, p. 77).

If we can take at face value the reported family tradition of making the child name what he desired, we can reasonably assume that Nietzsche's failure to utter a single word until forced to do so at $2\frac{1}{2}$ years aroused his mother's fears that she had a defective child. Indeed, such total absence of speech must be extremely unusual in unimpaired toddlers; the Nietzsches can hardly be faulted for their failure to realize that it was a sign of highly unusual cognitive capacities and not of some mental defect. Another family made a similar error with another genius—Albert Einstein—who continued to have difficulty putting his remarkably abstract thoughts into ordinary language well into middle childhood. Even the parents of Picasso, already aware of their son's artistic gifts, were unable to appreciate that his total inability to handle numbers resulted from his complete involvement with numerals as abstract designs—an aspect of genius as a draftsman rather than a deficiency in quantitative skills (M. Gedo, 1980a, p. 15). I believe that the mistaken judgment of parents about the worth of their atypical child is the source of that permanent defect in self-esteem that produces the lamentations of a Doctor Faustus. In terms of Nietzsche's nightmare at the age of 5, even his dead father preferred his brother Joseph, whom he embraced in his grave.

Ecce Homo, the Passion of Friedrich Nietzsche, is subtitled "How One Becomes What One Is." The poet already knew at 17 that he was a successor of Faust, a Euphorion; in the months following a premonitory episode of confusion (which preceded his collapse by less than a year), the climax of the philosopher's reactive outburst of creativity began with the plea: "*Above all, do not mistake me for someone else*" (1888, p. 217). Writing this intellectual self-portrait in his 44th year, Nietzsche defiantly expressed his gratitude for a life that had produced so many immortal

---

that is, Nietzsche's difficulty in communication must have extended to his parents' efforts to make themselves understood to the child. I have only encountered one instance of this kind in three decades of psychoanalytic practice, also involving a man of superior intellect, if one without the linguistic virtuosity of the mature Nietzsche. In that case, the early problems in communication also proved to have a devastating impact on the child's relationship to his parents.

works, and he went on to tell the world, in successive chapters, "Why I am so wise," "Why I am so clever," "Why I write such good books," and "Why I am a destiny." In equating his own greatness with his introduction of psychology into philosophy, Nietzsche also reiterated his insight into his own illness: "*Nausea* at man is my danger" (1888, p. 331).

III

HOW CAN WE summarize the implications of Nietzsche's life history for the relationship between genius and psychopathology? It would seem that his personality development was arrested by an overwhelming series of traumatic circumstances packed into a brief span of early childhood. His capacity for human intimacy was permanently impaired by these transactions, and there is reason to believe that he failed to develop expectable sexual interests in other people. "The great chill" had come before the age of 5. Yet his capacity to identify with his late father as a preacher and the richness of the creative play activities he organized shortly thereafter testify to the fact that Nietzsche's genius was already in evidence when he began his schooling. At first, his mother apparently could not grasp the favorable implications of the boy's fanatical commitment to his own enterprises, but she was assisted by her father's advice in adopting a more facilitating attitude. But we must not overestimate the extent of this shift; Nietzsche's mother, after all, never could learn to appreciate his actual contributions, however much she exploited his fame during the period of his tragic invalidism.

In adult life, the philosopher resigned himself to solitude after his disillusionment with Lou Salomé. Even if there was some validity to her suspicions that he harbored (surely unconsciously!) sexual feelings toward her, their emergence would have constituted the first return of an emotional tie to a woman since the rupture of Nietzsche's bonds to his mother during the third year of life—a resumption of development akin to the mobilization of an interrupted growth potential in psychoanalytic treatment (see Gedo, 1966, 1967; Gedo & Goldberg, 1973, pp. 135–149). The disappointment of his hopes for Lou confirmed Nietzsche in his posture of emotional aloofness. It is perfectly true, as Eissler has claimed in generalizing about the greatest creative minds, that his isolation made the philosopher more productive, but this result was only a consequence of his ability to manage attacks of incapacitating migraine more easily when he did not have to deal with other people.

It would seem, then, that Nietzsche's psychopathology was well portrayed by Mann through the figure of Leverkühn, even if Mann's implication that illness is a *necessary* by-product of such creative endeavors is false. On the contrary: An ill Nietzsche clearly found his only satisfaction in creative pursuits, and his pressing need to exercise his gifts must have arisen from this fact. As artist, philosopher, and secular prophet, he attempted to live up to the ideals he adopted from his father, from Schopenhauer, and probably from the revolutionary exile, Richard Wagner.

The misfortunes of his early childhood compelled Nietzsche eternally to repeat his traumatic disappointment in his mother. In this sense, his life history reflects that class of adaptive problems that lie "beyond the pleasure principle," as Freud put it in 1920 in the title of his most profound essay. Yet neither in childhood nor in any other period of his life did Nietzsche collapse in the face of a sea of troubles: His towering gifts can, in their turn, serve as prototypes for Phyllis Greenacre's thesis about the artist's recourse to "collective alternates" for the god that has failed (See Chapter 2).

Creativity as Prophecy: The Career of C. G. Jung

THE HISTORICAL studies that follow differ from those of the preceding section. Rather than focusing exclusively on the role of psychological factors in promoting or impeding the creative process, this material is also intended to clarify the role of the cultural context in these transactions. Interdisciplinary efforts by psychoanalysts generally underemphasize such issues; we not only tend to engage in psychological reductionism as a matter of professional preference, but we usually lack the requisite expertise in cultural history to wrestle with nonpsychological aspects of our subject matter. Perhaps not so incidentally, the same handicaps also diminish the power and cogency of our clinical case histories, for they are seldom grounded, as they ought to be, within a believable cultural matrix.

The major exception to the foregoing rule is the history of psychoanalysis itself in its varied aspects: as a succession of personalities; as an intellectual discipline; as a professional organization in the political arena. A steady trickle of historians manqués has sallied forth from our ranks to write about our discipline, and this literature on our psychoanalytic past is certainly familiar to every serious scholar within the field. Hence, in approaching creative activities in the psychoanalytic realm, I need hardly apologize for my excursions into the humanities: I have even had the joy of perusing unpublished documents, of providing the first commentaries on newly disclosed data, and of correcting certain false inferences drawn by previous scholarship (see my personal contributions to Gedo & Pollock, 1976).

In a volume on creativity, it therefore stands to reason that I am best able to demonstrate the interaction between the artist's subjectivity and his sociocultural circumstances by focusing on the subculture I know best, the psychoanalytic community. Within this context, I have chosen to discuss the career of one of the most creative individuals ever to enter the field, the Swiss psychiatrist Carl Gustav Jung. A man whose brilliant promise was widely recognized early in his career by Sigmund Freud among others, Jung participated in the Freudian enterprise for a few stormy years, only to become (for the reasons I shall elucidate below) the most celebrated defector from the psychoanalytic camp. He proceeded to found an independent therapeutic discipline with religious underpinnings, a discipline utterly different in its premises from psychoanalysis. Although Jung was extremely discreet about the religious nature of his psychology until he reached his ninth decade, he was very much aware of his identity as a prophet—he seemed to consider himself Nietzsche's successor inasmuch as he shouldered the burden of providing Western man with a modern belief system to replace Christianity.

Whatever our personal assessment of Jung's religious innovations may be (and we should keep in mind that it is very early indeed to render a historical verdict on his efforts, but see Homans, 1979), in my judgment there can be no question that his true vocation was prophetic, like that of van Gogh and Nietzsche. Compared to the original contributions he made after shedding the constraints of Freud's scientific humanism, Jung's efforts as a psychoanalytic apprentice were the prolific but uninspired scribblings of a bright student still searching for his proper field of activity. His example points to the fact that, within psychoanalysis, the mere possession of talent is never enough: It is necessary to share an intellectual and emotional commitment to a specific value system. In Chapter 11, I identify this value system of Western intellectual life as "the Socratic tradition," and I try to articulate the specific nature of Freud's personal commitment to this heritage as well as the manner in which it shaped its creative activities.

As the self-conscious heir of Nietzsche in using psychology for prophetic ends, C. G. Jung, that youthful native of Basel, gravitated toward psychiatry and was soon drawn into the orbit of the greatest psychologist of our era, Sigmund Freud. These men eagerly forged a *mésalliance*, each misled into false consensus by private hopes of having found a secret sharer who could be publicly acknowledged (cf. Kohut, 1976). The resulting disappointments were personally difficult for both protagonists, but much more so for the man at the threshold of his career, Jung, than for Freud, by then a world-famous professor in his mid-50s. As one might expect, the relationship had largely been structured on Freud's terms, and, as I attempt to demonstrate in Chapter 12, it provided an important stimulus for his creativity—even after the official rupture had taken place.

In Chapters 13 and 14, I review the climax of the Freud–Jung relationship, especially Jung's crisis of despair and renewal of hope after realizing that his need to erect Freud into a religious leader would be frustrated. This material could easily be understood by resorting to the conventional terminology of clinical diagnosis, but such an emphasis on Jung's psychopathological potential would be misguided. For Jung did not succumb to illness. Instead, he assumed the mantle of prophecy, thereby giving full scope to his creative potential. To be sure, this was not a *scientific* creativity, if we accept the conventional definition of science as systematized knowledge derived from observation and experiment (although, as Stepansky, 1976, has shown, Jung was interested in maintaining an empirical stance toward his experiences). Rather, Jung's immersion in occultism and magic, his certainty about his omniscience, and his gnostic reliance on his own experiences of the transcendental—these dimensions of his creative activity took him beyond the scientific pale and into the realm of religious innovation.

The last chapter in this section attempts to trace Jung's religious attitudes to some of their sources in his childhood experience. My conclusions about his case certainly confirm Jung's insistence that psychoanalytic theories reducing religious beliefs to derivatives of an infantile neurosis (i.e., to scars of the oedipal struggle) do not do justice to the facts. Of course, contemporary psychoanalysts generally hold considerably more sophisticated views about the genesis of religious beliefs (e.g., Rizzuto, 1980). But this fact notwithstanding, personalities shaped by familial influences analogous to Jung's would still have difficulty fitting themselves into the cultural context of the psychoanalytic community. Such difficulty does not boil down to the issue of religious faith versus scientific rationalism, even though the period of Freud's youth, dominated in this respect by the views of Feuerbach, frequently witnessed the erection of such a dichotomy. Science has its own set of *a priori* beliefs and commitments; Jung shared some of these beliefs (e.g., he adhered to the empirical position) but he rejected many others. As I will argue, his most decisive divergence from the Socratic tradition resided in his commitment to an essentially *pastoral* vocation.

If the lesson of Jung's flirtation with psychoanalysis is the sobering one that creativity is partly contingent on a social matrix able to nourish the specific kind of talent the artist has to offer, accelerating social change may actually bring to an end the centuries old dominance of the art of subjectivity, of the "journey into the interior" Erich Heller has detected in the work of the modern era. It hardly seems likely, however, that we face a classical renascence; indeed, it is very difficult to foresee the future of the humanities in the coming age of mass culture. In my Epilogue, I shall assess the position of the present-day artist in these changing cultural circumstances.

Chapter Eleven

Sigmund Freud and the Socratic Tradition

I

ONE OF THE PEAKS of the Athenian theater, Aristophanes's great comedy *The Clouds*, contains the earliest recorded attack on the ideal of a life dedicated to introspection. In his brilliant parody of the private encounters between Socrates and his students, Aristophanes provided a description that bears an uncanny resemblance to the setting of contemporary psychoanalysis.[1] A representative of the most conservative circles of the Athenian empire, Aristophanes disapproved of the Socratic goal of perpetual self-examination, although he may have been a personal friend of the philosopher. Paradoxically, his satire on the attempt to understand oneself turned into an accurate prediction of the judicial murder of Socrates at the hands of the Athenian democrats some 25 years later.

It is by no means certain that the passage of 25 centuries has taught mankind to distinguish more clearly between the actual aim of introspection, the unflinching examination of man's inner life as it is, and the goals Socrates was falsely accused of promoting, that is, the corruption of moral standards and other ideals. The self-preoccupation necessary for the introspective task has been accused of obstructing the dedication necessary to correcting undesirable social conditions. Hence contemporary conservatives still respond to psychoanalysis with suspicions echoing

1. Aristophanes mockingly named this school the "thinking shop" or "reflectory," and he characterized its students as unscrupulous delinquents who attend in order to learn rhetorical tricks to confute their creditors. When a young man-about-town applies his new learning to justify himself for reviling and beating his father, the latter burns down the thinking shop in revenge.

those of Aristophanes. Indeed, analysis has been the victim of judicial suppression at the hands of 20th-century popular democracies, especially those under Leninist rule, in which the sophisticated leadership is generally aware of the incompatibility of the ideals of the humanist tradition with those of their collectives. Even in America, many voices have condemned psychoanalysis as socially unconstructive and suggested that its practitioners should be encouraged or perhaps obliged to devote themselves to the solution of community problems.[2]

Did Sigmund Freud, founder of the modern introspective tradition embodied in psychoanalysis, consciously model himself on Plato's portrait of Socrates, as some of his Renaissance predecessors, the introspective humanists, had done? Strange to say, the question cannot be answered at present. In his formal autobiographical statements, Freud consistently disavowed any interest or expertise in philosophy. On the basis of surviving correspondence from his first year at the University of Vienna, however, we know that Freud's disclaimers on this score cannot be taken at face value. In fact, he had seriously considered supplementing his medical training with a degree in philosophy, and he had extensive personal contact with Franz von Brentano, the ranking philosophy professor at Vienna at the time (Gedo & Pollock, 1976, p. 13). Unfortunately, the records available to date do not reveal whether Freud's studies extended to Greek philosophy beyond the routine, superficial exposure to the subject at his secondary school, a classical gymnasium. At any rate, Freud's failure to comment on his adherence to the Socratic tradition and the paucity of references in his writings to either Plato or Socrates cannot be regarded as evidence on this score one way or the other.

At the same time, Freud did acknowledge his indebtedness to Athenian culture in a manner that was quite characteristic of his approach to intellectual life. He did so through his study of Sophocles, the tragedian who had transformed the Greek theater from enactments of dramatic rites

---

2. It may be in order to pause here to consider the meaning of the term "humanism." It designates a point of view focused on man himself, in contrast to the God-centered ethos of the European Middle Ages. From the vantage point of the Renaissance, this shift in perspective involved a return to the spirit of classical antiquity. But the application of the concept of humanism for developments prior to the 13th century is, in fact, anachronistic. In the intellectual life of the later middle ages, the *studia humanitatis* included poetry and rhetoric, history, and moral philosophy, with special emphasis on their classical sources. The specifically introspective bent of humanism is best illustrated by an anecdote about the great 14th-century Italian poet, Petrarch. While he stayed at the Papal court in Avignon, Petrarch climbed nearby Mt. Ventoux, taking the *Confessions* of St. Augustine along as reading matter. He abandoned mountaineering upon finding the following passage in the autobiography of the greatest psychologist of late antiquity: "Men go to admire the heights of the mountains, the great floods of the sea, the shores of the ocean, and the orbits of the stars, and neglect themselves" (see Kristeller, 1961, pp. 1–23, 84).

with primarily religious significance to portrayals of human psychology. In other words, Freud consistently displaced credit for his intellectual wellsprings from the realm of moral philosophy to that of art—in particular to the field of literature, with special emphasis on the drama. In implicit disagreement with Freud's attitude, I believe the arts of every era are permeated by recent advances in philosophy—or, if you will, that the tragedies of Sophocles and the educational procedures attributed to Socrates must have shared a common matrix in the thought of the previous generation. The thinkers of the age of Pericles, Anaxagoras in particular, had been on the verge of conceptualizing the human mind. And from a post-Freudian vantage point, it is appropriate indeed to interpret *Oedipus the King*, Sophocles's supreme achievement, as a morality play about the evil consequences of introspective failure.

II

WHATEVER DEGREE of skepticism we should preserve about Freud's professions of philosophical naiveté, study of his youthful letters amply confirms his predominant responsiveness to the appeal of literature (see Gedo & Wolf, 1970, 1973). It comes as no surprise that, in late adolescence, the authors whose works appear to have captured him most openly were some of the outstanding figures of one specific literary current. With some degree of license, it is legitimate to designate this type of literature as psychological. We must keep in mind, of course, that the list of Freud's favorites pertains to the early years of the 1870s, before the bountiful flowering of a literature explicitly concerned with man's psychology. Regarding my earlier assertion about the coterminous progression of philosophy and the arts, I see psychoanalysis and the literature of the past century as parallel developments, just as the contribution of Socrates and the sudden maturing of Athenian drama paralleled each other at the dawn of recorded Western thought. In any case, 100 years ago, a young psychological genius in search of idealizable models had turned to those psychological authors available to him: Cervantes, Shakespeare, Goethe, and Horace.

Before I undertake a more careful consideration of Freud's "modern" literary precursors, it may help to comment separately on the very interesting role of the Roman poet Horace—Quintus Horatius Flaccus—as one member of this quartet. In one sense, the fact that Horace exerted an important influence on Freud came about almost accidentally, in sharp contrast to the role of the other authors. Freud encountered Horace within the prescribed curriculum of his secondary school, whereas he discovered the others on his own. I believe that the boy destined to be a great German stylist acquired from this supreme master of Latin his aristocratic literary manners, his dominant tone of cultivated detachment and subtle irony. Freud derived the form of the bulk of his written production, that of the humanist letter, from the epistle, the favorite genre of Horace. And the content of the quasi-autobiographic verse in which Horace summed up the wisdom of the Augustan Age had confronted Freud for the first time with a person who devoted his entire adult life to self-examination. Incidentally, Horace had been eloquent in giving credit to Maecenas, the man who had made this life possible for him and whose name has therefore become synonymous with enlightened patronage.

I need only add that the Augustan literati exemplified by this "poet of sanity," as Horace has been justly called, were conscious heirs of Plato's Academy—although, to be sure, they were equally enthusiastic about other aspects of classical Greek culture as well. Because of the general loss of the ability to read Greek in the West before the Renaissance, the role of Roman followers such as Horace in transmitting Hellenic thought was extremely important. In fact, it was greater than the precision or depth of their understanding of the original sources might otherwise have warranted. Hence the Latin poet played a significant part in bridging the two millennia between the age of Socrates and the modern era. By the end of the 16th century, of course, Greek thought had once more been fully integrated by the European intellectual community. Thus a Shakespeare, who "had little Latin and less Greek," could study his Plutarch, for example, in adequate translation. For a man of the 19th century, such as Freud, there were innumerable channels for the reception of the Socratic tradition, and the role of Horace in this regard should not be overestimated.

On the other hand, we should not overlook the possibility that the influence of the Latin poet may have transcended the stylistic considerations I have cited or the countless explicit and unacknowledged quotations from his verse in Freud's writings. In our assessment of "On Transience," a vital document in the Freudian opus, for example, should we not recognize a prose version of Horace's autumnal lines: "Ah, how they glide by, Postumus, Postumus, The years, the swift years!" (*Odes*, book 2, #14)?

III

WITHIN THE CONFINES of this chapter, I cannot hope to substantiate the central relationship of specific works of Cervantes, Shakespeare, and Goethe to the tradition of humanist introspection. Nor has the actual influence of any of these great minds on Freud's life work been investigated systematically, however fascinating and important such studies would be. To invoke some idea of the probable import of these inspiring predecessors on Freud's development, let me only cite the fact that he began his reading of Shakespeare at the age of 8. One is tempted to conclude that this prodigious boy accomplished the leap from the parochialism of mid-19th-century Jewish life in the small towns of Eastern Europe to the forefront of 20th-century cosmopolitanism in one generation precisely with the help of such intellectual preceptors. As his correspondence reveals, by the time he had reached the age of 16 Freud had made his own a vast storehouse of Shakespearean ideas and phrases, largely in the original English; these acquisitions, moreover, were by no means confined to the better known plays. It should cause no surprise, then, that certain historians of Freud's intellectual development (e.g., Eissler, 1970) have concluded that his analysis of the Oedipus complex in *The Interpretation of Dreams* (1900) as the ambivalence of Hamlet toward both his parents was no mere illustrative device. Rather, they assume that Freud grasped the essence of this psychological configuration on the basis of what Shakespeare had taught him about it—or, if you will, Shakespeare and Sophocles in juxtaposition.

In the materials thus far made public, Freud has made no direct reference to the significance of his relationship to Shakespeare. I attribute this silence precisely to the primary importance of this relationship; much the same might be said about the influence of Goethe. Yet we may be able to gauge the import of these bonds on the middle-aged Freud from his espousal of the absurd hypothesis that the great Shakespearean oeuvre had been the work of the Earl of Oxford (Trosman, 1965). This fantasy betrays Freud's inability to tolerate any imperfection in a figure who remained essential for him—even the trivial disadvantage of relatively humble origins.

We are in a more fortunate position in trying to assess the function of Cervantes in Freud's intellectual development, perhaps because Cervantes's role assumed maximal importance at the time Freud went through the transformations of adolescence. In accord with the expectable needs of this developmental phase, Freud enacted some of the issues with which he was struggling in the setting of a peer group, resulting in the production of certain written records curiously focused on the world of Miguel de Cervantes y Saavedra.

In previous accounts of Freud's adolescent secret society, the Academia Castellana (Wolf, Gedo, & Terman, 1972; Gedo & Wolf, 1973), my colleagues and I have described how Cervantes had captured the imagination of the youthful Freud via the appeal of the figure of Don Quixote. The intensity of Freud's involvement may be gauged from the fact that he set out to teach himself Spanish for the express purpose of rereading the adventures of the knight of the rueful countenance in the original. The adolescent identification of the future discoverer of the psychoanalytic method with this embodiment of the neo-Platonic life of activity may seem surprising, but the sense of paradox disappears if we recall that Freud forever insisted that he was not so much an intellectual as a conquistador. I suspect that he nonetheless remained quite aware of Don Quixote's ultimate conclusion that the hardest kind of victory is achieved in the struggle to master oneself. In other words, I assume that Freud's claim meant he had conquered new territories for mankind in exploring the hitherto unknown realms of the unconscious. Perhaps that victory implies renunciation of fantasies about reforming the world by force of arms.

Be that as it may, Don Quixote should forever alert us to the error of looking on the Platonic categories of activity and contemplation as alternatives that are mutually exclusive. Like Socrates, who had distinguished himself militarily in the Athenian infantry, Freud was a man of great physical courage; let us only recall his defiance of the Gestapo at the time of the *Anschluss*.[3] Do we conclude that the introspective humanist will be ready to die for his beliefs in situations of appropriate gravity? Certainly this is the lesson Freud absorbed from Cervantes—a lesson tempered by humor about the countless potential miscarriages of intention that supervene in the fight for one's principles. And in this regard Cervantes had always lived up to his own precepts; not only had he earned glory on the battlefield by assaulting the Turkish flagship from a longboat at the battle of Lepanto; more impressively, as a prisoner of war in Algiers, his steadfast character had elevated him into a commanding position from which he won the universal respect of fellow prisoners and foes alike. These matters are of special interest, of course, because of Freud's own singular steadfastness of purpose in risking total professional isolation in the service of discovering psychoanalysis. Freud was fond of attributing his unwavering courage to his Judaic heritage, and he was candid about revealing his childhood identification with the Semitic warrior Hannibal, leader of the Carthaginian armies in their assault upon Rome. Although his interpretations undoubtedly have some validity, the records of his adolescence point in quite the opposite direction.

I am unable to judge whether the adolescent Freud was aware of the explicit identification of his model, Cervantes, the assailant of Moslem North Africa, with Hannibal's conqueror, the great Roman commander Scipio Africanus. But there is no question that Freud's adolescent fantasies followed Cervantes in this identification. The boy openly assumed the role of Don Cipion, based on one of the characters in Cervantes' astonishing novella, *The Colloquy of the Dogs*, and enacted a complex series of

3. Ernest Jones (1957, p. 226) recounts that when the Nazis demanded that Freud sign a document stating he had no reason for any complaint about the manner in which his emigration had been handled, "he asked if he might be allowed to add a sentence, which was: 'I can heartily recommend the Gestapo to anyone.'"

fantasies in this guise over a period of several years. Cervantes' novella, a work of the last decade of the 16th century, may well be the earliest example of the psychological novel—just as the contemporaneous plays of Shakespeare were the first serious presentations of the inner life on the stage since the age of Euripides. I shall return to the content of *The Colloquy of the Dogs* shortly.

But now I must attempt to put the sudden emergence of psychological understanding in the European literature of the late Renaissance into perspective. I will first note that the introspective tendencies in the work of both Shakespeare and Cervantes have on occasion been attributed to the influence of Michel de Montaigne. I believe that this circumstance is another example of the diffusion of a novel viewpoint through a whole culture as a consequence of a philosophical advance of the previous generation. Montaigne may well have been the only person in the history of the West to have devoted his mature life uninterruptedly to the task of introspection. The product of these labors, the celebrated *Essais* is, among other things, both a record of the personal changes brought about through relentless free association and a summary of the accumulated knowledge of antiquity and the Renaissance about the laws of human nature.

Montaigne's literal dedication to a life of contemplation in the 1570s and 1580s constituted a temporary reappearance of Socratic practice as a full-time activity, rather than a mere influence on some form of artistic expression. Compared to the intensity of Montaigne's self-scrutiny, the self-analytic efforts presently possible for busy practitioners responsible for the care of patients pale into tokenism. Of course, Montaigne was a uniquely fortunate man, the son of a benign father who fostered his humanist education and left him a large estate that relieved him of all economic burdens—a private Maecenas who had the discretion to pass on the inheritance shortly after the supreme crisis of Montaigne's emotional life, the loss of his friend La Boëtie. Lest we conclude that Montaigne's commitment to introspection came about through the absence of pressures from the outside, however, it should be kept in mind that his work as a humanist took place during the wars of religion, that is, during the most disastrous era in the history of France. In pursuing his introspective work, Montaigne resisted strong pressures for political commitment and tempting opportunities for a public career.

Elsewhere, I have compiled a résumé of Montaigne's psychology as a system of knowledge (Gedo & Wolf, 1976)—something the canny essayist had categorically refused to do himself. Taking into account certain omissions and differences in emphasis, this *summa psychologica* of the late 16th century bears a surprising resemblance to Freudian insights into man. Because of the complete lack of reference to Montaigne in Freud's writings, we can be reasonably certain that Freud had not made himself familiar with this work. As the Freud library contains a copy of

Montaigne's *Essais* bearing a 1916 dedicatory inscription from Lou Salomé (Trosman, personal communication, c. 1974), it is very unlikely that Freud had come across Montaigne before 1916.[4]

Montaigne's contribution had, in fact, been cut off from the culture of science by the philosophical developments of the early 17th century initiated by Descartes. In the 250 years from the 1620s to the 1870s, subjectivity had been largely banished from the purview of knowledge capable of scientific validation and assigned to the spheres of theology and the arts.[5] Freud, a 19th-century German adherent of natural science, could not possibly take Montaigne seriously as a scientific predecessor; at the same time, he could and did revere Montaigne's literary followers as purveyors of the most profound insights. By common consensus, the greatest names on the distinguished list of these heirs of the Gascon humanist are Cervantes, Shakespeare, and Goethe. A parallel to Montaigne's impact on literature would be Freud's influence on Thomas Mann's literature and the surrealists' painting.

It is one of those stunning coincidences, which take place with eerie frequency in the lives of men of genius, that the Spanish primer acquired by the young Freud used *The Colloquy of the Dogs* as its text.[6] In this

4. As even a brief summary of Montaigne's psychological viewpoint would overburden this presentation, I must content myself with asserting that practically nothing in his *Essais* is in disagreement with psychoanalysis. As Wolf and I have observed: "The differences between the introspective psychology of the sixteenth century and that of our age are attributable entirely to the fact that Freud succeeded in penetrating *further* into the opaque depths than Montaigne, or anyone else before him, had done. Thus Freud added to the accumulated knowledge of the Renaissance the psychoanalytic understanding of transference across a repression barrier, the compromise formations in dreams, parapraxes, and neurotic symptoms . . . the decipherment of the language of the unconscious . . . and [the] import of infantile sexuality for neurosogenesis" (Gedo & Wolf, 1976, p. 39). See also Wolf and Gedo (1975).

5. In an historical review of the development of psychology as a discipline, Rapaport (1974) attributes this intellectual trend to the impact of Descartes's philosophy. As he sees it, the seemingly unsolvable mind–body problem presented the thinkers of the early modern age with "intolerable tensions." For Descartes, in particular, "the originators of the tension were the age of skepticism in which he lived and the age of scholasticism from whose culture his mind had sprung. . . . He severed the tie between the two poles, separating body and mind to relax the tension" (p. 33). In this way, Descartes created a physiological psychology "centered on the concept of the motion of vital forces." Rapaport concludes that the laws of such a science could not apply "to reason or to the self"; it thereby became necessary "to place the unexplainable outside the domain of the newly created science" (p. 33).

6. Cervantes's novella, based on prototypes in the writings of Erasmus and Plutarch, is ultimately derived from the episode in Homer's *Odyssey* dealing with Circe's power to turn men into beasts. In the version of Cervantes, twin brothers have been turned into dogs. The narrative recounts the story of one brother, which has many similarities with the biography of the author. By implication, the dogs have come to die in a hospital for the indigent—the fate of artists who have been unable to find an "intelligent, generous, and magnanimous" patron, as Cervantes put it.

"setting for the jewel of truth," Cervantes's self-examination takes the form of a dialogue between a protagonist and a largely passive interlocutor—Don Cipion!—who takes on the function of promoting the flow of associations. On a deeper level, there can be no question that Cervantes is representing an internal dialogue within himself. Among other issues, the dog whose associations are recorded wrestles with the lack of appreciation in most societies for the artist–philosopher. No discriminating Maecenas and no provident father had saved Cervantes from the necessity of spending most of his life in menial labor. The Spain of Philip III was no more ready than the Athens of the Peloponnesian War to turn away from quixotic enterprises, to curb its presumption; the message of Cervantes was therefore no more welcome than that of Socrates had been!

From another vantage point, *The Colloquy of the Dogs* is the first statement of the introspective humanist's triumphant rejoinder to the inevitable hostility of the majority of mankind toward the partisans of the life of the mind. Self-scrutiny and the creativity that flows from it, Cervantes appears to say, amount to a pact with the devil that magically saves those who dare to make that choice from dependence on external recognition. We easily detect in this interpretation the theme that Goethe later infused into the Faust legend in making it the central myth of the modern age, that of man endlessly seeking fulfillment through the expansion of his knowledge, the broadening of his experience, and the expression of his creativity.

Did the adolescent Freud draw the same conclusion about the meaning of Cervantes's allegory? We do not know. But in following the enchanted hound Cipion into a life governed by Apollo's Delphic injunction, "Know thyself," I believe Freud indeed assumed the role he had enacted as a game in his adolescence, that of a 20th-century Socrates.

IV

THE DICHOTOMY of the *Naturwissenschaften* and *Geisteswissenschaften*, of science and humanism, or, as C. P. Snow put it more simply, of the two cultures, was too complete around the turn of the century to permit Freud to do more than pay tribute to his literary mentors for their intuitive insight into man's inner depths. In contrast to his eager enjoyment of their works, Freud was for a long time compelled to avoid altogether those of the writer whom he did acknowledge as his immediate predecessor as a depth psychologist, Friedrich Nietzsche. To be more precise, as an enthusiastic member of the Reading Society of German Students—the *Leseverein von deutschen Studenten*—at the University of Vienna, Freud had belonged to that small circle of admirers who appreciated the importance of Nietzsche's early work (see McGrath, 1974, pp. 53–83). From the context of Freud's writings, I believe it legitimate to infer that he really did not attempt to come to grips with the more significant, mature portion of the philosopher's output until after 1900. As Freud repeatedly stated, he avoided reading Nietzsche precisely because of his awareness of the fact that the philosopher had dealt with many of the issues that had confronted Freud in the course of discovering psychoanalysis.

But it is also clear that, in general terms, Freud was quite familiar with the later development of Nietzsche's ideas. Among the numerous ways in which such information reached him, I should like to single out one channel of communication. In 1884, one year prior to Freud's fateful study trip to Paris to learn about Charcot's pioneering experiments on hysteria, one of his closer friends, Josef Paneth, had met Nietzsche while doing research at Villefranche, on the Riviera. Paneth's fascinated reports about his contact with the famous author, which continued for several months, have been preserved in the Nietzsche archives (Förster-Nietzsche, 1914, pp. 189–196). The event was so meaningful for the young scientist that he gave Freud detailed accounts about it which are referred to in Freud's subsequent correspondence with Arnold Zweig (E. Freud, 1970, p. 78; cf. Kaufmann, 1980a, pp. 264–274). It is quite tempting to speculate that this exposure to the mature Nietzsche at the very time Freud completed his work on the psychiatric service at the Vienna General Hospital contributed to his change of interest from neuropathology to psychological medicine and thus figured in his decision to study with Charcot at the Salpêtrière when he won his traveling fellowship in 1885 (see Miller, Sabshin, Gedo, Pollock, Sadow, & Schlessinger, 1969).

Unlike the practicing neurologist Freud, Nietzsche was not restrained by any need for scientific respectability, and his identification with the humanist tradition of moral philosophy was both explicit and proud. One sign of this allegiance was Nietzsche's defiant designation of himself as "the immoralist." He entitled one of his books *Die Fröhliche Wissenschaft* (The Joyful Knowledge) as a direct reference to his beloved predecessor, Montaigne, who had termed his own introspective work *le gai savoir*. In a splendid discussion of the philosopher at the Vienna Psychoanalytic Society (Nunberg & Federn, 1967, pp. 25–33), Freud characterized Nietzsche's decade of productive self-scrutiny, after he resigned from his academic post at Basel, as leading to the most profound introspective insight ever achieved by a man. To be sure, Nietzsche himself has somewhat obscured the nature of his allegiances by repeatedly attacking Socrates for injecting an excess of rationalism into Hellenic thought. Nonetheless, I think he viewed himself as the first modern successor of Socrates—in his theatrical manner, he proclaimed himself "the first psychologist." And if we leave aside the era before the Cartesian revolution (and, for that matter, the introspective achievements of non-Western traditions, such as those of Buddhism and of Islamic Sufism) I think we can certainly concur with Nietzsche's judgment. His major accomplishment was the reintroduction of subjectivity into Western thought after a hiatus of two and a half centuries, and the birth of psychoanalysis in the next generation might well have been impossible without his assault on the illusions of rationality.

In his solitary campaign against a system of values that had outlived its usefulness, Nietzsche may ultimately have promoted Dyonisiac passion at the expense of Apollonian order, rather than seeking an appropriate balance between the two—hence his relative dissatisfaction with the Socratic reliance on reason. An explanation for this aberration must be sought in Nietzsche's personal history. As Thomas Mann has implied in his great modern version of *Faust*, Nietzsche's bargain with the devil must have had a particularly desperate quality, presumably because of the tragic tenuousness of his human bonds. Contrast this interpersonal alienation with Socrates's capacity to attract the best youths of Athens, with Horace's conviviality within the most exclusive imperial circles, with Montaigne's celebrated friendship with La Boëtie, or with Cervantes having been called mother and father to his fellow prisoners in Barbary. As is well known, Nietzsche's rare efforts to reach out to persons he could respect, such as Richard Wagner or Lou Salomé, were disastrously ill fated. Whatever the implications of his choice of objects, a quixotic quality of self-promoting grandiosity marks (and for many readers mars) much of Nietzsche's work, which is conspicuously lacking in the humor about his own presumption that elevates the writings of Cervantes to the highest sphere. And yet, it is natural enough that Nietzsche's letters should reveal his favorite piece of literature to be *Don Quixote*! Hence we must not take Nietzsche's denunciations of reason too literally. Nor should we forget that 100 years ago the world had not yet been endangered by the forces of modern irrationalism, so that it was natural to look upon the stifling of the passions as the source of civilized discontents.

In his emotional life, Sigmund Freud differed profoundly from Nietzsche. He too had made an adolescent Faustian bargain—to turn into Don Cipion, principal member of the Academia Castellana, who, in expectation of immortality, could bid his correspondents to guard his letters, preserve them, bind them together! But Freud had recoiled from his own grandiose speculative tendencies, and he had the humility and the perseverance to serve a 25-year apprenticeship in the school of scientific rationality before he undertook his great conquest of the unconscious through his self-analysis. In this way, Freud succeeded in fusing the humanist tradition of introspection with the accepted methods of science. The intellectual accomplishment was twofold: On the one hand, Freud's work eventually overthrew the prevailing materialist–positivist prejudices against data of observation obtained through the subjective methods of introspection and empathy; on the other, it has largely overcome the reluctance of humanists to submit the results of their introspective investigations to tests of validation. The significance for Western thought of building this bridge between the world of subjective meanings and the world of consensually validated sensory data cannot be overestimated.

Probably as a consequence of efforts on Freud's part to counterbalance the dangers of subjectivity in psychoanalysis, he has, to my knowledge, not been explicitly recognized as a Faustian figure, except for one allusion. In Thomas Mann's *Doctor Faustus*, Sigmund Freud is one of the series of great German humanists whose composite portrait is presented as the biography of one man, the composer Adrian Leverkühn. In a highly perceptive fashion, Mann chose to introduce Freud into the book by recounting the most traumatic episode of his life, the death of his grandson from meningitis. And, as if to indicate his awareness of the manner in which *this* particular Doctor Faustus differed from his fellows, Mann portrays the response of the bereaved genius as the enactment of the scene from Shakespeare's *The Tempest* in which Prospero renounces his possession of Ariel. In this view, then, Sigmund Freud is Prospero—a designation he was also accorded by the first scholar who attempted a major assessment of his position in intellectual history, Philip Rieff (1959). Implicitly, these observers would characterize the overall impact of psychoanalysis in Prospero's words of resignation:

> Now my charms are all o'erthrown,
> And what strength I have's mine own,
> Which is most faint. . . . Now I want [i.e., lack]
> Spirits to enforce, art to enchant,
> And my ending is despair,
> Unless I be relieved by prayer.
>
> (Epilogue)

V

WITH THESE WORDS of Prospero, I find myself face to face with the problem of Shakespeare's influence on Freud after all. Yet I shall adhere to the position I took earlier: The problem does not at present lend itself to fruitful discussion. On condition that we agree about the provisional nature of inferences based on a fragmentary approach, however, I think it may be fitting to make some comments about the place of *The Tempest* within the tradition I have been trying to characterize and to attempt to indicate some implications of the role of Prospero for the introspective humanist.

Let us begin with the reminder that, among the plays of Shakespeare, *The Tempest*, which was his valedictory, is most transparent in its debt to

Montaigne. Specifically, the play transcribes the latter's essay on the predictable destruction of the underdeveloped societies opened up to the forces of modernism by European exploration into the poetic metaphor of Prospero's potential dominance over every antagonist. It should be noted that Montaigne's intellectual impact on his contemporaries had been enormous: An English translation of the *Essais* was published by 1603, and prominent scholars went on pilgrimage to his château near Bordeaux. I do not believe it farfetched to see an idealized portrait of the great humanist himself in Shakespeare's Faustian protagonist. Whatever the degree of explicit modeling on Montaigne as a person, Shakespeare's Prospero was radically different from previous conceptions of Faust, such as Christopher Marlowe's. This evolution of the figure of the relentless seeker for knowledge might be construed as the consolidation of the rationality of the Socratic tradition at the threshold of the age of science—perhaps of that very ascendance of rationalism which Nietzsche was to anathematize almost three centuries later, when the seeming triumph of reason had called into question the significance and universality of man's poorly controlled passions.

To put this interpretation in another way, when Thomas Mann or Philip Rieff honors Freud as a Prospero, they are acknowledging not only the daemonic forces of creativity in him, for Freud, after all, had repeatedly called attention to the daemon that drove him ever since he had begun his self-analysis. In the figure of Prospero, these historians are referring to something more specific. Shakespeare's protagonist is the humanist whose introspection leads to the conclusion that his primary psychological task is the renunciation of magical thinking, or, more generally, of omnipotent strivings of all kinds. Modern man's Faustian bargain will not lead to damnation insofar as it avoids the exploitation of others as instruments of one's selfish goals: Shakespeare imposes on Prospero the sacrifice of having to set free his beloved servant, Ariel. But the same point was already implicit in Sophocles's drama, which teaches that the hubris of Oedipus must be curbed; man must bow to necessity. Yet, in *Oedipus at Colonus*, Sophocles required Antigone to accompany her father until his death. In *The Tempest*, Shakespeare denies the necessity for such self-sacrifice on behalf of a sacred hero; the drama records Prospero's effort to find a suitable husband for his daughter.

I do not presume to be able to judge the extent of Sigmund Freud's capacity to live up to these ideal standards in his personal life. In the next chapter, however, I shall attempt to show that he achieved precisely this kind of self-mastery in the course of his profoundly significant relationship with Carl Gustav Jung. In any case, the issue here is neither the attainment nor the maintenance of moral perfection by one man but, rather, the definition of the ultimate aims of psychoanalysis. If we accept the figure of Prospero as an idealized model of man made master within his own being through introspective effort, we should also agree with Philip Rieff (1959), who has called Freud the saving moralist of our culture. In accord with Apollo's injunction, to know oneself must lead in the direction of restraining one's quixotic presumption. If Friedrich Nietzsche led the overthrow of outmoded values to revitalize a civilization whose gods were dead, Sigmund Freud offers us a new version of the humanist tradition as a replacement.

VI

SELF-KNOWLEDGE is not given to many men, and neither is the capacity for self-mastery by way of introspective insight, even with the assistance of psychoanalytic treatment. If Sigmund Freud believed himself to be a conquistador (a fulfillment of his adolescent fantasies of heroic exploits in the picaresque mode), he earned this self-assessment through the unprecedented depth of his self-analysis. When in 1900 he published his magisterial treatise, *The Interpretation of Dreams*, a work copiously illustrated with autobiographical revelations, he had been pursuing the self-analytic effort for at least five years. From his recently published correspondence with Jung (McGuire, 1974), we have been able to reconfirm that this systematic introspective activity went on for at least another decade. Nor did Freud ever succumb to the temptation of looking upon his self-knowledge as complete or certain: In private correspondence, he called the self-analytic task "impossible" and averred that he was forced to extrapolate to himself much of what he had learned from his patients (Bonaparte, Freud, & Kris, 1954, pp. 234-235).

Freud's encounter with C. G. Jung was a pivotal event in the history of psychoanalysis not only because it led to a celebrated quarrel and the subsequent establishment of a rival school of psychotherapy but, more important from the standpoint of psychoanalysis, because its personal effects on Freud led him either to sharpen or redefine a number of key concepts. In the next chapter, I shall give some details about the substantive results of Freud's counterreaction to Jung's challenge. Here I wish only to note that these conceptual developments were, as was usual for Freud (see Gedo, 1968), based largely on his observations of his own relations with Jung. One prerequisite for these introspective insights (which were concerned with the complex interrelationships among narcissism, homosexual feelings, and paranoia) was Freud's mastery of his initial need to enmesh his younger colleague in his own scientific and personal enterprises—as if Jung had been a servant like Caliban, rather than an Ariel-like creature, to invoke once more the world of *The Tempest*. In order to take the first steps toward understanding the murky and explosive psychological problems that fueled his friendships and frequently ensured their dissolution, Freud had to stop the repetitive enactment of this pattern of living. I shall shortly recount how he succeeded in doing so; after the Jung episode, Freud would never again become embroiled in such an excessive and doomed relationship, although he lived on for another quarter of a century. In contrast, his early manhood had been marred by relationships quite similar to the one with Jung, with his mentors Ernst Brücke and Jean Martin Charcot, with his senior medical colleague Josef Breuer, and with his fellow psychobiological investigator, Wilhelm Fliess.

For his part, Jung also emerged from the ordeal of his dangerous dependence on Freud with enhanced creative powers, but his success was not attributable to the use of humanist introspection. Instead, he returned to modes of thought from which his attraction to Freud had temporarily diverted him—to magic, alchemy, occultism, and gnosticism. Probably in reaction to these activities of a former disciple whose name would forever be linked with psychoanalysis in the public consciousness, Freud seemingly felt constrained to assert categorically that the scientific discipline he had founded did not constitute a religion. In its most cursory form, this was tantamount to the claim that psychoanalysis does not create illusions (Freud, 1927). Today, we would be content to claim that we do not try to create them; contemporary philosophy of science will not abide by the positivist viewpoint that Freud espoused. Michael Polanyi, among others, has cogently demonstrated that certain *a priori* spiritual beliefs underlie every scientific discipline (Polanyi & Prosch, 1975). Thus, both science in general and, *a fortiori*, what I have called the "Socratic tradition" within it, may be plausibly regarded as a set of religious beliefs.

Of course, we should not be carried away by the ecumenical ethos of our time and overlook the fact that conflicting belief systems cannot be reconciled. The spiritual commitments of scientific humanism have no common ground with Jung's mystical beliefs or his resort to magical ideation (for convincing examples of such ideation, see Chapter 14). From a psychoanalytic perspective, Jung's therapeutic activities involved the indoctrination of patients with the psychiatrist's personal (and in Jung's case, idiosyncratic) opinions about the cosmos. As Frey-Rohn, a prominent contemporary Jungian, rightly observes, there is an "unbridgeable chasm" between the two systems of thought (1974, p. 132). Freud invariably focused on the psychology of the individual and on the concrete events of his life; Jung, on the other hand, sought out "aspects common to mankind," "archetypes" that are explicitly viewed as metaphysical in his system.

It follows from these considerations that creativity in psychoanalysis entails attributes and talents different from those required by the metaphysician. Jung's superb speculative capacities and expansive imagination could only make him impatient with the painstaking observational task intrinsic to Freud's methods. A man whose empirical interests led him to write a doctoral dissertation on parapsychology, as Jung had done in medical school, is unlikely to be the ideal collaborator for a Freud, who, at the same stage in his medical training, dissected several thousand eels to study the morphology of their testes. But in our Father's house, there are many mansions.

Chapter Twelve

A Promise of Magic

I

JUDGING FROM JUNG'S autobiography (1963), the most significant experience of his adult life was the encounter with Sigmund Freud. In its intensity, as well as in the bitterness that was its outcome, the relationship echoes the Nietzsche–Wagner idyll of the previous generation. Yet, the personal break between Freud and Jung remained inexplicable on the basis of the participants' contemporaneous statements about the matter (see also Jones, 1955). The only helpful observation made by either protagonist was Freud's judgment that Jung's ultimate divergence from psychoanalysis was due to his espousal of "a new religioethical system" (1914b, p. 62). But this self-evident conclusion explains neither what the two men originally had to offer each other, nor how they managed to become the closest of collaborators in the face of fundamental philosophical differences. In looking upon Jung's defection as an untoward event, Freud merely betrayed his failure to understand Jung's actual position throughout their relationship.

In Freud's rationalist view, Jung's abandonment of psychoanalysis was less significant as an intellectual phenomenon than the divergence of Alfred Adler—probably because he found Jung's modifications of analysis at the time of the split so "obscure, unintelligible and confused" (1914b, p. 60). Although the future may yet prove Freud right on this score, contemporary historians (e.g., Ellenberger, 1970) seem to view Jung as the more influential of the two early dissidents.

Freud's initial estimation of the individual worth of his former followers had also favored Jung. In the midst of Adler's impending defection from his circle, he wrote of him as a "poor fool" (McGuire, 1974, letter

A previous version of this material appeared in *The Annual of Psychoanalysis*, 7:53–82, 1979.

240^1); at a comparable point in his deteriorating relationship with Jung, he characterized the latter as a man of "exceptional talents" and "assured energy" (Freud, 1914b, p. 43). When the two men began their correspondence (*11*), Freud hailed Jung as "the ablest helper to have joined me so far" and soon voiced the expectation that this new collaborator would continue and complete his work (*18*). Six months later, he explicitly welcomed Jung as his successor (*20*), adding shortly thereafter that Jung's personal support assured the future of psychoanalysis (*27*). In April 1908, Freud declared that Jung possessed the seeds of greatness— the spark lacking in another new adherent, Karl Abraham (*84*). In fact, as Jones has noted (1955, p. 33), Freud looked upon Jung and Otto Gross as the only original minds among his early pupils.

In 1914, Freud frankly admitted (p. 43) that part of this enthusiasm had had a political motivation. As early as May 1908, he had pleaded with Abraham to make peace with Jung on the grounds that "it was only by his appearance on the scene that psychoanalysis escaped the danger of becoming a Jewish national affair" (Abraham & Freud, 1965, p. 34; cf. Selesnick, 1966). To Jung, he declared openly that the latter's character and *race* would command the public (*106*). But these prudential considerations should not be overestimated; Freud's generous estimation of Jung's abilities is hardly a function of the latter's status as a gentile. In October 1910, Freud tried to encourage Jung by reminding him how very superior he was to Adler (*218*); in December, he called Jung "the man of the future" (Jones, 1955, p. 140); and in July 1911, he predicted that if Jung applied himself, extraordinary rewards would come his way (*266*). In March 1912, when the approaching rupture seemed almost inevitable, Freud still assured Jung that he could not be replaced as friend, helper, and heir.

Jung's autobiography (1963) leaves no doubt that he was equally enthusiastic at the time of the encounter with Freud. In fact, aside from Jung's parents, Freud is the only person actually portrayed in this intriguing account of Jung's inner life. It follows that Freud was the person who achieved the greatest significance for Jung:

> Freud was the first man of real importance I had encountered; in my experience up to that time no one else could compare with him. There was nothing the least trivial in his attitude. I found him extremely intelligent, shrewd, and altogether remarkable. (1963, p. 149)

Further:

> I see him as a tragic figure; for he was a great man, and what is more, a man in the grip of his daimon. (1963, p. 153)

1. In this and the following two chapters, items in the Freud–Jung correspondence (McGuire, 1974) will henceforth be identified by number.

In a more objective vein, the aged Jung would give the following assessment of Freud's contributions:

> Freud's greatest achievement probably consisted in taking neurotic patients seriously and entering into their peculiar individual psychology. He had the courage to let the case material speak for itself, and in this way was able to penetrate into the real psychology of his patients. He saw with the patient's eyes, so to speak, and so reached a deeper understanding of mental illness than had hitherto been possible. In this respect he was free of bias, courageous, and succeeded in overcoming a host of prejudices. Like an Old Testament prophet, he undertook to overthrow false gods, to rip the veils away from a mass of dishonesties and hypocrisies, mercilessly exposing the rottenness of the contemporary psyche. He did not falter in the face of the unpopularity such an enterprise entailed. The impetus which he gave to our civilization sprang from his discovery of an avenue to the unconscious. By evaluating dreams as the most important source of information concerning the unconscious processes, he gave back to mankind a tool that had seemed irretrievably lost. He demonstrated empirically the presence of an unconscious psyche which had hitherto existed only as a philosophical postulate. (1963, pp. 168–169)

The recently published correspondence of Freud and Jung confirms the reliability of Jung's recollection of his admiring reaction to the older man. After visiting Freud in March 1907, Jung wrote of the "tremendous impression" Freud had made on him and vowed to demonstrate his gratitude and veneration through his work in psychoanalysis (*17*). Freud's positive reply evoked Jung's fear that his new mentor was overestimating his abilities (*19*), but he went on to assert that Freud's personality gave him faith in those aspects of psychoanalysis about which he lacked firsthand knowledge. Freud's generous response to Jung's qualms about his relative inexperience made the latter feel that he was "fighting not only for an important discovery but for a great and honourable man as well" (*44*). He experienced the friendship as an undeserved gift, a high point of his life (*72*). In August 1911, he was still overjoyed when he earned Freud's "paternal recognition" as the champion of his cause, and he was full of hope that his own work might serve as a stimulus for Freud's future discoveries (*269*).

In his autobiography, Jung summed the matter up in this way: "I found our relationship exceedingly valuable. I regarded Freud as an older, more mature and experienced personality, and felt like a son in that respect" (1963, p. 158). But he proceeded to claim that Freud had forfeited this paternal authority on the return voyage from their 1909 visit to America. It seems that during this trip the two men had engaged in attempts to analyze each other's dreams; when Jung, in this connection, asked for information about Freud's current life, Freud gave him "a look of the utmost suspicion" and refused, adding, "'But I cannot risk my authority'" (Jung, 1963, p. 158). It was this admission that Jung experienced as disillusioning; at the climax of his disappointment with Freud in December 1912, he would reproach the latter about this very incident (330). Yet, the correspondence between the two men does not bear out Jung's retrospective claim that his estimation of Freud changed at the time of this incident of 1909. In fact, the correspondence does not reveal a substantive change in the relationship until the fall of 1911, when other issues had supervened.

In some ways, Jung's "father complex," as both men referred to his awe of Freud, did not differ from the ambivalent reactions of Freud's other early adherents. On the one hand, Jung was alarmed by Freud's self-confidence (4); on the other, he decried his own resistances to certain Freudian conclusions (7). Yet, he had enough independence of judgment to condemn those of Freud's students who failed to take an empirical stance toward the clinical subject matter (17). Hoping that psychoanalytic work would bring him closer to Freud (24), in comparison with whom he felt deficient (9), he viewed his lack of insight as "morally inferior" (26). But Jung was quick to grasp the irrational nature of these initial reactions: By August 1907, he saw his jealousy of Karl Abraham and the "unconditional devotion" he felt for Freud as peculiar (39), and in October he ascribed his reserve in the relationship to shame over the erotically tinged crush he was then experiencing (49). He felt as if he had been in analysis with Freud and was anxious about the latter's potential reactions to these confessions (50).

Jung was insistent about avoiding a relationship of equality, pleading instead to be accepted in a filial role (72). Even implicit reproaches from Freud were very upsetting to him (83): He was particularly hurt when the latter expressed doubt about his hypotheses concerning dementia praecox (99). Every occasion of personal contact rekindled Jung's enthusiasm: The visits with Freud, as he put it, aroused his "complexes" (17). Notwithstanding his awareness of this fact, Jung felt these beneficial personal meetings should be repeated (111, 157, 165). Occasionally, Jung would state with excessive optimism that his most recent visit had freed him of his sense of Freud's oppressive paternal authority (138), only to relapse shortly thereafter into fantasies that the latter would chastise him (146). The most striking episode of this sort involved Jung's confession of a countertransference problem in his analysis of Sabine Spielrein, a Russian-Jewish psychiatrist who would join the Vienna Psychoanalytic Society in 1911. Jung decided that his infatuation with this Jewess represented the displacement of his feelings toward Freud (144).[2] This inability to overcome what he called his father complex

---

2. This association illustrates the manner in which Jung had given up "certain racial prejudices" (Freud, 1914b, p. 43) for the sake of Sigmund Freud. By current American

interfered with Jung's ability to communicate with Freud (cf. *180*); he was apparently humiliated at being unable to live up to the latter's expectations. As he once put it, he did not wish to wail to Freud about the complexes that plagued him (*175*).

We might ask at this juncture just what expectations Jung found it so difficult to fulfill. On receiving a gift of Jung's *Diagnostic Association Studies*, Freud initiated the correspondence in the hope of profiting from Jung's clinical experience with psychotic patients (*1, 8*), going so far as to present certain of his own observations of psychotics for Jung's consideration (*10*). His first New Year's greeting expressed the wish that Jung and he could work together without misunderstanding (*11*), and shortly thereafter Freud formally proposed that they collaborate on the problem of dementia praecox (*18, 23*). What he probably had in mind may be gauged from his request on May 23, 1907 (*25*) that Jung test in his clinical work a hypothesis Freud was developing to explain such psychotic conditions. Sometime later, he asked Jung to become the chief propagandist of the psychoanalytic cause because he felt that all hearts would open to him (*42*). Freud made it explicitly clear that he was not disturbed by partial differences between Jung's scientific views and his own; on the contrary, he was pleased by their partial agreement on certain matters (*84*). He did, however, seek harmony among his various followers, and to this end he asked Jung to work together constructively with Abraham (*87*), Otto Gross (*96*), and Sandor Ferenczi (*158*).[3]

By the summer of 1908, when Freud had apparently come to the conclusion that Jung was unfitted by temperament for scientific collaboration, he modified his stance by suggesting that Jung independently

---

3. In this regard, it should be noted that even at the height of their quarrel, Freud (1914b) credited Jung with training the most important of Freud's adherents, among his other great services to psychoanalysis. In a variety of ways, Abraham, Ferenczi, and Jones had each made contact with Jung before meeting Freud.

---

standards, the letters of both men are filled with racist attitudes. (For derogatory remarks about various nationalities, see *144, 223*, and *256*.) Such references were not predominantly negative in tone but emphasized ethnicity in a way that seems strange today. As an illustration, one can cite Freud's reaction on meeting Ernest Jones; he wrote Jung of experiencing "almost racial strangeness" (*87*). There were also references to Jung's "Germanic blood" (*106*) and Freud's indifference to "Teutonic women" (*84*). One might also recall Freud's letter to Abraham of October 11, 1908 in which he wrote of his efforts to guard against his own "racial preference" lest he do an injustice to Jung, the "more alien Aryan" (Abraham & Freud, 1965, p. 54). As for the permanence of Jung's relinquishment of anti-Semitism, Jones reports (1955, p. 103) that at the Munich psychoanalytic congress of 1913 Jung reproached him with the taunt "I thought you were a Christian" when Jones abstained from voting in favor of retaining Jung as president of the International Association. In his autobiography, it should be noted, Jones (1959, p. 224) gave a slightly different—and less conclusive—version of this incident (cf. Roazen, 1975).

carry out the task of extending psychoanalysis to the psychoses: "With your strong and independent character, with your Germanic blood which enables you to command the sympathies of the public . . . you seem better fitted than anyone else to carry out this mission" (*106*).

As late as January 1910, Freud was still delighted by Jung's occasional expressions of interest in theoretical discussions with him (*171*); by this time, however, he seemed more intent on ensuring Jung's political leadership of the psychoanalytic movement (*174*). Hoping that Jung would have sufficient self-confidence to be an effective president of the International Psychoanalytic Association (*185*), that is, that he could actually provide the organization with effective leadership, Freud pleaded with him to take his administrative responsibilities seriously and to devote himself to public relations to the full extent of his abilities (*205*). In February 1912, after noting unmistakable signs of Jung's disaffection, Freud continued to exhort him to attend to his organizational tasks; he was determined to safeguard the future by arranging "to see everything safe in [Jung's] hands when the time comes" (*301*).

Although Jung was evidently unwilling to engage in joint scientific work or to pour himself into administrative activities, his reluctance about these matters clearly did not trouble him; it follows that we must seek the sources of his difficulties with Freud at the more personal level of the relationship. It should be stated at the outset that these personal problems were compounded by Freud's unwavering conviction that Jung, like his other younger followers, was destined to exert all his efforts to demolish Freud's theories insofar as possible (*169*), that is, that Jung, like his other disciples, was destined to repeat the father murder Freud was then postulating in *Totem and Taboo* (1913)—thereby validating Freud's thesis in that work!

Binswanger (1957) has recorded that on the occasion of Jung's initial visit to Freud in March 1907, the former recounted a dream which Freud interpreted to mean that Jung wished to dethrone him. It is quite remarkable that in November 1907, Jung should protest that his dream of Freud as very old and frail had not been correctly understood: Instead of signifying hostile competitiveness, he claimed, it had served as a defense against his fear of being overwhelmed by Freud's personality (*50*). Although Freud did not respond to this correction at the time, it did not seem to have altered his basic assumptions about Jung's unconscious attitude. Indeed, there is some indication that he thought of Jung's alternative explanations of the dream as considerably less favorable prognostically and therefore preferred to discount them (cf. *52*).

Jones (1955, p. 146) has described another episode in which Freud claimed that Jung harbored unconscious death wishes against him—the occasion of their meeting in Bremen in 1909 en route to the American conference at Clark University. Freud insisted at the time that Jung's preoccupation with certain corpses found in the peat bogs near the city had the significance of unconscious death wishes (1963, p. 156); Freud also tried to force this interpretation on a dream he had during the journey (p. 159).[4]

It may be conjectured that a curious slip of the pen in Jung's second letter after the return from America (*159*) constituted his response to Freud's seemingly strained interpretations. This parapraxis (which depends on the similarity of the German *ihnen* [them] and *Ihnen* [you]) resulted in his writing that the scientific nature of psychoanalysis would have to be drummed into *Freud*! As Jung (1963) has provided the manifest content of this dream, it is indeed possible to confirm that Freud's interpretation about death wishes had been quite arbitrary and, as we shall see later, certainly missed the main purport of Jung's unconscious motivations at the time.[5]

Freud's admission that he expected Jung to join those who wished to demolish his work followed in December 1909. It was accompanied by the judgment that, like Adler (whom Jung despised), Jung was at the point of neglecting the study of the libido by concentrating on the ego (*169*). In his immediate reply, Jung said that his faith in himself had been shaken by these charges, and he complained about the difficulty of working alongside the "father creator" (*170*).[6] Thereupon he lapsed into miserable silence, only to be accused by Freud (in one of the few letters of the correspondence not to have been preserved) of having begun to vacillate in his adherence to psychoanalysis (see the ending of Jung's reply to the missing letter, *181*).

Freud's unempathic misconstruction of Jung's idealizing needs as a sign of hostile competitiveness did not play the primary role in spoiling his relationship with Jung; it was, in fact, an ineffectual attempt to deal with a problem he had misunderstood all along. It did however, add fuel to the fire and accelerate the inevitable deterioration of the situation. Jones (1955) has suggested, without much evidence, that the rupture was

4. To fend off what he experienced as an unjust accusation, Jung gave a spurious association to the dream which deliberately suggested that the "death wishes" were in fact directed against Jung's wife and sister-in-law. Winnicott (1964) has written an interesting essay on the significance of this lie on Jung's part.

5. I shall return to Jung's Bremen dream of 1909 in Chapters 13, page 255, and 14, pages 266, 267.

6. The severity of the jolt Jung had sustained is shown by the first appearance in the correspondence of paranoid ideation, here displaced to the irrelevant idea that Freud might have implied that Jung was unfit to study mythology. I believe this to have been a sign that Jung felt betrayed by Freud's attitude, particularly because it came in response to his ecstatic praise of Freud's case report on the so-called Rat Man (see *168*).

caused by Jung's neurotic resistance to Freud's sexual theories,[7] and he has defended this view by claiming that Freud did not become emotionally involved with Jung, as he had with Wilhelm Fliess a decade earlier (p. 33). Freud's lack of emotional involvement, for Jones, means that the rupture between mentor and student cannot be attributed to Freud's expectations in the relationship. But Freud's settled conviction that Jung wished to dethrone him is in itself sufficient to invalidate this contention. Moreover, the letters contain a great deal of additional evidence that Jung had indeed become an essential figure within Freud's psychological world. Consequently, the roots of the problem must be sought in the mutually contradictory personal requirements that the two men brought to their encounter.

II

THE EARLIEST indication of Freud's personal need for Jung, beyond the obvious desire to win the loyalty of a valuable recruit to the cause, cropped up in a letter of May 26, 1907, when he indicated that Jung's prompt replies to his letters had become important to him (27). He asked not to be forgotten during the vacation period that summer (36) and subsequently reported that his personality had become "impoverished" through the actual reduction in the correspondence during the holidays (38). In this same letter (38), a fantasy of psychic merger with Jung was revealed by Freud's statement that their collaboration would eliminate any distinction between their respective achievements. Secret sharers!

Following Karl Abraham's first visit to Freud, late in 1907, Jung seemed to have reacted with jealousy to the news that this potential rival had made a good impression; his letters subsequently became less frequent and less personal. Jung's dilatory responses finally evoked Freud's frank expression of concern that an estrangement had developed between them. The situation improved at the Salzburg congress of 1908, where Freud lectured for four hours about the case of the Rat Man. Jung fell under his spell once again: "I am under the reverberating impact of your lecture

---

7. Max Schur (1972, pp. 249–255) has hinted at the interpretation I shall offer below. (Both Jones and Schur, it should be noted, had access to the Freud–Jung correspondence in preparing their respective biographies of Freud.) Shengold (1976) has correctly blamed the difficulty on the participants' personal needs, but he has confined his explanation to the realm of the Oedipus complex, particularly in its homosexual aspects; such a view is exceedingly reductionistic, albeit relevant. In contrast, Loewald (1977) has tried to discern the deeper sources of the father–son entanglement that destroyed the relationship, especially its origin in early ideological commitments. His brief review, however, does not consider the roots of these commitments in personal experiences.

which seemed to me perfection itself" (*86*). Following Salzburg, Freud was able to express understanding of Jung's need for "negative oscillations." He stated that he no longer feared they would be "torn apart" and expressed satisfaction "to feel at one with you" (*87*). Of course, such an illusion could not persist, and when Jung became absorbed in professional activities, Freud was reminded of his earlier fear that his follower had "been alienated from [him] by some inner development deriving from the relationship with [his] father and the beliefs of the church" (*99*).

By the end of the summer of 1908, Freud realized that a personal meeting was needed "to demolish the resentment that is bound to accumulate . . . between two persons who demand a great deal from each other" (*106*). He must have grasped that his demands had exceeded Jung's capacity for closeness, but in the same letter he promised to "subordinate" his fondness for Jung. Freud's visit to Zurich at the end of September 1908 produced the desired results; in its afterglow, he was able to write: "Now that we can live, work, publish and enjoy a certain companionship, life is not at all bad and I should not want to change it too soon" (*114*). His New Year's greeting was simply: "May we remain close together in 1909!" (*123*).

But Jung was unable to remain adequately close for Freud's purposes. At the time Jung became preoccupied with Sabine Spielrein, Freud had to acknowledge his own sensitivity to the "dwindling correspondence." He frankly attributed his excessive vulnerability in this regard to the loss of his most meaningful relationship of the previous decade, his friendship with the charismatic Berlin physician, Wilhelm Fliess (*134*). Being appraised of this fact, Jung reassuringly responded: "You may rest assured not only now but for the future, that nothing like Fliess is going to happen" (*135*).

In March 1909, Jung went to Vienna to visit Freud a second time. On this occasion, those disadvantages of fantasied mergers that generally spoil such relationships made themselves felt. From Freud's point of view, one might say that the tail began to wag the dog in a most disagreeable way (cf. Schur, 1972, pp. 230–233, 251, 254; Jung, 1963, pp. 155–156). It was during this visit that Jung brought up the question of precognition, only to recall that Freud "rejected this entire complex of questions as nonsensical, and did so in terms of so shallow a positivism that I had difficulty in checking the sharp retort on the tip of my tongue" (1963, p. 155). Instead, Jung demonstrated in action that he could predict the recurrence of a "loud report" emanating from a piece of furniture. When this experiment proved successful, Jung recalled, "Freud only stared aghast at me" (p. 156). On his return to Zurich, Jung wrote, "It seemed to me that my spookery struck you as altogether too stupid and perhaps unpleasant because of the Fliess analogy. (Insanity!)" (*138*). How right he was!

The similarity of these developments to aspects of Freud's former relationship to Fliess was not confined to the fact that in both cases someone Freud felt he needed insisted that he accept a set of irrational beliefs held with messianic conviction. More importantly, in both instances Freud temporarily entered an encapsulated folie à deux with regard to such beliefs: The Fliessian mystical numerology that had won his allegiance in the 1890s was replaced in 1909 by Jung's parapsychological theory of precognition. Schur (1972) has carefully demonstrated that Freud's acceptance of some of Fliess's absurd "scientific" theories had not been entirely overcome with the termination of their relationship.[8] I think it very significant, in this regard, that the clearest evidence of the persistence of irrational Fliessian numerological preoccupations on Freud's part is to be found in the very letter he wrote following Jung's visit of March 1909 (*139*). It cannot have been accidental that the first part of this communication deals with Freud's rapid recovery from the effects of Jung's "spookery," whereas the subsequent "paternal warning" to his "dear son to keep a cool head" was sweetened with a confession about his own occasional reversion to irrational ideation.

It is difficult, then, to accept Schur's (1972) contention that Freud's recovery from Jung's spookery and his disabusing communication that he viewed it "as charming delusion" sealed the fate of their relationship. Jung did not discourage that easily; in his autobiography he stated, perhaps in a tone of satisfaction, that "it was some years before [Freud] recognized the seriousness of parapsychology and acknowledged the factuality of 'occult' phenomena" (1963, p. 155). In actuality, Jung's subsequent conclusion about the long-range effects of this incident seems more to the point—he felt that the incident aroused Freud's mistrust of him (1963, p. 156).

Several weeks passed before Jung responded to Freud's rejection of fantasied merger on *his* terms; he did so calmly, with the promise to exercise caution about the spooks, as Freud had advised (*140*). Freud had apparently drawn back from the relationship as well, for on this occasion he did not reproach Jung for his long silence. On the contrary, Freud specified that Jung need not write when he had nothing to communicate, whereas he himself might continue to write as frequently as he wished (*141*).

8. In his discussion of the Jung incident, Schur slurs over the fact that Freud acknowledged that he had accepted Jung's views, even though Schur quotes the relevant letter of Freud (*139*) in full. The relevant passage in Freud's text is: "I don't deny that your stories and your experiment made a deep impression on me. . . . My credulity, or at least my willingness to believe, vanished with the magic of your personal presence." Shengold (1976) has correctly discerned that in relationships like the one with Jung, Freud was seeking "the promise of magic."

Thus the incident had seemingly passed without damage. Jung was subsequently able to confide in Freud about his mishandling of the analysis of Sabine Spielrein (*144, 146, 148*) and was clearly reassured by Freud's understanding of the difficulties of the analytic beginner (*145*; see also *129*). The two men met in Bremen on August 20, 1909, and returned from their joint trip to America on September 29. This six-week period constituted by far the most personal contact between them; despite the difficulties resulting from rash efforts to interpret each other's unconscious motives, their companionship was outwardly untroubled, and their letters on returning home resumed on a positive note.

But this cordiality notwithstanding, Freud's cavalier interpretations of some of Jung's communications were probably responsible for the reduced frequency of the latter's messages. It was in reaction to these hurts that Freud once more accused Jung of murderous hostility toward him in December 1909. Jung's catastrophic reaction on this occasion has already been described; whether because Freud was able to grasp intuitively the futility of his need for Jung as an extension of himself, or for other reasons, Freud's subsequent letters do not exert the same kind of pressure on Jung that characterized the correspondence from mid-1907 through the end of 1909. Instead, he suddenly seemed to develop the scheme of handing over the political leadership of the psychoanalytic movement to Jung (cf. *174*), an intention on which he promptly acted at the Nuremberg congress of March 1910. Only a few months later, with Jung installed as president of the newly established International Psychoanalytic Association, Freud was forced to confess that he had pushed for the formation of this organization in a precipitous and politically counterproductive manner—and this because of his impatience to see Jung "in the right place" (*205*).

It is rather remarkable that this apparent shift in Freud's attitude toward Jung coincides with the establishment of a regular and satisfactory rhythm in the exchange of letters between them. The relationship did not become free of difficulties; on the contrary, the worst was yet to come. But throughout 1910 and 1911, whatever the vicissitudes of the personal tie, there was no interruption of regular correspondence. It is reasonable to conclude that Jung was not so much a poor correspondent (as Jones, 1955, believed) as a correspondent who modulated his letter writing on behalf of that "complex of self-preservation" he had vainly tried to bring to Freud's attention from the beginning (see *49*).

During the relatively tranquil period of their relationship in 1910 and 1911, the letters demonstrate a subtle but unmistakable return on Freud's part to a pattern of friendship that typified his adolescence (Gedo & Wolf, 1973). In the last chapter, we noted that during his last years at the gymnasium and his earliest ones at the university, Freud had formed a secret society, the Academia Castellana, with his friend Eduard Silberstein.

They communicated to a large extent in Spanish, but a Spanish heavily laced with a private code. The whole game, we pointed out, was a charming parody of Cervantes's *The Colloquy of the Dogs* in which self-examination took the form of a dialogue between the twin dogs Cipion and Berganza. Now, at the age of 54, Freud achieved a shared vocabulary with Jung that is strikingly reminiscent of the tone of "the records of the Academia Castellana" almost four decades earlier.

As if in response to the need to acknowledge the formation of a secret society, Jung jocularly proposed in the fall of 1911 the designation "Societas Psychoanalytica." This was to be abbreviated S. ψ A., on the model of S. J. for "Society of Jesus." Freud was delighted: "I feel sure that the sigla you invented . . . S. ψ A., will come into universal use" (*278*). Jung had not proved to be tractable as a symbiotic partner, but he did serve well as a fantasied twin brother, ghost of Cervantes's Don Berganza.

III

IN ORDER TO assess the impact of the relationship with Jung on Freud's creativity, one might well begin by noting that Jung had the happy inspiration, probably in the spring of 1910 at the Nuremberg congress, of calling to his mentor's attention the *Memoirs* of Daniel Paul Schreber. This book, then recently published, recorded the psychotic experiences of its talented author, formerly a respected judge in Saxony. Regardless of exactly when Jung commended this material to Freud, the latter reported soon after the congress that he was reading "the wonderful Schreber, who ought to have been made a professor of psychiatry" (*187*). The *Memoirs* turned out to contain material highly appropriate for illustrating Freud's hypotheses about the dynamics of paranoia, even though the correspondence with Jung reveals that Freud's insights in this respect were reached earlier, on the basis of his personal experiences with Wilhelm Fliess. In February 1908, Freud observed that "My one-time friend Fliess developed a dreadful case of paranoia after throwing off his affection for me, which was undoubtedly considerable" (*70*).

The events to which Freud referred in this statement had unfolded almost a decade earlier; presumably, they had affected Freud too deeply to permit him to develop scientific insights about them immediately after they transpired. It would seem, however, that the relationship to Jung had repeated, in a less intense and therefore more manageable manner, certain aspects of the earlier relationship to Fliess; as Freud gradually mastered his affective need for Jung as an extension of himself, he was able to turn his attention to the task of illuminating the genesis of paranoia in such intense, homosexually tinged transactions. On this level, Jung was capable, in mid-1910, of serving as a secret sharer. As Freud became immersed in writing his commentary on the case of Schreber (Freud, 1911), Jung wrote he was "touched and overjoyed to learn how much [Freud] appreciate[d] the greatness of Schreber's mind," particularly the psychotic verbalizations which Schreber termed "the basic language" (213). When Jung read the galley proofs of Freud's essay, he praised it as uproariously funny, brilliantly written, and—in my view, the crucial aspect of Jung's ability to assist Freud with his creative task—he expressed the wish that he had been able to create the study Freud had written (243). In other words, when Jung's own work was *not* at issue, he was spontaneously able to foster Freud's need for an illusion of identity in their respective thoughts.

Although we do not possess similar evidence about the effect of Jung's friendship on other works Freud produced during the era of their collaboration, on quantitative grounds alone we might conclude that the relationship facilitated Freud's productivity. Just as his early psychological writings were contingent on the supportive relationships he enjoyed with Charcot and Breuer, and just as *The Interpretation of Dreams* (1900) and *The Psychopathology of Everyday Life* (1901) (and the shorter papers that accompanied them) arose in connection with the Fliess episode, so a series of capital works seems to have grown out of the relationship with Jung. Freud had gone through a period of relative isolation after he broke away from Fliess; this isolated period lasted from 1901 to 1906. It is true that Freud was not unproductive in this interval: The main writings of those years were the *Three Essays on Sexuality* (1905b), a biological treatise that drew on the interests Freud had shared with Fliess, the case history of a young woman designated "Dora" whom Freud had analyzed before the break with Fliess (1905a), and *Jokes and Their Relation to the Unconscious* (1905c), Freud's most important excursion into aesthetics. These were major achievements, but—not to engage in qualitative judgments about their importance—they represented a relative diminution in Freud's usual rate of productivity.

From 1906 to 1914, while he was tied to Jung for better and for worse, Freud enjoyed one of his most creative periods, both quantitatively and qualitatively. To mention only the most significant of the works securely attributable to the Jung period,[9] Freud successively produced the case

9. According to Jones (1955, p. 341), Jung additionally claimed that Freud wrote his essay on Wilhelm Jensen's novel *Gradiva* (Freud, 1907) in order to please Jung, who brought the book to his attention. Jung may have been confusing the circumstances leading to the *Gradiva* essay with the later incident involving Schreber's book. If his report is accurate, however, it would mean that a portion of the Freud–Jung correspondence precedes April 11, 1906, the date of the earliest letter between Freud and Jung that has been preserved. In the extant correspondence, Jensen is first mentioned in the spring of 1907 (23), when Freud was at the point of sending the completed study to Jung.

histories of "Little Hans" (1909a) and the Rat Man (1909b), the lectures delivered at Clark University (1910a), the study of Leonardo da Vinci (1910b), the essay on Schreber (1911), *Totem and Taboo* (1913), along with important papers on psychoanalytic technique (1911–1915). Even the rupture with Jung stimulated Freud's creativity, leading directly to the writing of *On the History of the Psychoanalytic Movement* (1914b), substantially a polemic against Jung's dissidence, "The Moses of Michelangelo" (1914a), the deciphering of a prophet's wrath at his people's betrayal of his teachings, and two works that embody Freud's responses to Jung's substantive theoretical challenge, "On Narcissism: An Introduction" (1914c) and the case history of the Wolf Man (1918).

We can only conclude, as I did once before (Gedo, 1968), that Freud's subject matter principally involved introspective self-observations made in the context of his most significant personal relationships—human bonds he was most likely to forge with individuals capable of inspiring his admiration and evoking his unfulfilled archaic needs.

Chapter Thirteen

Magna Est Vis Veritatis Tuae Et Praevalebit*

*Great is the power of Thy truth, and it shall prevail!
(C. G. Jung to Sigmund Freud, November 11, 1908)

I

IN ORDER TO understand the collapse of the Freud–Jung collaboration, we must now try to grasp the converse of the matters we reviewed in the last chapter. In short, we must consider not only what Freud had expected of Jung—after many vicissitudes, they had apparently worked out a *modus vivendi* about this—but also what Jung had required of Freud. At the beginning of the relationship, this had not amounted to very much: Jung pleaded for understanding of the risks he incurred by espousing psychoanalysis publicly (*12*), and he expressed hurt feelings when Freud proved uninterested in his experimental work (*26*). After Freud began placing greater demands on him, in October 1907, Jung explained his reluctance to comply on the ground that this "veneration for [Freud] has something of the character of a 'religious' crush'" (*49*). He added shortly thereafter, "My old religiosity had secretly found in you a compensating factor" (*51*). Freud's reply to the first of these confessions is missing; to the second, he made a prophetic response: "A transference on a religious basis would strike me as most disastrous; it could only end in apostasy. . . . I shall do my best to show you that I am unfit to be an object of worship" (*52*).

A contemporary reader of the correspondence cannot quite agree that Freud presented himself to Jung as a person unfit for idealization. His proudest claim may have been a seemingly self-critical statement of December 1911 that preceded the final crisis of the relationship with

A previous version of this material appeared in *The Annual of Psychoanalysis*, 7:53–82, 1979.

Jung: "I was not cut out for inductive investigation . . . my whole make-up is intuitive . . . in setting out to establish the purely empirical science of ψA I subjected myself to an extraordinary discipline" (*288*). How admirable, this unsparingly critical inductivist able to trace his own imposing achievements not to innate aptitude for inductive work but only to an extraordinary capacity for self-discipline!

Compared with this admission, Freud's acknowledgment of his handicaps is not very striking. He wrote of his tendency to resist opinions different from his own (*8*), of his commitment to the routines of his life (*27*), of the inevitable personal distortions he had doubtless introduced into psychoanalysis (*34*). He also complained that people found his personality, ideas, and manner strange and repellent (*42*) while noting that his lengthy "splendid isolation" had made him unfit for the role of public leader (*84*). Most of all, he admitted himself to be a burdensome correspondent (*58*).

It is hardly surprising that Jung's propensity for idealization found a suitable object in Freud. For the most part, Jung tried to control this disturbing tendency by reducing the intensity of their contacts, but, as we have seen, this strategy offended Freud, who required greater intimacy. It was after their personal meetings that Jung tended to lose control of his "religious crush"; thus, Freud's visit to Zurich in the fall of 1908 produced this biblical outburst: "*Magna est vis veritatis tuae et praevalebit!*" (*113*).

Freud was clearly displeased with Jung's "theological style," and he tried to wean him from it by echoing it in a teasing manner. To this end, he characterized the commitment to psychoanalysis as being in league with the devil (*134*), and on asking Jung to assume analytic leadership in Zurich, he joked about having anointed him as his successor *in partibus infidelium.*[1] Needless to say, Freud's jocularity had no effect whatsoever on Jung, and Freud soon ceased to treat the matter in this light tone. There was no humor at all in Jung's declaration that he had fancied Freud to be "in possession of the highest esoteric wisdom" which Jung "as your *famulus* [a sorcerer's attendant] would have to emulate" (*144*). And Jung's reaction on reading the case history of the Rat Man was so worshipful that Freud could no longer tolerate it. "Like Herakles of old," he wrote to Freud, "you are a human hero and demigod, wherefore your dicta unfortunately carry with them a sempiternal value" (*168*). In his somewhat naive reply, Freud expressed disbelief that his errors could be worshipped as relics, and it was on this occasion that he added the hurtful accusation that Jung would try to destroy his work.

---

1. Literally, "in the domain of the unbelievers." Prelates with administrative appointments in Rome are given titular bishoprics in lands that are no longer inhabited by Christians.

Jung recovered from this blow after receiving a few friendly letters from Freud, and in February 1910, in response to Freud's inquiry about the possibility of joining forces with an "International Fraternity for Ethics and Culture" then being organized, he was quite explicit about his fantasies concerning psychoanalysis:

> If a coalition is to have ethical significance it should never be an artificial one but must be nourished by the deep instincts of the race. Somewhat like Christian Science, Islam, Buddhism. Religion can be replaced only by religion. . . . Only the wise are ethical from sheer intellectual presumption, the rest of us need the eternal truth of myth. . . . 2000 years of Christianity can only be replaced by something equivalent. An ethical fraternity, with its mythical Nothing, not infused by any archaic-infantile driving force, is a pure vacuum and can never evoke in man the slightest trace of that age-old animal power . . . without which no irresistible mass movement can come into being. I imagine a far finer and more comprehensive task for ψA than alliance with an ethical fraternity. I think we must give it time to infiltrate into people from many centres, to revivify among intellectuals a feeling for symbol and myth, ever so gently to transform Christ back into the soothsaying god of the vine, which he was, and in this way absorb those ecstatic instinctual forces of Christianity for the *one* purpose of making the cult and the sacred myth what they once were—a drunken feast of joy where man regained the ethos and holiness of an animal. . . .
>
> ψA makes me "proud and discontent," I . . . would like to affiliate it with everything that was ever dynamic and alive. . . . I have abreacted enough for today—my heart was bursting with it. Please don't mind all this storming. (*178*)

Freud responded with understanding: "Yes, in you the tempest rages; it comes to me as distant thunder"—but he was emphatic in disavowing Jung's aims: "You mustn't regard me as the founder of a religion." And, for good measure, he insisted that the need for a religion must be sublimated (*179*).

In Jung's striking self-revelation and Freud's unequivocal rejection of his program, we finally come face to face with the fundamental reason for their inevitable separation. Freud had, several months preceding this exchange, abandoned hope of structuring the relationship on his preferred terms; now, in the winter of 1910, Jung had to face the hopelessness of his own needs for Freud. As it happened, he did not accept the verdict immediately—in August 1910 he reiterated that psychoanalysis "has all the trappings of a religion." It was precisely because these religious trappings gave analysis the appearance of sectarianism and mysticism that Jung did not feel it could be presented to the public in undiluted form (*206*). In his secular way, Freud seemingly agreed: "We have let ourselves in for something bigger than ourselves" (*207*). The irreconcilable difference between them was henceforth left unspoken, even as each man now undertook a basic position statement on the subject of religion, Jung in *Symbols of Transformation* (1912), Freud in *Totem and Taboo* (1913). From time to time Jung expressed apprehension about Freud's expectable reaction to what he was writing (*230*; see also the letter from Emma Jung to Freud, November 6, 1911, in McGuire, 1974, pp. 455–457), and he wrote that he looked upon Freud as a "dangerous rival" on the topic of religion. Freud tried to reassure Jung that he had no reason to fear his opinion of Jung's work, although he expressed the hope that Jung would return from his mythological studies to "our medical motherland" (*232*).[2]

At the end of March 1911, Johann Honegger, Jung's friend, patient, and collaborator, committed suicide. Freud commented resignedly, "I think we wear out quite a few men" (*248*); Jung, for his part, confessed that "this blow struck home" (*252*). He blamed his own therapeutic inexperience for Honegger's death (cf. *259*), an idea Freud tried to dispel by expressing his disbelief that there had ever been any chance to save the man (*260*). Under the impact of this event, Jung tried once more to endow Freud and psychoanalysis with religious powers. In May, he was writing that "occultism is another field we shall have to conquer with the aid of the libido theory" (*254*)—a statement of faith that disproves Jones's contention that by this point in the relationship Jung had changed his scientific views. When Jung proceeded to immerse himself in the "magic perfumes of astrology," Freud was content to accept this new preoccupation as a potentially fruitful diversion. He predicted that Jung would return from his voyage into occultism "richly laden" and merely asked that this "colonial" venture not be unduly prolonged (*255*). When Jung reported making "incredible finds" with horoscopes (*259*), Freud replied that in such matters he would reluctantly credit whatever could be made to look reasonable (*260*). In August, when Freud hinted that he would communicate some important conclusions in *Totem and Taboo*, Jung was carried away by an excitement that pointed to his continuing religious needs:

> your letter has got me on tenterhooks. . . . I can't quite make out what is going on so enigmatically behind the scenes. . . . We [i.e., Jung and his wife] have reached surmises which . . . I would rather keep to myself. . . . I, too, have the feeling that this is a time full of marvels, and, if the auguries do not deceive us, it may very well be that,

2. As Stepansky (1976, p. 222) has emphasized, even in this difficult matter, the "collaborative understanding" between Freud and Jung persisted unbroken. He has rightly noted that repeated expressions of supportive interest and admiration fill the correspondence between them, despite the fact that they were struggling to articulate matters about which their underlying assumptions would prove irreconcilable.

thanks to your discoveries, we are on the threshold of something really sensational, which I scarcely know how to describe except with the gnostic concept of [*Sophia*], an Alexandrian term particularly suited to the reincarnation of ancient wisdom in the shape of ψA. I daren't say too much, but would only counsel you (very immodestly) to let my [manuscript] unleash your associations and/or fantasies: I am sure you will hit upon strange things if you do. (Provided, of course, that the mysterious hint in your letter has not already done so in anagrammatic form. With that letter anything seems possible.) (*269*)

But Jung's illusions were beyond the realm of the possible, and his anagrams proved empty. The crashing disappointment was postponed for a few weeks by Freud's second visit to Zurich, where he spent four days with Jung before they both proceeded to the Weimar congress. In mid-October, Freud recalled with pleasure the "splendid" days in Zurich and Weimar and their profitable exchange of ideas and hopes (*273*), and the letters continued to be full of friendly interchange well into December 1911. But Freud's prosaic statement of his actual views on religion (cf. *270*) proved more than Jung could bear.

A series of four letters from Emma Jung to Freud (in McGuire, 1974), written without her husband's knowledge, revealed the true state of affairs. She began (October 30, 1911) by expressing her concern about Freud's "resignation" over the fate of his "spiritual son." She thought this attitude might have been the product of Freud's disagreement with Jung's ideas in the manuscript of *Symbols of Transformation*; she had probably arrived at this false conclusion on the basis of Jung's recurrent concerns about Freud's anticipated disapproval of the work. In a second letter (November 6, 1911) that followed Freud's "kindly reply," she was able to attribute these worries to Jung's "parental complex." She went on to criticize Freud as a parent who gave excessively and expected a proportionate return, adding some strikingly insolent suggestions about the advisability of analysis for Freud's sons.[3] Her third letter (November 14, 1911) revealed that, although annoyed, Freud had been content to characterize such unwarranted intrusions as "amiable carpings." This exchange ended with Freud convincing Emma Jung that her husband's fears about him had not been based on reality. She ultimately came to see that her husband had resisted some necessary self-analytic work through his fantasies of Freud's disapproval.

At the end of November 1911, Freud communicated some disagreement with Jung's unselective use of mythological material in his manuscript—a point he had discussed at a meeting of the Vienna Society on November 8 (Nunberg & Federn, 1974, p. 307). He went on to indicate

3. Loewald (1977) has reacted differently to this interchange, stressing the good sense behind Emma Jung's warning that Freud was expecting too much of her husband.

that Jung had distorted the Freudian definition of libido in this work (*286*). Jung's reaction to these matter-of-fact criticisms demonstrates that his fear of Freud's disapproval reversed the actual state of affairs: It was Jung himself who proved to be unable to tolerate Freud's nonacceptance of his views. His rage over this injury to his self-esteem took the form of supporting the complaints of one of Freud's patients who had come to him to denounce Freud's nonsympathetic analytic stance toward her (cf. *291*).[4] As Jung must have anticipated, the woman duly reported her transaction with him in her analysis with Freud. In his next letter (*290*), Freud reiterated the technical inadvisability of personal overinvolvement with patients and then confronted the underlying issue openly: "If you really feel any resentment towards me, there is no need to use Frau C— as an occasion for venting it. . . . Just wait for my next misdeed and have it out with me directly." Jung attempted some lame explanations in a letter loaded with flowery compliments about Freud's undying fame (*291*). In fact, he accepted Freud's view of the incident seemingly without rancor, correctly adding that the criticism of Freud implicit in his remarks to Frau C— had not been based on frustrated wishes for affection: "In this respect, you would have more right to complain about me" (*292*).

Freud did not make an issue of this incident (*293*), but he clearly realized that Emma Jung's fears about the future of his relationship with Jung had been all too well founded. The correspondence subsequently became perfunctory until late February when a slip of the pen by Freud betrayed his strong sense of loss about Jung's estrangement (*298*). Jung picked up the fact that his uncommunicativeness had hurt Freud but excused himself on the ground that he was pouring himself into work "*ad majorem gloriam* ψA"—for the greater glory of psychoanalysis (*300*). Thus, psychoanalysis was still a manifestation of the Godhead for him, even if he had finally given up on Freud as a religious leader.

Freud's dignified response (*301*) acknowledged that he had been a demanding correspondent but did not permit Jung to rationalize his remissness in terms of mere irresponsibility (*300*). In the light of the latest developments, Freud reported, "I took myself in hand and quickly turned off my excess libido." In his reply, Jung acknowledged that he had behaved in an awkward and nasty manner, but he proceeded to resurrect the canard that Freud had taken offense at his divergent scientific views. He assumed a pseudomoral stance: "As one who is truly your follower, I must be stout-hearted, not least towards you" (*303*). As Jung himself would admit (*305*), Freud's answer was extremely kind. He pointed out

4. Stepansky (1976, pp. 231–232) has pointed out that Jung's rageful response was probably aggravated by the fact that he was utterly unprepared for Freud's definitive rejection of his views. Throughout the preceding period, he notes, Freud had in fact given Jung the impression that his revisions of libido theory would be received sympathetically.

that after the disappointment of his hope for "a reciprocal intimate friendship," he was now compelled to withdraw in order to defend himself. He protested that it was false to impute intellectual tyranny to him on the basis of his need to protect himself emotionally. Freud then expressed his continued willingness to resume intimacy whenever Jung might be ready to tolerate it: "During the transition to this attitude of reserve, I have complained very quietly. You would have thought me insincere if I had not reacted at all" (*304*).

There matters stood until the end of May 1912. About a dozen letters were exchanged in the interval, specifying the increasing differences in the writers' scientific views but lacking personal commentary. At Whitsun, Freud made a hurried trip to Switzerland to visit Ludwig Binswanger, who was thought to be dangerously ill. He was apparently hoping that Jung might join him in Kreuzlingen and thus wrote to him about the prospective journey (*316*). As Jones has recounted (1955, p. 144), Jung proceeded to construct a grievance: On the basis of erroneous assumptions about the dating of Freud's letter, he convinced himself that Freud had intentionally informed him of his visit to Binswanger too late for Jung to join them and had thereby snubbed him. In his reply (*317*), Jung took the stance of a patient martyr. He accused Freud of having slighted him because of "displeasure at my development of the libido theory" (*318*). Freud again answered in an equable tone, affirming that scientific differences need not alter their personal relations and correcting Jung's misinterpretations of his visit to Binswanger. Jung's reply was angrily assertive and unmistakably paranoid: "I understand the Kreuzlingen gesture" (*320*). In August, he offered to have the membership of the International Psychoanalytic Association review the matter of his presidency to test "whether deviations are to be tolerated or not" (*321*).

Jones (1955, pp. 93–95) quotes a letter (September 14, 1912) in which Freud expressed appreciation for a very friendly note from Emma Jung (see McGuire, 1974, p. 514), discreetly dissociating her from her husband's hostile attitude. This exchange occurred during the summer when a "committee" of Freud's most loyal adherents was established; it was clearly intended to replace Jung as the standard-bearer of psychoanalysis. Jung had left Zurich on September 7, 1912, for a lengthy lecture tour in America, and he did not get in touch with Freud until his return in early November. At that time, he continued to insist he had been dealt "a lasting wound" by the "Kreuzlingen gesture," and he still attributed the gesture to Freud's alleged resentment over his theoretical innovations. He protested in advance that his views could not be ascribed to resistance; he further betrayed his real feelings about having been confronted with his hostility toward Freud the previous December by exclaiming that he wouldn't tolerate being "treated like a fool riddled with complexes" (*323*). Freud's reply assumed a much more formal tone than any of his previous letters, and he was explicit about the fact that his affection had cooled: "You have successfully broken me of that habit." He once again expressed puzzlement about Jung's insulting remarks concerning Kreuzlingen and reiterated his belief that scientific differences need not interfere with their collaboration (*324*). The fact that this stance was emotionally unacceptable to Jung was reconfirmed by his next letter: "Since you have disavowed me so thoroughly, my collaboration can hardly be acceptable" (*326*).

Jones (1955, pp. 145–147) has reported the temporary dissolution of Jung's paranoid attitude in the course of an administrative meeting in Munich in late November 1912. On this occasion, Jung acknowledged his misconstruction of Freud's visit to Binswanger and "became extremely contrite." According to Jones, Freud "did not spare him a good fatherly lecture. Jung accepted all the criticisms and promised to reform" (p. 145). It was at the luncheon following this confrontation that Freud underwent a fainting episode that was probably related to memories of his rupture with Wilhelm Fliess—a loss that had been prefigured by a fainting episode on his part in the very same dining room! Nothing could have been more damaging to the reconciliation that had just taken place. As Jung records in his autobiography, "Everyone clustered helplessly around him. I picked him up, carried him into the next room, and laid him on a sofa. As I was carrying him, he half came to, and I shall never forget the look he cast at me. In his weakness he looked at me as if I were his father" (1963, p. 157).[5]

Even Freud's refusal to be the prophet of a therapeutic religion could not have been as disillusioning as this "weakness." In retrospect, the previous fainting spell in Bremen now appeared in the same light: "The fantasy of father-murder was common to both cases" (Jung, 1963, p. 157). Nonetheless, Jung's very next letter confirmed his distress over his own lack of insight and affirmed his intention of maintaining the relationship with Freud, having come to realize how very different he and Freud were. He closed with expressions of personal concern and good wishes (*328*). In his answer, Freud thanked him for his friendliness and gently implied that Jung's resentment of the scientific differences between them had been at the root of the trouble. Although this interpretation was certainly correct, it overlooked Jung's need to idealize him; that is, it overlooked the probability that the scientific differences had initially arisen because of the disappointment Freud had caused Jung by disclaiming omniscience. Hence it was quite disastrous for Freud to go on

5. In Chapter 14, where the special difficulties of the religious innovator are considered through the illustrative example of Jung's struggle to find his calling, I shall begin the exposition by reconsidering this incident.

to confess that he had not yet found the time to analyze his fainting spell (*329*): This admission of inability to understand his own reactions repeated the disappointment once again.

On December 3, 1912, Jung responded in a furious, accusatory tone. He charged Freud with being unable to value Jung's contribution because of his own neurosis, the persistence of which he now attributed to Freud's uncooperativeness on the occasion of Jung's attempt to analyze his dreams on the trip back from America in 1909. He also tried to head off the rejoinder that these attitudes were manifestations of a father complex (*330*). Jung must have repented of this outburst at once, for on December 4 he appended the following note to a business communication dealing with publishing arrangements he had negotiated on behalf of the International Psychoanalytic Association: "I hope you weren't offended by my last letter. I wish you the best of everything and I shall not abandon you. You shouldn't be distressed on my account" (*331*). But it was too late; Freud's willingness to compromise had come to an end. "Let each of us pay more attention to his own than to his neighbor's neurosis," he commented drily (*332*), and when Jung made a slip of the pen that betrayed his lack of allegiance to psychoanalysis (see *335*), Freud curtly pointed it out (*337*). This elicited still another rageful letter in which Jung, extremely provocative and arrogant in tone, dismissed his own slip "in comparison with the formidable beam in my brother Freud's eye. I am not in the least neurotic—touch wood!"—this last, apparently, on the basis of having been "analyzed," unlike Freud (*338*).

On January 3, 1913, Freud broke off the personal relationship because of the impossibility of dealing with Jung's unrealistic accusations (*342*). Jung's resignation from the editorship of the *Jahrbuch* folowed in October 1913. In April 1914, he resigned the presidency of the International Association, and in July he withdrew from the Zurich Society. Freud might well have consoled himself with the very advice he had given Jung early in 1909, when the latter had been so troubled about the difficulty of being a psychoanalyst: "*Navigare necesse est, vivere non necesse.*"[6]

II

JUNG'S OWN survival as a fallen angel was quite precarious at first. "After the break with Freud," he recalled, "all my friends and acquaintances dropped away. My book was declared to be rubbish; I was a mystic, and that settled the matter. Riklin and Maeder alone stuck by me" (1963, p. 167). Furthermore: "a period of inner uncertainty began for

6. It is necessary to sail, not to survive—a motto taken from Plutarch's *Life of Pompey*.

me. It would be no exaggeration to call it a state of disorientation. I felt totally suspended in mid-air. . . .[7] I lived as if under constant inner pressure. At times this became so strong that I suspected there was some psychic disturbance in myself" (pp. 170, 173). By the autumn of 1913, the threat to Jung's psychic integration had progressed to the point of a vague delusional system: "The pressure which I had felt was in *me* seemed to be moving outward. . . . It was as though the sense of oppression no longer sprang exclusively from a psychic situation, but from concrete reality" (p. 175).

In October 1913, when he was initiating his actual withdrawal from the psychoanalytic community, Jung was "seized by an overpowering vision" of a catastrophe destroying Europe in a sea of blood. This frightful fantasy recurred several times, leading Jung to decide "that I was menaced by a psychosis." Over the following months, this disturbance took on an increasingly megalomaniacal flavor; in June 1914, Jung dreamt of the destruction of the European heartland by frightful cold "descended from out of the cosmos" except for his own "tree of life . . . whose leaves had been transformed by the effects of the frost into sweet grapes full of healing juices. I plucked the grapes and gave them to a large, waiting crowd" (Jung, 1963, p. 176). Thus had Jung himself become "the soothsaying God of the vine" whose prophet he had wanted Freud to be.

We can put this differently by stating that Jung saw himself as another reincarnated Christ, freed from the undesirable encrustations through which his divine message had been distorted by institutional Christianity. From such a perspective, a Jewish precursor, Sigmund Freud, takes on the significance of a John the Baptist. In this regard, it is highly suggestive that Jung was never able to accept Freud's secular attitude at face value. A half century after their break, he continued to insist that Freud had been a deeply religious man who had unfortunately needed to erect defensive barriers against this essential component of his own nature: "He gave me the impression that at bottom he was working against his own goal and against himself; and there is, after all, no harsher bitterness than that of a person who is his own worst enemy" (1963, p. 152). The passage is reminiscent of the picture of the mortified Judas who had to commit suicide in reaction to his betrayal of Christ.

In my view, these claims of the elderly Jung show that he never overcame the confusion of his own goals and values with those of Freud. Thus, when Freud explained the heuristic necessity for the libido theory as the need to anchor psychoanalysis within biology, thereby preventing

---

7. This candid self-description bears a striking resemblance to the reports and imagery of analytic patients who, having established archaic transferences with their analysts, suddenly find themselves cast upon their own resources.

its engulfment by a "black tide of occultism," Jung could not see this as a statement about intellectual issues; he interpreted it in terms of his personal psychology, which he then proceeded to attribute to Freud. He assumed, in other words, that, like himself, Freud had been menaced by the threat of regression into magical thinking.[8] Contrary to Jung's version of this incident, which depicts Freud communicating this idea with a "deeply moved expression," the letters provide a rather matter-of-fact, written statement on the issue: "In the sexual processes we have the indispensable 'organic foundation' without which a medical man can only feel ill at ease in the life of the psyche" (*84*, dated April 19, 1908).

As for Jung's "discovery" that Freud had erected sexuality into a crypto-religious entity, a *"deus absconditus"* or concealed god, the correspondence suggests that the idea may have originated in Jung's concretization of one of Freud's favored metaphorical expressions. In the spring of 1911, Freud had characterized Adler's theories as "heresy against the offended Goddess Libido" (*238*). Was it on the basis of this phraseology that Jung later wrote, "Freud [was] trying to outdo the church and to canonize a theory. To be sure, he did not do this too loudly; instead, he suspected *me* of wanting to be a prophet" (1963, p. 154)? Elsewhere, however, Jung was proud to own up to his own prophetic ambitions and to adjudge his life a series of irruptions of the "imperishable world" into this "transitory one" (1963, p. 4). He saw the Freudian exploration of the depths as a search for the lost God who would be found "below, not above" (1963, p. 151). In the manner characteristic of certain thought disorders, that is, Jung had taken the epigraph of *The Interpretation of Dreams* (1900) in a completely literal way: *Flectere si nequeo superos, Acheronta movebo* means "If I cannot bend the higher powers, I shall move those of the Underworld." Loewald (1977) has evaluated Jung's misperception of Freud on this score similarly.

In Jung, the process of psychic disintegration set in motion by the disappointment of his hopes in Freud was apparently halted by the outbreak of the World War in August 1914. Convinced by this cataclysm that his personal psychic experience "coincided with that of mankind in general," Jung was confirmed in the role of messiah. He felt possessed of demonic strength and of the "unswerving conviction that I was obeying a higher will" (1963, pp. 176–177). He was not without insight into the nature of the experiences he was undergoing:

> I [ran] into the same psychic material which is the stuff of psychosis
> and is found in the insane. This is the fund of unconscious images

---

8. Jung (1963, pp. 150–151) claims that his interchange occurred during a conversation of 1910 in Vienna. In fact, Freud and Jung met twice in 1910, in Nuremberg and Munich (as I have already recounted), but not in Vienna. To be sure, the conversation may actually have taken place at another time or in another place, but Jung's slip in memory calls his entire account into doubt.

which fatally confuse the mental patient. But it is also the matrix of a mythopoeic imagination which has vanished from our rational age. (1963, p. 188)

He was able to continue his practice and his family life; he was reassured by these routines because he knew that psychotics could not maintain them:

> These were actualities which . . . proved to me again and again that I really existed, that I was not a blank page whirling about in the winds of the spirit, like Nietzsche. (1963, p. 189)

It was not until 1918 or 1919 that he settled down sufficiently to embark on a half century of productive scholarship in a unique and newly found discipline that tried to return psychology to a transcendental system.[9]

In a letter of March 1911 (241), Freud had written Jung that symbol formation may be the initial stage in the development of a concept. The metaphors Jung used in describing psychoanalysis in his letters are thereby revealing of how Jung himself increasingly understood this discipline; as we have seen, the metaphors were consistently religious. Among the more striking examples of this proclivity, Jung wrote that becoming a psychoanalyst, like eating from the tree of paradise, made one clairvoyant (28); for him, the act of representing Freud at a psychiatric meeting constituted an "apostolic journey" (41); in analyzing his own dreams, he felt he was making his "morning devotions" (204); at one congress, he felt like Luther at the Diet of Worms (239).[10]

In spite of his refusal to concede that Freud had an irreligious attitude, Jung did indeed grasp that the Freudian empire clearly had nothing in common with the City of God. In his autobiography (1963, pp. 179–181), he reported that on December 18, 1913, one year to the day after he wrote the letter that caused Freud to break with him (338), he had a dream of killing the hero Siegfried. I shall discuss this revealing material in greater detail in the next chapter; here I only wish to note that Jung's associations revealed that Siegfried stood for a part of himself: "the attitude embodied by Siegfried, the hero, no longer suited me"; it had to

9. In a discussion of an earlier version of this chapter at the San Francisco Psychoanalytic Society (October 13, 1975), Erik Erikson pointed out that Philip Rieff (1966) was inexact in characterizing Jung's private religion as "God-centered"; it was in fact, closer to certain Eastern faiths that do not conceptualize a definite deity. In this sense, Jung may have succeeded in overcoming his earlier need for an idealized other.

10. In contrast, Freud's metaphors were invariably political: He pleaded for harmony among his followers with "we mustn't quarrel while we are besieging Troy" (87), compared himself to Moses, and called Jung his Joshua, destined to take possession of "the promised land of psychiatry" (125). Jung was, variously, his "crown prince" (139) who would lead the cause to victory (174), his "dear son Alexander" (182), and his adopted son Augustus (205) who would establish the psychoanalytic empire.

be abandoned for the sake of "higher things." The secular aims promoted by Freud, the offer of psychoanalytic empires, had to be rejected.[11] Jung did not connect this dream with Freud, but its occurrence on the anniversary of his murderous message and the choice of Siegfried, son of Siegmund, to represent himself, suggest that he felt pushed into the role of the hero by Freud's "paternal authority."

Jung has claimed that Freud forfeited this authority by refusing the risk of losing it in the course of their mutual dream analyses of 1909. A dream of his own from this very time (Jung, 1963, pp. 158–161)—the dream that Freud appealed to in documenting his conviction that Jung wanted him out of the way—shows that Freud's lack of authority actually stemmed from his refusal to play God. This complex dream involved descent through a succession of levels in Jung's house, each more archaic than the one above, into a prehistoric cave containing scattered bones and broken pottery. In the deepest recesses of his own mind, in other words, Jung portrayed only devastation. This was the void he sought to fill by eating the fruit of the psychoanalytic tree of paradise.

Between the ages of 3 and 4, shortly after being separated from his mother who had been temporarily hospitalized for an emotional disturbance, Jung had his "earliest dream." This dream, which preoccupied him for the rest of his life (1963, pp. 11–13), also involved descent into an underground cavern; here, a huge phallic shape of naked flesh sat upon a magnificent golden throne. The dreamer heard his mother's voice warn him that this was the man-eater. It was the desperate need to idealize a male figure implied in this nightmare that Jung eventually directed onto Sigmund Freud. Instead of the Godhead, however, he would only find the archeological science of psychoanalysis. Creatively, he solved his dilemma by finding the divine in his own unconscious, a solution I shall explore in greater detail in Chapter 14.

Jung's own statement about what he had been seeking in the relationship with Freud is both explicit and insightful: "My whole being was seeking for something still unknown which might confer meaning upon the banality of life" (1963, p. 165). Hence, he became scornful of Freud's viewpoint that, except for the various "all-too-human" limitations, nothing much is to be found in Man. As Jung put it, "That cabbages thrive in dung was something I had always taken for granted" (p. 166).

---

11. Jung was striving for an empire of the spirit, to be the founder of a great new religion, like Ikhnaton, the originator of monotheism. How very wrong Jones's interpretation (1955, pp. 146–147) about the explosion in Munich in November 1912 had been! Jung's frantic protest about Karl Abraham's view of Ikhnaton did not originate in a need to disavow patricidal impulses—throughout his life, Jung had striven to erect a father adequate to his needs, not to destroy one. In the Munich incident, the originator of a new theogony was rightfully defending his life's work against the pejorative implications of an inadequate application of psychoanalytic drive psychology to his essential personal aims.

Philip Rieff (1966) may have been the first to perceive Jung's defection from psychoanalysis as the successful transformation of psychological treatment into a new form of religion; he dubbed the sage of Bollingen the prophet of an original Revelation. Jung protected his creation from the ossification inevitable in institutions by confining it to the private arena of dyadic therapeutic relationships. Present-day Jungians tend to be quite forthright on this score; Meier (1977), for instance, asserts that the effects of therapy "cannot be understood by psychological knowledge alone"; the "riddle" of mental healing is a "miracle" that must be attributed to "the religious factor" (p. 5). Meier acknowledges that such considerations can find no scientific explanations.

Irrational though Jung's solution for understanding man's spirituality may have been, we cannot afford to avoid the challenge it poses. If psychoanalysis continues to neglect such questions, we may yet have to echo the philosopher–emperor Julian's despairing concession to the forces of irrationality he had tried to stem: "Thou hast conquered, Galilean!"

Chapter Fourteen

The Air Trembles, for Demi-Gods Draw Near*

*2 Faust II: 3—On the Lower Peneus

I

IN A RECENT commentary on C. G. Jung's *Answer to Job* (1952), Harry Slochower (1981) has brought to light a remarkable letter the Swiss psychiatrist wrote to Hans Illing in 1955. In this document (presently unavailable for exact quotation), Jung, in his own terms, reaffirmed the profound divergence between his psychological system and that of Sigmund Freud. In Slochower's view, Jung's religious commitments were sequelae of his relationship to Freud, that is, of feelings toward Freud that Jung himself had characterized as a "religious crush" in the fall of 1907. As the letter of 1955 demonstrates, Jung certainly continued to nurse a quasi-paranoid sense of grievance about the rupture between himself and Freud. As I have discussed in the last chapter, the source of Jung's feeling of injury was the disappointment of his desperate need to idealize Freud as the prophet of a new therapeutic cult. Despite the clear persistence of this aspect of Jung's archaic reaction to Freud, I see an explanation of Jung's religiosity at the level of a transference interpretation to be so partial as to be misleading. In order to place this issue in a wider context, I will amplify the psychological portrait of Jung that I began to sketch in the preceding two chapters, placing particular emphasis on two issues uppermost in the recently discovered letter of 1955: Jung's attitudes toward Nazism and toward the Jews.

As a point of entry into this material, we may recall the fateful meeting of November 24, 1912, in the Park Hotel in Munich, where, for the last

A previous version of this material appeared in *American Imago*, 38:61–80, 1981.

time, Freud succeeded in dispelling Jung's paranoid attitude toward him (see Jones, 1955, pp. 145–147). Following this successful reconciliation, the luncheon conversation focused on Karl Abraham's thesis that the religious innovations of the Egyptian pharaoh Ikhnaton could be explained in terms of patricidal motives. While Jung was vigorously taking issue with this interpretation, Freud had a fainting episode that ultimately struck his student as an enactment of Freud's fantasy that Jung harbored unconscious death wishes toward him (Jung, 1963, p. 157). At the time, however, Jung preferred to imagine that Freud was physically ill and quickly sent him a note full of solicitous good wishes; it was Freud himself who, in his reply of November 29, diagnosed the fainting spell as symptomatic of a piece of neurosis he had not yet bothered to analyze (329). This confession deprived Jung of his defensive disavowal of what he had perceived; as he reflected half a century after the fainting incident: "I shall never forget the look he cast at me. In his weakness he looked at me as if I were his father" (p. 157).

This transference repetition of Jung's childhood experience with a powerless father (cf. Jung, 1963, pp. 52, 55) was apparently traumatic enough to provoke the first of those rude and arrogant letters (December 3, 1912; 330) that would soon convince Freud of the need to terminate the personal relationship with his rageful disciple altogether. As I have described in Chapter 13, Jung's paranoid attitude had initially supervened— probably in the summer of 1911 but no later than May 1912—as a result of Freud's explicit insistence that he could not be regarded as the founder of a new religion as Jung then needed to view him (cf. 269, 270). Thus the Munich discussion about Ikhnaton, the originator of monotheism, was a thinly veiled restatement of the fundamental divergence of aims between the two men. Freud must have realized that Jung's passionate argument that religious innovation cannot be reduced to aspects of an infantile neurosis (as Freud was then trying to do) demonstrated the hopelessness of retaining his allegiance. Freud's loss of consciousness in that context, echoing the loss of his vital relationship to his friend Wilhelm Fliess a decade earlier,[1] must have served as an emergency defense against that painful realization. It seems reasonably certain that Jung was never able to maintain a realistic view of Sigmund Freud: Unless he could attribute magical powers to him he tended to view Freud as a reincarna-

---

1. Schur (1972, pp. 264–271) has discussed the probable significance of Freud's fainting spells *in extenso*—without satisfactorily resolving the matter in my judgment. Because the fainting spells in Jung's presence repeated two similar episodes with Fliess, it may not be possible to penetrate their meaning without information about the specifics of the Freud– Fliess rupture. Freud's experience with Jung, that is, may have constituted a transference repetition of the earlier transaction with Fliess.

tion of his inadequate father.[2] The emotional consequences of the emergence of such a negative father transference may be discerned most clearly by examining one of Jung's "secret" childhood experiences, as Slochower (1981) terms it. I am referring to Jung's fantasy about the so-called cathedral. Before turning to this material, however, we should note that Jung's "pseudoidealization" (see Gedo, 1975) of Freud—the insistence that he was "an Old Testament prophet" (Jung, 1963, p. 169)—did not form part of the father transference. On the contrary, it constituted a vigorous defense against it. Moreover, there may have been a childhood precedent for Jung's transference relationship to Freud. Specifically, his tendency to erotize his attachment to Freud was probably related to another early secret memory, that of the admired man who had seduced him as a child; the disillusionment that followed this incident probably put an end to Jung's initial efforts to escape the consequence of his disappointment in his father.

The cathedral fantasy took place shortly after Jung began to attend school in Basel at the age of 11 (1963, pp. 36–41). This was a time of disillusionment with his family, allegedly because the boy finally grasped how modest their circumstances were. In a shameful but exhilarating vision, Jung imagined that God destroyed the *Münster* of Basel by defecating on it; he felt like a "chosen one" in being given this sign of divine contempt for the Protestant church. The significance of this fantasy is transparent if we recall that Jung's father was a Protestant clergyman, a minister whose faith was hollow by his son's standards.

I think there can be little doubt that Jung attempted to force on Freud the role of a prophet of the vengeful God (Yahweh?) at the same time as he sought to transform psychoanalysis into a post-Christian creed that might provide modern man with an intoxicating "irresistible mass movement" (see *178*). Hence his reaction to Freud's definitive rejection of these transference projections was, once again, an anally tinged attack from a megalomanic posture (e.g., on December 18, 1912, he wrote: "You go around sniffing out all the symptomatic actions in your vicinity. . . . For sheer obsequiousness nobody dares to pluck the prophet by the beard" [*338*].)

In childhood, Jung had a need to disavow his grandiose ideation and the cathedral fantasy reached his awareness only in the face of strong resistance. He conceptualized his anxiety about the fantasy as a reaction to the possession of a dark and terrible secret, a frightful revelation,

2. See, for example, Jung's letters of December 14, 1909: "You are a human hero and demigod" (*168*) and of August 29, 1911: "Thanks to your discoveries, we are on the threshold of something really sensational, which I scarcely know how to describe except with the gnostic concept of [*Sophia*]" (*269*).

something evil and sinister. Given Jung's anxiety about this memory, I tend to doubt a conjecture put forward by Homans (1979, p. 122) that Jung's secret childhood ritual that involved manipulating a manikin of his own creation involved his need "to idealize a male figure"; more likely, this ritual was the behavioral concomitant of megalomanic fantasies in which the boy wielded omnipotent control over a microcosm. After the break with Freud, Jung either chose to confront this aspect of himself or lacked the strength to maintain his former defenses: In either case, for the next several years Jung engaged in that confrontation with the unconscious that Ellenberger (1970, p. 672) has termed his "creative illness."

Perhaps his lasting grievance against Freud resulted from the latter's decision to dissociate himself from Jung's personal struggles. Be that as it may, much of the material Jung has revealed (1963) about the turmoil that followed his split from Freud is openly grandiose. Consider his fantasy of October 1913, the period when he was initiating his official withdrawal from the psychoanalytic community, about a catastrophe that would cover Europe with a sea of blood. By June 1914, he was dreaming about himself as a divine personage. Ultimately, Jung would characterize such experiences as irruptions of the "imperishable world" into the "transitory" one (1963, p. 4). Sometime during World War I, he gained the "unswerving conviction" that he "was obeying a higher will"; he thereby felt possessed of "demonic strength" (p. 177). His subsequent career as psychologist and sage of Bollingen was a thinly disguised effort to found a modern religion (cf. Gedo, 1972d, pp. 199–205, 219–221, and Chapter 13).

II

IN HIS AUTOBIOGRAPHY (1963, pp. 10–13), Jung provided information that permits us to trace these issues back to his early childhood; Slochower (1981) refers to the material in question as the "secret dream" of the phallus. We touched on this dream at the end of the preceding chapter: During a separation from his emotionally disturbed mother at the age of 3, the boy dreamt of a huge naked phallus on a golden throne in an underground cavern. In the dream, his mother's voice warned him that this phallus was the man-eater. I believe this imagery represents a compromise between the child's need to idealize a paternal figure (the need that leads to the fellatio fantasies and homosexual anxieties that beset Jung in his contacts with Freud) and his subject-centered grandiosity, the latter expressed in fantasies of being a divine phallic entity. Let us again recall Jung's dream of June 1914 (1963, p. 176) in which he fed the waiting multitudes "sweet grapes full of healing juices" from his own "tree of life." Here, at the threshold of his most productive years, the dreamer was confident of his capacity to provide in the active mode whatever men may need to incorporate; homosexuality had been converted into a sacrament.

It follows that Jung's complex relationship to the man-eating, cruel God he was to identify with Yahweh (1963, p. 201) both preceded and outlasted his transference reaction to Freud. Jung himself was quite aware of this fact; in the prologue of his autobiography, he noted that "people are established inalienably in my memories only if their names were entered in the scrolls of my destiny from the beginning, so that encountering them was at the same time a kind of recollection" (1963, p. 5). Hence, in disagreement with Slochower's (1981) view, I believe that Jung tried to make use of Freud as long as possible as a relatively healthy alternative to the maximally regressive modes of object relationship that emerged after their rupture. We might think of his efforts in this respect as part of a defense through maturational progress. Like Jung's own father, however, Freud did not lend himself to being used as a pseudoidealized figure.

Perhaps the best way to substantiate this point is to return to the dream that reportedly occurred on December 18, 1913, the first anniversary of the letter Jung had written Freud (*338*) that led the latter to break off contact. Jung wrote: "I was with an unknown, brown-skinned man, a savage, in a lonely, rocky mountain landscape. It was before dawn. . . . I heard Siegfried's horn sounding over the mountains and I knew that we had to kill him. . . . We shot at him, and he plunged down, struck dead" (1963, p. 180). The dream filled Jung with "unbearable guilt," and he thought he would have to shoot himself unless he could "understand" it. His interpretation was that "the attitude embodied by Siegfried, the hero, no longer suited me"; it had to be abandoned on behalf of "higher things."

In order to grasp the significance of Jung's terse statement about the meaning of his dream, we must recall that aspect of Wagner's *Ring of the Niebelungs* to which he was alluding. In this saga, the hero Siegfried was the son of Siegmund, a fact that points to Jung's frustrated wishes to force Freud into the role of an idealized father—or into the role of the prophet of Yahweh. Thus the dream expressed Jung's desperate wish to transcend his longing for Freud. Although he aspired to loftier aims than those of Siegfried (which he depreciated as standing for the German ambition to impose on others), Jung actually represented the repudiation of his loyalty to Freud as a savage deed. A few days before this dream, Jung had had a vision in which he first sighted the corpse of Siegfried in a cave to which he was admitted by a dwarf (p. 179): Obviously, he knew himself to be on the side of the evil Niebelungs!

Jung's profound guilt in reaction to the dream betrayed the fact that he had no rational justification for provoking the rupture with Freud. His obsessional idea of suicide did not constitute a plan to expiate his guilt because his "understanding" of the dream amounts to nothing but a transparent rationalization. But then, Jung had no more justification for the secret contempt of his father embodied in his cathedral fantasy. It follows, I believe, that the "higher things" for which he abandoned both his father and Freud were tied to his grandiose ambitions in the religious sphere. In terms of the Judeo-Christian tradition, neither man fit into his narcissistic world by playing the part of a minister of Yahweh; in the parallel Nordic myth, neither could embody the will of Wotan as Jung required them to do. When nobody was available to contain Jung's grandiosity in this manner, he began to feel that his own unconscious was divine.

It is with these considerations in mind that we may be able to comprehend Jung's later references to Nazism. Hitler succeeded in creating an intoxicating mass movement with an ideology that offered modern man an alternative to religious traditions he could no longer espouse with enthusiasm. Perhaps the most significant statement of the dilemma to which Nazism attempted to provide a "world historical answer" (Jung's phrase in the letter of 1955 [see Slochower, 1981]), at least for populations of German culture, was provided by Nietzsche, who had proclaimed that God was dead and the values of Christianity were to be overthrown (see Chapter 10). I believe Jung was trying to condemn Hitler's "negative" response to the challenge Nietzsche had posed without discrediting the need to provide a valid answer to it—as he had in fact attempted to do in his life work.

In this connection, it is relevant to recall that Jung dismissed the value of theological thinking among his relatives by stating that in their discourse "the name of Nietzsche did not occur at all" (1963, p. 73). As a student at the university, he hesitated to study the writings of his great Basel predecessor, "held back by a secret fear that I might perhaps be like him, at least in regard to the 'secret' which had isolated him . . . like me, he was a clergyman's son" (p. 102). One of Jung's formative intellectual experiences had been reading *Thus Spake Zarathustra*, a work that had an impact on him comparable to Goethe's *Faust*. Jung looked upon the personal disaster that had overtaken Nietzsche as a cautionary tale: He concluded that he must never publicly reveal "this *arrheton*, this thing not to be named" (p. 73) that constituted his religious inspiration. He was guided, in this respect, by his realization "that one gets nowhere unless one talks to people about the things they know" (p. 103).

On the intellectual plane, Jung was attracted to psychoanalysis because he viewed Freud's emphasis on sexuality as a counterweight to "Nietzsche's deification of the power principle" (1963, p. 153); nor could he ever understand the libido theory in any context without imputing religious meaning to it (cf. Chapter 13, p. 253). After the rupture with Freud, he

THE AIR TREMBLES, FOR DEMI-GODS DRAW NEAR

compared his turmoil to that of Nietzsche in his isolation (1963, p. 177), and he viewed the exploration of his grandiose religious ideation as a link "in the *Aurea Catena*" [the Golden Chain, i.e., the succession of great alchemists] that was to follow the Goethe of *Faust* and the Nietzsche of *Zarathustra* (p. 189).

Yet Jung was not simply a follower of Nietzsche; he was quite serious in his belief that he would succeed in encompassing in his own system the divergent perspectives of psychoanalysis and the will to power. He quoted Jacob Burckhardt's prophetic warnings about the fateful consequences of German hubris as closer to his own attitude than "the archetypes of Wagner . . . and the Dionysian experience of Nietzsche—which might better be ascribed to the god of ecstasy, Wotan" (1963, p. 235). Because the elderly Jung could look back upon 50 years of successful struggle with "the challenging riddles" posed for him by "the restless Wotan-Hermes of [his] . . . ancestors" (p. 318), he was able to view Hitler's enactment of *Götterdämmerung* with more empathy than others could command in the face of cruel divinities. Yet, in striking confirmation of Jung's perspective, Auden, in a poem entitled *September 1, 1939* (quoted in Waite, 1977, p. ii), termed Hitler "a psychopathic god" as early as 1939, whereas Robert Waite (1977, pp. 424–426) has more recently documented the dictator's identification with Wotan.

Jung's cryptic statement in the 1955 letter—"It is always the case of a man who does his best, [that he] falls into his worst"—must refer to enterprises of limitless ambition, such as Hitler's and his own. The manifest content of his Siegfried dream actually acknowledges his hubris, although his own interpretation of the dream repudiates this "German" aspect of himself. Yet, the unbearable guilt that follows the murder of Siegfried in the dream indicates that here Jung has fallen into *his* worst. Could it be that the brown-skinned savage who assists him in this deed is the Wild Huntsman, Wotan the Destroyer? Consider Slochower's (1981) astute observation that the Yahweh of Jung's *Answer to Job* (1952) represents an aspect of Jung himself as an unjust, cruel divinity—perhaps the man-eater of his secret phallus dream—that is no longer disavowed, as it had been 40 years earlier.

Hence we may reasonably conclude that Jung's paranoid attitude in his transactions with Freud in 1912 had been an attempt to project his own cruelty onto the latter; it was the failure of this defense that brought him face to face with the evil within himself. Surely, when he alluded to Yahweh's treatment of Job as a parallel to Nazism in his letter of 1955, Jung must have meant that Hitler–Wotan had played the part of the ruthless divinity even as the Jewish people were compelled to assume the status of their legendary martyr. In the context of Jung's mature religious thought, this interpretation is hardly exceptional. As Stepansky (1980) has shown, Jung's religious outlook emphasizes that God is to be feared *precisely* because He "fills us with evil as well as with good" (Jung, 1952, p. 461).

III

CAN WE CONCLUDE, then, that the intellectual content of the divergence between Freud and Jung concerns their respective emphases on different psychological issues? This is the thesis proposed by Homans (1979), who views Jung's psychological system as an early (and therefore understandably imperfect) effort to explore the terrain mapped out over the past decade in the work of Heinz Kohut (1971). There is, of course, a germ of truth in the contention that the two men were primarily interested in somewhat different clinical problems in 1912–1913, although I would not choose to characterize these problems in terms of the modish categories invoked by Homans.

The second decade of the century was a period that Freud utilized to test the limits of conclusions he had reached during the preceding decade on the ground of the "transference neuroses." Freud's initial aim in seeking a collaboration with Jung was to check the applicability of his theories to the psychoses by making use of the latter's expertise in this area (see *1, 8, 106*). In this sense, Jung's legitimate need repeatedly to bring up his own psychological concerns could only be a source of irritating distraction to the founder of a new discipline—however high Freud's estimation of Jung's talents may have been, after all, he was dealing with a neophyte barely past 30 when they met.

From the autobiographical data Jung chose to disclose at the age of 80, we can discern that, for him, the most pressing issue until middle age was the problem of evil. In 1913, Freud's psychological system was still so narrowly focused on the realm of sexual conflicts that it could not deal with such matters. Hence, from the standpoint of the traditional categories of psychoanalytic explanation, Jung was pushing Freud in the direction of the conceptual advances the latter would make seven years later in *Beyond the Pleasure Principle* (1920). Freud, that is, eventually proposed the concepts of the repetition compulsion and the death instinct as explanatory constructs that could encompass the full breadth of the problem of human aggression. In view of the fact that Freud did move on to these issues within a very few years, we must look for a more fundamental divergence to understand the intolerance with which the two would-be collaborators rejected one another's work.

In his letter of 1955, as on a number of previous occasions (listed in Slochower, 1981) Jung tried to explain this divergence in terms of the putative differences between the "characteristic psychology" of particular ethnic groups—in this specific instance, between the psychology of Jews and the psychology of Christians of German descent. In the present context, the vexing question of Jung's possible antisemitism need not concern us, for the issue at hand is that of the *nature* of these alleged racial differences, whatever Jung's valuation of them may have been. My own guess is that Jung was, in fact, perfectly justified in rejecting accusations of prejudice against Jews. By current standards, his attitudes were racist, but such views were neither unusual nor disreputable before the Nazi cataclysm. Cocks (1979) has reviewed Jung's actual behavior during the Nazi era; in his judgment, the latter did not compromise himself in any way.

In Jung's terminology, the inherited imprints of a collective unconscious capable of producing distinct psychological phenotypes in diverse ethnic groups are classified as archetypes. Clearly, Jung was convinced that his conceptualization of the archetypes represented an empirical biological discovery, an alternative to Freud's drive theory in anchoring his psychology in the natural sciences. Conversely, as I have already emphasized, he was able to grasp the concept of instinctual drives only as the covert introduction of the divine into Freud's system (cf. Jung, 1963, pp. 150–151). However skeptical we may be about Jung's speculative biologizing, the phenotypes he was concerned about may obviously come into being on the basis of cultural transmission rather than as a result of constitutional endowment alone. And, as a matter of fact, Jung's allusions to "Jewish psychology" in the letter to Illing of 1955 implicates the cultural heritage of the Jewish people—this despite his peculiar statement of 1934 that the Jews had never created a "cultural form" of their own (see Slochower, 1981, p. 6).

One can only assume that, at the height of Hitler's success in Germany and before the actualities of the New Order had made themselves manifest in their full horror, Jung was temporarily carried away by the promise of a messianic leader—a figure of the kind he wanted Freud to be a generation earlier. Thus, he blundered into depreciating Jewish culture on the basis of the Jews' presumed inability to organize a nation–state. Yet, in characterizing them in the letter as "nomads" Jung was actually acknowledging, in a most left-handed manner, the fact that Jews had cherished and preserved their distinctive culture through the two millenia of diaspora.

In the 1955 letter, Jung summed up his conception of Jewish psychology in terms of the "chosen people complex." He gave a concrete example of what he meant in describing Freud's personality as the personality of a man who had supreme confidence in the validity of his own introspective insights. Jung traced these flinty qualities to the nature of the Judaic deity, Yahweh, whom he called "Guardian of Law and Custom, though he is himself unjust" (in Slochower, 1981, p. 5). In his

Answer to Job (1952), he further characterized Yahweh as the embodiment of perfectionism, a divinity without love for mankind. Finally, in his autobiography (1963, p. 202), Jung criticized Judaism, along with the Protestantism of his forebears, as exclusively patriarchal in spirit, paying no heed whatsoever to the feminine principle.

Whether or not Jung's understanding of Judaism was an adequate basis for this judgment—a question I am not competent to answer—it was this conception that led him to classify psychoanalysis as a typically Jewish product. Because he thought of psychoanalysis, not unreasonably, as Freud's exclusive creation, the foregoing aspects of his conclusion may be translated into the following statements about Freud: The latter could not be persuaded to give greater weight to the clinical reports of others than to his own clinical experiences (presumably including the experience of his self-analysis); he insisted that psychoanalysis should be restricted to the procedure he had devised (i.e., that technical modifications should clearly be labeled as nonpsychoanalytic); he failed to value Jung's original contributions but demanded a high level of performance at tasks that his disciple found uncongenial (a set of circumstances Jung experienced as unfair); he withdrew his affection when confronted with Jung's volcanic ambivalence; and, as of 1913, he espoused clinical theories that underemphasized the role of the mother of earliest childhood in personality development. I believe that Jung was largely correct in these judgments, but it is difficult to see what any of these issues has to do with Freud's Jewishness. Moreover, it is hardly probable that a man who was Freud's junior by 20 years would have founded a separate psychological discipline on the foregoing grounds alone less than 15 years after Freud's creation of psychoanalysis. Complaints of this kind would simply not predispose a student an entire generation younger than a teacher of Freud's stature to desert the field after so brief an apprenticeship. To get to the heart of Jung's defection from psychoanalysis, then, we must look beyond his understanding of "Jewish psychology" to his own "Aryan" alternative.

IV

BY HIS OWN testimony, Jung's first encounter with the need to differentiate his viewpoint from psychoanalysis took place when he and Freud were about to embark on their trip to America from Bremen in August 1909. The two men, we have observed, tried to analyze each other's dreams every day; in this setting, Jung (1963, pp. 158–161) had a dream strikingly reminiscent of the secret dream of the phallus of his early childhood. In its new version, Jung descended into the underground cavern through a long series of cellars beneath his house only to find dust, scattered bones, and broken pottery. As I pointed out in the preceding chapter (p. 255), this dream must have been Jung's attempt to communicate to Freud his dissatisfaction with psychoanalysis, a scientific enterprise that, like archeology, lacked religious significance.

Jung deliberately misled Freud about his actual associations to this material: "It would have been impossible for me to afford him any insight into my mental world"—that is, into the world of Jung's childhood grandiosity that he was to keep secret for another half century. He rationalized this decision on the grounds of Freud's allegedly rigid commitment to the preeminent importance of sexual issues—a leaky argument, indeed, in view of the overt sexual content of the original version of the dream. At any rate, in 1909 Jung came to terms with his propensity to form megalomanic fantasies, an aspect of mental life he had always found extremely frightening—presumably because such ideas struck him as *prima facie* "crazy"—by devising the concept of a "collective unconscious"; that is, he disclaimed responsibility for unacceptable ideation by attributing it to his racial heritage (cf. Jung, 1963, p. 148).

It is of some interest that Jung juxtaposed his account of Freud's vain attempt to analyze his archeological dream of descending into the underground cavern with a report of the first episode of Freud's fainting in his presence (1963, p. 156). This occurred during a conversation about certain prehistoric mummified corpses excavated in the region; Freud was apparently quite irritated by Jung's preoccupation with this topic and regarded it as an indication that his disciple harbored death wishes toward him. As on the later occasion of the Munich discussion about Ikhnaton, Freud's interpretation was almost certainly inexact. The interpretive crux of the matter was contained in Jung's archeological dream, regardless of whether it preceded or followed Freud's fainting spell. Jung disclosed the connection between the mummified corpses and his dream in reporting a slip he made in discussing the corpses; he had mistakenly reported that they were found in the *cellars* of Bremen (1963, p. 156), that is, the very cellars which, in the context of Jung's Bremen dream, pointed to the religious emptiness of psychoanalysis. I think it very probable that Freud's loss of consciousness served to avoid the threatening insight that Jung's preoccupations (and his dream, if it in fact preceded this incident) were harbingers of the inevitable break between them. In terms of Freud's psychological system of 1909, Jung's problems were indeed prehistoric and therefore indecipherable (cf. Winnicott, 1964).

Kaufmann (1980b, p. 388) has discussed Jung's remarks of 1934, in a Nazi-controlled psychiatric journal, about the differences between the psychology of Jews and Aryans. He quotes Jung's claim that the Aryan unconscious "contains explosive forces and seeds of a future yet to be born . . . [it] has a higher potential than the Jewish." I believe Jung meant that, for good or ill, the primitive forces within himself and within the German people could lead to an "archetypal outbreak"—such as the

Nazi regime proved to be. In comparison, Freud was indeed the quiet voice of reason—as he was proudly to claim in *The Future of an Illusion* (Freud, 1927, p. 53). I am unable to judge whether Jews were everywhere destined to be the natural heirs of the Enlightenment, as Jung's statements would imply, but it is now an historical commonplace that this was indeed the case throughout the 19th century in the reactionary world east of the Rhine (see Gay, 1978; Schorske, 1981). Moreover, as Goya predicted at the end of the 18th century: *El sueño de la razón produce monstruos* [the sleep of reason produces monsters]. But Jung's needs propelled him toward gnosticism, alchemy, and certain other features of the Middle Ages.

He showed his understanding of this issue in the manner of concluding his autobiographical chapter on the relationship with Freud: He gave an account of a complex dream that, for him, prefigured their rupture. In the dream, he portrayed Freud as a sour, elderly Austrian customs official, paradoxically destined for immortality; I believe this imagery amounts to an acknowledgment that Jung had illegitimately tried to smuggle something alien into the Freudian system. The dream then contrasted this latter system with Jung's own psychological world, portrayed by means of the symbol of a 12th-century crusader knight. One can only agree with Jung's own conclusion: "my own world . . . had scarcely anything to do with Freud's. My whole being was seeking for something still unknown which might confer meaning upon the banality of life" (1963, p. 165). Jung was to find what he was looking for in the expressions of the "chthonic spirit" that were to preoccupy him for the rest of his life (p. 168).[3]

Jung described the first several instances of this kind several days after his receipt of Freud's letter breaking off their personal relationship. Around Christmas of 1912, Jung had a dream in which a dove was transformed into a marvelous girl child (and back again into a bird) while contrasting herself with a male dove "busy with the twelve dead" (1963, pp. 171–175). Jung had just arrived at the realization that "the Christian myth" was no longer meaningful for him, and he associated the twelve Apostles to the dead of the dream. Had word of the formation of the secret committee of Freud's loyal adherents reached him? Although he offered no interpretation to this effect, I think it fairly clear that, having lost the old religion and its Holy Spirit (Freud?), Jung had a desperate wish to make contact with a myth based on the feminine principle. Not long after having this dream, he built an altar on his property. As he was completing this task, he recalled for the first time in decades "the under-

3. Kaufmann (1980b, pp. 358–363) has interpreted this material more boldly; in his view, even the figure of the knight may conceal Jung's disavowed longing for Freud.

ground phallus" of his childhood dream and felt that he was on the way to the discovery of his own myth. This was the process Rieff (1966) has called Jung's theogony.

V

IN RECORDING the history of his spiritual quest, Jung has given us detailed evidence that permits identification of the roots of his inability to adhere to Freud's scientific humanism. It is quite true, as Homans (1979) has pointed out, that Jung's religious experiences were principally related to childhood events *preceding* the development of a full-scale Oedipus complex, as the crucial dream he had at the age of 3 already demonstrates. But it is not adequately illuminating merely to classify Jung's psychological world as preoedipal (and therefore "narcissistic" if one invokes Kohut's 1971 criteria)—or, for that matter, as weighted on the side of the feminine principle. In order to characterize it with greater precision, we must consider some additional data Jung himself provided.

Following his realization that he needed to create a private religion, Jung more or less worked through his separation from Freud in connection with the Siegfried material I have already discussed. From the religious point of view, he looked upon the "archetypal" male companion in the dream as his "shadow": a personification of everything he had theretofore refused to acknowledge about himself (1963, p. 181). In his autobiography, after recounting the Siegfried dream, Jung described a fantasy in which he encountered the Prophet Elijah and a blind Salome; Elijah assured Jung that the two "belonged together from all eternity." The "wise old prophet" thereby became a personification of an aspect of Jung himself. Analogously, Jung designated the female figure in the fantasy his "anima," that is, the representation of his unconscious femininity.[4]

Although he apprehended these images as his own creations, Jung simultaneously regarded them as distinct entities with a reality of their own. Thus, he discussed his internal guru, eventually called Philemon or Ka, as the revenant of another person (1963, p. 184). He further claimed to

---

4. Kaufmann (1980b, pp. 358–363) has astutely pointed out that the choice of Salome as Jung's "anima" was very likely based on the fact that Freud's favored female student at that time was the beautiful Lou Salomé—the very person Nietzsche had hoped to enlist in a similar role! It follows that the Jewish prophet, Elijah, must also refer to Sigmund Freud. Kaufmann even believes that, in a drawing Jung later made to represent this fantasy (reproduced in 1980b, p. 362), the "wise old prophet" physically resembles Freud.

It should be noted here that Kaufmann's work, which covers much the same ground as Section IV of this volume, is generally marred by a lack of empathy for Jung's position.

write down his associations so that the anima would have "no chance to twist them into intrigues," all the while acknowledging that "the insinuations of the anima . . . can utterly destroy a man" (pp. 186, 187). When his anima "left" him, Jung literally felt deprived of his soul, and he experienced "parapsychological phenomena" of being haunted by the spirits of the dead as a consequence (p. 191). Because of his access to this source of supernatural wisdom, Jung concluded that his "life belonged to the generality" (p. 192). Yet he summed up these matters insightfully:

> As a young man my goal had been to accomplish something in my science. But then, I hit upon this stream of lava, and the heat of its fires reshaped my life. That was the primal stuff which compelled me to work upon it, and my works are a more or less successful endeavor to incorporate this incandescent matter into the contemporary picture of the world. (p. 199)

From a psychoanalytic perspective, Jung's decision to focus exclusively on the common features of his own strange psychological world and those of mankind in general constitutes an avoidance of personal conflicts. At the same time, it is a perfectly legitimate pursuit, probably optimally adapted to the religious goal Jung had chosen. Hence, it is not valid to look upon him as a dissident from psychoanalysis; he is something entirely different, a genuine visionary. His religious movement, like that of Mary Baker Eddy, continued to straddle the frontier between the realm of the supernatural and that of psychobiological adaptation.

In the context of explaining the connection between his religous ideas and the tradition of alchemy, Jung (1963, pp. 213–215) recounted a dream that throws light on the childhood roots of his mysticism. He dreamt of entering a wing of his house he had never visited before; it consisted of his father's workroom and a room belonging to his mother. The former was set up as a zoological laboratory, even though its subject matter was Christianity; the mother's room was haunted and terrifying. The whole complex was hidden behind a public lobby full of worldly joviality. I will not try to interpret this material beyond observing that in mature life Jung viewed his parents in terms of polar opposites: The world of his father, like that of Sigmund Freud, was empirical and rational; the world of his mother was uncanny and numinous. Jung was well aware that he hid his private complexities behind a mask of bonhomie. His published work presented his thinking in the guise of empirical science (cf. Stepansky, 1976), but, in an isolated part of his being, he identified with an irrational mother. As he put it, "what a dreary world it would be if the rules [i.e., the laws of nature] were not violated sometimes!" (1963, p. 191).

We know very little about Jung's early relationships beyond his own testimony: "The feeling I associated with 'woman' was for a long time that of innate unreliability. 'Father,' on the other hand, meant reliability and—powerlessness" (1963, p. 8). In part, his feelings must have been a reaction to his separation from his mother when she was hospitalized at the time he was 3; in part, they were probably determined by her ambivalence toward him. He recorded a prayer she taught him that the boy understood to mean that he should ask to be devoured by Jesus (p. 10). This, then, would be the origin of the words attributed to his mother in the secret dream of the phallus about the divinity as man-eater. The fact that the prayer made Jesus sound like the mother's agent led the child to develop a phobia of Jesuits, whose long habits he confused with feminine dress. Ultimately, then, he must have experienced his mother as a potentially destructive phallic being.

It is of some interest that Jung's irrational dread of Catholicism finally lifted in St. Stephen's Cathedral in Vienna when he was in his 30s (1963, p. 17)—that is, when he was on a visit to Freud and felt connected to a man whom he did not regard as ineffectual. Jung also recalled that before he was six he kept pestering his mother "to read aloud . . . an old, richly illustrated children's book, which contained an account of exotic religions, especially that of the Hindus" (p. 17). Although his mother spoke of "heathens" with contempt, it cannot have been a coincidence that this was the shared activity her son singled out for mention 75 years later. In my judgment, the exotic divinities in their picture book represented the child's conception of his mother's qualities:

> My parents were sleeping apart. I slept in my father's room. From the door to my mother's room came frightening influences. At night Mother was strange and mysterious. One night I saw coming from her door a faintly luminous, indefinite figure whose head detached itself from the neck and floated along in front of it, in the air, like a little moon. (p. 18)

The personification of castration emanated from her; no wonder the anima can destroy a man!

It would greatly oversimplify matters to imply that Jung experienced his mother only as Kali-Mata, to use the Hindu pantheon. Like her son, she also had an affable surface, that of "a kindly, fat old woman, extremely hospitable, and possessor of a great sense of humor" (p. 48). But behind this façade, Jung found her "unexpectedly powerful: a somber, imposing figure possessed of unassailable authority." When her "uncanny" aspects emerged, what she said "usually struck to the core of [his] being, so that [he] was stunned into silence" (p. 49). This side of her "was like one of those seers who is at the same time a strange animal, like a priestess in a bear's cave. Archaic and ruthless; ruthless as truth and nature" (p. 50). Jung actually believed that she was capable of divination, and he literally claimed to possess similar omniscience: "In the course of my life it has often happened to me that I suddenly knew something which I could not really know at all." The truth would automatically come to both mother and son "like a voice wielding absolute authority, which said exactly what fitted the situation" (p. 51).

It is, of course, all too easy to yield to the temptation to take a patho-biographical approach toward this material. After all, no less an authority than Winnicott (1964) has characterized Jung's life as a successful adaptation to a childhood psychosis. I have no quarrel whatever with that diagnosis. As I have outlined elsewhere (Gedo & Goldberg, 1973), I believe every personality has a core that might well be described meaningfully in such terms. But it is not Jung's pathology that was remarkable; rather it was his successful adaptation. It is this adaptation, in turn, that we must examine as the motive force behind his intellectual work.

Jung attempted no less than to attain "priority of place as the [organizer] of the next phase of the psychohistorical process," to borrow a phrase of Rieff's (1966, p. 234). In the manner of all religious authorities, Jung messianically claimed to be in possession of ultimate truth about those matters that are of greatest general import. Insofar as he repudiated Jesus in earliest childhood, we might well think of him as a modern anti-Christ, a born-again Faust or Zarathustra. Until his rupture with Freud, Jung was terrified at the megalomanic potentialities of his true self and tried to project these qualities, including the intolerance of dissenting viewpoints, onto his mentor. Deprived of this last-ditch defense, he gained access to his primitive core without a permanent disruption of his personality. Moreover, he used this contact with his archaic self to "draw ethical conclusions" (1963, p. 192); he knew that he "was not a blank page whirling about in the winds of the spirit, like Nietzsche" (p. 189).

From the rationalist perspective of psychoanalysis, the crudeness of Jung's magical thinking in his autobiographical revelations is both shocking and faintly ludicrous. Yet we should recall that our "severe and chill antidoctrine" (Rieff, 1966) is never likely to have broad appeal, whereas Jung's modern mystery cult packaged in psychological garb has more potential to gain influence with the general public. After all, the fact that the masses need myths and slogans for their edification was already clear to Plato. Our primary aim is to *know*; Jung's was the cure of souls. It is an enterprise about which, in our disdain of the irrational, we have learned all too little.

The Artist and the Age of Mass Culture: Prophet in the Wilderness

I

AS I HAD OCCASION to note in Chapter 2, Gilbert Rose (1980), paraphrasing Freud, termed the individual's continuous, evolving personality development "the creativity of everyday life." Unobjectionable as his witty proposal seems to be, I would prefer in all seriousness to reserve the term "creativity" for activity that involves devising some valued product—if only a thought that can be recorded through some form of symbolic notation. In accord with such a definition, "the creativity of everyday life" might be better understood as manifestations of the universal human propensity to reach for new configurations that occur outside the traditional areas of creative endeavor, that is, outside of art, science, religion, humanistic scholarship, or public affairs.

Western culture has, until quite recently, followed the leadership of its educated elites, deferring to their collective consensus about the very definition of civilized values. This mandarinate has had a monopoly on the production of high culture and has provided the great majority of its consumers as well. Individuals unable to enter these prestigious circles (the storied *nekul'turny* of Russian invective) never dared to challenge the cultural establishment before the advent of democratic populism in our own era. In the past half century, we have witnessed a profound revolution, a turn to mass culture in every advanced industrial society; paradoxically, the so-called popular democracies of the Eastern bloc bring up the rear in this advance toward egalitarian ideals. The entire population of the West has participated in this fulfillment of the Nietzschean prophecy of the triumph of nihilism: as the philosopher himself stated, "from now onwards [people] exist on the mere pittance of inherited and decaying values" (quoted in Heller, 1976, p. 179).

These radical changes have affected us all, and they have altered our conceptions of creativity in ways we may find very difficult to realize. The difficulty stems from our lack of self-awareness about these insidious shifts in our system of values. In this concluding chapter, I shall argue that these altered conceptions have generally taken the direction of vastly broadening both the acceptable boundaries of high culture and the nature of the creativity that sustains it. At the same time, these cultural changes have radically compromised the position of the artist committed to high culture—he has become unable to compete for public attention, much less public favor, with the providers of mass entertainment, pop psychology, and "the media."

Traditional culture has tended to value creativity to the degree that it has separated the result from the person of the creator. By contrast, the mass audience, more openly identified with its idols, often uses the product merely as the conduit through which to make contact with its superstars. Perhaps the past decade has witnessed a decisive breakdown of this distinction: We are in the era of operatic tenors and politicians who become television personalities, of museum exhibits in which a producer documents the production of the documentary product ostensibly being exhibited! At any rate, much of the creative activity that was in the past officially excluded from serious consideration and held in public contempt was discredited on grounds that seem somewhat arbitrary today— for instance, on the grounds that the product in question was a fiction featuring the creator as its protagonist.

Yet the borderline between art and imposture is ever a hazy one: If the impostor eventually exposes himself, the record of his experience qualifies as autobiography or middlebrow sociology—witness the success of a recent book about the writer impersonating a professional athlete. But the indefinite prolongation of a successful hoax is never quickly forgiven by the cultural establishment. The works of the forger van Megeren, for instance, were good enough to pass muster on the open market as the lost early works of Jan Vermeer; once the guardians of historical truth exposed the hoax, however, these marvelous paintings were completely withdrawn from public exhibit. The passage of time may ultimately permit the admission of such creations into the corpus of high culture. Consider, for example, the early 20th-century pseudomedieval works of the celebrated "Spanish Forger" which are now receiving scholarly attention and should soon reappear on museum walls.

Successful imposture is much more common in the realm of public affairs than in art or science, although the relatively recent example of the Soviet biologist Lysenko imposing his charlatanry on a vast empire shows that the exploitation of human gullibility does not stop at the threshold of our laboratories. Yet charlatans generally succeed only if they are genuinely convinced of the validity of their theses; I therefore assume that Lysenko, in his conviction, was actually the creator of a most persuasive bit of science fiction—not so dissimilar from Orson Welles's radio drama about an invasion from Mars. Of course a key difference remains: Welles considered himself a playwright, whereas Lysenko mistakenly thought he was a scientist.

In the clinical setting of psychoanalysis, we sometimes have the opportunity to observe the creation of such private dramas, albeit of generally lesser scope than the creations of a van Megeren or a Lysenko. Phyllis Greenacre (1958b) was probably the first to call attention to the artistic quality of many of these achievements, although she rightly emphasized the pathological attributes of imposture—the pathetic fact, if you will, that the impostor is unable to make use of his often considerable talents for very much beyond attempted self-improvement, his "creative" activity presumably being required to repair some profound disarray. I do not disagree in the least with Greenacre in her judgment that imposture is *prima facie* pathological, but I would like to call attention to the other side of the coin, namely, the probability that, in order to succeed at all, the impostor must create something coherent, lifelike, even insightful. In other words, he is an *artiste manqué* precisely because his talents are used up in his need to rescue himself.

I may be able to illustrate my point by citing the instance of a patient whose modest talents were in the area of fashion and costume design. For various complex reasons, this young woman had turned her back on these fields of endeavor when she made her vocational choice in late adolescence and was floundering without a settled occupation when a host of grave difficulties brought her into treatment. Her appearance and manner were those of a highly seductive, old-fashioned ingénue preoccupied with teasing men. It took about two years of analytic investigation to expose the total inauthenticity of this role. We found that it was rather used in desperation to hide a clumsy masculine identification and homosexual orientation that this woman found completely unacceptable. But the point I wish to stress here is that her defense against the anxiety-provoking wishes she needed to repudiate made quite specific use of her genuine talent for enacting a role—in *costume*! It may not have been good enough for Broadway, but one often sees work less meritorious on stage at university theaters.

With analysands of greater talent, the "fraudulent" accomplishment may be a great deal more impressive. I know a trial lawyer, for example, whose compulsive procrastination made any serious preparation for court appearances impossible. When his clients could no longer tolerate endless postponements, he would be propelled into action, not as an advocate but as a covert arbitrator whose clever blandishments could not be ignored by the opposition. He could then persuade his clients to compromise with their mollified opponents. In this manner, he entirely avoided going to court for a number of years, playing a confidence game of supreme skill. Many years later, after a lengthy, difficult, but seemingly fruitful analysis, this man became a highly respected judge, widely known for the equity of his rulings. In other words, he became capable of using his talents creatively in the public arena.

II

IF IMPOSTURE occupies the pathological end of the spectrum among the creative activities of everyday life, perhaps its most exact counterpart in the well-adapted range consists of related efforts to present the individual's authentic self to a relevant public. Although these activities are universal, women have in most periods been given greater scope to exercise their gifts in this manner. It is easiest to describe their creative efforts in selecting (or making) their clothing, but the totality of a person's grooming involves many other matters, from coiffure and make-up through jewelry and accessories to posture and movement. There is no need to go into detail here about the miracles certain talented people are often able to effect from relatively unpromising materials. It may be sufficient to note in this regard that personal beauty is probably the summation of countless subtle *activities*. It is only necessary to observe the kaleidoscopic changes in the appearance of analytic patients from day to day—changes we can generally correlate with moods and/or the picture the individual wishes to present to the world—to be disabused of the notion that beauty is a stable property of the flesh.

Actually, the striving for some form of sexual appeal is so widespread that it is probably the least interesting aspect of these activities. The effects people are able to create through grooming are, in fact, much subtler than simply wishing to be maximally attractive. Women from the upper class present themselves in a manner absolutely typical for their group, utterly different from actresses or fashion models, but these distinctions are not apparent to the uninitiated. In the same way, prostitutes give themselves away even when they are not plying their trade. One of the most humiliating moments of my professional life occurred when I was consulted by a sad-faced young woman who wanted me to tell her how people could continually identify her as a streetwalker no matter how hard she tried to act respectable. I did not know!

Of course, it is by no means easy to determine the limits of authenticity in the realm of creative self-improvement. Nobody would dispute the legitimacy of mastering a foreign language, a musical instrument, or an athletic skill or of acquiring an art collection; but we begin to approach a more dubious type of self-expression when certain devotees of physical culture produce a "body beautiful" through extensive programs of muscle building, sometimes involving the use of pharmacological agents. How is such an alteration of the body substrate to be differentiated from the achievement of apparent changes in secondary sexual characteristics though the use of hormones, surgery, or both? Is energetic dieting more authentic than cosmetic surgery? Are padded brassieres less imposturous than silicone implants—or codpieces? It has taken less than a century to render Oscar Wilde's fantasies in *The Picture of Dorian Gray* technologically feasible!

Nor has the human ambition to tinker with nature stopped at these bizarre forms of satisfying the demands of vanity. The tendency to concretize the sense of one's limitations often takes the form of hypochondriasis, and the attempted remedies may run the full medical gamut all the way to the implantation within the body of the latest products of biomedical engineering. Another variant of such aberrant creativity is the messianic character who repeatedly persuades various surgeons of the need to remove some part of his bodily substance. Certain individuals are so skilled at this grim game of body sculpture that the activity has received the name of "polysurgical addiction." Yet these *formes frustes* of attempted self-creation are not so different, at bottom, from the effort to alter various character traits by means of psychoanalytic treatment.

In this context, I am reminded of an analysand of the highest moral standards who, at the age of 7, made a serious attempt to cut off his own penis. The point of this attempt, the successful execution of which was barely prevented by his parents, would have been to disprove the continuing insinuations of his psychotic stepmother that the boy had illicit sexual designs upon her. This child did not suffer from the concretization of thought demonstrated in hypochondriasis; on the contrary, his intention to mutilate himself was a harbinger of major creative capacities, for the castration he intended to perform on himself was to be understood *metaphorically*, as a token of moral purity. In other words, he had devised a dramatic scenario, parallel to the blow with which Billy Budd smashes Claggart in Melville's allegory of good and evil. Most probably, therein lies the crucial distinction between art and self-improvement. Comparably, imposture may be differentiated from dramatic art whenever it lacks symbolic overtones.

In general, the further an activity is removed from the individual's physical person, the more likely the guardians of high culture are to accept it as legitimately creative. Thus we may often admire people for their skill in dressing with good taste or high style, but we are not much more likely to credit their appearance a creative accomplishment than we would tend to think of a strong tennis game in such terms. Yet, competitive tennis does require tactical skills of a certain order, even if they do not quite measure up to the requirements of championship chess or military leadership. Similarly, the accomplishments of a "clothes horse" depend on many of the same attributes we would acknowledge as the basis for creative success in a field such as interior design. It is generally understood that professional success in all of these fields entails a large measure of creativity—dress or costume designers, athletic coaches, interior decorators, strategists, businessmen, and bridge and chess players may occasionally be honored in this regard. Their innumerable counterparts in the world of amateurs, however, were in the past seldom viewed in the same light. This elitism seems to be passing from public favor now.

III

THE ILLUSTRATIONS I have offered thus far tend to suggest still another gradient widely used to determine whether an activity qualifies for consideration as a major creative effort: The further it is removed from immediately practical ends, the more likely it is to receive such acknowledgment. One of the most inventive people I know is a professional tradesman, equally skilled at carpentry, plumbing, and electrical work—painter, machinist, jack-of-all-trades, and problem solver extraordinary. In one of our recent wars, the air force put him to work salvaging reusable parts from wrecked planes—and I am practically ready to believe that he could make an armored car fly. People of his kind seldom realize how rare their abilities are or how miraculous the results they produce seem to others; yet they possess practical genius in the realm of things concrete.

In the clinical setting, I have heard of another person of this type who was somewhat more self-conscious about her abilities and therefore became a virtuoso instructor in a school of industrial arts. Her son, who was my analysand, grew up to be passionately involved with artistic endeavors. From his vantage point, that is, from the vantage point of one totally committed to high culture, her activities lacked aesthetic merit because of their concreteness—despite the fact that she was supremely skilled in most craft techniques.

It is quite instructive to compare this mother's activities with those of her son because their respective endeavors had so much in common. Yet the mother always confined herself to the "creativity of everyday life," even in her choice of a vocation, whereas the son's approach to everything he undertook—work, study, play, social activities—appeared to propel him into the most elevated kind of creative efforts far removed from "everyday" concerns. Both mother and son did whatever they tried extremely well; there was no difference in their degree of commitment to the task or in the standards they set for themselves. What distinguished them, rather, was the guiding ideal each had chosen: The mother was absolutely wedded to the value of pragmatism to such an extent (and with such fervor) that she could not appreciate her son's enterprises, which generally struck her as quixotic; my patient, on the other hand, was primarily interested in ethical matters. At the age of 7, he had picked out Albert Einstein as his idealized model and subsequently felt obliged to abandon his parents' church because it taught that salvation was reserved for those who, unlike Einstein, had been baptized. The same moral grandeur infused his activities as an adult, and it was this quality that lent all his accomplishments the aura of artistic achievements. Yet, in a different sense, he seldom ventured beyond the boundaries of the creativity of everyday life before his analysis: It is, after all, a very private matter to change one's religious affiliation, even if this move is motivated by moral issues. As a piece of creativity, it cannot *in principle* be distinguished from tinting one's hair or choosing to drive an unusually fine car.

But our traditional culture placed greater value on moral and ethical achievements than on pragmatic ones, so we tend to respond to ordinary activities that are visibly infused with ethical meaning almost as if they constituted works of art. Witness the manner in which the analysand I am describing made use of the ultimate success of his analysis: He devoted a period of several years to seeing his father—a very difficult person who had always treated him with ill-concealed jealousy—through the latter's terminal illness. Magnanimity is no less moving in everyday life than it is when Shakespeare portrays it through the figure of a Prospero! It was also characteristic of this patient that he expressed to me his gratitude for the fact that our work had made it possible for him to create the relationship with his dying father that the latter had been unable to offer him in childhood.

Without such moral overtones, the establishment of human relationships is seldom regarded as a creative achievement per se. Leporello may sing with envious admiration about the catalogue of Don Giovanni's conquests, but off the stage Don Juanism is still widely regarded as a disease of the soul. Yet, even in our age of libertinage, juggling a number of simultaneous affairs is no mean feat; it requires a great deal of ingenuity at the very least! I suppose that in some ways such an ability is regarded in the same light as mass entertainment or popular farce—interesting but déclassé! But I believe my point is valid for other types of relationships as well, even when there is no question of a conflict with our ideals. Thus the single most important area of human creativity—the upbringing of the next generation—simply does not qualify for inclusion on any list of the pillars of high culture, even though everyone actually knows it to be a task that is maximally difficult to do well.

In point of fact, this general verdict on the status of childrearing is perfectly just, for the optimal raising of our children is simply an extension of our self-enhancement. And this judgment is certainly proved by the occasional exception: Great achievement on behalf of the children of other people is usually highly honored, whether the activities are carried out privately and on a small scale or in a broader public arena, as is the case with work that leads to the creation of major social institutions—the work of a Pestalozzi, a Florence Nightingale, or a Mother Teresa. In the case of these individuals, I infer that we respond to the moral grandeur implicit in their work as much as to their organizational success: After all, do we remember individuals who set up self-serving bodies such as professional societies?

IV

WE HAVE THUS FAR discussed three distinguishing criteria that have been used to separate the creativity of everyday life from the achievements of high culture: The products of everyday creativity need not possess the same degree of authenticity; they may represent direct attempts at self-improvement (without symbolic significance); and they are generally lacking in moral and ethical content. In other words, creative achievements have been regarded as significant to the extent that they possess universality and moral value while, at the same time, they genuinely represent the creator's passionate convictions. Of course, many intermediate possibilities exist, activities to which these valid distinctions have always been too difficult to apply; moreover, the ethical message is often encoded in formal attributes alone, as I have discussed in Chapter 2.

Perhaps it may be easiest to illustrate one of the grey areas of creativity by citing certain works that are initially held in the highest esteem but gradually lose respect because, rightly or wrongly, subsequent generations are unable to discern the authenticity of their sentiment. In our secularized and sexually permissive culture, many works with religious subjects or moralizing works like those of the Victorian era strike large segments of the audience as arch, syrupy, maudlin, or false. Occasionally, even a very great artist may produce so many works of this type that his reputation declines. It is only by comparing these specific pieces with others, which we are able to appreciate as well as the artist's contemporaries, that we regain sufficient perspective to avoid dogmatic judgments. Do certain masters of the Italian baroque, like Guido Reni, deserve to be ranked among the giants of their art, or did they paint too many commissioned pictures filled with trite religious exaltation? Judging on the basis of Guido's skill in depicting other emotions, we are inclined to condemn many of these religious works as unconvincing. Yet we may well be wrong; the deficiency may be our own, incapable as we generally are of tolerating open displays of strong feeling.

Although it would be tempting to discuss the borderline of creativity by examining other examples of apparent failures on the part of acknowledged masters, I wish to return to the other side of the problem and continue to focus on activities that seem to fill most of the relevant criteria but might be excluded nonetheless as a matter of principle. As an illustration, we might consider talented individuals who pour themselves into quasi-artistic activities such as the production of jokes or pornography. Obviously, I do not agree with Arieti (1976, p. 128) that jokes necessarily constitute small works of art! His view represents the coming age of mass culture. In my judgment, the overwhelming majority of these efforts fail to produce anything that should be accepted as art because the resulting creations generally lack ethical content. Yet we cannot be categorical in making such an assumption, for great works of art may be full of humor as well as sexual appeal; this is to say that neither wit nor prurience necessarily excludes the possibility of an ethical message, as readers of Aristophanes, Rabelais, Shakespeare, or Balzac well know.

In fact, the rarity of great art on erotic themes and, for that matter, in the comic vein, suggests it may be unusually difficult to transcend the direct gratifications provided by such subject matter by infusing it with additional values. To put this differently, it seems to require mastery of a highly elaborate, not to say artificial, tradition to transmute openly erotic content into public art. Hindu temple sculpture and the court art of Louis XV—Fragonard's paintings along with novels such as *Manon Lescaut* and *Les Liaisons Dangereuses*—come to mind as the most relevant examples of successful works of this kind. And comedy all too easily degenerates into farce, mockery, or empty clowning.

Clearly, in marginal areas of this kind, shifting public fashions are decisive in determining the limits of what the audience is capable of experiencing aesthetically. Much of Fragonard's erotica was destroyed in the puritanical moral climate of prerevolutionary France; today it can be appreciated as a sublime representation of profound human experience. Comedy tinged with sadism toward certain ethnic groups may become entirely witless within a single generation: In the era of Karel Woytila, Czeslaw Milosz, and Lech Walesa, a civilized person cannot laugh at slurs against the Poles.

To return to the people who confine their creative endeavors to efforts to stimulate others to laughter or sexual excitement—forms of self-enhancement through the indirect exercise of power—psychoanalytic practice sometimes gives us opportunities to witness the transformation of such behavioral patterns into activities that possess public value. I have treated one woman who spent several years working as a chorus girl in tawdry striptease joints, full of sadistic glee about stimulating and frustrating the pathetic men who came to gawk at her. For a girl from a respectable lower-middle-class Jewish home, this attitude not only pointed to the specifically perverse meaning of her exhibitionism; it also embodied a rageful effort to spite the parents who had refused to support her cultural aspirations. But the two strands of her motivation could be understood as aspects of the same childhood *ambiance*. In the manner traditional to such families, the parents of this woman had overtly lavished admiration on their eldest son for his intellectual prowess; the patient had consequently developed intense competitive hatred for men that specifically focused on the phallus. Hence her triumphant performances on stage constituted an assertion of the superiority of her own genital equipment over that of the voyeurs she induced to masturbate in the course of her display.

When the patient had mastered these problems by means of analytic insight, she began to make use of long dormant talents to fulfill her secret, lifelong ambition to become a painter. Because she married and left town soon after the completion of our work, I do not know about her subsequent progress as an artist. From the sample of her work she exhibited before her departure, I formed the impression that she was correct in her self-assessment: She seemed to have sufficient talent to achieve a modest professional success. Clearly, to exhibit the cherished products of her creativity, knowing that they did not match the achievements of the masters, required mastery of her conflict about her brother. But it perhaps makes more sense to give this insight an alternative formulation: As long as this patient's conflicts prevented her from trying to achieve professional status in the creative activity for which she possessed some talent, her need to assert her own worth remained focused, in a childlike and concrete manner, on her body as a sexual stimulus. In addition to the handicap of being bound to her person, her preanalytic performances also failed aesthetically because they lacked symbolic connotations.

I can cite another example of this kind from my clinical work, one in which rather similar childhood vicissitudes drove a girl, in accord with the nature of *her* specific (verbal) talents, into compulsive clowning. When this patient mastered her competitive anxieties vis-à-vis males, the neurotic compromise through which she destroyed the value of her creativity by relentlessly focusing it on fugitive trivia became superfluous; she found herself effortlessly composing poetry in her head. Once again, I was most impressed by the strong exhibitionistic need resulting from the inability to make use of a real talent—a need that markedly diminished when the creative paralysis was overcome.

To turn now to the frontier of creativity as it interfaces with the issue of pragmatism, we must, of course, seek most illustrations in the realm of science rather than the humanities, the latter having relatively few practical applications. The most striking example to come to my attention concerns a pair of brothers, one of whom was active in pure mathematics, the other in nuclear engineering. Although within their respective specialties the stature of each brother was, in fact, comparable, there was absolutely no question in the mind of either man about the preeminence of the mathematician as a creative person. Of course, these men represented a deeply conservative stratum of our society. Technological inventiveness has brought tremendous rewards, particularly in financial terms, but it had to reach levels of extraordinary excellence to overcome the traditional bias against acknowledging it as a feat of sheer originality.

The conceptualization of the double-helical structure of DNA by Watson and Crick or of the benzene ring by Kekulé may have struck us as poetic achievements, "works of art in the medium of pure thought," to borrow a phrase from the psychoanalyst Hans Loewald. Only the rarest of engineering feats, like some of the structures of Pier Luigi Nervi, elicited comparable responses. Of course, one reason for this prejudice is the simple fact that one cannot appreciate the elegance or originality of specific solutions in most technical fields without a great deal of specialized knowledge. But this factor applies to complex scientific endeavors as well, and our admiration for contemporary natural science is never dampened by our lack of understanding of its abstruse theories.

Perhaps this issue might best be clarified by approaching it from the vantage point of its pathology, namely, the destructive pressure certain families bring to bear on children who develop creative aspirations— pressure rationalized on the grounds that the activities relevant for realizing such ambitions are useless, impractical, and essentially selfish (see Chapter 6). These prohibitions are applied just as frequently to scholarly or scientific pursuits as to artistic ones, and they often succeed in diverting the child from creative activities altogether. The belief system fueling these educational efforts is not merely the unexceptionable preference for bourgeois success over bohemian fecklessness; it is the philistine attitude epitomized in the famous aphorism placed in the mouth of Schlaggeter by Nazi playwright Hans Johst in his 1933 play bearing the same name: "When I hear the word 'culture,' I reach for my holster!" In this caricature of opposition to creativity, we may discern the mirror image of the traditional antipragmatic bias.

V

THIS SURVEY OF aspects of the creativity of everyday life has now probably covered sufficient ground to warrant a few inferences about its counterpart, the achievements always accepted as valued additions to high culture. I have described several interrelated criteria differentiating these major efforts to find significant novel configurations: separation of the product from the person of the creator; its authenticity in representing the latter's point of view; the degree to which it transcends concrete existence by transmitting symbolic meanings; and the extent of its disregard of utilitarian goals and/or its commitment to ethical values—if only in its meticulous attention to formal or technical perfection.

If we assume that becoming an artist—and for purposes of discussion in this volume, it will be recalled that within this designation I have consistently included not only practitioners of literature, music, and the visual arts, but scientists, scholars, religious innovators, and persons creative in the public arena as well—requires the capacity to function automatically in accord with these complex guidelines, what kind of personal qualities must the artist possess in order to make this possible? It would seem that, among many other attributes already discussed in this volume, the most essential one in this regard could well be an early commitment—generally made in adolescence or even earlier—to a disciplined tradition, one that implicitly espouses the requirements of the profession in question.

The continuing assault upon cultural traditions characteristic of our century, aptly named the age of the avant-garde, has made it progressively more difficult (especially in the "arts" in the narrower sense) for adolescents to idealize their chosen disciplines. In certain circles, idealization of revolutionary change has provided a watered-down substitute—in the dada movement, for instance, that formed a small nucleus of international protest against World War I. The enfeeblement of tradition is equally apparent, to give only a few examples, in the relative lack of concern about technical fundamentals in the visual arts, about communicative power in music, or about narrative content and social observation in literature. As a result, the artist has had to turn his focus more and more upon himself, with less and less pretension of offering aspects of his own experience as specific examples of certain human universals. Moreover, the mandarinate is embarrassed about professing any value system at all, as Polanyi and Prosch (1975) have eloquently demonstrated. Under these circumstances, all creative activities threaten to become all too pragmatic quests for fame and fortune.

Two centuries of modernism have effectively overthrown the dominance of Western civilization by its intellectual elite. Today, we can scarcely differentiate the bulk of contemporary cultural production from our television commercials. And hardly anyone seems to care.

BIBLIOGRAPHY

Abraham, H., & Freud, E., eds. (1965). *A Psycho-Analytic Dialogue: The Letters of Sigmund Freud and Karl Abraham, 1907-1926*, trans. B. Marsh & H. Abraham. New York: Basic Books.

Andersen, W. (1971). *Gauguin: Paradise Lost*. New York: Viking.

Arieti, S. (1976). *Creativity: The Magic Synthesis*. New York: Basic Books.

Arlow, J. (1961). Ego psychology and the study of mythology. *Journal of the American Psychoanalytic Association*, 9:371-393.

Armstrong, R. (1971). Joseph Conrad: The conflict of command. *The Psychoanalytic Study of the Child*, 26:485-534.

Baglione, G. (1642). *Le Vite de'Pittori, Scultori, et Architetti*. Rome.

Battisti, E. (1960). *Rinascimento e Barocco*. Torino.

Bergmann, M. (1973). Limitations of method in psychoanalytic biography. *Journal of the American Psychoanalytic Association*, 21:833-850.

Binion, R. (1968). *Frau Lou: Nietzsche's Wayward Disciple*. Princeton: Princeton University Press.

Binswanger, L. (1957). *Sigmund Freud: Reminiscences of a Friendship*. New York: Grune & Stratton.

Blum, H. (1956). Van Gogh's chairs. *American Imago*, 13:307-318.

Bonaparte, M. (1933). *The Life and Works of Edgar Allan Poe: A Psychoanalytic Interpretation*. London: Imago, 1949.

Bonaparte, M., Freud, A., & Kris, E., eds. (1954). *The Origins of Psycho-Analysis*. New York: Basic Books.

Brassaï, [Halász] G. (1966). *Picasso and Company*, trans. F. Price. New York: Doubleday.

Breuer, J., & Freud, S. (1895). Studies on hysteria. *Standard Edition*, 2. London: Hogarth Press, 1955.

Bychowski, G. (1951). Metapsychology of artistic creation. *Psychoanalytic Quarterly*, 20:592-902.

Ciardi, J. (1960). *How Does a Poem Mean?* Boston: Houghton Mifflin.

Cinotti, M., dell'Acqua, G., & Rossi, F. (1973). *Immagine del Caravaggio: Mostra Didattica Itinerante—Catalogo*. Milano: Pizzi.

BIBLIOGRAPHY

Cocks, G. (1979). C. G. Jung and German psychotherapy, 1933–1940. *Spring: An Annual of Archetypal Psychology and Jungian Thought*, pp. 221–227.

Colquhun, A. (1968). Guiseppe di Lampedusa. In G. Lampedusa, *Two Stories and a Memory*. New York: Grosset's Universal Library.

Coltrera, J. (1965). On the creation of beauty and thought. *Journal of the American Psychoanalytic Association*, 13:634–703.

Corbin, E. (1974). The autonomous ego functions in creativity. *Journal of the American Psychoanalytic Association*, 22:568–587.

Decker, H. (1980). A tangled skein: The Freud–Jung relationship. In E. Wallace & L. Pressley, eds., *Essays in the History of Psychiatry*. Columbia, S.C.: South Carolina Department of Mental Health, pp. 103–118.

Delay, J. (1956–1958). *La Jeunesse d'André Gide*, 2 vols. Paris: Gallimard.

Ehrenzweig, A. (1953). *The Psychoanalysis of Artistic Vision and Hearing*, 3rd ed. London: Sheldon, 1975.

Ehrenzweig, A. (1967). *The Hidden Order of Art*. Berkeley: University of California Press.

Eissler, K. R. (1961). *Leonardo da Vinci: Psychoanalytic Notes on the Enigma*. New York: International Universities Press.

Eissler, K. R. (1963). *Goethe: A Psychoanalytic Study*. Detroit: Wayne State University Press.

Eissler, K. R. (1967). Genius, psychopathology, and creativity. *American Imago*, 24:35–81.

Eissler, K. R. (1970). *Discourse on Hamlet and "Hamlet."* New York: International Universities Press.

Eissler, K. R. (1971). *Talent and Genius*. New York: Quadrangle.

Eissler, K. R. (1978). Creativity and adolescence: The effect of trauma in Freud's adolescence. *The Psychoanalytic Study of the Child*, 33:461–518.

Ellenberger, H. (1970). *The Discovery of the Unconscious*. New York: Basic Books.

Erikson, E. (1958). *Young Man Luther: A Study in Psychoanalysis and History*. New York: Norton.

Erikson, E. (1963). *Gandhi's Truth: On the Origins of Militant Nonviolence*. New York: Norton.

Esman, A. (1979). The nature of the artistic gift. *American Imago*, 36:305–312.

Ferenczi, S., & Hollós, S. (1922). *Psycho-Analysis and the Psychic Disorder of General Paresis*. New York: Nervous and Mental Disease Publishing, 1925.

Förster-Nietzsche, E. (1912). *The Life of Nietzsche: I. The Young Nietzsche*, trans. A. Ludovici. New York: Sturgis & Walton.

Förster-Nietzsche, E. (1914). *The Life of Nietzsche: II. The Lonely Nietzsche*, trans. P. Cohn. New York: Sturgis & Walton.

Fraiberg, L. (1956). Freud's writings on art. *International Journal of Psycho-Analysis*, 37:82–96.

Freud, E., ed. (1970). *The Letters of Sigmund Freud and Arnold Zweig*, trans. E. Robson-Scott & W. Robson-Scott. New York: Harcourt, Brace & World.

Freud, S. (1900). The interpretation of dreams. *Standard Edition*, 4 & 5. London: Hogarth Press, 1953.

Freud, S. (1901). The psychopathology of everyday life. *Standard Edition*, 6. London: Hogarth Press, 1960.

Freud, S. (1905a). Fragment of an analysis of a case of hysteria. *Standard Edition*, 7:7–122. London: Hogarth Press, 1953.

Freud, S. (1905b). Three essays on the theory of sexuality. *Standard Edition*, 7:135–243. London: Hogarth Press, 1953.

Freud, S. (1905c). Jokes and their relation to the unconscious. *Standard Edition*, 8. London: Hogarth Press, 1960.

Freud, S. (1907). Delusions and dreams in Jensen's *Gradiva*. *Standard Edition*, 9:3–98. London: Hogarth Press, 1953.

Freud, S. (1909a). Analysis of a phobia in a five-year-old boy. *Standard Edition*, 10:5–149. London: Hogarth Press, 1955.

Freud, S. (1909b). Notes upon a case of obsessional neurosis. *Standard Edition*, 10:153–250. London: Hogarth Press, 1955.

Freud, S. (1910a). Five lectures on psycho-analysis. *Standard Edition*, 11:9–55. London: Hogarth Press, 1957.

Freud, S. (1910b). Leonardo da Vinci and a memory of his childhood. *Standard Edition*, 11:59–138. London: Hogarth Press, 1957.

Freud, S. (1911). Psycho-analytic notes on an autobiographical account of a case of paranoia (dementia paranoides). *Standard Edition*, 12:3–84. London: Hogarth Press, 1958.

Freud, S. (1911–1915). Papers on technique. *Standard Edition*, 12:85–174. London: Hogarth Press, 1958.

Freud, S. (1913). Totem and taboo. *Standard Edition*, 13:1–164. London: Hogarth Press, 1955.

Freud, S. (1914a). The Moses of Michelangelo. *Standard Edition*, 13:211–236. London: Hogarth Press, 1955.

Freud, S. (1914b). On the history of the psycho-analytic movement. *Standard Edition*, 14:3–66. London: Hogarth Press, 1957.

Freud, S. (1914c). On narcissism: An introduction. *Standard Edition*, 14:73–102. London: Hogarth Press, 1957.

Freud, S. (1916). Some character types met with in psycho-analytic work. *Standard Edition*, 14:310–355. London: Hogarth Press, 1957.

Freud, S. (1918). From the history of an infantile neurosis. *Standard Edition*, 17:7–122. London: Hogarth Press, 1955.

Freud, S. (1920). Beyond the pleasure principle. *Standard Edition*, 18:3–66. London: Hogarth Press, 1955.

Freud, S. (1923). The ego and the id. *Standard Edition*, 19:3–67. London: Hogarth Press, 1961.

Freud, S. (1926). Inhibitions, symptoms, and anxiety. *Standard Edition*, 20:77–178. London: Hogarth Press, 1959.

Freud, S. (1927). The future of an illusion. *Standard Edition*, 21:3–57. London: Hogarth Press, 1961.

Freud, S. (1928). Dostoevsky and parricide. *Standard Edition*, 21:177–198. London: Hogarth Press, 1961.

Freud, S. (1936). A disturbance of memory on the Acropolis. *Standard Edition*, 22:238–249. London: Hogarth Press, 1964.

Frey-Rohn, L. (1974). *From Freud to Jung*. New York: Putnam.

Friedlaender, W. (1955). *Caravaggio Studies*. New York: Schocken, 1969.

BIBLIOGRAPHY

Frommel, C. (1971). Caravaggio und seine Modelle. *Castrum Peregrini*, 96:21–56.

Gay, P. (1976). *Art and Act. On Causes in History—Manet, Gropius, Mondrian.* New York: Harper & Row.

Gay, P. (1978). *Freud, Jews and Other Germans.* New York: Oxford University Press.

Gedo, J. (1966). The psychotherapy of developmental arrest. *British Journal of Medical Psychology*, 39:25–33.

Gedo, J. (1967). On critical periods for corrective experience in the therapy of arrested development. *British Journal of Medical Psychology*, 40:79–83.

Gedo, J. (1968). Freud's self-analysis and his scientific ideas. In J. Gedo & G. Pollock, eds., *Freud: The Fusion of Science and Humanism* [*Psychological Issues*, Monograph 34/35]. New York: International Universities Press, 1976, pp. 286–306.

Gedo, J. (1970a). The psychoanalyst and the literary hero: An interpretation. *Comprehensive Psychiatry*, 11:174–181.

Gedo, J. (1970b). Thoughts on art in the age of Freud. *Journal of the American Psychoanalytic Association*, 18:219–245.

Gedo, J. (1972a). Caviare to the general. *American Imago*, 29:293–317.

Gedo, J. (1972b). On the psychology of genius. *International Journal of Psycho-Analysis*, 53:199–203.

Gedo, J. (1972c). On the methodology of psychoanalytic biography. *Journal of the American Psychoanalytic Association*, 20:638–649.

Gedo, J. (1972d). The dream of reason produces monsters. *Journal of the American Psychoanalytic Association*, 20:199–223.

Gedo, J. (1975). Forms of idealization in the analytic transference. *Journal of the American Psychoanalytic Association*, 23:485–505.

Gedo, J. (1978). Some contributions of psychoanalysis to a science of man—A grammar for the humanities. *The Annual of Psychoanalysis*, 6:67–102.

Gedo, J. (1979a). *Beyond Interpretation: Toward a Revised Theory for Psychoanalysis.* New York: International Universities Press.

Gedo, J. (1979b). A psychoanalyst reports at mid-career. *American Journal of Psychiatry*, 136:646–649.

Gedo, J. (1979c). Magna est vis veritatis tuae, et praevalebit! *The Annual of Psychoanalysis*, 7:53–82.

Gedo, J. (1981a). *Advances in Clinical Psychoanalysis.* New York: International Universities Press.

Gedo, J. (1981b). Measure for measure: A response. *Psychoanalytic Inquiry*, 1:289–316.

Gedo, J., & Goldberg, A. (1973). *Models of the Mind.* Chicago: University of Chicago Press.

Gedo, J., & Pollock, G., eds. (1976). *Freud: The Fusion of Science and Humanism* [*Psychological Issues*, Monograph 34/35]. New York: International Universities Press.

Gedo, J., & Wolf, E. (1970). The "Ich." letters. In J. Gedo & G. Pollock, eds., *Freud: The Fusion of Science and Humanism* [*Psychological Issues*, Monograph 34/35]. New York: International Universities Press, 1976, pp. 71–86.

Gedo, J., & Wolf, E. (1973). Freud's *Novelas Ejemplares.* In J. Gedo & G. Pollock, eds., *Freud: The Fusion of Science and Humanism* [*Psychological Issues*, Monograph 34/35]. New York: International Universities Press, pp. 87–114.

Gedo, J., & Wolf, E. (1976). From the history of introspective psychology: The humanist strain. In J. Gedo & G. Pollock, eds., *Freud: The Fusion of Science and Humanism* [*Psychological Issues*, Monograph 34/35]. New York: International Universities Press, pp. 11–45.

Gedo, M. (1979). Art as autobiography: Picasso's *Guernica*. *Art Quarterly*, 2:191–210.

Gedo, M. (1980a). *Picasso—Art as Autobiography*. Chicago: University of Chicago Press.

Gedo, M. (1980b). Art as exorcism: Picasso's "Demoiselles d'Avignon." *Arts*, 55:70–83.

Gedo, M. (1981). The archaeology of a painting: A visit to the city of the dead beneath Picasso's "La Vie." *Arts*, 56:116–129.

Gedo, M. (1983). Looking at art from the empathic viewpoint. In J. Lichtenberg, ed., *On Empathy*. Hillsdale, N.J.: Erlbaum.

Gilot, F., & Lake, C. (1964). *Life with Picasso*. New York: McGraw Hill.

Gombrich, E. (1954). Psychoanalysis and the history of art. *International Journal of Psycho-Analysis*, 35:401–411.

Greenacre, P. (1957). The childhood of the artist. In *Emotional Growth*, vol. 2. New York: International Universities Press, 1971, pp. 479–504.

Greenacre, P. (1958a). The family romance of the artist. In *Emotional Growth*, vol. 2. New York: International Universities Press, 1971, pp. 505–532.

Greenacre, P. (1958b). The relation of the impostor to the artist. In *Emotional Growth*, vol. 2. New York: International Universities Press, 1971, pp. 533–554.

Greenacre, P. (1960). Woman as artist. In *Emotional Growth*, vol. 2. New York: International Universities Press, 1971, pp. 575–591.

Greenacre, P. (1971). *Emotional Growth*, 2 vols. New York: International Universities Press.

Heimann, P. (1942). A contribution to the problem of sublimation and its relation to processes of internalization. *International Journal of Psycho-Analysis*, 23:8–17.

Heller, E. (1976). *The Artist's Journey into the Interior*. New York: Harcourt, Brace, Jovanovich.

Helson, R. (1971). Women mathematicians and the creative personality. *Journal of Consulting and Clinical Psychology*, 36:210–211, 217–220.

Hess, J. (1971). Almost every place but Picasso's town noting his 90th birthday. *The New York Times* (October 23, 1971).

Hildesheimer, W. (1982). *Mozart*. New York: Farrar, Straus, & Giroux.

Hollingdale, R. (1965). *Nietzsche, the Man and His Philosophy*. Baton Rouge: Louisiana State University Press.

Homans, P. (1979). *Jung in Context*. Chicago: University of Chicago Press.

Horace (1967). *The Odes*, trans. J. Michie. Harmondsworth, England: Penguin.

Jaspers, K. (1935). *Nietzsche*, trans. C. Wallraff & F. Schmitz. Tucson: University of Arizona Press, 1965.

Jones, E. (1953). *The Life and Work of Sigmund Freud*, vol. 1. New York: Basic Books.

BIBLIOGRAPHY

Jones, E. (1955). *The Life and Work of Sigmund Freud*, vol. 2. New York: Basic Books.

Jones, E. (1957). *The Life and Work of Sigmund Freud*, vol. 3. New York: Basic Books.

Jones, E. (1959). *Free Associations*. New York: Basic Books.

Jung, C. (1912). Symbols of Transformation. *Collected Works*, 5. Princeton: Princeton University Press, 1967.

Jung, C. (1952). Answer to Job. *Collected Works*, 11:355–470. Princeton: Princeton University Press, 1958.

Jung, C. (1963). *Memories, Dreams, Reflections*, trans. R. Winston & C. Winston. New York: Vintage.

Karl, F. (1979). *Joseph Conrad: The Three Lives*. New York: Farrar, Straus, & Giroux.

Kaufmann, W. (1962). *20 German Poets*. New York: Modern Library.

Kaufmann, W. (1968). *Nietzsche: Philosopher, Psychologist, Antichrist*, 3rd ed. New York: Vintage.

Kaufmann, W. (1980a). *Discovering the Mind, II: Nietzsche, Heidegger, and Buber*. New York: McGraw Hill.

Kaufmann, W. (1980b). *Discovering the Mind, III: Freud versus Adler and Jung*. New York: McGraw Hill.

Kitson, M. (1969). *The Complete Paintings of Caravaggio*. New York: Abrams.

Kleinschmidt, H. (1967). The angry act: The role of aggression in creativity. *American Imago*, 24:98–128.

Kohut, H. (1957). Observations on the psychological functions of music. In *The Search for the Self*, vol. 1, ed. P. Ornstein. New York: International Universities Press, 1978, pp. 233–253.

Kohut, H. (1960). Beyond the bounds of the basic rule. In *The Search for the Self*, vol. 1, ed. P. Ornstein. New York: International Universities Press, 1978, pp. 272–303.

Kohut, H. (1968). The psychoanalytic treatment of narcissistic personality disorders: Outline of a systematic approach. In *The Search for the Self*, vol. 1, ed. P. Ornstein. New York: International Universities Press, 1978, pp. 477–509.

Kohut, H. (1971). *The Analysis of the Self*. New York: International Universities Press.

Kohut, H. (1976). Creativeness, charisma, group psychology: Reflections on the self-analysis of Freud. In *The Search for the Self*, vol. 2, ed. P. Ornstein. New York: International Universities Press, 1978, pp. 793–843.

Kris, E. (1952), *Psychoanalytic Explorations in Art*. New York: International Universities Press.

Kris, E. (1956). The personal myth: A problem in psychoanalytic technique. In *Selected Papers*. New Haven: Yale University Press, 1975, pp. 272–300.

Kristeller, P. (1961). *Renaissance Thought*. New York: Harper.

Lichtenberg, J. (1978). Psychoanalysis and biography. *The Annual of Psychoanalysis*, 6:397–427.

Linsday, J. (1969). *Cézanne—His Life and Art*. New York: Harper & Row, 1972.

Loewald, H. (1977). Transference and countertransference: The roots of psychoanalysis. *Psychoanalytic Quarterly*, 46:514–527.

Lubin, A. (1972). *Stranger on the Earth*. New York: Holt, Rinehart & Winston.

Mack, J. (1971). Psychoanalysis and historical biography. *Journal of the American Psychoanalytic Association*, 19:143–179.

McDonald, M. (1970). Transitional tunes and musical development. *The Psychoanalytic Study of the Child*, 25:503–520.

McGrath, W. (1974). *Dionysian Art and Populist Politics in Austria*. New Haven: Yale University Press.

McGuire, W., ed. (1974). *The Freud/Jung letters*, trans. R. Manheim & R. F. C. Hull. Princeton: Princeton University Press.

Meier, C. (1977). *Jung's Analytical Psychology and Religion*. Carbondale: Southern Illinois University Press.

Meyer, B. (1967). *Joseph Conrad: A Psychoanalytic Biography*. Princeton: Princeton University Press.

Miller, J., Sabshin, M., Gedo, J., Pollock, G., Sadow, L., & Schlessinger, N. (1969). Some aspects of Charcot's influence on Freud. In J. Gedo & G. Pollock, eds., *Freud: The Fusion of Science and Humanism* [*Psychological Issues*, Monograph 34/35]. New York: International Universities Press, 1976, pp. 115–132.

Milner, M. (1969). *The Hands of the Living God: An Account of a Psychoanalytic Therapy*. New York: International Universities Press.

Modell, A. (1965). On having the right to a life: An aspect of the superego's development. *International Journal of Psycho-Analysis*, 46:323–331.

Modell, A. (1970). The transitional object and the creative act. *Psychoanalytic Quarterly*, 39:240–250.

Moraitis, G. (1979). A psychoanalyst's journey into a historian's world: An experiment in collaboration. *The Annual of Psychoanalysis*, 7:287–320.

Morgan, G. (1941). *What Nietzsche Means*. New York: Harper, 1965.

Nagera, H. (1967). *Vincent van Gogh: A Psychoanalytic Biography*. New York: International Universities Press.

Nass, M. (1971). Some considerations of a psychoanalytic interpretation of music. *Psychoanalytic Quarterly*, 40:303–312.

Nass, M. (1975). On hearing and inspiration in the composition of music. *Psychoanalytic Quarterly*, 44:431–449.

Niederland, W. (1967). Clinical aspects of creativity. *American Imago*, 24:6–34.

Niederland, W. (1976). Psychoanalytic approaches to artistic creativity. *Psychoanalytic Quarterly*, 45:185–212.

Niess, R. (1968). *Zola, Cézanne, and Manet*. Ann Arbor: University of Michigan Press.

Nietzsche, W. F. (1888). *Ecce Homo*, trans. W. Kaufmann. In *"On the Genealogy of Morals" and "Ecce Homo."* New York: Vintage, 1967.

Noy, P. (1966). On the development of artistic talent. *Israel Annals of Psychiatry*, 4:211–218.

Noy, P. (1968). The development of musical ability. *The Psychoanalytic Study of the Child*, 23:332–347.

Noy, P. (1969). A revision of the psychoanalytic theory of the primary process. *International Journal of Psycho-Analysis*, 50:155–178.

Noy, P. (1972). About art and artistic talent. *International Journal of Psycho-Analysis*, 53:243–249.

BIBLIOGRAPHY

Nunberg, H., & Federn, E., eds. & trans. (1962). *Minutes of the Vienna Psychoanalytic Society, vol. 1: 1906–1908.* New York: International Universities Press.

Nunberg, H., & Federn, E., eds. & trans. (1967). *Minutes of the Vienna Psychoanalytic Society, vol. 2: 1908–1910.* New York: International Universities Press.

Nunberg, H., & Federn, E., eds. (1974). *Minutes of the Vienna Psychoanalytic Society, vol. 3: 1910–1911*, trans. M. Nunberg. New York: International Universities Press.

Nunberg, H., & Federn, E., eds. (1975). *Minutes of the Vienna Psychoanalytic Society, vol. 4: 1912–1918*, trans. M. Nunberg. New York: International Universities Press.

Oremland, J. (1975). An unexpected result of the analysis of a talented musician. *The Psychoanalytic Study of the Child*, 30:375–404.

Parens, H. (1979). *The Development of Aggression in Early Childhood.* New York: Jason Aronson.

Parmelin, H. (n.d.). *Picasso: Women*, preface by D. Cooper. Paris: Cercle d'Art, 1964.

Pfister, O. (1922). *Expressionism in Art.* London: Kegan Paul, Trench, Trubner.

Piaget, J. (1923). *The Language and Thought of the Child*, trans. M. Gabain. Cleveland: World Publishing, 1955.

Pletsch, C. (1977). *F. W. Nietzsche.* Unpublished doctoral dissertation. University of Chicago, Chicago, Ill.

Polanyi, M., & Prosch, H. (1975). *Meaning.* Chicago: University of Chicago Press.

Posner, D. (1971). Caravaggio's home-erotic early works. *Art Quarterly*, 34:301–324.

Rank, O. (1924). *The Don Juan Legend*, ed. & trans. D. Winter. Princeton: Princeton University Press, 1975.

Rapaport, D. (1974). *The History of the Concept of Association of Ideas.* New York: International Universities Press.

Rewald, J. (1954). *Paul Gauguin.* New York: Abrams.

Rewald, J. (1962). *Post-Impressionism from van Gogh to Gauguin*, 2nd ed. New York: The Museum of Modern Art.

Rieff, P. (1959). *Freud: The Mind of the Moralist.* New York: Viking.

Rieff, P. (1966). *The Triumph of the Therapeutic.* New York: Harper & Row.

Rizzuto, A. (1980). *The Birth of the Living God.* Chicago: University of Chicago Press.

Roazen, P. (1975). *Freud and His Followers.* New York: Knopf.

Rose, G. (1980). *The Power of Form* [*Psychological Issues*, Monograph 49]. New York: International Universities Press.

Rosen, V. (1964). Talent and character style. *Psychoanalytic Quarterly*, 33:1–2.

Rothenberg, A. (1971). The process of Janusian thinking in creativity. *Archives of General Psychiatry*, 24:195–205.

Röttgen, H. (1974). *Il Caravaggio: Ricerche e Interpretazioni.* Roma: Bulzon.

Salerno, L. (1974). The art-historical implications of the Detroit "Magdalen." *Burlington Magazine*, 859:586–593.

BIBLIOGRAPHY

Salerno, L., Kinkead, D., & Wilson, W. (1966). Poesia e simboli nel Caravaggio. *Palatino*, 10:106–117.

Schapiro, M. (1956). Leonardo and Freud: An art-historical study. *Journal of the History of Ideas*, 17:147–178.

Schnier, J. (1950). The blazing sun. *American Imago*, 7:143–162.

Schorske, C. (1981). *"Fin-de-Siècle" Vienna*. New York: Vintage.

Schur, M. (1972). *Freud: Living and Dying*. New York: International Universities Press.

Segal, H. (1957). A psycho-analytical approach to aesthetics. In M. Klein, P. Heimann, & P. Money-Kirle, eds., *New Directions in Psycho-Analysis*. New York: Basic Books, pp. 384–405.

Selesnick, S. (1966). Carl Gustav Jung. In F. Alexander, S. Eisenstein, & M. Grotjahn, eds., *Psychoanalytic Pioneers*. New York: Basic Books, pp. 63–77.

Shengold, L. (1976). The Freud/Jung letters. *Journal of the American Psychoanalytic Association*, 24:669–683.

Skira-Venturi, R. (1952). Caravaggio, a new interpretation of visual experience. In L. Venturi, *Italian Painting from Caravaggio to Modigliani*, trans. S. Gilbert. New York: Skira, 1952, pp. 25–36.

Skura, M. (1981). *The Literary Use of the Psychoanalytic Process*. New Haven: Yale University Press.

Slochower, H. (1981). Jung's "secret" confrontations with Freud: Freud as Yahweh in Jung's "Answer to Job." *American Imago*, 38:3–39.

Solomon, M. (1977). *Beethoven*. New York: Schirmer.

Spear, R. (1971). *Caravaggio and His Followers*. Cleveland: The Cleveland Museum of Art.

Spector, J. (1973). *The Aesthetics of Freud*. New York: Praeger.

Stepansky, P. (1976). The empiricist as rebel: Jung, Freud, and the burdens of discipleship. *Journal of the History of Behavioral Science*, 12:216–239.

Stepansky, P. (1980). Toward a future without illusion: Feuerbach and Jung as religious critics. Unpublished manuscript.

Sterba, E., & Sterba, R. (1954). *Beethoven and His Nephew*. New York: Pantheon.

Sterba, R., & Sterba, E. (1956). The anxieties of Michelangelo Buonarroti. *International Journal of Psycho-Analysis*, 37:325–330.

Stern, J. P. (1978). *Friedrich Nietzsche*. New York: Penguin.

Stokes, A. (1945). Concerning art and metapsychology. *International Journal of Psycho-Analysis*, 26:177–179.

Stokes, A. (1963). *Painting and the Inner World*. London: Tavistock.

Stoller, R. (1975). *Perversion: The Erotic Form of Hatred*. New York: Pantheon.

Sugana, G. (1972). *L'Opera Completa di Gauguin*. Milano: Rizzoli.

Tartakoff, H. (1966). The normal personality in our culture and the Nobel Prize complex. In R. Loewenstein, L. Newman, M. Schur, & A. Solnit, eds., *Psychoanalysis—A General Psychology*. New York: International Universities Press, pp. 222–252.

Tralbaut, M. (1969). *Vincent van Gogh*. New York: Viking.

Trosman, H. (1965). Freud and the controversy over Shakespearean authorship. In J. Gedo & G. Pollock, eds., *Freud: The Fusion of Science and Humanism*

[*Psychological Issues*, Monograph 34/35]. New York: International Universities Press, 1976, pp. 307–331.

van Gogh, V. (1959a). *The Complete Letters of Vincent van Gogh*, 2nd ed., vol. 1. Greenwich, Conn.: New York Graphic Society.

van Gogh, V. (1959b). *The Complete Letters of Vincent van Gogh*, 2nd ed., vol. 2. Greenwich, Conn.: New York Graphic Society.

van Gogh, V. (1959c). *The Complete Letters of Vincent van Gogh*, 2nd ed., vol. 3. Greenwich, Conn.: New York Graphic Society.

van Gogh-Bonger, J. (1959). Memoir of Vincent van Gogh. In *The Complete Letters of Vincent van Gogh*, 2nd ed., vol. 1. Greenwich, Conn.: New York Graphic Society.

Venturi, L. (1952). *Italian Painting from Caravaggio to Modigliani*, trans. S. Gilbert. New York: Skira.

Waelder, R. (1930). The principle of multiple function: Observations on over-determination. In *Psychoanalysis: Observation, Theory, Application*, ed. S. Guttman. New York: International Universities Press, 1976, pp. 68–83.

Waelder, R. (1965). *Psychoanalytic Avenues to Art*. New York: International Universities Press.

Waite, R. (1977). *The Psychopathic God: Adolf Hitler*. New York: Basic Books.

Weissman, P. (1965). *Creativity in the Theater: A Psychoanalytic Study*. New York: Basic Books.

Weissman, P. (1971). The artist and his objects. *International Journal of Psycho-Analysis*, 52:401–406.

Westermann-Holstijn, A. (1951). The psychological development of Vincent van Gogh. *American Imago*, 8:239–273.

Winnicott, D. W. (1964). Review of C. G. Jung, *Memories, Dreams, Reflections*. *International Journal of Psycho-Analysis*, 45:450–455.

Winnicott, D. W. (1967). The location of cultural experience. *International Journal of Psycho-Analysis*, 48:368–372.

Wittkower, R. (1965). *Art and Architecture in Italy, 1600–1750*, 2nd ed. Harmondsworth, England. Pelican.

Wolf, E., & Gedo, J. (1975). The last introspective psychologist before Freud: Michel de Montaigne. *The Annual of Psychoanalysis*, 3:297–310.

Wolf, E., Gedo, J., & Terman, D. (1972). On the adolescent process as a transformation of the self. *Journal of Youth and Adolescence*, 1:257–272.

Wysuph, C. (1970). *Jackson Pollock: Psychoanalytic Drawings*, New York:

INDEX

Italicized page numbers indicate illustrations.

INDEX

Brassaï, H. G., 105, 285n.
Brentano, F. von, 214
Breuer, J., 45, 227, 241, 285n.
Brücke, E., 227
Burckhardt, J., 263
Bychowski, G., 29n., 285n.

C

Camus, Albert, 19
Caravaggio, M. M. da, xviii, 101, 162–
187, *164, 166, 168, 170, 171,*
174, 176, 178, 180, 182, 193
early works of, 163–169
exile of, from Rome, 181–184
family of, 162, 163
later period of, 181–184
middle period of, 169–181
paranoia of, 177, 181, 183–187
violence of, 169–181, 183–187
Carlyle, T., 157
Castration complex, 2, 19, 47, 48
Cervantes, M. de, 93, 97, 103n., 216–
221, 223, 240
Cézanne, P., 32, 33, 90, 91, 91n.,
149n., 187–193, *189–192*
Charcot, J. M., 222, 227, 241
Cherubini, L., 181
Ciardi, J., 39n., 285n.
Cinotti, M., 162, 177n., 285n.
Cocks, G., 265, 286n.
Cocteau, J., 110
Colloquy of the Dogs, The (Cervantes),
218–221, 240
Colquhoun, A., 58, 286n.
Coltrera, J., 28, 286n.
Competition, 47–50
father–daughter, 65
guilt and, 48, 49
humiliation and, 49–50
Confidentiality
absence of clinical information and,
23, 24, 42, 85, 86
breach of, 24
Conrad, J., 16–21, 59, 105, 110, 111,
120
Conversion symptoms, 45
Corbin, E., 34, 286n.

Creativity
autonomy and, 46
childbearing and, 49, 60–62
humor and, 281, 282
imposture and, 274–276
narcissism and, 35
paralysis of, 45–59
competition and, 47–50
illusions in, 50–54
impact of, 58, 59
organization of self in, 54–58
subjectivity in, 45, 46
in women artists, 67–70
pragmatism and, 278–280, 282, 283
in self-improvement, 276–278
sexuality and, 14, 87, 88, 281, 282

D

Dalton, E., xviii
da Vinci, L., xv, xvii, 9, 12–16, 22, 35,
97, 194, 242
Defenses, 10
hierarchy of, 31
Degas, H., 151
de Haan, J. M., 157
Delacroix, F., 105, 120, 149
de la Tour, G., 165
Delay, J., 84, 286n.
dell'Acqua, G., 162, 177n., 285n.
Descartes, R., 220, 220n.
Diagnostic Association Studies (Jung),
233
Doctor Faustus (Mann), 194, 195, 199,
207, 208, 223, 224
Donatello, 74
Don Quixote (Cervantes), 217, 218, 223
Dostoevski, F. M., xix, 9
Dreams, 9, 34, 88, 95n., 217, 226, 241,
253, 266–270

E

Ego, 27, 28
Ehrenzweig, A., 30–37, 39, 39n., 40,
88, 286n.

Messerschmidt, F. X., 187
"Methodology of the Psychology of
    Poets" (Graf), 9
Meyer, B., 16–22, 110, 120, 139, 149,
    291n.
Michelangelo, B., xv, 74, 84, 162, 188,
    193
Miller, J., 222, 291n.
Milner, Marion, 23, 291n.
Misogyny
    of Conrad, 18, 19
    of Gauguin, 151–155
    homosexuality and, 80–84
Modell, A., 29, 82, 291n.
Models of the Mind (Goldberg), xiii, 43
Moir, A., 167n.
Monet, C., 91n., 188n.
Montaigne, M. de, 103n., 219, 220,
    220n., 222, 225
Monte, Cardinal del, 163, 167, 173
Moraitis, G., 195, 291n.
Morgan, G., 198, 201, 204, 291n.
Motherhood
    self-esteem and, 66, 67
    symbiotic needs and, 68–70
    as theme of Gauguin, 141–143, 145
    women artists and, 60–62, 65–70
Movement in art, 39
Mozart, L., 95, 110
Mozart, W. A., xxii, 2, 27n., 35, 91,
    91n., 110
Music
    development of talent in, 37
    movement in, 39
    as symbolic form, 36
    as transitional activity of infants, 29,
        30
    two dimensions of, 35

N

Nagera, H., 2, 130, 133, 135, 140n.,
    291n.
Narcissism, 23, 24
    creativity and, 35
Nass, M., 35n., 36, 291n.

Nazism, 257, 262, 263, 265, 267, 268
Nevelson, L., 62
Niederland, W., 23–25, 291n.
Niess, R., 188n., 291n.
Nietzsche, E., 202–206
Nietzsche, Franziska, 202, 203, 205
Nietzsche, Friedrich, 52, 70, 84, 95,
    101–103, 108, 109, 111, 113,
    120, 195–208, 210, 225, 226,
    229, 254, 262, 263, 269n., 272
    brain disease of, 198, 199, 203, 204
    education of, 199–203
    family of, 201–206
    influence on Freud, 221–223
    loneliness of, 196–198, 201, 202,
        204, 205, 207
    sexuality of, 205, 205n., 207
    symbiotic needs of, 204–207
    Wagner and, 197, 198, 198n.
Noy, P., 34, 36–38, 291n.
Nunberg, H., 9, 10, 222, 247, 292n.

O

Oedipus complex, xv–xvii, 2, 24, 25,
    217
    in father–daughter relationships,
        63–65
    resolution of, 15
Olivier, F., 111
*On the History of the Psychoanalytic
    Movement* (Freud), 242, 287n.
Oremland, J., 24, 25, 292n.
Overbeck, F., 196

P

Pallarés, M., 110
Paneth, J., 222
Paranoia
    of Beethoven, 12
    of Caravaggio, 177, 181, 183–187
    of Cézanne, 187–193
    Freud's study of, 240, 241
    of Jung, 235n., 249, 250, 257, 258,
        263

INDEX

Tomasi, G., 58
Totem and Taboo (Freud), 234, 242, 246, 287n.
Tralbaut, M., 107, 108, 293n.
Transference, 43
  Freud's study of, 264
  in Jung–Freud relationship, 258–260
Trosman, H., 217, 220, 293n.

U

Unconscious Structure in "The Idiot" (Dalton), xviii, xix

V

van Gogh, T., 57, 108, 113, 115, 115n. 117, 119, 120, 124, 130–133, 135, 137, 157, 202
van Gogh, V., 4, 5, 6, 88, 94, 95, 98, 101, 105–109, 113–139, *123, 126, 134, 136, 138,* 140, 140n., 141, 143, 145, 149n., 153n., 155, 155n., 157, 186, 194, 197, 202, 210, 294n.
  alienation from mother, 127, 128, 133, 137
  Arles catastrophe of, 3, 124, 131, 132, 145
  childhood of, 132
  depression of, 130, 135–137
  excitability of, 57, 172n.
  loneliness of, 131
  physical illness of, 129, 130
  Picasso's interest in, 105–107, 111, 113, 128
  religious interests of, 117–127, 131, 133, 149
  self-mutilation of, xvi, 2, 3, 124, 131–133
  suicide of, 113, 130, 132, 147
  symbiotic needs of, 107, 108, 115–117, 124, 130, 133–135, 137–139
van Gogh-Bonger, J., 117, 294n.
vanMander, K., 172

Velázquez, D., 105, 107, 111, 165
Venturi, L., 163, 294n.
Verbalization, interpretation of, 13
Victorianism, xx, xxi
Visual arts
  development of talent in, 37
  movement in, 39
  subjectivity in, 32, 33
Vittrice, P., 177

W

Waelder, R., xix, xx, 27, 28, 294n.
Wagner, C., 198, 198n., 202
Wagner, R., 162, 186, 197, 198, 198n., 202, 204, 208, 223, 229, 261, 263
Waite, R., 263, 294n.
Walter, M.-T., 109, 111
Weissman, P., 29, 42, 294n.
Westermann-Holstijn, A., 132, 294n.
Wignacourt, A. de, 183, 184
Wilde, O., 84, 277
Wilson, E., xix
Wilson, W., 167, 293n.
Winnicott, D. W., 28, 29, 38, 97n., 235n., 267, 272, 294n.
Wittkower, R., 163, 294n.
Wolf, E., 97, 97n., 103n., 200, 202, 215, 217, 219, 220n., 239, 288n., 294n.
Women artists, 60–73
  creative paralysis of, 67–70
  culture and creativity of, 62–65
  family impact on, 70–73
  identification with mother and, 65–70
  motherhood and, 60–62
Wound and the Bow, The (Wilson), xix
Wysuph, C., 24, 294n.

Z

Zola, E., 187n., 188n.
Zweig, A., 222